Praise for Chris Donnelly's *Doc, Donnie, the Kid, and Billy Brawl: How the 1985 Mets and Yankees Fought for New York's Baseball Soul*

"A rollicking look back at the pre–Wild Card era."
—PATRICK J. SAUER, *New York Intelligencer*

"Chris Donnelly captures the essence of how entranced both fan bases were, as their respective teams battled at the top of their divisions, as they played meaningful baseball in both Yankee and Shea Stadium through September."
—JERRY MILANI, *Sports Media Report*

"Donnelly's latest is a must-read for sports fans everywhere. His attention to detail along with the firsthand accounts of so many players and personalities involved brought me back to the summer of '85 and that unforgettable baseball season."
—DAVID A. PATERSON, former governor of New York

"Although many readers already know the outcome of the 1985 season, Donnelly does a good job of building suspense. A solid choice for both Mets and Yankees fans."
—*KIRKUS REVIEWS*

"The author has done a thorough job exploring the intense rivalry between the talent-rich '85 Mets and the equally loaded Yankees for supremacy in the city during what were the generally bleak days of the mid-eighties. . . . [An] entertaining trip down memory lane."
—MARK LEVINE, *Booklist*

"Fun. Nostalgic. Contagious. *Doc, Donnie, the Kid, and Billy Brawl* is a manual for Yankees and Mets fans to read cover to cover, and to use as ammunition for just who was a better team in 1985, and why."
—*OBSERVER-DISPATCH* (Utica)

"A really fun look back at the summer of 1985 when the Mets and the Yankees flirted for the very first time with giving us a Subway Series. Fine work by Chris Donnelly."
—MIKE VACCARO, *New York Post*

Praise for Chris Donnelly's *Road to Nowhere: The Early 1990s Collapse and Rebuild of New York City Baseball*

Named a Best Baseball Book of 2023 by *Sports Collectors Digest*

"If you're a Yankees or Mets fan, there's a lot here for you."
—ANDY McCUE, *Nine: A Journal of Baseball History and Culture*

"*Road to Nowhere* is an excellent history of New York City baseball in the early 1990s. With its thorough use of primary and secondary sources, it should be of interest to baseball history scholars and baseball fans alike."
—ANASTASIA L. PRATT, *Journal of Popular Culture*

"The battle for New York has always been a rich part of the city's baseball tapestry, and there was a time it seemed the Mets would own its soul forever. In Chris Donnelly's meticulously reported and wonderfully written book *Road to Nowhere* we learn just how the Yankees regained their swagger—and, just as important, their sway over the best baseball town of all."
—MIKE VACCARO, *New York Post* columnist and author of *1941—The Greatest Year in Sports*

"What a gift Chris Donnelly has given to baseball fans in New York and all those who live and die with the Mets and Yankees. *Road to Nowhere* is an insider's look, chock-full of entertaining anecdotes and revealing details based on extensive research, at the period in the early and midnineties when the Big Apple became a Yankees town once again. Colorful, legendary characters abound in a delicious tale of baseball in Queens and the Bronx."
—ANDREW MARANISS, author of *Singled Out: The True Story of Glenn Burke*

"Chris Donnelly is an utmost authority on New York baseball during the 1990s. In *Road to Nowhere* he has written the definitive book tying in the end of a mostly glorious 1980s decade. . . . It is a beautifully written book with plenty of fresh content from those who played on these two New York teams. A must-read for any baseball fan interested in that period."
—ERIK SHERMAN, author of *Two Sides of Glory: The 1986 Boston Red Sox in Their Own Words*

Get Your Tokens Ready

Chris Donnelly

Get Your Tokens Ready

The Late 1990s Road to the Subway Series

University of Nebraska Press | Lincoln

The University of Nebraska Press is part of a land-grant institution with campuses and programs on the past, present, and future homelands of the Pawnee, Ponca, Otoe-Missouria, Omaha, Dakota, Lakota, Kaw, Cheyenne, and Arapaho Peoples, as well as those of the relocated Ho-Chunk, Sac and Fox, and Iowa Peoples.

Library of Congress Cataloging-in-Publication Data
Names: Donnelly, Chris, author.
Title: Get your tokens ready: the late 1990s road to the Subway Series / Chris Donnelly.
Description: Lincoln: University of Nebraska Press, [2025] | Includes bibliographical references and index.
Identifiers: LCCN 2024033112
ISBN 9781496230805 (hardback)
ISBN 9781496243591 (epub)
ISBN 9781496243607 (pdf)
Subjects: LCSH: New York Mets (Baseball team)—History—20th century. | New York Yankees (Baseball team)—History—20th century. | Baseball—New York (State)—New York—History—20th century. | Sports rivalries—New York (State)—New York—History—20th century. | World Series (Baseball)—History—20th century.
Classification: LCC GV875.N45 D642 2025 | DDC 796.357/64097471—dc23/eng/20240812
LC record available at https://lccn.loc.gov/2024033112

Set in Minion Pro by A. Shahan.

With so much love and appreciation to Jamie, Erin, and Charlie, who make anything possible with their support.

In loving memory of my father, Tim, a devoted Mets fan who missed most of 1999 NLCS Game Five because he was visiting me at college, and my buddy Chris "Big" Singer, with whom I was on the phone when Piazza flied out to end the Subway Series.

Contents

Acknowledgments

This book was not supposed to be a stand-alone project. As noted in my previous book, in the summer of 2019, shortly after *Doc, Donnie, the Kid, and Billy Brawl* came out, I had an epiphany while listening to a YouTube clip of John Sterling announcing George Steinbrenner's banishment in July 1990. *Doc, Donnie*, I realized, was just the beginning of the story around the fight between the Yankees and Mets for New York City's baseball soul.

I began writing the next part of the story, which was supposed to be a book about the entirety of 1990s baseball in New York, ending with the Subway Series. I quickly realized that was too much for one book. There were simply too many stories to tell and too much information to share to fit into one book. I wanted to include as much as possible. This is the era in which I grew up watching baseball. Researching this time period and interviewing the players who were part of it brought back a million fond memories: watching games with my friends; debating who was the better shortstop, Jeter or Ordóñez; watching the postseason and talking to my buddies through Instant Messenger as the Mets and Yankees both advanced. I view it as a golden age of baseball in New York, not just for what it meant to me on a personal level but also for what it meant to the fans of both teams and baseball in general.

I loved writing this book, and I hope it lives up to the memories of those who participated in these events or watched them from afar. As always, no one does it alone. And so my sincere thanks to the following people: my amazing wife, Jamie, and my two incredible kiddos, Erin and Charlie; my mother, Sandy; my brothers, Tim and Mike; my sister-in-law, Taylor; my future sister-in-law, Liliana; my brothers-in-law, Glenn and Derek; my mother- and father-in-law, Karen and Roy; the Donnellys, Kassabs, Praschils, Leahys, Dudases, Salzanos, and Kennedys; my friends, from Lincoln to Lakeside to PLHS to TCNJ; my wonderful work friends, from the state government years to Avoq; my editor, Rob Taylor, and everyone at the University of Nebraska Press who has helped over the course of this trilogy; Michael Kay, for blessing my usage of his famous call of David Justice's ALCS home run as the title of this book. And last, all who have picked up one of my books over the years and felt it was worth their time.

Get Your Tokens Ready

Jelly-Legged Him

Dave Mlicki, chewing on his gum and sporting a long-sleeved undershirt despite the mid-June temperature hovering near 70 degrees, got the sign from catcher Todd Hundley. He did not dissent. It was the bottom of the first inning of the first-ever regular season game between the New York Mets and New York Yankees. Standing on the mound at Yankee Stadium, Mlicki could hardly believe he was actually here this moment.

Yes, Dave Mlicki, of all the Major League players to have come and gone, was the guy on the mound for this moment. The Ohio native—Cleveland at first, then Columbus. Well, Upper Arlington to be exact. "It's where Jack Nicklaus is from. Ohio State's right there," Mlicki proudly points out. It's understandable that Mlicki grew up a big Ohio State fan. He also loved baseball and began watching the sport as the Cincinnati Reds' Big Red Machine was mashing its way to consecutive world championships in the 1970s. Mlicki and his brother, Doug, would find the box score from the previous day's game and reenact the action in their yard with a ball and bat, right down to imitating the players. They'd flap their arms if they were Joe Morgan or crouch down low if they were Pete Rose.

Once or twice a year, Dave and Doug's parents would pile them into the car and drive down to Cincinnati. They'd stop first at the Montgomery Inn for its world-famous ribs, then head over to Riverfront Stadium to see a game in person. When Dave reached his high school years, his father got a new job in Colorado, and the family relocated to Colorado Springs. There, at Cheyenne Mountain High School, people found out something: Dave Mlicki was really good at baseball. His small stature had caused him to be overlooked in Ohio, but once he got to Colorado, he experienced a substantial growth spurt. Mlicki began to draw attention, not as a pitcher, but as a shortstop. Then he went on a recruitment trip to Wichita State with Mike Lansing, an up-and-coming shortstop prospect who eventually made it to the Majors. "I saw him and I'm like, 'Oh my god, that guy's way better than me,'" said Mlicki. It was enough to make Mlicki focus more on being a pitcher. As it turned out, he could pitch too.

Now, 1,700 miles away from Colorado Springs, Mlicki was on the mound for the New York Mets on June 16, 1997. His team had already jumped out to a 3–0 lead in the top of the inning, delighting the large contingent of Mets fans who'd risked the trip into Yankee Stadium.

The Yankees were trying to mount a comeback, having already put a runner on second base with no outs. But Mlicki retired the next two batters and was now looking at a 1-1 count to the Yankees' designated hitter, Cecil Fielder. Mlicki took the sign from Hundley and came to a set position on the mound. He then turned his head quickly, glaring at Derek Jeter as the Yankees' shortstop took his lead off second base. Mlicki turned back, looked into his glove, then turned to stare at Jeter one more time. Quickly he brought his right arm straight down, parallel to his body, then heaved the baseball toward home plate. Just before releasing the ball, he flicked his wrist in a violent downward motion. The result was a pitch that began at and appeared to be headed toward Fielder's neck.

The Yankees' cleanup hitter began his long, violent hitting motion thinking a fastball was coming, one that was about to strike him in the upper body. He abruptly stopped his motion, waiting for the inevitable pain that comes with taking a five-ounce solid object thrown at ninety-plus miles per hour to the body. Instead, as the ball raced toward home, it plummeted downward but remained over the plate, catching the strike zone just above Fielder's knees. Fielder stood helplessly as home plate umpire Tim Tschida signaled a strike. The count was now 1-2.

"Jelly-legged him," said Steve Lyons, a former player who was doing color commentary for FX during the nationally broadcast game. The term was baseball nomenclature for when a batter, not recognizing a breaking ball, stops his swing and acts as though the ball might hit him, only to watch helplessly as it crosses the plate. Fielder had just perfectly exemplified it. "Not those legs," said former Mets manager Jeff Torborg, also doing commentary in the booth; "he's got legs coming out of his shirt, he's so big."

Torborg's metaphor was clumsy but not far off. Fielder was known as "Big Daddy," a nickname befitting a man who dwarfed just about every other player in the Majors. At 6 feet 3 inches and a generously listed weight of 230 pounds, Cecil had been among the game's most consistently dangerous hitters since the start of the decade. In 1990, after returning from a year in Japan and having spent four seasons in Toronto during the late 1980s, he'd taken the American League by storm by crushing 51 home runs for the Detroit Tigers. In fact, his fiftieth and fifty-first home runs had been launched from the very same batter's box Fielder now occupied. He followed up with 44 home runs in 1991 and 35 in 1992, not to mention that he led the league in RBIs in all three of those years. Two strike-shortened seasons had dented his home run totals somewhat, but in 1996, a season he started with Detroit and ended in New York, he notched another 39. All told, from 1990 to 1996 Fielder hit 258 home runs.

Then it happened. It happens to all ballplayers at some point in their careers. Sometimes it happens gradually over the course of many years. Sometimes it happens in the blink of an eye. In Fielder's case, it was the latter. For hitters the hand-eye coordination slows down, and their sense of timing decreases just enough that they can't get around on a fastball the same way they used to. Coaches, managers, scouts, and even casual observers pick up on it quickly. More important, however, pitchers pick up on it and exploit it for all it is worth.

Somewhere between the last out of the 1996 World Series and the first game of the 1997 season, that's what happened to Cecil Fielder. Expected to provide pop as the team's designated hitter (DH), he went twenty-two games into the year before hitting his first home run. It was hoped that first shot, coming in a 5-5 performance against the White Sox, would be the start of a torrid run by Big Daddy. It never materialized. This was his only home run of the month. He hit just two in May and had a total of only five extra-base hits. Fielder had always generated a ton of strikeouts, a consequence of his long, swing-as-hard-as-he-could effort in the box. But he was not striking out any more than in other seasons, meaning that he was making contact at essentially the same rate he always had. He just was not driving the ball anymore.

This was no secret to the Mets, especially not to Mlicki or Hundley. Conventional wisdom might have indicated that now, with a 1-2 count and Fielder having just buckled from a curve, it would make sense to try the same pitch again. The thought surely must have crossed Fielder's mind. Instead Hundley signaled for a fastball. Mlicki, as he would do for the remainder of the night, nodded in agreement. He checked Jeter just once this time, then fired a fastball toward the outer part of the plate. Fielder, likely expecting

3

that curveball again, swung late, missing the ball as it popped loudly into Hundley's glove for strike three.

Mlicki tugged at his uniform just above his left shoulder, then performed a 360 spin after his follow-through, so his momentum took him toward the Mets' dugout on the third-base side. The Mets fans in the crowd stood and applauded while Yankees fans sat and sulked. The first inning of the first-ever regular season game between the Mets and Yankees had been eventful. But the rest of the night would be the Dave Mlicki Show, cementing his name in the history books of both clubs with a performance that would still be talked about decades later. For now, though, it was just a 3–0 game headed to the top of the second inning.

2 Not Any Nastier

Ticker tape fluttered all throughout the Canyon of Heroes on a crisp Tuesday afternoon in October 1996. An estimated 3.5 million people had crowded into lower Manhattan to watch a cavalcade of cars carry the reigning world champion New York Yankees team personnel, coaches, manager, and players and their spouses from the tip of the island to City Hall. Included in this parade of honorees was the team's owner, one George M. Steinbrenner III. And boy, was the owner pissed off for a man whose ballclub had just won its first World Series in eighteen years.

"Get your fucking wives off the float," the owner screamed at Jim Leyritz and John Wetteland, two of the team's postseason heroes.[1] Steinbrenner was livid that wives were gathering on the parade floats, where they would be given equal time with the players as they were chauffeured up Broadway. The parade was meant to honor the guys who won it, not showcase the wives. The wives and their husbands, however, refused to relent, angering Steinbrenner even further. He "went fucking ballistic," said one team official, and like any bully, since the players had stood up to him, he directed his rage elsewhere, largely at the team's marketing director, Debbie Tymon.[2] He continued to fume as the parade began moving north through the city.

For the public, though, it was all smiles on this day. Fans were elated to celebrate a team that had won not just the championship but also the hearts of countless New Yorkers and even fans across the country. The Yankees were filled with Hollywood-type stories, from the young matinee-idol shortstop Derek Jeter to the feel-good tale of manager Joe Torre's brother getting a heart transplant the day before the Yankees won it all. For decades baseball fans around the country had reveled in despising the Yankees. The 1980s and early 1990s had been an especially enjoyable time for these fans, as the team had sunk to all-time lows in performance and morale. But these Yankees? These Yankees were actually kinda likable.

Now fans filled Broadway to bask in the post-championship glow. One even brought a python snake to mingle among the crowd. "I've never seen a ticker-tape parade like this one, and I've been in a few of them," said Yan-kees legend Joe DiMaggio, who had won nine championships as a player.[3]

The players themselves were on cloud 9. Of the twenty-five on the World Series roster, only five had won a championship before, and only one of them, Darryl Strawberry, had won it in New York. Most of them had never experienced anything like this.

"Ticker tape being an obsolete relic, people hurled everything from shredded paper to confetti to toilet tissue," reported the *New York Times*. "In fact, several government agencies near City Hall dumped entire boxes of public and confidential records out the window, without troubling to shred them. Down came checks issued by the New York City Housing Authority and records of unemployment checks from the New York State Department of Social Services."[4]

Steinbrenner, meanwhile, soaked up the adulation and attention, sitting on stage at City Hall in what would soon emerge as his standard fall outfit: blazer with a turtleneck. No sooner had the pomp and circumstance of the ceremony ended, though, when the Boss set his sights on 1997. Raised sternly by a perpetually unsatisfied father, Steinbrenner carried forward this inability to be satisfied, to lose out on what it meant to truly be happy. It meant that Charlie Hayes's squeezing the last out of Game Six might as well have been another lifetime by November 1, 1996, because the only thing better to the Boss than his team being world champions was being repeat world champions.

The march to a twenty-fourth title began just days later with a decision that altered the course of the franchise and, ultimately, baseball history. John Wetteland had performed solidly in two seasons as the team's closer. His forty-three saves in 1996, the second highest single-season total for a Yankee to that point, led the league and happened despite countless ulcer-inducing performances for fans. In the World Series he had saved all four New York victories, earning him Series MVP. It was rare for a reigning World Series MVP to leave his ballclub. Wetteland was also just thirty years old, with plenty of good baseball left in him. The Yankees, however, were ready to move on. "Yankees executives have spoken privately about the frequency with which Wetteland nearly blew games," noted *Newsday* that off-season.[5] Fortunately for them, they had someone waiting in the wings.

Mariano Rivera, "Mo," had overwhelmed American League hitters as the team's setup man in '96. His 130 strikeouts were second on the team, despite the fact that he pitched out of the bullpen, and his strikeouts per nine innings rate was just shy of eleven, a remarkable number in a time when most batters still swung for contact. Rivera earned himself a third-place finish in the American League Cy Young Award voting. His performance did not wane in the postseason either. During the Yankees' playoff run, Rivera threw fourteen and a third innings and allowed only one run while striking out ten. The Yankees envisioned a future where Rivera would use these talents pitching in the ninth inning instead of the seventh and eighth.

That left no room for Wetteland. When he became a free agent in the first week of November, the Yankees made clear they would not be bringing him back. The closer's role would now be Mo's. A month later Wetteland signed with the Texas Rangers, where he pitched for four seasons before retiring.[6]

Turning to Rivera was by no means a slam-dunk decision. He had been incredible in 1996, but he had faltered so badly as a starter in his rookie year of 1995 that he had been sent back down to the Minors. There was also, for some pitchers, a big difference between being on the mound in middle relief and being there in the ninth inning, when a mistake could result in an immediate loss. Wetteland was battle tested, even if he tended to allow the tying or winning runs to reach base before saving the game. Would Rivera provide the same stability? Time would tell.

Wetteland was the World Series MVP, but the most memorable Fall Classic moment had been provided by Jim Leyritz. "The King" was the senior member of the team, having arrived in 1990 as the Yankees were in the midst of their worst season in almost seventy years. His nickname did not come from admiration; rather it was a commentary from teammates about Leyritz's innate ability to tell anyone and everyone how good he was. Leyritz didn't care if it was meant pejoratively. He loved it.

Over the years the King had endured playing on bad teams, having been sent down to and back up from the Minors multiple times, and in 1993 he saw his playing time cut when Mike Stanley emerged as the team's everyday catcher. But in two postseasons he'd provided two of the most memorable moments in team history. The first was his fifteenth-inning game-winning home run against the Mariners in Game Two of the 1995 Division Series. The second was his eighth-inning three-run game-tying home run in Game Four of the 1996 World Series against the Braves. The home run, which brought the Yankees all the way back from an early 6–0 deficit, changed the course of the Series and solidified Leyritz as one of the more clutch performers in postseason history. Years later the cover of Leyritz's autobiography, *Catching Heat*, would feature a picture of Leyritz hitting the World Series home run in Atlanta.

All the postseason heroics in the world did not change the fact that Leyritz had no permanent role with the team heading into 1997. Joe Girardi was the everyday catcher, and highly touted prospect Jorge Posada was expected to be with the team that year, learn from Girardi's tutelage, and eventually take over as the full-time catcher. The designated hitter spot was taken by Cecil Fielder. Leyritz had played third base and outfield in the past, but those positions already had multiple people set to play them or serve as backups.

Leyritz had no desire to be, at best, a bench player. He had been promised for years, first by Buck Showalter and then by Joe Torre, that he would get more playing time than he'd had the year before. It never happened, though, and he was not going to wait any longer. Leyritz asked for a trade to a team where he was going to get at bats every day. It turned out that the Yankees were all too willing to comply.

During Game One of the World Series, Leyritz had ignored the team's scouting reports by calling for Andy Pettitte to throw fastballs to Braves' rookie outfielder Andruw Jones. Jones homered. Twice. After the 12–1 loss, Steinbrenner grew incensed when he learned what Leyritz had done. "I spend hundreds of thousands of dollars on scouting, and your dumbass players don't follow instructions," he barked at general manager (GM) Bob Watson. "I want Leyritz traded. Right now!"[7]

Leyritz, of course, could not be traded in the middle of the World Series. But the Steinbrenner rant still rang true weeks later, even after the King's big Game Four home run. Torre was not sorry to see him go either, having tired of Leyritz's constant griping about playing time. The Yankees traded him to the Angels for two Minor League players.

Five days after the Leyritz trade, another World Series hero departed. Jimmy Key had come to the Yankees before 1993, a consolation prize after the team had failed to land Greg Maddux. In his first two seasons in New York, he had been remarkable, winning thirty-five games and finishing fourth and then second in the American League Cy Young Award voting. After missing most of 1995 because of a torn rotator cuff, he'd returned in 1996 and, while not the same pitcher, won twelve games. In the postseason, Key pitched eight strong innings to earn the win in Game Three of the American League Championship Series (ALCS). Then in Game Six of the

World Series, he held the Braves to just a single run over five and a third innings of work, earning the win in the Series clincher.

Key's time in New York was over though. The Yankees did not plan to bring back a thirty-five-year-old pitcher with a recent severe arm injury. On December 10 Key signed with the Baltimore Orioles, a coup for Orioles owner Peter Angelos. The Orioles had chased the Yankees all summer long in 1996 for the division title and then, after winning the wild card, had fallen to them in five games in the ALCS. Using a key member of the Yankees' championship team to try and overtake the Yankees certainly must have appealed to Angelos.

Steinbrenner felt he could lose Key in part because he was desperately trying to sign free agent Roger Clemens, "the Rocket." The pitcher—who had already won three Cy Young awards and an MVP award—had unceremoniously been dropped from the Boston Red Sox's future plans after the team decided he was on the down side of his career. Loving the idea of swooping up the Red Sox ace—not to mention adding the greatest pitcher of the last ten years to his team—Steinbrenner met with Clemens at the pitcher's Houston home in November. The Boss felt confident that he had sold Clemens on becoming a Yankee.

A few weeks later, Steinbrenner called Toronto Blue Jays president Paul Beeston, with whom he was friendly. Steinbrenner knew that Beeston had just paid a visit to Clemens too and wanted to both see how the visit had gone and crow that he felt his odds were good at landing the Rocket. Beeston had some bad news. He had left Clemens's home with a signed contract. Clemens would play for the Blue Jays. "You fucking Canuck," Steinbrenner yelled. "How did you do that? You can't afford him!"[8]

With Clemens now off the table and just two weeks left in the year, the Yankees had lost three important pieces to their championship puzzle and had nothing to show for it other than a hope that Mariano Rivera would become a reliable closer. The team decided to gamble. After talks with former Braves lefty Steve Avery broke down over asking price, they signed lefty David Wells to a three-year, $13.5 million contract.

Wells had long fascinated Steinbrenner. In 1989 the Blue Jays were considering hiring Lou Piniella as their manager, but Piniella was under contract with the Yankees. Wells was one of the players New York was going to ask for in return for allowing Piniella out of his deal. It never came to that, but six years later Steinbrenner nearly traded Rivera to the Detroit Tigers for Wells. Instead the Tigers dealt Wells to Cincinnati. The Yankees tried one more time to trade for him after the 1995 season, but the Reds' asking price was too much, and Boomer, as he was nicknamed, went to Baltimore.

Wells had spent his early years in Toronto but had been something of a vagabond of late, playing for three different teams between 1995 and 1996. His numbers in 1996 had been among the worst of his career, though some of those could be attributed to his having to pitch in hitter-friendly Camden Yards for the Orioles. The flip side was that Wells was an innings machine with pinpoint control, often averaging around only two walks per nine innings. He had a big, looping curve that paired well with a sneaky fastball. To that point, he was 10-1 with a 2.93 ERA at Yankee Stadium in his career. Wells was also something of a Yankees fanatic, having idolized Babe Ruth growing up. He would say that if he could be reincarnated as anyone, it would be Ruth. He hoped to wear a number with "3" in it when joining the team, to honor the Babe. He eventually settled on 33.

There was another element to Wells, though. He had grown up in the rough San Diego neighborhood of Ocean Beach, and his father had walked out shortly after his son's birth in 1963. Wells's mother dated members of the Hells Angels and relied on welfare at times to get by. Growing up in this kind of environment shaped Wells's character, and it was not surprising that he went on to have problems with authority. He had challenged manager Cito Gaston in Toronto, the two once getting into a screaming match on the mound. The portly pitcher liked having a good time, whether that was eating or drinking whatever he wanted, listening to his kind of music, or just being crude. He was who he was, and he didn't care what people thought. "I've been big my whole career," said Wells when the topic of his weight came up after signing with the Yankees. "You don't run the ball over the plate, right?"[9]

Wells's problems with authority were no secret to most of the Majors. Torre may have tipped his hand early on about the confrontations that would soon occur between the two. "I'm partial to the guys who were on the club last year, especially Jimmy Key and what he fought back from," said Torre when hearing of the signing. "Jimmy Key proved he can win in the postseason. We'll see if David Wells can do that."[10]

Wells, on the other hand, could barely keep the smile off his face. "I think more than anything he's so thrilled to say he's a New York Yankee," said his agent, Gregg Clifton, after inking the deal. "He's finally able to be with the team he's always wanted to be with."[11]

Two weeks later the Yankees signed Mark Whiten, a power hitting out-fielder who would provide depth on the bench. Then they stopped making moves of any kind. Steinbrenner, having vowed to get to work on another championship before the team had time to enjoy its current one, pumped the brakes. The Yankees had subtracted more than they had added but felt they had the pieces in place to win it all again. They knew it would not be easy, that their feel-good story would melt away on the first pitch of Opening Day because everyone guns for the champions. What they did not realize, however, is that the difficulties the team would face throughout 1997 would largely be self-inflicted. The result was a season nearly as chaotic as the losing years of the early 1990s.

• • •

They would not admit it, but to sit through the off-season and watch the Yankees be feted across the country—to even be deemed likable—was embarrassing for the New York Mets. They had struggled nearly the entire decade of the 1990s, going through five managers, three general managers, and a conga line's worth of players, all to finish no better than third in four of seven seasons. They had suffered through a myriad of clubhouse and off-the-field scandals, from bleach spraying to firecracker throwing to allegations of rape and sexual misconduct. Star players had come to New York and either grossly underperformed, like Vince Coleman, or run afoul of fans and the media, like Bobby Bonilla and Bret Saberhagen. The year 1996 was supposed to be a rebound following a surprise second-place showing in 1995. Instead, they went 71-91 and fired their manager in August. Now, amid all such problems, they had to stare at their TV screens as two of the franchise's biggest stars—Dwight "Doc" Gooden and Darryl Strawberry—participated in a Yankees championship parade. Not just Gooden and Strawberry but David Cone too. Hell, even their former pitching coach, Mel Stottlemyre, was riding on a parade float.

Something needed to change with the Mets. Their ineptitude had lasted too long, enabling the Yankees to become the city's beloved team. This could not continue. The previous August the team had fired manager Dallas Green and replaced him with Bobby Valentine. Green had been an old school manager who believed tough love was the way to success. You could do things Green's way, or you could leave. But many viewed Green's gruff attitude as an act, and even if it wasn't, how many times was the same harangue or door slam or overturned table going to change anything?

Valentine certainly had his detractors. His first managing gig in Texas had brought mixed results. There were some good seasons but nothing approaching expectations. And Valentine rubbed some the wrong way with his style. He was brusque and a know-it-all, some thought. "He was said to be an egomaniacal schemer who would say or do anything to get what he wanted," noted the *Bergen Record*. "He was said to never assume responsibility for anything but things that went well."[12]

After being fired by Texas in 1992, Valentine made his way into the Mets' organization and was managing the team's triple A club when he got the call to take over the big-league team. He appeared to have changed in that time, learning to communicate better with players. And Valentine was not your typical run-of-the-mill manager. He had engaged in competitive dancing as a teenager and had even appeared on *The Dating Game*. He could be cutting in his remarks, but he could be funny too. He also knew what players went through, having been a highly touted prospect himself before a leg injury derailed his career. Valentine could make things work in Queens if he had the right group of players.

That was the problem, though. The Mets did not have the right group of players and hadn't for some time. "When I got hired, I didn't think it would be in the middle of a season," said Valentine. "And I didn't think that that season could be saved. So when I came in, I wanted to do a true evaluation and not make any decisions until I was comfortable with it."[13]

Valentine spent the remaining weeks of the 1996 season evaluating what the team already had and where it was lacking. He spoke individually with players to get a better sense of the culture and where the organization might be obtuse on clubhouse issues. "I met with every player, three players a day," said Valentine. "Sometimes I'd skip batting practice so I could hold these meetings. I just wanted to hear what everyone had to say."[14]

Once the season ended, Valentine had a plan in mind to alter the team both on and off the field. Still, as the Mets entered the off-season, wholesale changes were not in the offing for 1997. Valentine's plan would have to be implemented in steps. The team had trimmed payroll during the 1995 season, shipping away its biggest paid stars, and instead had invested hope in a group of young players and low-risk, high-reward signings and trade returns. For the offense, Rey Ordóñez, Edgardo Alfonzo, Butch Huskey, and Carl Everett represented a youth movement in which the organization saw huge potential, even if all these players had struggled through 1996.

Free-agent-signing Bernard Gilkey, on the other hand, had had a career year, as had free-agent-signing Lance Johnson. Todd Hundley had finally broken out, setting the single-season record for home runs by a catcher and for a Mets player.

As for pitching, the team had come to grips with the fact that Generation K—Paul Wilson, Bill Pulsipher, and Jason Isringhausen—was never going to pan out. Wilson, perhaps the most talented of the bunch, had already thrown his last pitch as a Met. Injuries would keep him out of baseball until 2000. Pulsipher, the quirky left-hander who had shown promise in 1995, had not thrown a pitch in 1996 due to a torn elbow ligament. He would not pitch again until 1998. Isringhausen had been felled by injuries and inconsistency in 1996 but was the only one of the three slated to throw a pitch in 1997. The top three starters of 1996—Mark Clark, Bobby Jones, and Pete Harnisch—were assumed to be part of the rotation again. Outside of John Franco, who had had perhaps the best season of his career, the bullpen had been spotty at best.

That left the Mets with three pressing needs going into 1997: back end of the rotation starting pitchers, at least one more dependable arm in the bullpen, and another starting infielder at either first base or third base. There was a dearth of any such options on the free-agent market; this meant the Mets were going to have to trade their way toward filling most of these gaps.

First up was the bullpen, which had blown twenty-three save opportunities in 1996, the third most in the National League. Two days before Thanksgiving, the team acquired Greg McMichael from the Braves. Though he had struggled during the Braves '96 postseason, McMichael was a vastly underrated bullpen arm who had been solid for Atlanta for four years. His herky-jerky, somewhat three-quarters motion provided a sharp drop on his pitches, making it difficult to lift the ball against him. In nearly 318 career innings, he had allowed only sixteen home runs. Even more important, he ate up innings, having, outside of the strike-shortened '94 year, averaged over eighty-six innings per season for his career. It was a strong, if understated, start to the off-season.

On Thanksgiving Day the Mets traded for Colorado starter Armando Reynoso. He had been with the Rockies since their beginning, though injuries had stunted his progress over the years. His numbers were not overly impressive, but there was hope that removing him from the thin air of Coors Field could improve his performance.

Rather than go after another starter, the Mets ultimately opted to go in-house. Rick Reed was born in the West Virginia town of Huntington, nestled on the Ohio River across from Ohio. Born into poverty, Reed found escape through baseball and earned a scholarship to Marshall University as a pitcher. He showed promise with a mix of off-speed pitches, so the Pirates drafted him in the June 1986 amateur draft. Although he was initially a reliever, Pittsburgh turned Reed into a starter in 1988. That season he made his debut by throwing eight shutout innings against the eventual National League East Division champion Mets.

Over the next few seasons, though, Reed struggled to find success. He bounced around from the Minors to the Majors and from team to team, from Pittsburgh to Kansas City to Texas and finally to Cincinnati. Reed was in the Reds' Minor League system when the 1994 players' strike began. As the strike continued, in the spring of 1995 the owners decided to use replacement players to both have a season and to force the players into accepting the owners' terms. Reed was offered a spot as a replacement player. This was no small decision. Crossing the picket line would brand Reed a scab among Major Leaguers and possibly ruin any chance he had of every making or even being accepted by a big-league club. But Reed did not think he had a choice. His mother, Sylvia, was a diabetic who did not have medical insurance. He needed to pay for her insulin. So he crossed the line. Just before the season was to start with replacement players, the strike ended. Reed went back down to the Minors, fully aware that he could now be a marked man. "There's going to be some hard feelings, but not as much as there would have been if we had played in regular season games," said Reed. "And I think these guys [Major Leaguers] realize that we were put between a rock and a hard place. We had to make a decision RIGHT NOW, and we had to think of our families."[15]

Reed became a free agent after the 1995 season, and the Mets signed him and sent him to Triple A Norfolk. His numbers there, 8-10 but with a 3.16 ERA, impressed the organization's higher-ups. Valentine wanted to give him a chance heading into spring training in 1997. The manager gauged what the feeling would be if Reed made the Opening Day roster. The reaction was mixed, though John Franco was the most adamant in his opposition. Ultimately Franco acquiesced, mostly for the sake of team harmony. "If he's going to help us win, that's fine with me," he told reporters that spring.[16]

The team now needed to find an infielder. Butch Huskey had played first base for nearly half of the previous season and, with the Mets having traded Rico Brogna to the Phillies, they had no other viable option. They preferred that Huskey be in the outfield while occasionally filling in at third or first to help to give someone a day off. With Edgardo Alfonzo slated to play third full time and Carlos Baerga at second, it made sense that the team would explore options for a first baseman. On December 20 they found one.

John Olerud had not panned out exactly as the Toronto Blue Jays had hoped. Growing up in the Pacific Northwest, he had baseball in his blood. Olerud's father had been a Minor League player. As he followed in his father's footsteps, Olerud's baseball talent was clear from an early age because he was both a tremendous hitter and perhaps even a better pitcher. Drafted out of high school by the Mets in 1986, he opted instead to attend Washington State University (WSU). There Olerud became not just a star but also possibly one of the greatest collegiate baseball players of all time. In his sophomore season he went a staggering 15-0 pitching while hitting .464 with twenty-three home runs. Baseball America named him College Player of the Year.

Olerud was drawing national attention when, in late 1988, he began to experience intense headaches. Initially he kept the headaches to himself. In January 1989 Olerud was running laps at WSU's Hollingbery Fieldhouse. "I had run about three-quarters of a mile and then decided that was enough of that for a while," said Olerud. "When I stopped running, I got one of those headaches again. I remember thinking, what are these things?"[17] Then Olerud collapsed. He woke up an hour later, unsure of what had just happened.

The seizure Olerud suffered ultimately led to the discovery of a brain aneurysm. Surgery removed the aneurysm, but as a result Olerud spent the rest of his baseball career wearing a batting helmet at all times, even in the field. He returned for his junior year, and while his pitching numbers plummeted, his hitting was still sharp. That June he informed any MLB team that would listen that it was his intention to complete his senior year at WSU. The Blue Jays, however, were in love with Olerud's hitting ability. Rather than let some other club scoop him up, they took a chance and drafted him in the third round. After months of Olerud's rejecting Toronto offers, the Jays put an $800,000 signing bonus on the table, along with a promise that he would go straight to the Major Leagues. That was enough for Olerud.

Olerud emerged just as Toronto was going on a run of dominance in the American League East, winning the division in four of five seasons. Olerud was a contact hitter with a strict sense of the strike zone. He fit in perfectly with a Toronto team loaded with talent. That talent also covered Olerud in some obscurity. He was not as big a name as Dave Winfield or Roberto Alomar or Joe Carter or Jack Morris. Perhaps because he was surrounded by marquee names on a team in the midst of winning back-to-back world championships, Olerud's 1993 season remains one of the most impressive and least talked-about performances of the 1990s. As late as August 2, he was hitting .400, creating serious buzz that he might be the first batter to achieve that mark over a full season in fifty-two years. His numbers faded in September, but ultimately Olerud hit .363. It was the highest single-season average of any American League player in the '90s, and because he had hit .31 points better than the next closest player, it was the highest differential of any American League batting champion for the decade. His season was about more than batting average, though. Olerud led the league in doubles, his fifty-four being the seventeenth highest single-season total in baseball history to that point. In addition to batting average and doubles, he led the league in on-base percentage (OBP), On-Base Plus Slugging (OPS), and even intentional walks. Not bad for a guy who topped out at twenty-four home runs.

Olerud made the All-Star team and finished third in MVP voting. The Blue Jays had high hopes for the future of their first baseman. But Olerud failed to live up to those expectations in the proceeding years, in part because Toronto pushed him to try and hit with more power. The result was a failure across the board. His average never got above .300 again with the Blue Jays, and his power numbers never came close to matching those of his '93 season. As the Yankees, Orioles, and Red Sox emerged as leaders in the AL East, Toronto faded away. After a disappointing 74-88 season in '96, the Blue Jays decided it was time to cut bait on their first baseman. In came the Mets, offering pitcher Robert Person five days before Christmas. The deal was done, the Mets had their first baseman, and ultimately the trade would prove to be one of the best in team history.

The Mets had checked off all the boxes for the off-season. They added a backup catcher too, signing Todd Pratt just before Christmas. Pratt had been a member of the Phillies team that had surprised many by capturing the National League pennant in 1993. He had never been a starter and in fact had missed the entire '96 season. But he was a serviceable backup option for Hundley. The remainder of the off-season was largely quiet.

• • •

The Yankees had seen this before: David Cone on the mound, flustered; Ken Griffey Jr. circling the bases; over fifty-seven thousand Mariners fans going berserk. They'd seen it during the eighth inning of Game Five of the 1995 Division Series, and they were seeing it now in the third inning of Opening Night in 1997. The Kingdome had for years felt like a house of horrors for New York. The Yankees had played worse in other ballparks, but something about the manner and frequency with which they lost there seemed to stick out more. The losses were often crushing, with the crowd taking extreme delight in breaking the heart of the big-money, elitist group from the East Coast.

Opening Night 1997 was no different. The defending champs started the season knowing that they now had a target on their back. They responded by taking a 1–0 lead in the first inning and a 2–1 lead after the second. But in the bottom of the third, Cone, sporting a new pitching motion that saw him raise both hands above his head before delivering a pitch, hung a breaking ball that former Yankee Russ Davis belted into the left-field stands to tie the game. Three batters later, Cone threw Griffey a 3-2 splitter on the outside part of the plate. The pitch was good enough to fool Griffey, but Griffey was good enough to still extend his arms and send the ball just over the wall in right field for his second home run of the game and a 4–2 Mariners lead. "I got too much of the plate with the splitter," said Cone. "I didn't think it would go out though."[18] Fans couldn't help but watch it and feel as though they were watching a repeat of that Division Series. The Yankees failed to score again. It was their fifteenth loss in their last seventeen games at the Kingdome. "Three mistakes," added Cone, who threw 119 pitches in his first start of the year. "That's my night."[19]

Opening Night had been disappointing, but the second game of the year provided a preview of what the Yankees could expect from their first baseman in 1997. Tino Martinez had come to New York with the burden of replacing Don Mattingly, possibly the most beloved athlete in the city's history. Martinez had delivered, hitting twenty-five home runs and driving in a team-leading 117 RBIs. In October, however, Tino had struggled mightily, going just 9-48 and failing to drive in a single run. When the World Series shifted to Atlanta and the Yankees lost the designated hitter option, Torre decided to bench Martinez in favor of Fielder. It was the right move, as Fielder put in an MVP-worthy performance.

Martinez quickly left any talk of postseason struggles behind when in game two of the 1997 season he hit three home runs off Seattle pitching while driving in seven in a 16–2 drubbing of the Mariners. It was the beginning of what would be a historic year for Martinez.

Still, in the initial goings, the defending champs could not find their groove. When the Yankees moved to Oakland, the bullpen spoiled a solid team debut by Wells when it blew a 2–1 lead in the eighth. Two days later an error by Boggs in the eighth inning overshadowed a dominant performance by Cone, leading to another loss. In between the Yankees won their second game of the year but at a cost.

Dwight Gooden had not felt quite right during the winter and through the spring. He had discomfort in his groin, so he informed the team medical staff in spring training. An MRI showed no issue, and staff suggested it was merely a muscle strain. It was actually a hernia, and in Gooden's first start of the year, he ruptured the muscle wall in his groin. He had to have surgery now to fix the issue, a necessity that cost him the next two and a half months of the season. Doc was not happy. "I'm relieved that they finally found out what it was, but at the same time I'm ticked off," said Gooden after learning of the true diagnosis. "I mentioned to them before Christmas that I was having discomfort in my groin, and I'm not getting it taken care of until next week. After being out of the game for a year and a half and missing more time late last year because of a tired arm, I didn't want to miss any time this season."[20]

Returning home with a 3-3 record, the Yankees hoisted their 1996 championship banner with the help of an old friend, Don Mattingly. He had given the Yankees his blessing in November 1995 to move on without him, though he had refrained from officially retiring from the game. In January 1997, however, at a press conference at Yankee Stadium he made it official: his playing days were over. Mattingly's career had been sandwiched between two World Series appearances by the team, a reflection more on the poor state of the organization during his time there than on Mattingly's performance. "He taught Bernie Williams and a lot of guys here how to play the game," said Cone. "I think Donnie was part of the championship."[21]

The Yankees announced that they would retire his number 23 in August, and now he was back at the stadium to hoist their twenty-third championship banner during a sun-splashed day in the Bronx. "It's a little different seeing Opening Day from this perspective," said Mattingly.[22]

The home opener was setting up to be the perfect day. When Paul O'Neill drove in a run in the seventh, it gave the team a 1–0 lead behind the dominant pitching of Cone, who struck out twelve A's. Then in the ninth, protecting that lead and making his first Yankee Stadium appearance as the team's official closer, Mariano Rivera began the inning by throwing a middle-of-the-plate fastball to Oakland slugger Mark McGwire. On his way to hitting fifty-eight home runs that year between the A's and Cardinals, McGwire swung and demolished the pitch, sending it into the black seats in centerfield for a game-tying home run. It was the first home run Rivera had allowed to a right-handed batter since September 1995 and just the sixth hit he had allowed to the first batter he faced since the start of the 1996 season. The stadium went silent outside of the celebratory noise coming from the Oakland dugout. "We had everything in place going to the ninth inning," said Torre. "Then that big monster tied it up, and we couldn't do anything."[23]

New York lost the game three innings later, and people started to ask: Did the Yankees make a mistake entrusting Rivera as the closer? Absurd as the question may seem in hindsight, it was not ridiculous at the time. Three days earlier Rivera had blown a one-run ninth inning lead in Anaheim, a game the Yankees also lost in extra innings. Four days after the McGwire shot, entrusted with a one-run lead at home against the Angels, Rivera gave up a two-out, two-run double to former Yankee Jim Leyritz, leading to a 6–5 defeat. He was booed off the mound. In one week Rivera had blown three out of four save opportunities. In nine total innings for the year, he'd allowed fourteen hits and four runs. Meanwhile, Wetteland was a perfect 4-4 in save opportunities in Texas and had not allowed a run.

"Less than two weeks into the season, the decision not to re-sign John Wetteland and to promote Rivera looks dubious," wrote Jack Curry of the *New York Times*.[24] Curry was especially pointed in his writing, noting that the Yankees just assumed Rivera would slip into the role with no problem and that they had played it cheap by refusing to offer Wetteland a contract. "Mariano Rivera, we have seen John Wetteland. You are not John Wetteland. Not yet. Maybe never," Curry wrote two days after the Angels game.[25]

Rivera, who rarely looked or felt rattled on the ballfield, was putting an intense amount of pressure on himself. The blown saves appeared to be hurting his confidence. After the Leyritz game he sat at the buffet table in the clubhouse and "jabbed at his food, stared at a can of soda and looked perplexed."[26] "I told him, 'You're the guy I want out there saving my games,'" Cone explained to Rivera after one of the blown saves. "I wanted Mariano to know that I have faith in him."[27]

In-mid April Torre called Rivera into his office to talk with him and Stottlemyre. You're pressing, Torre told Rivera. The manager explained that Mariano was trying too hard to make the perfect pitch, to try and convince people he had what it takes to be the team's closer.

Rivera had gotten away from what had made him so successful, Stottlemyre said to the pitcher. By trying to do too much, he was taking away some of his aggressiveness and hurting his command. He was the team's closer. He was their guy, and the team wanted him to be that guy, and that was not going to change, Torre explained.[28]

The conversation put Rivera at ease. He converted his next twelve consecutive save opportunities, allowing only two runs in the process.

Rivera was not the only one struggling early on. On April 17 the bullpen blew a 4–1 lead in Milwaukee. The Yankees fell to 5-10 and a shocking six games out of first, despite the season's not even being three weeks old. In desperate need of turning their season around, the Yankees finally went on a run. They took three of four from the White Sox in Chicago, swept a two-game series at home against the Brewers, and then took two of three from the White Sox and Mariners at home before heading to Kansas City and winning two of three there. Overall they won eleven of fifteen games at the end of April and into the first week of May.

Leading the charge was Tino Martinez, who, after his three-home-run game in Seattle had gone homerless for ten games before exploding. He hit two home runs and drove in five runs in Chicago, a series where he batted .412. He drove in seven runs during the two-game sweep of Milwaukee, then hit two home runs and drove in five more against the White Sox and Seattle. For April, Martinez batted .327 with a 1.005 OPS and drove in a then-record thirty-four RBIS.

Bernie Williams was following up his best season with an even better performance. During a fifteen-game run, Williams batted .441 and scored nineteen runs while driving in sixteen. Cone recovered from his Opening Night loss and was among the league leaders in ERA and strikeouts. "This is the best I've felt in years, back to early Mets days," said Cone of his start. "I really feel like the more windup I've incorporated has really helped."[29]

Wells had turned in several solid performances, eating up innings along the way. Rivera recovered from the early season blown saves to convert all six opportunities during the run, allowing only five hits in seven and two-thirds innings.

Perhaps most noteworthy was a seventh-inning home run hit at Kaufman Stadium during the final game of the Kansas City series. After fifty Major League at bats, Jorge Posada had final gone deep. "It's awesome," said Posada of the moment. "I thought I wouldn't get it until the end of the season."[30]

It was a signature moment for the catcher. Born in Puerto Rico, Posada's father, Jorge Senior, had been a stellar athlete in Cuba: swimming, basketball, baseball. You name it, Senior could excel at it. Then Castro took over the island, and Senior fled, the full promise of his athleticism never realized. He landed in Puerto Rico, where he passed that athleticism on to his son, who from an early age "loved swinging a bat and watching the ball fly off it in the Puerto Rican sky."[31] His ability was obvious, and various parts of his upbringing, such as taunts from classmates that included calling him "Dumbo" because of his ears, stiffened Posada's resolve to never give in.

Posada ended up at Calhoun Community College in Decatur, Alabama, not as a catcher but as an infielder, largely playing second base. Speaking with a thick Spanish accent in the heart of the deep South was not the easiest experience, and he encountered brutal racism along the way. But his performance in Decatur was enough to convince the Yankees to draft him in 1990. He did not sign immediately, continuing to play for Calhoun and even, in the summer of 1990, playing ball for a semipro team in nearby Hartsell. Because many of his teammates had day jobs that sometimes kept them from making games, it was there that Posada played catcher for the first time. He eventually inked a deal with New York just before becoming eligible again for the draft.

As he made his way through the team's Minor League system, it became clear that Posada could hit and hit for power. It also became clear that he was not going to cut it at second base. The organization felt he just wasn't fast enough to play the position. Posada was not thrilled, but as a Single A player he did what the Yankees wanted. It took a while. He committed thirty-eight passed balls in 1993. The more he caught, though, the better and more self-assured he got. But Posada incurred a setback while playing for Triple A Columbus in 1994. While he was blocking home plate with his left leg exposed, a runner barreled into him. The collision resulted in a broken leg and ankle. "I was alternating screaming and gritting my teeth," said Posada. "I tore at the ground, grabbing fistfuls of dirt."[32]

Posada thought his career might be over as he writhed in the dirt. But in six weeks he was walking without assistance. Over many months of rehab, he was able to rejoin Columbus in 1995. That year word started getting around that Posada could hit. Teams began inquiring about him in possible trades with the Yankees, and in September Jorge became the last of what would eventually be known as the Core Four players—Pettitte, Rivera, Jeter, Posada—to make his big-league debut. It came as a ninth-inning defensive replacement, and it was the only appearance he made during the 1995 regular reason. When the Yankees made the playoffs, manager Buck Showalter decided to include Posada on the roster as a third-string catcher. Inserted as a pinch runner in the bottom of the twelfth inning of Game Two, he scored the tying run on a Rubén Sierra double. He was replaced in the lineup immediately thereafter, giving him an interesting career stat line to that point: two games, no plate appearances, one run scored.

Posada appeared in a handful of games in 1996, garnering his first career hit. Now, with Leyritz playing in California, the team was ready to make him their backup catcher to Girardi. He would learn from the veteran catcher, get used to Major League pitching, and, in a year or two, assume the role of full-time catcher. Girardi, graciously, offered no resistance, taking Posada under his wing, knowing full well that doing so would eventually cost him his job. Posasda did not hurt his case by hitting .357 with two home runs that spring, taking home the James P. Dawson Award for best rookie in camp.

The Yankees returned home and lost their first game against Minnesota before starting another streak, winning eight of nine games. Their record stood at 24-16, the same as it had been through forty games during their championship season. The only thing that stopped them from being in first place this time was a torrid start by the Baltimore Orioles. Having come within three wins of a World Series appearance the year before, Baltimore set about to plug holes in the roster. Jimmy Key replaced Wells in the rotation. Former Yankee Scott Kamienicki signed with Baltimore and had his best season in the big leagues. Mike Bordick, the surehanded A's shortstop, came to the Orioles as Cal Ripken Jr. officially moved over to third base. While Eddie Murray and Bobby Bonilla had left via free agency, holdover players would uniformly put in solid seasons for Baltimore. Eight of the nine starting regulars had double-digit home run seasons.

Even if the records were the same, the Yankees did not seem the same as the championship team from just a year ago. Controversy and off-the-field distractions were permeating the clubhouse. And they were not going to end until the last pitch of the season.

• • •

Uncertainty is what best described the Mets as they gathered in Port St. Lucie in the spring of 1997. This was largely the same team that had won just seventy-one games the year before. Had that team underperformed? Or were those seventy-one wins more representative of who the Mets were as a club? Time would tell. Mets GM Joe McIlvaine was so bold as to suggest this Mets team could win ninety-one games, just one fewer than the reigning world champions had won the previous year.

The players, sporting a new orange button on the top of their caps, headed to San Diego for Opening Day, and when Hundley hit a two-run home run in the season's third inning, all felt right for the Mets. An inning later Gilkey added two more runs on a single. It was only the fourth inning of the first game of the year, but the Mets were rolling. Until the sixth inning.

Pete Harnisch had been going through withdrawal for nearly a week after he had quit chewing tobacco. He had barely slept leading into his Opening Day start. "The last five nights I haven't gotten any sleep at all other than 90 minutes at one stretch last night, and woke up shivering and sweating," he said after the game.[33] That made his performance even more impressive, as through the first five innings he allowed only two hits to the defending NL West champions. Sitting on a 4–0 lead, he began the sixth inning by allowing a home run to Chris Gomez. Then one to Rickey Henderson. Then another to Quilvio Veras. That trio would ultimately hit only eleven more home runs combined the rest of the year. In the span of fourteen pitches, the Mets lead had gone from 4–0 to 4–3. Harnisch came out, and Yorkis Pérez came in. He sandwiched an out around two hits while allowing the tying run to score, leaving a runner on for Toby Borland. A serviceable reliever for the Phillies previously, Borland was making his team debut. He walked the first batter he faced, retired the next, then walked the next two. Borland departed the game for Barry Manuel, also making his team debut. Manuel proceeded to:

Hit a batter, allowing a run.

Walk in a run.

Give up a two-run single.

Give up a two-run double.

All told, the Padres scored eleven runs, seven of them with two outs, to take an 11–4 lead. It was one of the worst innings in the history of the Mets and the most runs any National League team had allowed in one Opening Day inning during the twentieth century. "In one horrendous sequence Tuesday, the Mets showed they're really no different than they were a year ago," wrote the *Bergen Record*'s Rafael Hermoso.[34] The team lost 12–5. Yorkis Pérez's ERA for the season was 54.00, Borland's was 81.00, and Manuel's was 20.25.

One bad game out of the gate was no reason to panic. There were 161 more games to play. But the Mets looked sluggish and overmatched as the first few weeks of the season played out. Fighting hard for their first win in the second game of the year, John Franco could not hold a 4–3 lead in the ninth. With two out in the top of the eleventh, Olerud lined a single to center to plate the go-ahead run. In his first two games as a Met, the first baseman hit .500 with four RBIs. The bullpen could not hold it. A sacrifice fly in the bottom of the inning tied the game before Toby Borland gave up the game-winning hit with two outs. The pen had now given up eleven runs in its first eight and one-third innings of the season.

Salvaging the third game of the series against San Diego helped alleviate some of the pressure on the Mets. Still, they lost two of three in San Francisco, then lost two heartbreakers in Los Angeles. In the first loss, the bullpen kept the team in the game with six shutout innings before allowing the game-winning hit with two outs in the fifteenth. The Mets' offense mustered only seven hits in the game. In the rubber match of the series, the bullpen again stood strong, holding the Dodgers scoreless for five innings before losing the game in the fourteenth. The offense went 1-16 in extra innings.

The Mets returned home and promptly got rained out for the opener and the next game. Playing a home-opener double header against the Giants in front of only twenty-two thousand fans, they lost the first game. Hoping to avoid a sweep, they took a 2–1 lead into the eighth of the second game, when former Met Jeff Kent hit a go-ahead two-run home run off McMichael. Valentine surprised reporters when, between games, he said the mound at Shea was higher than the league's ten-inch limit. Perhaps, he implied, that was to blame for starter Mark Clark's poor performance.

New York was 3-9 on the season, in dead last and floundering. The starting pitching had provided pleasant surprises in the performances of Dave Mlicki and Bobby Jones. Harnisch, however, was dealing with personal issues that would keep him out for months. Quitting tobacco had made him jittery but also tired while unable to sleep. Overall he just did not feel right. While Harnisch would dispute that tobacco withdrawal was the sole cause of it, he was suffering from clinical depression. Initially the Mets kept the news internal. After his Opening Day start, the team pulled him from his next scheduled appearance, and Harnisch disappeared from the clubhouse. In late April he held a conference call with reporters and admitted, for the first time publicly, his diagnosis. "I just felt very withdrawn," said Harnisch. "I was having trouble communicating. I felt very much to myself. The sleeping problems had come back from the previous week. I had a lot of anxiety."[35]

Harnisch began taking antidepressants and sought counseling. He would not return until August. Outside of Olerud, the offense was sputtering. Hundley, Gilkey, and Huskey were all hitting below .200, with Huskey having a higher batting average than OBP. Ordóñez, Everett, and Baerga had no extra-base hits among them in ninety-nine total at bats. Edgardo Alfonzo was hitting .129 with a .454 OPS. On April 14 the starting lineup featured six players with an OBP lower than .289. "Guys are just trying to do too much," said Valentine. "It usually happens at a time like this early on. They want to impress and they are trying to do too much. I am hoping they will relax and do the kind of job they are capable of doing."[36]

The Mets finally won their first home game of the year on April 15, but that was not the story. That night Major League Baseball celebrated the fiftieth anniversary of Jackie Robinson's breaking the game's color barrier. With President Bill Clinton in attendance, acting commissioner Bud Selig announced that baseball was retiring Robinson's number 42 forever. Players already wearing number 42, including the Mets' Huskey and the Yankees' Rivera, would be grandfathered in. Otherwise, "No. 42 belongs to Jackie Robinson for the ages," declared Selig.[37]

Ultimately the Mets went 5-6 during their first home stand of the year. They headed to Montreal and lost the first two games of the series, dropping them to 8-14 on the year. It's a long season, but the first month's worth of games indicated that the 1997 Mets would mimic the 1996 Mets, creating another long, fruitless summer in Queens.

That feeling only grew stronger when Isringhausen broke his wrist hitting a plastic garbage can. The pitcher had been rehabbing his shoulder and elbow in Norfolk in the hopes of joining the Mets' rotation. After a bad outing, he let fly on the receptacle. It delayed his progress. Then Isringhausen started feeling chest pains and having difficulty breathing. Concern grew that he might have cancer. Instead tests revealed tuberculosis, a bacterial infection that had been deadly before advancements in medicine in the middle of the twentieth century. There was immediate relief that it was not cancer but also a feeling of incredulousness that a Mets pitcher had contracted a disease that afflicted less than .0001 percent of all Americans. Isringhausen's season would get even weirder when, on September 10, he ended up stabbing himself in the thigh while opening a wheel lock.

On Sunday, April 27, Ordóñez slapped a single into right field off the Expos' Lee Smith in the top of the tenth to give the Mets a 5–3 lead and the eventual win. It was the last decision of Hall of Famer Smith's career, a footnote in a game that would ultimately mean more to the Mets. From that point on until the end of May, the team went on a 22-9 run, a .710 pace of winning ball the team had not experienced since the start of the decade.

After the thrilling win against the Expos, the Mets bashed the Reds for eighteen runs in a two-game mini sweep. They did not lose a series in May, including a sweep of the Cardinals in St. Louis that featured dramatic back-to-back home runs by Everett and Huskey off Dennis Eckersley in the third game to give the Mets the game in the ninth. The win put the Mets above .500 for the first time all season. Returning home, they took four of six from the Astros and Rockies, winning the final game of the home stand, yet again in dramatic fashion. They were down a run in the ninth when Olerud hit a two-run walk-off home run. His teammates went berserk as they waited for him at home plate, exuding the emotion of a team that had just won a playoff game.

Free from the pressure of having to try and hit home runs, Olerud was a revelation. The only player to hit consistently through the early going of the season, after forty-three games he was batting .350 with twelve doubles, seven home runs, and thirty-three RBIs.

By the end of May the Mets were 30-23, sitting in third place and waging an all-out fight for first. The offense had woken up in May, and Olerud no longer had to carry the load on his own. Hundley went on a tear, hitting .347 for the month, with six home runs and twenty RBIs. He was not fully replicating his 1996 numbers, but he was coming close, and his 1.016 OPS led the club.

Baerga, looking to reinvigorate a career that had stalled in Cleveland, hit .368 for the month, with six games of three hits or more. Huskey came to life, hitting .338 in May with seven home runs, nineteen RBIS, and a .663 slugging percentage.

Armando Reynoso pitched like a bona fide Cy Young candidate. He was 4-0 with a 2.95 ERA and had given the Mets a quality start in all but two of his appearances (he was 1-0 with a 2.70 ERA in those two non-quality starts). In his first June start Reynoso tossed a shutout against the Marlins. Rick Reed, the replacement player who had spent all the previous season in the Minors, was throwing even better than Reynoso, having allowed two earned runs or fewer in seven of his first nine starts. By the end of May his ERA stood at 1.70, and he'd walked only eight hitters in sixty-eight and two-thirds innings.

Credit for the winning also went to Bobby Valentine. The Mets' manager had his team playing with a zest for the game that had been missing for years. He introduced unorthodox methods, such as constantly changing the lineup around. This not only kept all the players on their toes but also kept them vested in each day's game since they might be hitting second or eighth or not playing at all. Valentine also tried to communicate directly with each player on his line of thinking during a game: why he was bunting; why he wasn't stealing; why he was not making a move. The idea was to prevent something of which Valentine himself had been guilty back in the day: having a player openly second-guessing the manager.

"Some of the things Valentine does, some of his lineups, make you scratch your head," said John Franco at the time. "But it all seems to work, so you go with the flow. He's kept everyone involved and everything positive. We have a great attitude and you have to give Bobby credit for that."[38]

Valentine also gave each player a portable monitor to use on flights. The idea was for each player to review tapes specifically created for him to help him improve his game. It would eventually become commonplace but was novel at the time.

The Mets were not only winning, but they were also exciting. On June 1 they even had a better record than the defending world champs and were fewer games out of first place. They remained in third place in what was turning out to be the highly competitive NL East when the Red Sox came to

Shea for the two teams' first-ever interleague match-up. It was an exciting moment, as the teams had not faced each other in a meaningful way since Game Seven of the 1986 World Series. At the same time, it was somewhat bittersweet: a reminder of the dynasty that was meant to begin on that night but never materialized. It also represented a touch of irony: of the eight active players who had participated in that World Series, none still played for either team, but three—Gooden, Strawberry, and Boggs—played for the Yankees, an unthinkable scenario in 1986.

Mookie Wilson threw out the first pitch and, coincidentally, the second-base umpire was named Bucknor (spelled differently than the former Boston first baseman). Carl Everett hit the first interleague pitch ever thrown to a Met for a home run. It was not enough. The Mets lost, 8–4. The loss went to Reed, who, after starting off with an ERA of 1.27, by mid-May had won only a single game in his last seven starts. The next day Mark Clark created a buzz when he took a no-hitter into the eighth inning. No Met had ever thrown a no-hitter before, and Clark made it all the more intriguing when he homered in the fifth. Clark allowed a leadoff single in the eighth, though, losing the no-hitter but eventually getting the victory.

Losing four of the first six interleague games, the Mets were glad to get back to National League opponents. They swept the Pirates, doing so yet again with excitement and walk-off wins. In the first game of the series, John Franco gave up a game-tying three-run home run with two outs in the ninth. It could have been a deflating moment. Instead, in the bottom of the inning, Jason Hardtke, a backup infielder who had made his season debut two innings earlier, singled in the winning run, one of just sixteen career RBIs for Hardtke.

Three days later, after Franco again blew a ninth-inning lead with two out, Everett came to the rescue with a three-run home run in the tenth. The Mets were becoming the walk-off kids, making the best of blown leads that could have deflated team morale.

The four-game sweep of Pittsburgh fed into the first big divisional match-up of the season: three games at home against the Braves. With the Mets six games out of first, the series presented a key opportunity to make up ground in the division while making a statement that the Mets were for real.

Everett again provided the heroics, hitting a two-run home run in the sixth of the first game off John Smoltz that gave the Mets the lead for good. In the second game, the Amazin's did it again, this time with Baerga playing hero. With the team down two in the eighth, Baerga swatted at an outside fastball and sent it just over the wall in left field, putting the crowd of twenty-six thousand into a frenzy as he pumped his fist rounding first base. After McMichael struck out Eddie Pérez with the based loaded in the ninth, thrilling the crowd so intensely that the television cameras visibly rocked back and forth, Baerga singled against a drawn-in infield in the bottom of the inning to win it.

Shea Stadium shook. Literally. The Mets were just four games out of first and playing a brand of ball that made every night a thrill ride. The Braves avoided the sweep, but the Mets had made their point. They were not going to be bullied anymore. The Mets closed out the first half—how else?—with a walk-off win against the Marlins courtesy of an Everett single. "This is a nice little way to end the first half, with a little exclamation mark," said an excited Valentine after the game. "I think the first half was a good half for building. We still have improvements to make and we still have places to go from here."[39]

They entered the break 48-38, their best first-half record in seven years and only half a game worse than their crosstown rivals. "It is the All-Star break and the Mets are still playing for something this year," wrote the *Bergen Record*'s Steve Adamek. "Their second half matters for the first time since Bud Harrelson was the manager and Bobby Bonilla was in Pittsburgh."[40]

"Same time last year, Bobby Valentine was sacking out on worn out mattresses in cheap motels, scraping his nickels together for phone calls home and sneaking back for drink refills at roadside burger places. . . . Valentine never dreamed that he'd be where he is today: living in his hometown of Stamford, Conn., managing the team he cheered as a child and being an early front-runner for National League Manager of the Year," noted the *Star-Ledger*'s Lawrence Rocca.[41]

The Mets would open the second half with four big games in Atlanta, their first time playing at the new Turner Field. It would be yet another opportunity to make a statement and show that they would not fade in the second half. Not this time.

• • •

As quickly as the Yankees won eight out of nine, they lost eight out of ten, with seven of the losses coming against division rivals. One of those wins came courtesy of Charlie Hayes, who hit a two-run walk-off home run against the Red Sox. The home run was noteworthy, but Hayes would soon become embroiled in a controversy of his own making. In Baltimore on June 3 he emerged from an elevator with several teammates when a fan approached him looking to shake his hand. Hayes refused and allegedly made a racially charged remark, though neither he nor the fan would directly address that with the media. Hayes at first denied that the incident took place, then was forced to apologize. "The biggest thing is to get this behind me," Hayes said. "I know I am a good person. I told [the fan] I was sorry for everything. He accepted my apology."[42] The fan did not accept the apology, though, and the entire incident soured Steinbrenner's feelings about the third baseman. Hayes was as good as gone once the season was over.

There was more. In the off-season Fielder had griped about being bench for Game One of the 1996 American League Division Series (ALDS), demanded a contract extension, demanded a trade when an extension was not offered, and at times had gone AWOL when Torre tried to reach him to discuss everything. "Fielder still doesn't understand how bad he looked or sounded, and how quickly he forfeited his title as the hippest, coolest, fat guy ever to play for the Yankees," wrote the *Bergen Record*'s Bob Klapisch just after Opening Day.[43]

Fielder's general unhappiness seeped into spring training as he was still demanding a trade. No team wanted him, thanks to the $7.2 million he was due. Fielder dropped his trade demand, but it was too late to assuage any hurt feelings. When players were introduced during the home opener, some in the crowd booed the postseason hero. When Fielder went 0-5 to drop his season average to .122, they booed some more. "That's the way they feel; I can't control the way they feel," said Fielder of the crowd reaction. "That's their way of saying they didn't appreciate what went on over the winter, all the things that went on. I understand. That's fair."[44]

Steinbrenner himself was the cause of much of the drama. During the off-season the Boss had announced a deal with Adidas providing the company exclusive rights for ten years to bedeck Yankees uniforms, Yankees apparel, and Yankee Stadium with its trademark logo. In exchange the Yankees would receive $95 million. The deal was shocking, especially to acting commissioner Selig, who was in the midst of implementing a national marketing plan for the game. This coincided with a new labor agreement that introduced revenue sharing among all teams and a luxury tax on teams whose payrolls exceeded a certain amount. Steinbrenner deplored both actions, perceiving them as punishment meted out specifically on the Yankees and no one else. The Adidas deal was a way to get around them.

Shortly after the deal went public and after the Yankees had slapped the Adidas logo on nearly everything within Yankee Stadium short of the urinals, Selig announced that the Yankees could not move forward with it. They were not allowed, in any way, to brand anything with the Adidas logo. On May 6 Steinbrenner, along with Adidas, responded by suing Major League Baseball, each of the twenty-nine other teams, and a handful of baseball personnel. As punishment the Boss was removed from baseball's Executive Council and its realignment committee.

That turned out not to even be the biggest Steinbrenner-related distraction in May. That prize belonged to Steinbrenner's dogged pursuit of a pitcher who had never set foot on a Major League mound in the United States. During the 1990s, as international free agents became more and more popular, Steinbrenner became more driven to sign them. It wasn't just what one player could do on the field; it was the additional fans and revenue a pitcher from, say, Central America or Japan could bring to the table.

Japan was one area the Yankees had pursued with little success. In January 1997 the Padres acquired the rights to pitcher Hideki Irabu. The big right-hander had dominated Japanese baseball with a fastball that usually hit the high nineties and a split-finger that seemed to drop off the planet. American coaches and players who had seen him testified to Irabu's being the real deal. "He's got a nasty forkball and an eephus curveball," said former Yankee Hensley Meulens, who had played three years in Japan. "This guy is definitely a better pitcher than Hideo Nomo. This guy is definitely going to be an impact player."[45] "He's blessed," noted Valentine, who had managed Irabu in Japan. "He has a special arm. Not many guys throw like he does."[46] He was the Japanese Nolan Ryan or Roger Clemens. Steinbrenner wanted him. Badly.

The Padres had acquired the rights to Irabu largely because they had fostered a relationship with the Chiba Lotte Marines, Irabu's team in Japan. No other team was allowed to negotiate with the pitcher, a move that the Boss loudly decried. "I think the young man has certain rights, too," Steinbrenner said after the Padres deal was announced. "We sure would like to have him play for us."[47]

Steinbrenner's wish was going to come true. Though San Diego had acquired the rights to sign Irabu, the pitcher made clear he would leave

Japan for one team only: the New York Yankees. It boxed the Padres in and gave them almost no leverage in trying to make a deal. Other teams, including the Mets, were desperate for Irabu's services. The Mets offered San Diego pitcher Mark Clark and two Minor League pitchers. "We were going to make the best offer we could," said Mets owner Fred Wilpon. "We were going to try to be as responsive as we could to them, and we were. We were never going to be irresponsible. We did what we thought was appropriate. We made a hell of an offer."[48]

But the Padres had only two choices. They could either try to force Irabu—who already had a reputation for being moody and distant—to play for them or deal him to the Yankees at a discounted rate. When they initially asked about having Jeter or Rivera be part of a trade, the Yankees laughed. The fact that it had come to this aroused suspicions that the Yankees were guilty of tampering. Any allegations came to nothing, though, and ultimately on May 29 the Yankees sent Rubén Rivera, three prospects, and $3 million to San Diego for Irabu. They also gave Irabu a $12.8 million contract, including a club record $7.5 million signing bonus.

In a clubhouse filled with guys whom Steinbrenner had tried to short-change in arbitration or refused to sign to long-term deals, such a contract was bound to cause a problem. "I think it's bullshit that he's getting all that money, but if he can get it, he can get it," said Wells. "Does he deserve it? Fuck, no. Personally, I don't care but a lot of guys in here are going to be offended when the deal gets done."[49] Jeff Nelson added, "Everyone seems to be getting tons of money, even players out of college and high school. It's kind of tough to swallow when you haven't thrown a pitch in the majors."[50] "[They] think of Irabu as a media creation, someone who's made a career out of slaying Japanese hitters and American castoffs such as Pete Incaviglia and Tom O'Malley," wrote Klapisch.[51]

Irabu had not even set foot in Yankee Stadium yet, and his teammates were already resentful of him. The press smelled blood in the water. "The Yankees had better pray he doesn't become the next Brien Taylor, a former No. 1 pick who became a bust after injuring his shoulder in a street fight," wrote Claire Smith of the *New York Times*.[52]

With Irabu now set to work his way through the Minors and Hayes and Fielder drawing unwelcome headlines, the Yankees attempted to right themselves on the field. Losing eight out of ten had dropped them eight games out of first place. June could be a make-or-break month for the club as the Orioles gave no indication they were going to let up in the AL East. They responded by going 17-8 for the month, chopping two and a half games off their deficit. Still, June was not without its moments. While they were playing their first-ever interleague game in Miami, Cone took a shutout into the ninth inning against the Marlins, only to allow a game-tying two-out single. The Yankees stranded six runners in extra innings before losing in the twelfth. The next night, Wells cemented his forever rickety relationship with Torre.

Wells had created problems before even putting on a Yankees uniform. In January a misunderstanding over the location of Wells's car keys resulted in his punching someone outside a San Diego bar. "When I saw them fighting, I just thought it was five drunks and I'd see a good fight," said one eyewitness. "Then I saw one guy hit another guy and hit the deck. He went down like a stone."[53]

Wells avoided being charged with assault but broke a bone in his pitching hand. When he showed up for spring training, he became afflicted with gout, a form of inflammatory arthritis that causes joint point. Some Yankee personnel grumbled that the gout could be attributed to Wells's questionable eating and drinking habits. Then came June 14 in Miami. Wells had gotten shelled in the first inning, capped by a Gary Sheffield grand slam. In the top of the second, Wells, forced to bat in a National League park, stood in the on-deck circle and began jawing with the home plate umpire, Greg Bonin, over the strike zone. Bonin threw him out of the game. Torre was livid. The Yankees' bullpen was exhausted and could hardly afford to pitch two innings that day, let alone eight. The game was eventually rained out, but Torre and Stottlemyre were no less angry. They stopped talking to Wells, giving him the cold shoulder for days. They saw his ejection as the act of a selfish person who had already caused them enough headaches. "I was more than aggravated," Torre said after the game. "That was unprofessional. There's no excuse for it. He left us hanging."[54]

Eventually Wells apologized, but the damage was done. Even Cone had confronted the pitcher about his action in the clubhouse. The Yankees won the make-up game in Florida the next day, the first of a doubleheader. In the second game they scored two runs in the ninth, the last on a Pat Kelly triple, to take a one-run lead into the bottom of the inning. But with the based loaded and one out, Kelly allowed a tailor-made double-play ground ball to roll between his legs, giving Florida the game.

Less than two weeks later Wells again faced the ire of Torre. A well-known admirer of Babe Ruth, Wells purchased a Yankees cap in which the Babe had played during his final season with the Yankees. Showing it around the clubhouse, Wells told Torre he'd like to wear it on the mound during the game. Players were not allowed to wear whatever they wanted on the field. Torre told him he'd have to get permission from the league to do so, and if he planned on doing that, he should let Torre know first so he could get the necessary approvals. Torre was not keen on the idea, though. In the first inning of his June 28 start against the Indians, Wells took the mound wearing the sixty-three-year-old item. FOX, broadcasting the game nationally, immediately picked up on it, zooming onto Wells's head to show Ruth's cap. After Wells got out of the first without allowing a run, an angry Torre told him he had to take the hat off. "I made him take it off," Torre said after the game. "I didn't know he had it on until he was out in the middle of the diamond. It wasn't the standard uniform."[55] Torre fined Wells $2,500 for the incident.

The manager was now understanding why the lefty had worn out his welcome just about every place he went. Wells, meanwhile, didn't understand the big deal. "I was very nervous but it's just a hat," he said during an interview not long after.[56]

Perhaps the most important event, however, occurred not during a game but before it. The Yankees were in Detroit in late June when, hours before the game, Rivera was playing catch with fellow Panamanian Ramiro Mendoza in front of the team's dugout. As they threw more and more, Mendoza began to complain that Rivera's tosses were moving too much. They kept breaking in toward Mendoza's right side, almost like sliders, except they were not off-speed pitchers. They were fastballs. Mendoza thought Mariano was messing with him, and he was having so much trouble catching the ball that he thought he might get hurt. "We keep playing catch. I throw the ball to him again and the same thing happens. It breaks about a foot right when it is on top of him, and again he almost misses it completely," recalled Rivera.[57]

Mendoza, fearing for his safety, ended the game of catch. Rivera, not knowing what was going on, went to bullpen catcher Mike Borzello and then Stottlemyre to see if either of them knew what was happening. "He threw it at first and I'm like, 'OK, what was that?'" said Borzello. "We took that ball out—maybe it was scuffed—and he did it again. I go, 'What are you doing?' He goes, 'I don't know.'"[58]

Rivera was gripping his fastball the way he always did, in what is known as a four-seam grip. Four-seam fastballs, sometimes referred to as rising fastballs, often have little vertical or horizontal movement. They rely on the speed with which the pitch is thrown to overpower hitters, who often believe the pitch is rising, though that is just an optical allusion. Rivera had dominated hitters so far with this pitch, possibly in part because his small form deceived hitters from realizing just how fast he was capable of tossing the ball.

Rivera's four-seam grip was now acting more like a cut fastball. This kind of pitch has movement like a slider in that it breaks right to left when released by a right-handed pitcher. But it's thrown at a higher velocity than a slider, and that is part of what makes it so effective when thrown correctly. How Rivera was now doing this was a mystery to both Borzello and Stottlemyre. He was using the same grip and the same motion and was not throwing it any harder or softer than normal. Yet the movement was incredible, and Rivera's initial reaction was concern—concern that he would no longer be able to control his fastball.

Over the next few weeks Rivera worked with Stottlemyre to home in the pitch and better command it to his advantage. The result would be one of the most unhittable pitches in the history of baseball.

Rivera's cutter had movement like few had seen before. As his career went on, switch hitters would sometimes opt to bat right-handed against Rivera for fear of having his cutter jam them from the left side of the plate. One result was that Rivera's strikeout totals, while still impressive, would never match his 1996-level dominance. Instead the cutter would simply shatter bat after bat after bat over the years, resulting in weak contact. What became more maddening was that hitters often anticipated the pitch coming and still could not make solid contact. The Tampa Bay Devil Rays used to joke about Rivera's tipping his pitches because they all knew the cutter was coming.

Rivera acclimated to life with the cutter, and there's never been a full understanding of just how it happened. "How can I explain it any other way than as one more incredible gift from the Lord," said Rivera, a deeply religious man, in his autobiography.[59]

Heading into the All-Star break, the Yankees were seven games out of first, four games worse than they had been at the same point in 1996. The slow start to the year had cost them, but there was still another half of the season to play. And they had something the Orioles would not have in that half season of baseball. They had the Japanese Nolan Ryan joining their starting rotation.

• • •

Turner Field, named for the Braves' longtime eccentric owner Ted Turner, had been built to showcase the 1996 Summer Olympic Games in Atlanta. Situated across the street from Fulton County Stadium, Centennial Olympic Stadium, as it was first called, was converted into a baseball-only facility in time for the 1997 season. Unlike many of the ballparks built in the 1990s, Turner Field did not possess quirky angles or monstrous walls. The outfield dimensions were nearly identical, with right field being slightly further in the power alley than left. An abundance of blue filled the stadium, from the seats to the outfield walls. It was a simple but enjoyable place to take in a game, even though its location and lack of parking made some fans hesitate to make the commute to downtown Atlanta.

On July 10, 1997, the Mets played their first game ever at the new ballpark. Over the course of the next four years, no other stadium, outside of their own home of Shea, would play as important a role for the team.

Starting the All-Star break in third place and trailing Atlanta by eight and a half games, the Mets did in the first game against Atlanta what they had done all year: they won in thrilling fashion. Trailing 5–1 after five innings, they chipped away at the lead until Hundley nailed a Mark Wohlers fastball for a three-run home run in the eighth to give the Mets the lead. The bullpen gave the lead back, but as had already happened countless times in the season, the Mets persevered rather than crumbled. A Manny Alexander triple and an Alfonzo single gave them the lead back while John Franco struck out the side to end the game.

The next night the Mets did it again. Trailing 5–1 in the sixth, they strung together five singles and a walk off Tom Glavine, all with two outs, to tie the game. Atlanta took the lead back in the seventh, so the Mets clawed back with four in the eighth, with Matt Franco's pinch-hit double giving the team the lead for good. "It's been unbelievable the way we've been coming back," said John Franco afterward. "It's getting to the point where we're down 5–1, 6–1 and we still think we're going to win. That's an incredible attitude to have. It seems like we have to be two or three runs down to start playing well."[60]

After losing the third game of the series, the Mets proceeded to pull off the comeback win of the season in the fourth and final game. On national television as part of ESPN's *Sunday Night Baseball*, Atlanta battered Bobby Jones for six two-out runs in the first, and it looked like the Braves would pull off a split of the series. Instead Huskey hit two-run and three-run home runs over the course of three innings, putting the Mets right back in the game. The Mets tied it in the fifth, and the game stayed tied at 6–6 until the tenth inning. There Alex Ochoa, who had shown promise in '96 but had struggled mightily in the early goings of '97, hit a solo home run. The shot, just his second of the year, was enough as John Franco got his third save of the series. "Can you tell me something?" bullpen coach Randy Niemann asked Franco as they walked back into the clubhouse. "Can you tell me how we did that? How did we do that?"[61] "The Amazin' Mets of 1997 just keep raising the bar of improbability. And they keep clearing it," wrote the *Star-Ledger*'s Lawrence Rocca.[62]

The Mets had come into Atlanta and taken three of four, moving them to within six and a half games of Atlanta for first. Perhaps more important, it put them just a game and half out of the wild-card lead. Meanwhile, as the team contributed one comeback win after another, behind the scenes, change was on the horizon.

Joe McIlvaine had endured a tumultuous run as general manager since coming back in 1993. Having been with the team during the 1980s heydays, he returned to an organization in chaos. With ownership looking to cut costs, McIlvaine oversaw the dismantling of the team's high-priced stars who had never worked out: Bonilla; Saberhagen; Coleman; Murray. All gone. The organization moved toward lower-maintenance players and a youth movement. It had not worked in 1995 or 1996, though that was not entirely McIlvaine's fault. Now the team was undergoing a resurgence, and co-owners Fred Wilpon and Nelson Doubleday did not necessarily think that was McIlvaine's fault either.

The general manager had never really felt comfortable in the position. McIlvaine loved evaluating young talent. Often he was not at Shea Stadium but following one of the organization's Minor League clubs. That just was not the role of the GM, and the co-owners, along with many others in the organization, began to tire of McIlvaine's absences, Wilpon especially. The co-owners had asked McIlvaine to set up regular calls to review various aspects of the organization. McIlvaine did the calls but not regularly.

Wilpon and Doubleday wanted someone who would be in the thick of things at Shea, someone who could develop relationships and handle the media, two things at which McIlvaine was not adept. On July 15 in Pittsburgh, McIlvaine "greeted an approaching group of reporters by suddenly turning and ducking into the players' bathroom."[63]

It was one of McIlvaine's last acts as general manager. Later that night he learned from a group of reporters that he had been let go. "I think making the move now . . . gives us a better chance to make some progress with reinforcements," said Wilpon in a not-so-subtle jab at McIlvaine's ability to improve the team as GM.[64]

Wilpon further explained that with McIlvaine's contract up after the year, the co-owners would not be offering him an extension. That meant they wanted to have someone in place now who could prepare them for the stretch run but also be ready for the expansion draft that was set to take place that November. "We think this team is close and we want to do what we can for this team right now, this season," added Wilpon.[65]

McIlvaine was gracious about the change, heading to Shea Stadium the next day to debrief and provide notes on recent trade discussions to the man who would be taking his place: thirty-four-year-old assistant general manager Steve Phillips. The new GM had played infield in the Mets' Minor League system in the 1980s before retiring and earning a degree in psychology from the University of Michigan. It was actually McIlvaine who, as a scout, had discovered Phillips and had coaxed him into joining the organization's front office in 1990. Phillips worked his way up the ladder—some said by being a "yes" man—to become McIlvaine's assistant. Now he was getting the big chair. "Joe has handled this with class and dignity," said Phillips, who was also concerned about the perception that he might have orchestrated McIlvaine's ouster. "We had a great conversation. He's been my tutor and personal friend."[66]

In Phillips's first game as GM, Reynoso had to leave early with elbow and shoulder soreness. Initially the team thought it would result in just one missed start at worst. It turned out he needed season-ending shoulder surgery.

Phillips's first win as GM came, appropriately enough, thanks to a walk-off single by Huskey against the Cubs. It was the first of what would be five wins in a row and eight wins over nine games, pulling the team into a tie with the Marlins for the wild-card lead. Meanwhile, the July 31 trade deadline came and went without any deals, surprising and angering fans who felt the Mets did not have all the key components they needed to stay in contention. Phillips, however, was attempting to find just such components and, a week later, completed a deal with the Cubs that brought outfielder Brian McRae and relief pitchers Mel Rojas and Turk Wendell to the Mets.

Wendell proved to be the centerpiece of the deal, even though the entire transaction was by no means considered a blockbuster. Born Steven John Wendell, he got the nickname "Turk," according to him, because, "My grandfather nicknamed me after one of his buddies because I was always doing stupid, rebellious things."[67] It fit. Wendell was, by baseball standards, different. He had a series of routines that, in time, would make him stand out among his colleagues: eating black licorice and brushing his teeth between innings; hopping over the foul line; drawing crosses in the dirt; slamming the rosin bag down after throwing his warmup pitches. All of these labeled Wendell as an eccentric, a label that overshadowed his workhorse behavior and ethic on the baseball diamond. Wendell's fastball was not overpowering, but he used his motion and an effective changeup to deceive hitters. He'd had a career year with the Cubs the season before, saving eighteen games. He had struggled with Chicago in 1997, and the Mets hoped a change of scenery would revive him.

In exchange, the Mets sent Lance Johnson, Mark Clark, and Manny Alexander to Chicago. Johnson had turned in a fine season, though not as strong as his 1996 performance, when he had made the All-Star team. He had been stricken with shin splints in early May and missed six weeks. His .385 OBP was among the highest on the team, but his playing time had decreased as had his stolen bases and extra base hits, making him expendable.

On the day of the trade New York stood three games back of Florida in the wild card. The Marlins, who had gone on a free-agent spending spree during the off-season to secure their first-ever playoff appearance, were proving to be formidable contenders, even challenging the Braves for first place. As the season headed through the dog days of August, the question now was whether the Mets could keep pace and overtake them for a playoff spot.

• • •

Perhaps no mid-July home game against the Tigers had ever drawn as much buzz for the Yankees as the one on July 10, 1997. Starting off the second half of the season on a sultry Thursday night in the Bronx, Hideki Irabu made his Major League debut in front of 51,901 energized fans. The game was televised live in Japan, 8:30 a.m. local time, with Tokyo putting up giant televisions in public spaces. Steinbrenner made sure that sushi was served in the press dining room. An estimated three hundred reporters, one hundred of whom were from Japan, covered the event.

The crowd could not wait to finally catch a glimpse of the man who, despite all the attention garnered over the past three months, still largely remained an enigma, both professionally and personally. Could this man possibly live up to the hype George Steinbrenner and the media had created over him?

The answer, after the first two innings, appeared to be a resounding yes. Irabu, who was wearing a long-sleeved undershirt even though the temperature hovered around 80 degrees, struck out Bobby Higginson and Travis Fryman to end the first, then fanned Bob Hamelin and Damion Easley to end the second. The movement on Irabu's pitches was incredible. The strikeout of Higginson happened on a splitter that dropped a foot horizontally while moving a foot vertically into the opposite batter's box. Fryman, Hamelin, and Easley all went down swinging on splitters as well. The crowd ate it up, with some fans posting the letter "K"—the traditional symbol for a strikeout—in Japanese along the facing of the upper deck.

Irabu ran into trouble in the third, allowing his first hit and his first run. But after Martinez homered to give the Yankees the lead in the bottom of the inning, he struck out the side in the fourth. In the fifth, after Irabu had allowed one more run, Stottlemyre visited the mound to attempt to tell Irabu, in Japanese, that he was overthrowing. He then said, in English, "Keep your arm up. Do you understand that?" Irabu nodded, but just to be safe, Martinez tried a different tactic. "Suave," the first baseman told the pitcher in Spanish, meaning "relax." The surrounding infielders, led by Jeter, laughed at the exchange.[68]

Irabu departed with two outs in the seventh, yielding to the man who had most vocally criticized all the Irabu hoopla: Jeff Nelson. "He was outstanding, unbelievable, you couldn't ask for anything better," said Wells, another critic of Irabumania.[69]

All told, Irabu struck out nine and earned a loud curtain call, with flashbulbs popping all around the park as he emerged from the dugout, at the insistence of Cone, to doff his cap. The Yankees won the game, 10–3. "The experience was more than I dreamed of," said Irabu through his interpreter.[70]

Perhaps more than the win—for George Steinbrenner anyway—the night had gone off perfectly: a large crowd; lots of strike outs; a Yankees victory; building excitement for the next Irabu start.

The next start, however, was anything but perfect. Though he still picked up the victory, the Indians smacked Irabu for nine hits and five runs in five innings. Worse still, they were not even remotely impressed by what they saw. "He doesn't throw any harder than anybody else in the league. His split-finger is not any nastier than anybody [else's] in the league," said Indians outfielder David Justice.[71]

Five days later the Brewers got Irabu for six runs. When he came out of the game, he appeared to spit in the direction of the fans, as if sending them a message, though Irabu denied having done so. Then the Mariners teed off on him at Yankee Stadium, driving him out of the game after two innings and six runs allowed. In the three starts since his magical debut, Irabu had allowed sixteen earned runs in just under fourteen innings. That included six home runs against just seven strikeouts. His pitches had seemingly lost any movement. His fastball, while not losing velocity, was coming in straight as an arrow. Irabu was now learning that Major League hitters would hit a straight fastball no matter how hard it was thrown.

The Yankees sent him down to the Minors to work on his mechanics, a development that deeply embarrassed Steinbrenner. "He's not himself," said Steinbrenner in the pitcher's defense. "He's going through a period that a lot of pitchers go through. He's going through a dead-arm period. I'm not a baseball player, but my baseball people said everyone goes through it. He's going to be a good pitcher."[72]

When Irabu returned on August 13, he put in two solid starts, one against the Royals and one in Anaheim. But in Oakland on August 27 he allowed three home runs and five runs and failed to get out of the fourth inning. In his next start in Philadelphia he gave up nine hits and five runs in just three innings. Fans started joking that Irabu was actually pronounced I-Rob-You.

Joe Torre had seen enough. With Irabu's ERA standing at 7.68 and his having surrendered twelve home runs in his last thirty-one and a third innings, Torre yanked him from the rotation with the full support of the owner. "I have seven dozen Hideki Irabu T-shirts that I'm going to give to the Little Sisters of the Blind," Steinbrenner said as his prized overseas acquisition landed in the bullpen.[73]

On September 5 Pettitte was struck in the face by a Cal Ripken line drive and had to leave the game after the first inning. Irabu replaced him and gave up six earned runs in just over five innings. As the Yankees fought for a playoff spot the rest of the month, Torre made every effort not to use Irabu out of the bullpen. On the last day of the year he let Irabu start the game. By then the Yankees had already secured the wild card, and the outcome had no bearing on the team's future, outside of what it could possibly do for Irabu's mindset. He got the win, bringing his season to a merciful end with a 5-4 record and a 7.09 ERA. He then refused to report to the Arizona fall league, as the team wanted. Instead he remained in Tampa at the team's minicamp.

While Irabu struggled through his early starts, clubhouse controversy continued to embroil the team. In early June Steinbrenner had given a wide-ranging interview to some of the team's beat reporters. He was unsparing in his comments. When asked about pitcher Kenny Rogers, who had complained about the Yankees' acquisition of Irabu by asking what they needed another starting pitcher for, Steinbrenner said, "All you have to do is watch Rogers and you know what we need [Irabu] for."[74] When asked about the Boss's remarks, Rogers responded with, "Oh yeah . . . my buddy."[75]

The writing was on the wall. Rogers's second season in pinstripes had gone worse than his first. He was 3-3 at the time, with a 5.65 ERA, having failed to allow fewer than four runs in each of his last three starts. He continued to underperform and lost his spot in the starting rotation in late June. Just before the All-Star break the Yankees worked out a deal with the Padres, sending Rogers to San Diego for outfielder Greg Vaughn in a six-player deal. Vaughn was coming off a forty-one-homer season but had struggled during the first half of the year. While several of Rogers's teammates felt it was the best thing for him, Rogers himself did not want to leave the Yankees. He still believed he could figure out his issues, whatever they were, in New York.

The trade took place on a Friday, and Rogers packed his things, got on a plane, and headed to California. On Saturday the Yankees were on their way to an 8–0 win in Toronto when an announcement made its way through the press box in the fourth inning: the deal was off. Vaughn had failed his physical due to a torn right rotator cuff. The Padres disputed the finding. "As far as our medical staff is concerned, Greg Vaughn is healthy," said Padres manager Bruce Bochy.[76] Steinbrenner did not care what the Padres were saying, noting that the Yankees were "not going to take a wounded solider at $12 million, or whatever it is."[77]

Rogers jumped back on a plane to return to New York. It turned out that Vaughn was not the only one injured. Rogers was playing with a bum shoulder, an injury that limited him to only three appearances in July. He rejoined the rotation in August but gave up exactly six runs in each of his last three starts of the year and played no role in the postseason.

Rogers was not the only one to catch shrapnel from Steinbrenner's interview. Mariano Duncan had been a surprise sparkplug for the 1996 team, batting a career high .340. His "We play today, we win today. Das it" expression had become a team motto. The second baseman had started out strong in 1997, batting .333 through April. His numbers started to plummet in May, though, and his defense became an issue when his range became noticeably more restricted. "We've got to do something at second base," said Steinbrenner after he'd taken his shot at Rogers. "I don't think the feeling is Duncan has the range. He's made an awful lot of misplays lately."[78] He then suggested that Duncan would be better off in the outfield, where he had not played regularly in five years.

Duncan, already upset that the Yankees had not extended his contract after his stellar '96 season, was caught off guard by the comments. He had to have a meeting with Torre to ensure he was not now the team's backup outfielder. Torre said that was not the case, but a still irked Duncan let loose. "If that's the way they feel, I'll go back to being a backup," he told reporters. "If they don't want me, I know I can play for somebody."[79]

Over the next eight weeks, as Duncan's playing time became nearly non-existent, he continued taking jabs at Steinbrenner in the hopes of forcing a trade. "That was unfortunate, it really was," said Torre later in the year. "To me, Mo had more class than that. He overreacted and got himself bent out of shape. It bothered me because of what he meant to the team last year."[80]

At least three separate times a deal for Duncan was broached with the Giants, only to fall apart when Steinbrenner demanded too much in return. Duncan was also included in the Padres deal for Vaughn that fell apart. Finally, on July 29 around 10 a.m., Duncan was informed by Watson that he had been traded to the Blue Jays.

"I have peace of mind now," Duncan told reporters afterward. Then he took a parting shot at the Boss: "I don't have to show nothing to nobody. And I don't put much into what someone says if they don't say it to my face. Even if he apologized to me now, that wouldn't be good enough for me."[81] When Tino Martinez asked him for whom he had been traded, Duncan replied, "It doesn't matter. They could trade me for a piece of garbage."[82]

The trade also ended what had been a nightmare situation for Torre. He had an unhappy player in his clubhouse who, every day for over a month, had been taking pot shots at Torre's boss. "I think there will be a little less tension," Torre responded when asked about the deal. "Waiting to be traded makes for some uneasiness. . . . I'm happy it's over with right now, and I have nothing but great memories."[83]

Meanwhile, if there was anyone on the Yankees who had been unhappier than Duncan, it was Wade Boggs. The discontent had started in the off-season when the team had extended Charlie Hayes's contract, despite the fact that Boggs still had another year left on his deal. "By the way, does anyone believe for a minute that Wade Boggs is 'delighted' that Charlie Hayes got a contract extension? That's what his agent Alan Nero said," noted Bob Klapisch that off-season.[84]

Boggs and Hayes were equally unhappy when they reported to spring training, realizing that neither would be given the starting third-base job outright but would have to earn it over the other. Boggs won out and started the year in typical Boggs fashion, batting .311 with a .442 OBP in April. May, however, proved brutal for the future Hall of Famer. He went 8-56, a .143 clip, with only three extra-base hits. As his performance fell, Hayes, who had been unhappy with his role on the team, saw more and more playing time. When Hayes caught fire in late June, going 7-19 with two home runs and five RBIs over a five-game stretch, the third-base job was officially his.

On the same day that the Vaughn deal fell apart, Boggs had walked into Torre's office and conceded that he was no longer the team's starting third baseman. He then made it known to the press that he wanted out of New York. "I've conceded the job, and it's better for the team for him to play every day," Boggs told reporters in reference to Hayes.[85]

Three days later Boggs's agent reached out to the Rangers about a possible deal of third basemen: Boggs for Dean Palmer. After a massive 1996 season, Palmer had struggled to repeat his numbers in 1997 and was a pending free agent. But he earned substantially more than Boggs, a factor that was enough to squash any interest from the Yankees. "There's a big difference in money," Watson told reporters when asked about the proposal. "This is not as clean as it looks. . . . I don't know if I'd be interested."[86]

No deal with Texas happened, but Boggs insisted he wanted out. "Like Johnnie Cochran said, 'If you don't fit, you got to get rid,'" said Boggs, mangling the actual quote from Cochran.[87]

For two weeks the specter of Boggs leaving hung over the clubhouse. Then, on July 15, Fielder broke his thumb. It gave Boggs an opportunity to play at DH. He responded by going 6-7 in two games at Chicago, the start of a ten-game hitting streak. Boggs, whose average had fallen to .240 on July 6, finished the year hitting .292 and even regained the starting job at third when Hayes went down with a viral infection in late August. "I just felt I wasn't helping this team playing once a week or whatever it was and that it would have been better for all concerned for me to go somewhere else," said Boggs after becoming the regular third baseman again. "As it turned out, not getting traded may have been the best thing for me."[88]

Still, the general unease around the team did not dissipate. Factions began forming in a way that had largely been absent in 1996. "You have the Latinos hanging together. You've got the white guys hanging together. You've got the black guys hanging together. You've got the pitchers hanging together, the infielders, the outfielders, and there was none of that on our [1996 team]," said outfielder Tim Raines.[89]

On August 30 the tension nearly came to a head between two guys who seemingly liked each other: Steinbrenner and Wells. The pitcher had just come out of a game against Montreal, trailing 6–0. Earlier in the game Wells had given up a home run to Darren Fletcher when a fan reached over O'Neill and the top of the right field wall to snare the ball. Wells was annoyed by the incident, and he ran into Steinbrenner in the clubhouse after his outing was over.

"Hey, George, you need to get some security out there in right field. Build a wall or something," said Wells.

"Never mind about the fucking security, you just worry about pitching. You better start winning some games, because you're not the pitcher I thought you were," retorted Steinbrenner.

"Is that right? Well, you can go fuck yourself. If you don't like it, you can trade me."

"Believe me, I would, but no one wants your fat ass."

"You better get the fuck out of this room, before I fucking knock you out."

"Go ahead, do it. Try it. You think I'm afraid of you?"[90]

The incident remained under wraps for two weeks before word broke to the press. Wells refused to discuss it while Steinbrenner issued a cheeky statement about his own workout habits. "Now you guys have me taking on Wells," read the statement, addressed to reporters. "The only thing that really bothers me about that is I really need him down the stretch. I'm counting on him! So why hurt our chances?"[91]

Surprisingly though, the Yankees played their best ball of the season, despite Irabu's struggles, the clubhouse unhappiness, and the injuries.

Jeter, who even in his second season knew how much O'Neill disliked people telling him how well he was hitting, could not help but bait his teammate that summer. He would walk by the right fielder in the locker room and shout, "O'Neill, you can hit!"[92] Jeter was correct: O'Neill could hit. He set career highs in doubles and RBIs that year while posting the second-highest batting average of his career, .324. He hit .428 with runners in scoring position, a league best, with eighty-four RBIs.

Williams, despite missing a month's worth of games, drove in one hundred runs on his way to winning his first Gold Glove. Martinez was on his way to hitting forty-four home runs, the most by a Yankees first baseman since Lou Gehrig.

On August 13 the team brought back former Yankee Mike Stanley in a trade with the Red Sox. Stanley, the fan favorite whose departure from the team had caused fans to initially boo Girardi in 1996, served as a backup first baseman and DH the rest of the year.

Pettitte put in arguably his best season, setting a career high in innings pitched while winning eighteen games and leading the league in fewest home runs allowed per nine innings. Gooden returned after his hernia operation and won six games over the last two months of the season.

Even the lopsided losses brought moments of levity. On August 19 in Anaheim, the Yankees had fallen behind, 12–4, after five innings. With their bullpen badly depleted, Torre turned to Boggs to pitch the bottom of the eighth. Boggs, who was known for tinkering with a knuckleball during pregame warmups but had never pitched in a big-league game before, walked the first batter he faced. He then retired the next three with a mix of knuckleballs and slower-than-slow fastballs. He struck out Todd Greene to end the inning, drawing laughs from the dugout and cheers from the crowd. "It's pretty special, because I grew up idolizing Phil Niekro and I've thrown a knuckleball since I was 10 years old," said Boggs. "It took me 16 years to break it out, but it was well worth it. Joe asked me if I would do it, and I didn't give him the opportunity to say no. I just ran to the bullpen."[93]

Baltimore had simply been too good during this time for the Yankees to reach first place. In fact, the defending champs never held first at any point during the '97 season. Still, on September 20 they clinched a postseason berth, claiming the wild card with a walk-off win against Toronto. Despite the trials and tribulations of the season, the 1997 Yankees and the 1996 Yankees had remarkably similar seasons. The '96 team hit 162 home runs, while the '97 team hit 161. The '96 team slashed .288/.360/.436, while the '97 team slashed .287/.362/.436. The pitching staffs had similar strikeout totals, hits allowed, and home runs allowed. The '97 team's ERA, however, was over half a run better, an improvement that may have accounted for the four additional wins that the '97 team had over the championship team, finishing 96-66. All that was left now was to march through Cleveland in the Division Series, face off against familiar foe Seattle or Baltimore in the ALCS, then head back to the World Series.

• • •

August 9–26 proved a brutal seventeen-game stretch for the Mets where little went right. It began with three straight losses to Houston and extended through a road trip that saw them get swept in Colorado. Afterward the clubhouse was left searching for answers. The fatigue of a long trip was one of the issues. "We're at the end of a real long journey, and we were on a little less than a full tank of gas," said Valentine.[94]

They went 4-5 on a return trip home, but each loss seemed to coincidence with a Braves or Marlins win while each victory often failed to gain them any ground on either. Worse still, the tension got to the clubhouse.

Valentine was good friends with Hundley's father, Ray, a former big leaguer himself. Ray had approached Valentine earlier in the year to inform him that his son had a sleeping problem, a euphemism for his son's drinking and being out at night. Valentine offered to help Todd through it, and during the course of the year, he would sit with Hundley after particularly rough nights.

On August 20 the Mets were rained out at home. Valentine took questions from reporters, one of whom asked about Hundley's playing time, especially the lack of it in day games. Valentine responded, "He had a little trouble sleeping at night. Day games are a problem."[95] He expanded further, talking about Hundley being up until 4 a.m. once but clarifying that he did not mean that he was out partying.

Reporters immediately went to Hundley for a response. The catcher, whose relationship with Valentine had been strained at best to that point, fired back. "You guys know him well enough to know he'll come up with things that have nothing to do with this earth," he told the press.[96] Hundley continued, saying he had no idea what the manager was talking about and that, despite Valentine's saying that he might have discussed the issue with him, this was the first time Hundley was hearing about this concern. Eventually people began to wonder if Valentine had merely created an issue to deflect from the team's slump. Either way, Hundley continued to make his displeasure known. "I don't get paid enough to have a relationship with that guy," he said the day after Valentine's original comments. "You couldn't pay me enough." A day later Hundley approached Valentine and offered a peace between the two.[97]

On August 29 the Mets started a three-game series in Baltimore with a crushing loss to the Orioles. The bullpen could not maintain a 3–0 lead heading into the seventh and Cal Ripken Jr. singled in the winning run off John Franco in the twelfth. "We made a couple of mistakes," said Valentine. "They came back to haunt us."[98]

The loss put the Mets ten and a half games back of the Braves, effectively ending any chance the team had of winning the division. It also put them six back of the Marlins for the wild card, with the Giants also ahead of them for the final playoff spot.

More controversy engulfed the Mets when, the day after losing to Baltimore in the twelfth, they designated Harnisch for assignment. The pitcher had returned earlier in the month from his leave for clinical depression and gotten hit hard in three starts. The team moved him out of the rotation and into the bullpen, angering the pitcher. He made one more appearance, allowing two runs in an inning of work. Finally, the team decided to let him go. Harnisch decided to let loose. Hours after his release, he called into WFAN, New York City's flagship sports station, and lit into the organization, focusing much of his ire on Valentine. "On a personal, humane level . . . Bobby Valentine is a very low-grade person," Harnisch said from his hotel room. "I think from the front offices to umpires to players on down, there's not a whole lot of people that like Bobby Valentine."[99] It took less than twenty-four hours for the Mets to trade Harnisch to Milwaukee for a prospect who never made it to the Majors.

It had been a difficult stretch, but the team was not giving up. It rebounded to win the series against Baltimore and then swept the Blue Jays at home. A week later Olerud became the seventh player in franchise history to hit for the cycle. The feat was even more remarkable considering that it included Olerud's only triple of the year, his first triple since August 11, 1994.

Two days later the Mets mounted their most exciting comeback at Shea of the year. At home against Montreal, the Expos had jumped out to an early lead and were winning 6–0 heading into the ninth. The Mets had two runners on but had already recorded two outs in the inning. And then:

Single; two runs score.

Single.

Single; bases now loaded.

Up came Carl Everett. The Mets had had high hopes for Everett heading into 1997. He had not lived up to them. Everett had gotten off to a slow start that year, his slugging percentage lagging below .400 until mid-June. He had gone through a hot streak that month but had ultimately cooled again. He had never lived up to the power numbers the team felt he should be producing, and he was striking out too much for someone who was not producing enough extra base hits. Coming into this at bat with the bases loaded and as the tying run, Everett had hit just one home run in the last nine weeks. Still, he received unanimous support from the crowd as the count moved full. With fans and players on their feet, Everett pulled one over the right field wall, tying the game.

"We got a brand new, shiny one," yelled Mets play-by-play announcer Howie Rosen as the crowd screamed in excitement. It had been a long time since a Met had hit that big of a home run at Shea Stadium. It was to be Everett's last, and possible only, memorable on-field moment with the team. He may not have known it, but his Mets future had been sealed weeks earlier when a child-care worker at Shea Stadium noticed bruises on Everett's five-year-old daughter. The child, along with her four-year-old brother, was immediately taken out of the custody of Everett and his wife, Linda. Ultimately a family court judge ruled that both had been neglectful in the care of their children and that there was evidence of "excessive corporal punishment" inflicted on the kids by Linda.[100] While both Carl and Linda never admitted to having done anything wrong, they had to undergo and attend parenting classes before they could have custody of their children again, both of whom had been placed in foster care. The entire situation played out as the Mets were attempting to make the postseason. Coupled with Everett's performance and generally standoffish attitude, it meant that his time in New York would be done once the season ended.

The game moved into extras, where, in the twelfth, Bernard Gilkey came up with two runners on and two out. Like in the case of Everett, the Mets had been expecting much out of Gilkey when the season began. His performance in 1996 had been one of the best all-around offensive seasons in team history: 44 doubles, 30 home runs, 117 RBIS, a .955 OPS. Like Everett, though, he also started slowly in 1997. By late June it was clear he was not going to repeat his past season's performance. As pressure mounted to put up better numbers, Gilkey began getting advice from anyone who thought they knew something about baseball. It was overwhelming and unhelpful. "I was getting too much information. 'Try this, try that,'" said Gilkey. "In past years, I really didn't think too much about anything."[101] Even after he stopped listening, Gilkey never really found a groove during the season until the final weeks of September.

Now, though, Gilkey put that all behind him for one at bat as he drilled a game-winning home run into the mezzanine level at Shea. It was an exhilarating win, and when Mlicki and McMichael combined to shut out the Expos the next day, the Mets guaranteed their first .500 season in seven years.

It was becoming obvious at this point, though, that for all the Mets magic that year, it was ultimately not going to be enough to catch the Marlins. Even with the wins against Montreal, New York still trailed Florida by six games in the loss column with fourteen games left. When the Mets lost five games in a row to Atlanta, Philadelphia, and Florida, it put them on the brink of elimination. During those games Ordóñez set a team record for most consecutive hitless at bats by a position player after going 0-37. New York remained alive with three wins in Miami but lost the first game after returning home. At 10:55 p.m., five minutes before the loss, the Marlins won their game, clinching the wild card and officially knocking the Mets out of contention. The Marlins ultimately beat the Indians for their first-ever championship.

The mood in the Mets' clubhouse was somber as they walked in after the loss. "We put on a good show," said Valentine as he joylessly sipped a beer after the game. "People can say anything they want about why we didn't win more games or how we lost the games."[102]

The Mets had defied expectations and provided some of the most memorable moments at Shea in years. They had done it despite getting two combined wins from Generation K, both coming from Isringhausen, the only member of the group to appear in 1997.

There had been some clubhouse distractions for sure, but the Mets had actually been less of a zoo than their Bronx counterparts and, in many ways, a lot more fun to watch. The Mets had maintained hope all summer that they could actually pull off a postseason berth, making the official end all the more difficult to swallow. It was especially hard for players like Hundley, who had joined the team just as the franchise had begun to crumble and endured some harsh seasons in Flushing. Now, with his body starting to break down on him thanks to an injured right elbow, he began to wonder if he'd ever get to the playoffs. "You only have so many major league seasons in you," said Hundley after the game. "This is one that's lost."[103]

The Mets provided their fans one last thrilling win, coming back from a 1–0 eighth inning deficit to beat the Braves in walk-off fashion in the penultimate game of the year. The Mets finished 88-74, four games out of a playoff spot. It was, by far, their most successful season since 1990. The success and the manner in which it happened, with thrilling win after thrilling win, reinvigorated the fan base. Their forty-six come-from-behind wins led the Majors. "If the Mets had eliminated the Marlins instead of the other way around, we would be talking about what a magical season this had been, and about how this outfit had replaced the 1969 Mets as one of the greatest overachieving teams in sports history," wrote the *Bergen Record*'s Mike Celizic.[104]

Nearly two hundred thousand more people had come out to Shea than the year before, a welcome figure for a franchise that had been hemorrhaging ticket sales the last few years. The ending had been disappointing, but the journey had been amazing. It left genuine hope that the team would take the next step in 1998. Now all that was left to do was sit back and hope the Yankees did not win back-to-back titles.

• • •

In the 1996 postseason everything had gone the Yankees' way. A bad bounce always happened in their favor. A mistaken call by the umpire always benefited them. A hanging slider was thrown to them but not by them. These were the kinds of breaks that all championship teams enjoy.

When the 1997 postseason started, it looked like the Yankees were destined to enjoy all those breaks again. Facing off against the Central Division champion Indians, the Yankees fell behind 5–0 before they had sent a batter to the plate in the series. Cone, third in the American League in strikeouts that year and having allowed only eight first-inning runs all season, was not fooling Cleveland at all. Singles, hit batters, wild pitches, and a three-run home run by Sandy Alomar Jr. put New York in a huge hole. When the Indians tacked on a sixth run in the fourth, that was it for Cone. He had struggled all night, unusual for him in a postseason game. Moreover, he had look uncomfortable from the beginning, walking to the mound "shoulders slumped, no juice in his step."[105] But Cone's issue went beyond a lack of control or missing spots. He was nursing a sore shoulder, though he would not admit how much of an issue it actually was. The problem was caused by tendinitis and inflammation in his rotator cuff. It would keep him out of the rest the series.

Then the mystique of the previous year seemingly returned. The Yankees chipped away, scoring runs in the fourth and fifth and then another in the sixth to make it a 6–4 game when Tim Raines came up with two out and a runner on first. Raines had missed two months of the season with pulled hamstrings, but overall, his .321 average and .403 OBP were his best in ten years. Put into the starting lineup as the designated hitter against Orel Hershiser, whom he had faced numerous times when they had both been in the National League, Raines had already driven in a run. Now, against Eric Plunk, "whose pitching implosions were unforgettable during his 2½ seasons as a Yankee," Raines drilled a hanging breaking ball into the right-field stands to tie the game.[106]

"I was looking for a fastball, because he had gotten behind throwing breaking balls," said Raines. "The forkball kind of stayed up, and I was able to get a good swing on it."[107] It was the first, and as it would turn out, only postseason home run of Raines's career. Torre looked like a genius yet again for putting the right player in the lineup at the right moment.

The crowd had barely settled down when Jeter turned on an 0-2 fastball and hit it into the left-field stands to give the Yankees a 7–6 lead. The pitch had been so far inside that Jeter's left elbow nearly made contact with his stomach as he swung. The Indians replaced one former Yankees reliever, Plunk, with another former Yankees reliever, Paul Assenmacher. He jumped ahead of Paul O'Neill, 0-2, then tried to sneak in a fastball. O'Neill knocked it over the center-field fence. It had never happened before in the postseason: back-to-back-to-back home runs, one to right, one to left, and one to center.

"After last year, we had a feeling that we'd always come out of a tight spot, and we did Tuesday night," said Raines.[108] "That's not the type of game we want to play against Cleveland," said Torre, acknowledging that Cleveland's offense was more potent than that of the Yankees. "I'm not saying we can't slug it out with the Indians, but I wouldn't want to make a habit of it."[109]

Game One had all the makings of another Yankees' postseason of timely hitting, timely pitching, and timely luck. When they jumped out to a 3–0 lead in the first inning of Game Two, it looked like nothing was going to stop them from advancing to the ALCS. Then the mystique began to fade away, and Torre's warning came to fruition. In the fourth inning, with two outs, Pettitte gave up three consecutive singles and then a two-run double to former Yankee Tony Fernández. Cleveland added two more runs in the fifth. The Yankees kept putting runners on base but could never get the big hit to drive anyone in. They loaded the bases with one out in the eighth and scored on a hit-by pitch, but Boggs popped up and Raines grounded out. The Yankees lost a game that a year earlier it felt like they would have won.

The series moved to Cleveland, where an O'Neill grand slam and superb pitching by Wells put the Yankees just a win away from advancing. In the first inning of Game Four they scored two runs and had two on when Hayes singled to left field for what appeared to be another run. But Martinez was thrown out at home plate, changing the entire trajectory of the game. Again the mystique fading away, piece by piece. Dwight Gooden, yet to win a postseason game in his career but 5-0 against Cleveland lifetime, held the Indians to just one run, and the Yankees had a 2–1 lead with two outs in the eighth and Rivera on the mound.

Sandy Alomar Jr. came to the plate. It had been a dream season so far for the Cleveland catcher. He had set career highs in nearly every single offensive category, including home runs and RBIs. At that year's All-Star game, played in Cleveland, Alomar's seventh-inning home run gave the American League the lead and eventual victory. He took home the game's MVP. Now here he was facing the guy for whom he had caught the final three outs of that game.

With the count 2-0 on Alomar, Rivera threw a fastball over the outer half of the plate. Alomar guessed the pitch was coming and started his swing early. "It was a chance to cheat a little bit," said Alomar. "I did, and I hit the ball hard."[110] Alomar's shot went just over the wall in right field to tie the game. It was the first run allowed by the Yankees' bullpen in the series. "To me, I don't feel that was a good pitch," Rivera told reporters after the game. "It was outside and he was able to put some wood on it. He surprised me. It was not even close to the strike zone. He was up there hacking."[111]

The Yankees had not lost. The game was not over yet, and even if it had been, there was still one more game to play. But the home run knocked the wind out of the Yankees' playoff momentum. It felt impossible that they would give this lead up, especially with Rivera on the mound. The '97 season had always just felt different from the '96 season. Now this moment had cemented that feeling. "Giving up that homer is the greatest failure of my young career," Rivera later lamented.[112]

New York failed to score in the top of the ninth. In the bottom of the inning, a single, a bunt, and a single off the glove of Ramiro Mendoza that deflected just out of the reach of Jeter ended the game. "It came so fast that I couldn't make a backhanded play," said Mendoza of the game-winning hit. "I turned my glove inward, and the ball went off the heel. When I looked behind me, I knew the game was over. There was nothing Jeter could do."[113]

Again the little things, like a deflected ground ball, were not benefitting the Yankees. "The way we lost just didn't make sense," said O'Neill.[114] The clubhouse was quiet afterward. Players spoke of winning Game Five and having all that had just happened not matter. But their expressions and demeanor betrayed these platitudes. "Pick an adjective of disaster, devastating, draining, agonizing, horrible, gut-wrenching, pin it on this one, and don't worry about overstating the hurt, because that's not possible," the *Bergen Record*'s Mike Celizic wrote of the Game Four loss.[115]

Game Five, played the next night and the first-ever winner-take-all postseason game in Cleveland's history, felt like an inevitable loss after the Indians jumped out to a 4–0 lead. The Yankees chipped away, but again the big hit or a lucky break alluded them. In the seventh, Cleveland first baseman Jim Thome snared an O'Neill lined shot that would have put the tying run on third with no outs. In '96 that ball would have gotten through. "I was sure we were going to win the game," said Torre. "When we got it back to 4–2, I was sure we were going to win the game. But Thome's play was the big play. First and third, nobody out, who knows where we go from there?"[116]

In the eighth, Manny Ramirez cut off a Boggs single that otherwise could have scored the tying run. In '96 that ball would have made it to the wall. In the ninth, with two out and still down a run, O'Neill lined a first-pitch fastball into right-center field. "The liner smacked about halfway up the fence," O'Neill wrote in his autobiography. "Another six feet higher, about the length of two baseball bats, and it would have been a game-tying homer."[117]

In '96 it would have left the yard to tie the game. O'Neill, running hard out of the box, dashed to second base. "Because I hit the ball so hard, the [center] fielder retrieved [the ball] quickly and I had to hustle, scramble, and slide awkwardly on my right side to get into second and secure a double," added O'Neill.[118] The series-tying run now in scoring position, Bernie Williams flied out softly to left field. There would be no repeat.

"I thought all the way to the last out we were going to win," said Jeter. "Last out, Bernie at the plate, runner at second, we had a chance. It didn't happen. There's nothing more you can say."[119]

Several Yankees sat on the dugout bench, their eyes glazed over as they contemplated how this could have possibly happened. They had been up three runs in Game Two and lost. They had been up one run with four outs to go in Game Four and lost. They had had the tying run on base in the sixth, seventh, eighth, and ninth innings in Game Five and lost. It was not supposed to be this way. They were supposed to be headed to Baltimore for an ALCS rematch with the Orioles. Instead, one by one, they filed into a quiet clubhouse, left to wonder how and where things had gone wrong.

3

Square in the Back

Dave Mlicki did not think he was ready. Out of high school, he'd had surgery on his pitching arm to remove bone chips. He hadn't pitched much for Oklahoma State, his college of choice after high school. Plus, he really wanted to play in the College World Series at some point. For all those reasons, when the Seattle Mariners selected Mlicki in the twenty-third round of the 1989 amateur draft, he decided not to sign with them. "It was more me than the organization. It had nothing to do with Seattle or anything like that," said Mlicki. "There were some goals and stuff that I didn't really finish yet in college and I was still just a skinny kid."[1]

Mlicki waited a year and then was drafted by and signed with the Cleveland Indians. Though he had been a Reds fan growing up, signing with Cleveland was in many ways a dream come true for Mlicki. Cleveland was close enough to where he had grown up, and in fact his family had relocated back to Columbus at this point. It only took two years for him to work his way through the Minors before Cleveland called him up to start on September 12, 1992. The Indians were in Chicago, where Mlicki's then girlfriend and future wife, Annie, was from. Annie was in college at the University of Arizona at the time, but her parents, Mlicki's parents, and a slew of relatives were in the crowd that night.

Mlicki was nervous, as could be expected. He'd never pitched in front of so many people before. Not even close. Before he knew it, he was starring in at Joey Cora, the first Major League hitter he would face. "I was looking around and I couldn't feel my hand. I couldn't feel anything. I just decided I was going to throw this thing as hard as I could," he recalled. Mlicki reared back, fired . . . and hit Cora square in the back with his first big league pitch.

Five years later Derek Jeter might've thought for a second that Mlicki was trying to relive that first-pitch moment. Jeter seemed certain that the ball headed toward him was going to make contact with his body. It was now the bottom of the third inning, and the Yankees' shortstop was batting with one out, a runner on second, and his team trailing, 3–0.

Jeter's wiry frame dove into pitches as they headed toward the plate; his right-handed stride made him exceptional at driving outside pitches to right field for singles and extra-base hits. It also made him susceptible to getting hit by the ball. In his rookie season the year before, he'd been plunked nine times, the tenth most in the American League. It was the first of seven times Jeter placed in the top ten in the league in that category.

Mlicki had no intention of hitting Jeter, though. Instead he was settling into a rhythm, the conductor of which was Todd Hundley. "I don't think he gets enough credit for how he helped me," said Mlicki of Hundley. "We had so many conversations on team planes and hotel rooms on how to pitch guys and what to do. I had amazing catchers my whole career but I had a better connection with Todd."

The bottom of the second had been almost laughable in its ease. Working off a scouting report that told them to swing early in the count, the Yankees had gone down in order while making Mlicki throw only five pitches. He'd done so using his fastball, which each hitter had been expecting. But Mlicki's fastball had just enough movement and just the right amount of placement to keep Tino Martinez, Charlie Hayes, and Mark Whiten from doing any damage with it. Beginning in the third, he used the same pattern when Chad Curtis led off:

Fastball.

Strike one.

Fastball.

Meek ground ball to third.

Catcher Joe Girardi came to the plate. Hundley decided if it was not broken, there was no need to fix it.

Fastball.

BAAM!

Girardi drilled it to the gap in right-center field, easily reaching second base for a double. The crowd came alive. Yankees fans knew it was early enough for this team to come back, especially against a guy with a 2-5 record.

Hundley now decided it was time for a change. Following the pattern of the first nine batters in the Yankees' order, Jeter would be expecting a fastball. Instead:

Curve.

Jeter, like Fielder before him, jelly-legged instantly as the ball fell over the middle of the plate for strike one. When the count moved to 1-2, there was a sense in the crowd of what was coming. Hundley set up on the outside part of the plate. Mlicki came set, delivered, and flicked his wrist again. The pitch missed Hundley's intended location. It was far more in than the catcher had wanted. It didn't matter. By the time Jeter recognized what was coming, it was too late. In the milliseconds he had to make a decision, he had not committed to swinging.

Curve.

Strike three.

Jeter walked back to the dugout. He had no argument to make. The pitch was a strike, and he knew it. "Mlicki pretty much pitched perfect," said Jeter.[2]

Pat Kelly stepped up next. To this point Mlicki had thrown a first-pitch strike to nine of the first ten batters. Kelly, having just returned from the latest of a string of injuries that had sidelined him over the years, was feeling the pressure of this game perhaps more than any other player. Two days earlier he had committed an error in the bottom of the ninth, turning a 5–4 win into a 6–5 loss to the Marlins.

Mlicki gave Kelly no quarter. He quickly moved him into a 1-2 hole, the second strike coming on another massive curveball. "He has been like a pitching machine out there," remarked FX broadcaster Chip Caray after the sharp break of the pitch. "This guy's 2-5, how's that possible?"[3]

Kelly worked the count full. Again the crowd sensed what was coming. By this point many of the players must have as well. Hundley set up on the outside corner of the plate. This time Mlicki did not miss. Kelly stood and watched, as Fielder and Jeter had before him, as the ball left Mlicki's handed, spun, then dropped what seemed like ten feet.

Curve.

Strike three.

Kelly walked away, dejected and looking a mixture of bemused and confused. He flipped and then caught his bat with his right hand as he headed back to the dugout to grab his glove. Mlicki walked off the mound, over the foul line, and to the dugout. Three innings in, and he had yet to give up a run while striking out each of the Yankees' first four hitters in the batting order. More important for the Mets, though, Mlicki and Hundley were now working in perfect synchronicity.

4   A Viable Man

The Marlins, fresh off their seven-game World Series triumph in 1997, immediately set about dismantling the team. Now that owner Wayne Hezinga had his championship, it was time to slash Florida's $53 million payroll. First went outfielder Moisés Alou to the Astros, then relief pitcher Robb Nen to the Giants and outfielder Devon White to the Diamondbacks. Outfielder Jeff Conine went to the Royals. All of this within a nine-day span in November. In December pitcher Kevin Brown went to the Padres. Three days later the Mets got in on the act, acquiring relief pitcher Dennis Cook from Florida to solidify a bullpen that, outside of John Franco, had few reliable left-handed pitchers. Cook had been spectacular during Florida's postseason run, allowing only a single hit and no runs in nine innings of relief while also earning the win in Game Three of the World Series.

Florida was not done. On February 6, 1998, the Mets sent three Minor Leaguers to the Marlins for starting pitcher Al Leiter. It was not the splashiest move of the Major League off-season. It may have been the most important one, though, in shaping the future of any club. "My history of following the Mets goes back to when I was three years old, upstairs in our house in Toms River, N.J., listening to the '69 Mets in the World Series," said Leiter, who grew up about sixty miles away from Shea and Yankee Stadiums.[1]

After Leiter had dominated hitters while pitching for Central Regional High School in Bayville, a section of Berkeley Township in New Jersey, the Yankees drafted him in 1984. He had electrified the home crowd when, in his September 15, 1987, debut at Yankee Stadium, the first six outs of his career were strikeouts. Two starts later, he struck out ten Orioles en route to his second career win. He began drawing comparisons to Ron Guidry as fans imagined a bright future with Leiter leading the rotation for years to come. But Leiter got hit hard in two of his four appearances that year and had a propensity for getting too picky with his pitch location. It led to lots of walks and high pitch counts. Leiter was also a ball of nervous energy. Some believed they had never played with such a high-strung person before. Occasionally viewers could hear his follow-through grunt on TV.

Billy Martin, the Yankees' manager to start the '88 season, was highly impressed with the lefty, and Leiter began that season in the club's starting rotation. He responded by winning his first three starts of the year, striking out twenty-three in twenty innings. In May he began to experience issues with a blister and back pain, forcing him to constantly be removed early from starts or to miss appearances all together. In six starts between May 6 and June 21, he threw just sixteen and a third innings. The injuries forced him out of action from late June until September.

Leiter began the 1989 season in the rotation again. It was his second start of the year that ultimately may have been the most impactful of his career. On a cold, damp April night in the Bronx, Leiter walked nine Twins and struck out ten more on pace to throwing 162 pitches in eight innings. It was an obscene number in any scenario, one made worse by the weather conditions and the fact that it was just his second start of the year. No one has thrown that many pitches in a game for the New York Yankees since. "That was just abuse," Leiter later said. "Two starts later, I could barely lift my arm. That derailed my entire career."[2]

Those two starts had not gone well, and Leiter was 1-2 on the season with a 6.08 ERA. The Yankees decided they could no longer wait for Leiter to become Ron Guidry. They traded him to the Blue Jays for outfielder Jesse Barfield. Leiter was devastated. "If I had started off 4-0 and was cruising, I feel certain the trade wouldn't have been executed," he said after hearing the news. "But I'm still in that potential mode. I'm struggling and they're wondering when this world of potential would erupt."[3]

The Blue Jays had taken a substantial risk. Leiter had already shown a tendency for injuries, and his 162-pitch performance should have been a red flag. They either ignored the signs or hoped they would not matter. But they did. Leiter made one start for Toronto and promptly injured his shoulder, an injury he was certain happened as a direct result of his start against Minnesota. Over the next four seasons Leiter made a total of nine appearances with Toronto, limited by multiple shoulder injuries and issues with tendinitis.

Leiter became a mainstay in the Blue Jay pitching staff in 1993, appearing mostly out of the bullpen as he eased his way back into being a full-time pitcher. He even picked up a win in relief in Game One of that year's World Series. He joined the rotation the following year, though his numbers were less than spectacular: a 5.08 ERA and a 1.18 strikeout-to-walk ratio. He came into his own in 1995, finishing with eleven wins and making twenty-eight starts, by the far the most he'd done in any season up to that point. He had also led the league in walks, and his habit of never giving in to a hitter, coupled with an inability to sometimes hit the strike zone, would remain a constant for his entire career.

Now a bona fide quality starter, Leiter signed his first big contract that off-season, heading to Miami. Florida's investment in the lefty paid off immediately. On May 11, 1996, Leiter threw the first no-hitter in team history. He finished the year 16-12 with a 2.93 ERA, accomplishing his first two-hundred-strikeout season, making his first All-Star team, and garnering his first Cy Young Award votes.

The Marlins had enough confidence in Leiter to hand him the ball to start Game Seven of the 1997 World Series. Leiter, in turn, gave up just two runs in six innings, keeping the game close enough for Florida to eventually come back and win the title in extra innings.

While Leiter's overall performance in 1997 had fallen from the previous year, the fact remained that there just were not that many high-quality left-handed starting pitchers in baseball. Leiter was now a hot commodity, and with a salary of nearly $3 million a year, an expensive one for the payroll-shedding Marlins. In the last of the team's fire sale moves that off-season, Florida traded Leiter to the Mets. "I knew I was getting traded," said Leiter. "I heard the Cubs mentioned a lot. Pat Gillick was the Orioles GM—he was with me during my Blue Jays days—and I heard I was getting traded to the Orioles for a couple of players, and that year the Devil Rays ended up drafting one of the players in the deal, so the way it turned out, I got traded to the Mets and I was thrilled."[4]

The trade gave credibility to the Mets' starting rotation. Yes, the team had gotten solid performances from its starters the previous year. Those guys, however, were still largely unknown around the league, and it was questionable if they would continue to be quality starters. Leiter was a known entity who had just been showcased on baseball's biggest stage to a national audience. Not since August 26, 1992, the day before the Mets had traded David Cone to the Blue Jays, had the team possessed such a marquee name in the rotation.

Leiter and Cook were key additions to the team that off-season. They were not, however, what co-owner Fred Wilpon meant when, after the previous year ended, he had indicated that significant changes were coming. The Mets had tried, and failed, to acquire Expos pitcher and reigning NL Cy Young Award winner Pedro Martinez. Their offer was rebuffed, and Martinez, much to the Yankees' chagrin, ended up going to their AL East rival, Boston. The Mets then tried to trade for the Mariners' Randy Johnson, who was in the final year of his contract and almost certainly was going to sign elsewhere after the 1998 season. Nothing came of it. In addition to obtaining Leiter and Cook, the team had also tried to pry away Gary Sheffield from Florida. A possible deal fell apart after Florida refused to pay a sizable portion of Sheffield's contract.

Any of those three players—Martinez, Johnson, Sheffield—would have been game changers for the organization (and ultimately two of the three would wear a Mets uniform toward the end of their careers). With none of those deals panning out, the next biggest transaction the Mets made that off-season was not an addition but a retention. John Olerud became a free agent after the '97 season, and it was uncertain if he would resign. Rumors had begun swirling late in the season that Olerud wanted to move on from New York and sign with the Mariners. Olerud himself never said anything to that affect publicly, though he was from Washington state. In the off-season Seattle offered him only a one-year deal, which he rejected. The Mets offered him three years. He rejected that too, instead asking them to make it two. "I felt the four-year contract I signed in Toronto didn't work out as I had hoped," said Olerud. "I wanted to keep it short, which gives me an opportunity to have a couple really strong years on top of what I did in 1997 and show people that's the player I am."[5]

"Well, you're stuck with me another two years," Olerud told Mets hitting coach Tom Robson by phone after inking the deal.[6] The two had gotten close after Robson had suggested Olerud stop trying to pull everything and just hit his natural way. That change was largely credited with the boost in Olerud's numbers.

The Mets also added one more pitcher to their rotation. The team had been in talks with Dwight Gooden for a return to Shea, but GM Phillips felt Gooden's asks were not realistic. Gooden ended up signing with the Indians. The Mets could not rely on Isringhausen to fill the starter role after the pitcher was lost for the year due to elbow surgery in January. That injury prevented a possible trade to the Marlins for pitcher Kevin Brown. The Mets looked outside the United States and found Masato Yoshii, a starting pitcher with the Yakult Swallows. "He's not a power pitcher with an exploding fastball," Phillips said of Yoshii the day of the signing. "He's a pitcher. He throws strikes, changes speeds and mixes up his pitches."[7] In short, he was what the Mets needed: someone who could keep the team in the game, eat up innings, and give New York a chance to win.

Ultimately the Mets headed into spring training in 1998 stronger than the year before but with some significant shortcomings. The quality of their outfield was suspect. Huskey was coming off a strong year, but Gilkey had faltered, and in fact the Mets had tried to trade him that off-season with no luck. McRae had not been overly impressive in his two months with the club. Everett was now an Astro, traded in the off-season for little return, largely so that the team could be rid of a headache and any pending legal troubles in which he might find himself. Meanwhile, at catcher, the Mets simply did not have one. Hundley had undergone reconstructive elbow surgery in the off-season and would be out until the second half of the season. Hoping they could get by long enough to await his return, the Mets opted not to bring in a full-time catcher. Instead they went with two career backups: Alberto Castillo and Tim Spehr. Collectively the two had hit .198 for their careers with just thirty-one extra-base hits in 424 at bats.

Hope still hung in the air, though. This was a team that had surprisingly won eighty-eight games the year before and had not been eliminated from contention until the season's final week. With improved pitching and some key offensive performances, the team could very well see its first playoff appearance of the decade.

• • •

It had been a remarkable forty-eight hours in the Yankees' organization. On February 1 Bob Watson informed George Steinbrenner that he was done as general manager. From the moment he had started the job in the fall of 1995, Watson felt marginalized. Steinbrenner failed to inform him of trades that were in development or players the team was targeting to sign. When the Yankees traded for Tino Martinez, Jeff Nelson, and Jim Mecir in December 1995, Watson had been out of the loop. The details were left to Gene Michael, the man Watson had replaced but who was still a valued member of Steinbrenner's inner circle. After the team signed Cone, Watson said the Yankees were done with free-agent signings for the off-season. That's what he had been told, anyway. "Ten days later, we signed Kenny Rogers and I was called a liar," said Watson.[8]

In 1996 Watson denied the team was going to sign Darryl Strawberry, unaware that Steinbrenner had already decided the team needed an infusion of power despite being in first place. Just weeks later Strawberry was in a Yankees uniform. When the team traded for Graeme Lloyd and Pat Listach from the Milwaukee Brewers, both of whom were injured, Steinbrenner went ballistic and began privately telling people that Watson would be history. Listach had to be sent back to Milwaukee while Lloyd became one of the team's many postseason heroes that year.

The year 1997 had been just as bad: the team's dogged pursuit of Irabu; the failed deal of Rogers for Vaughn; the loss to the Indians after Steinbrenner had spent a record $62 million in team payroll. Despite winning a World Series and getting to the postseason again in 1997, Steinbrenner refused to give Watson a raise. It was all too much for the general manager. In April 1997 he'd had to check himself into a hospital after having chest pains. Doctors told him to reduce stress levels, a laughable proposition given his position. Then after the season, in mid-November, the Montreal Expos traded reigning Cy Young Award winner Pedro Martinez to the Red Sox. Steinbrenner was livid. The Yankees had been trying to acquire the future Hall of Famer, and Martinez had wanted to go to New York. "I asked to be traded to the Yankees 3 times before I got to Boston," Martinez said. "I was the last one left on [Montreal's] rotation and when I was asked where I wanted to be, at that exact moment [the] Yankees were taking off, I wanted to be somewhere that I could win."[9]

Steinbrenner focused his wrath on Watson for not having completed the deal and for allowing the Red Sox, of all teams, to get Martinez. He was even angrier that the Red Sox had used Tony Armas Jr. in the deal, a pitcher whom Boston had acquired that August from the Yankees for Mike Stanley. If the Yankees had just kept Armas, Steinbrenner reasoned, they could have had Martinez. In reality, Montreal's general manager, Jim Beattie, was a one-time Yankees pitcher whom Steinbrenner had once publicly berated during Beattie's rookie season. Beattie had decided that he would not make any deals with the Yankees if he could avoid doing so. In this case, with the Red Sox offer, he could. It was Steinbrenner's fault, but Watson took the blame. Watson, for his own well-being, could not take being in the Boss's orbit anymore.

Watson began doing the things that a few others had done before to push Steinbrenner to fire him. He reportedly came into work some days, walked into his office, locked the door, and remained there all day watching television. Weeks after the end of the season, Watson had publicly stated that Steinbrenner's baseball people were "little people that run around in his head."[10]

Then on February 1 Steinbrenner called Watson with exciting news. Chuck Knoblauch, the Minnesota Twins second baseman, was available by trade. The Yankees could not resist. Knoblauch was an elite second baseman: a four-time All Star who got on base, stole, and was coming off his first Gold Glove season. Steinbrenner wanted Watson to call the Twins and offer them Bernie Williams and Andy Pettitte for Knoblauch. Watson was aghast. Knoblauch was great, but he was not worth *that*. He refused to make the offer.

"Are you defying me?" Steinbrenner asked.

"Yes," Watson replied. "Bottom line, you cannot trade Bernie Williams and Andy Pettitte for Chuck Knoblauch. I'm not going to hurt the team."

"If you don't do it, you're fired," threatened Steinbrenner.

Watson had had enough. "You don't have to go that far. Instead of you firing me, I quit."[11]

That was that. The Knoblauch deal was the final straw. "He had the trade made, and I packed my little box under my desk and that was it," Watson later said.[12] The two met the next day and discussed the terms of Watson's leaving.

"It did shock me. I just hope it has nothing to do with Bob's health," Steinbrenner told reporters when word leaked out, making reference to numerous health-related issues Watson had endured over the years, including a bout with prostate cancer. "I don't know if I drove him out or if it was cancer, but Bob is not as full of energy as he used to be, and I'm a demanding boss."[13] In many ways it was a typical Steinbrenner statement. Even if his behavior had caused Watson to leave, it was still Watson's fault for not being up to the task of working for the Boss.

"Nobody forced him to come here," Steinbrenner added. "He knew what he was getting into when he took this job. As far as I'm concerned, there's no malice at all between us. If he's not comfortable with me, that's fine. I'm me. I can't help that. I want to win for New York in the worst way imaginable. For some people, that may not be their cup of tea. I think it takes a lot more time than Watson was willing or able to give."[14]

Four days later the team completed the Knoblauch deal. The Yankees were giving up a lot, including Eric Milton, a highly touted left-handed pitching prospect; Brian Buchanan, their 1994 first-round pick; Cristian Guzmán, a speedy middle infielder; and pitcher Danny Mota. The whole thing seemed worth it, though. "He can play deeper than most second basemen because he has such a good arm," Orioles assistant general manager Kevin Malone said about Knoblauch at the time of the trade. "He can move toward the middle or go deep in the second-base hole to get a ball—he's got that athleticism—and he's got enough arm strength to make a throw off balance."[15]

The Yankees had not had a second baseman of his caliber in seven years, when Steve Sax had manned the position. Knoblauch would bat leadoff, allowing Derek Jeter to move down to the number two spot, creating more RBI opportunities for Jeter and putting two on-base machines at the top of the order for O'Neill.

Meanwhile, taking Watson's place as the seventeenth GM under Steinbrenner's rule was his assistant, Brian Cashman. He had been with the organization for over a decade, and at thirty years old, he was the second youngest GM in baseball history. Gradually he worked his way up the ladder, leading to his meeting with Steinbrenner shortly after Watson informed a shocked yet excited Cashman that he was George's pick to replace him. The Boss asked him if he felt he could handle the job.

"I think I can, sir, but I want to prove to you I'm the right man for the job," Cashman replied. "That's why I'd like a one-year contract."

"One year," replied a confused Steinbrenner.

"Yes, sir. I want to show you I'm the right man, but I feel that right now, any more than one year wouldn't be right for either of us," said Cashman.[16]

Impressed, Steinbrenner agreed. That one-year deal would end up outlasting every single player and coach on the team and even Steinbrenner himself. After being introduced as the new general manager, Cashman said he was not blind to the challenges of working for Steinbrenner. "I know it's going to be a drain. I know it's going to be a marathon. People came in before and said it was going to be different. I'm not saying that. I know what it is. I've been here for 10 years."[17]

"How could you know?" quipped Watson's wife, Carol, when she heard Cashman's comments. "This is analogous to reading a book about having a baby."[18]

Cashman was not wrong about the challenges ahead. No general manager had lasted more than two years under Steinbrenner except for Gabe Paul and Gene Michael, and their tenures coincided with Steinbrenner's two suspensions from the game. But the Boss was all smiles for his new GM. "I tell you, Cashman is a very bright young man, studies hard and did a lot of work for Bob during his recovery time," Steinbrenner told reporters before adding a somewhat backhanded compliment. "I could go outside and bring in a figurehead name, a well-known guy, but after 10 years this guy deserved a chance."[19]

The Knoblauch deal, which Cashman completed as his first assignment as GM, was the last piece of an off-season puzzle in which the Yankees attempted to leave no lineup hole unfilled. They also wanted to rid the team of those most responsible for causing clubhouse problems in '97. After the drama of the Boggs/Hayes situation the previous year, they were not going to have two full-time third basemen on the roster anymore. Boggs, coming off his worst, though still productive, season as a Yankee left as a free agent and signed with his hometown expansion Tampa Bay Devil Rays. Steinbrenner was so annoyed with Hayes's response to being platooned and his incident with a fan that he traded the third baseman to the Giants and agreed to pay all of Hayes's salary for 1998. "George wanted him gone, so he's gone," said Hayes's agent, Tommy Tanzer. "The conflict with Boggs wore everybody down and eventually it gobbled up Charlie."[20]

A week before the Hayes deal, the team at long last traded Kenny Rogers for someone who would not fail a physical. Rogers departed for Oakland in exchange for Scott Brosius. Born and raised in Milwaukie, Oregon, Brosius had been a great athlete in high school but particularly excelled at baseball. Inheriting a love of the game from his father, who adored Mickey Mantle, Brosius was a late-round draft pick by the A's in 1987. He made his way through the Minors just as Oakland's incredible clubs of the late 1980s were starting to fall apart. Joining the team full time during a period of rebuilding allowed Brosius to garner significant playing time, albeit not at the position for which he later became known. During his first years in Oakland Brosius played everywhere: second, third, first, short, left field, right field, and center field. It wasn't until 1996 that he began to see the majority of his playing time at third.

Brosius had potential, but he was coming off the worst season of his career, having hit just .203 with only eleven home runs, both career lows for any full season he had played. When Oakland called Cashman, then serving as assistant general manager, and asked if the Yankees would want Brosius, Cashman feigned disinterest.

"I don't think so," Cashman replied, "but let me check with my people."[21] Cashman's people said yes, the team should be interested in Brosius. He'd had a bad year in 1997, but in 1996 he'd hit twenty-two home runs with an OPS of .909, so something was there, somewhere. It was just a matter of flushing it out and hoping that 1997 had been an outlier. Not to mention that he was an excellent defender. The team made the deal, but just in case, New York signed veteran infielder Dale Sveum as insurance.

Cecil Fielder would not be returning as designated hitter. Big Daddy took his bat to Anaheim, but the speed that had eluded him the previous year did not return. The Angels released him in August. He spent a month with the Indians, was released again, and retired with 319 career home runs. To fill Fielder's literally large shoes, the Yankees brought in a veteran with more career home runs. Chili Davis had long quietly been one of the game's most consistent power hitters, good for around twenty-five home runs and eighty to ninety RBIs a year. In 1997 with Kansas City, he had hit a career high thirty home runs. Not only would Davis bring even more power to the lineup, but he would also add a veteran presence with postseason experience and a championship ring with the 1991 Twins to his credit.

The Yankees had, in essence, removed every player outside of Wells and Irabu, who had caused headaches during the 1997 season. Hayes, Boggs, Fielder, and Rogers were now gone, joined also by Pat Kelly, who would not be returning, and Gooden, now with Cleveland. For Joe Torre this was all addition by subtraction. They had also gotten lucky in the expansion draft, losing only relief pitcher Brian Boehringer off the big-league team even though Girardi and outfielder Chad Curtis were left unprotected.

In Knoblauch, Brosius, and Davis the Yankees had filled holes at second, third, and DH. That left every position claimed heading into the season, with only catcher being split between two players. Even that, though, was by design and not because of a potentially acrimonious situation. Girardi and Posada would split time nearly evenly throughout the year, with Girardi counseling Posada and preparing him to take the reins in a more permanent role in 1999. Both players understood the situation. There would be no griping in the papers about playing time from either of them.

The chatter around the team as spring training headed to a close was about as positive as had been around any Yankees team in decades. Big things were expected from this club.

• • •

It could have passed for a midsummer weekend game. Shea Stadium was packed. There was a buzz of excitement in the air. And it was 80 degrees. Opening Day 1998 for the Mets was just about picture perfect. With the team's coming off a surprise eighty-eight-win season, expectations were high. Moreover, many of those eighty-eight wins had come in dramatic fashion, featuring a bevy of comeback and/or walk-off wins. Once the first game of the year was over, there was every reason to believe these kinds of wins would continue into the new season.

For eight innings the Mets' offense was shut down by the Phillies' starting pitcher, Curt Schilling. Fresh off a season in which he had struck out 319 batters, Schilling had allowed just three base runners in these eight innings of work. Meanwhile, Bobby Jones was not too bad himself, keeping Philadelphia scoreless through six. From there the bullpen picked it up, allowing only five hits over eight innings. Turk Wendell, who had gotten battered after joining the team in 1997, began this season by throwing two scoreless innings after entering the game in the thirteenth. The game, which had started bathed in afternoon sunshine, entered the bottom of the fourteenth in twilight. That tied a National League record for most innings played on Opening Day. The Mets managed to load the bases with two outs when Castillo, who had been in the clubhouse getting hot chocolate when he saw on TV that he was being summoned to pinch-hit, lined a 3-2 pitch into right field to win it, 1–0. "I know what's thought about Albert," said Valentine. "But I managed him in Class AAA. And he'll have some ugly at-bats. But the one thing I always say in my meetings is he gives you a good one when you need it. And he gave us one there."[22]

Castillo was the last position player available on the team. "The last man and our first hero this year," said Castillo.[23]

"Last year, Opening Day was like a conga line with all the runs that were scored against us," said Franco, referring to the team's 12–5 loss to the Padres in 1997. "Everything is different now."[24]

After the Mets split the first two games with Philadelphia, Pittsburgh came to town, and remarkably, the Mets won the first two games of the series in walk-off fashion. The second of those two wins came after New York had trailed 6–3 entering the ninth. While much of New York was talking about whether Joe Torre would get fired a week into the season, the talk around the Mets was exhilaration—the idea that this Mets team was going to erase the years of distress and bad play that had permeated Shea for too long.

On April 19 the Mets collected sixteen hits, including four home runs, in a 14–0 drubbing of the Reds. Leiter pitched seven scoreless innings, moving his record to 3-1, with a 1.44 ERA. The win put the Mets a half game ahead in the division. It was only three weeks into the season, and no one was popping champagne bottles just yet. Still, the Mets were emerging as a feel-good story in a season that would be full of, in the moment, feel-good stories.

Three days later Jim Tatum, a journeyman utility infielder/outfielder playing on his fifth team in five seasons, hit a two-out, three-run home run in the bottom of the ninth to give New York a 10–7 win. It was only his second of three career home runs, but it was a big one.

The Mets had fallen into second place but were just a half game out. It was the closest they would be to first for the rest of the season. A six-game losing streak at the end of the month, coupled with a Braves team that was off to a 20-9 start, dropped them five and a half games back. The losing streak also exposed a much deeper problem with the club that was now obvious to everyone: the Mets needed a catcher.

The duo of Castillo and Spehr was not working out. On May 4 the Mets lost to Arizona and fell to .500. In that game Spehr went 1-4, a performance that actually boosted his average to .137. At that point, he'd recorded only seven hits on the season, just one of which, a double, was for extra bases. He had driven in just three runs. In the May 4 loss to the Diamondbacks Spehr broke a bone in his left wrist while applying a tag, sending him to the disabled list. He did not play again until September, at which point he was a Royal. Castillo had handled the pitching staff well but had been no more potent on offense. The day Spehr suffered his injury, Castillo had been hitting .257 (he'd recently gotten his average above .200 by going five for his last ten), with only two extra base hits and two runs driven in for the year. The Mets had only five runs driven in from the catcher's spot through the first month of the season. After Hundley had broken the single-season home run record for a catcher in 1996, the Mets were now twenty-eight games into the 1998 season without having a single home run from any catcher.

They traded for Rick Wilkins to replace Spehr. Wilkins went 2-for-15 with no extra-base hits in his five-game Mets career.

It is possible that the struggles at backstop would not have been as notable if the rest of the team's offense had not also been flaccid. While Olerud was putting in another strong season, McRae, Baerga, Huskey, and Ordóñez were all struggling at the plate. The four hit just two home runs in the first five weeks of the season. Edgardo Alfonzo had just begun hitting his stride when, in early May, he went on the disabled list with a shoulder injury. Gilkey had been stinging the ball, hitting .314 through April, but without a single home run. On April 26 he too landed on the disabled list with an injured elbow. He would struggle the rest of the season.

The Mets just were not scoring runs and were struggling to stay afloat and relevant through mid-May. Worse still, at least as far as Mets ownership was concerned, fans were no longer seemingly enamored with the club. An eight-game home stand at the start of May, which included two weekend games and two games against the Cardinals' Mark McGwire, who was already on pace to break Roger Maris's single-season home run record, never drew a crowd over twenty thousand in any game. The walk-off wins had stopped, and now this team was just . . . boring.

Some kind of move had to be made. On Friday, May 15, there was a blockbuster trade made by a National League East team to acquire a catcher. The catcher was Mike Piazza, and the team acquiring him was not the Mets. It was the Florida Marlins.

Piazza had been the best catcher in baseball for five years. A sixty-second round draft pick in the 1988 MLB amateur draft, Piazza had been selected by the Dodgers as a favor to his father, who happened to be good friends with Dodgers' manager Tommy Lasorda. Piazza was a first baseman, but Lasorda told him to switch to catcher to increase his chances of making it to the Majors. Not much was expected of Piazza. Not much is ever expected of the 1,390th pick in the draft. Yet he tore up A ball pitching in 1991, hitting twenty-nine home runs. He followed that up with twenty-three more in Double A and Triple A ball in 1992, with a 1.000 OPS. The young catcher from Pennsylvania torched his way through the Minors and made the team full time as a rookie in 1993. That year he hit thirty-five home runs, batted .318, and easily won National League Rookie of the Year. Season after season Piazza tallied ridiculous numbers that no catcher had cumulatively put up before. In 1997 he hit forty home runs, batted .362 with a .638 slugging percentage, and was runner-up in MVP voting.

Piazza wasn't just the greatest catcher in baseball; he may have been the greatest player. A free agent after 1998, he wanted the Dodgers to pay him like he was the greatest player. Willing to work out an extension, Piazza asked the Dodgers for the first $100 million contract in baseball. They refused, going as high as $81 million. The stalemate lasted through spring training and into the early weeks of the season. The Dodgers' owners decided they were not going to give Piazza what he wanted, instead opting to at least get something for him before he left via free agency. On May 16 Piazza was traded to—of all places—the Marlins, in a mega deal that exchanged several players. The trade was shocking, if for no other reason than that Florida was still continuing its post-championship fire sale. In fact, the deal was done without the general managers of either team knowing. Instead the hierarchy of both clubs negotiated the trade. "I was adamant that we needed to keep Mike, entering the peak years of his career," said Dodgers general manager Fred Claire. "I told [Dodgers team president] Bob Graziano that it was very important we keep him on the team. . . . This is why this absolutely was a jolt out of the blue."[25]

Mets fans were irate. Why couldn't their team have gotten Piazza? They grew even angrier when, in the days following the trade, the Mets said they had no interest in trading for the All-Star catcher. Phillips told Hundley directly that the Mets were not going after Piazza. Co-owner Nelson Doubleday was also unhappy. He did not like the team's lethargic play, that fans had no interest in coming to the ballpark, or that the Mets had somehow just lost out on a major upgrade to a team that was trying to reduce payroll. "I thought Mr. Piazza was a viable man for the New York Mets and a viable man for New York City and one hell of a star and we ought to take a shot at him," said Doubleday.[26]

Additional pressure came from WFAN. Mike Francesa and Chris Russo, hosts of the country's most popular sports talk program, *Mike and the Mad Dog*, were apoplectic that the Mets had not been in on Piazza.

All of these combined elements pushed the Mets to move. The Marlins had made it known, almost immediately, that they were willing to deal Piazza. The Mets had an advantage because, having made the Leiter and Cook trades in the off-season, they already knew which players in their system were of interest to Florida. Wilpon had some concerns, believing that making such a big trade would give Piazza leverage in any contract extension or off-season contract negotiations. But too many people within the organization wanted to make this happen. Phillips reached out to Florida general manager Dave Dombrowski, and just one week after they had acquired him, the Marlins sent Piazza to the Mets for outfielder Preston Wilson and pitchers Ed Yarnall and Geoff Goetz. "Angry calls to sports-talk radio stations are not a normal ingredient in baseball trades, but in this instance it seemed clear that the Mets' owners were sensitive to the discontent and pushed Phillips to get the deal done," noted Jason Diamos in the *New York Times*.[27]

While many saw the trade coming, it was still a coup. The deal would, in time, rival that of the December 1984 trade for Gary Carter as the most important in team history. "Whether Piazza actually makes the Mets better remains to be seen," wrote the *Bergen Record*'s Bob Klapisch. "They'll have an answer by July. But for one day, we all experienced an intense rush of déjà vu, back to a time when the Mets, not the Yankees, were the big movers in town."[28]

"It felt like the Mets were back in the baseball business yesterday," wrote the *Daily News*' Mike Lupica. "Yes, the Mets contended for a wild-card playoff spot last September. Yes, you can look at this team and see a chance at the playoffs again once Todd Hundley is back in the lineup, maybe as soon as July. But they give you this chance in front of empty seats, in a ballpark that was once the most important sports room in town. They give you this chance inside a terrible quiet, up against all the roar of the Yankees."[29]

Piazza immediately improved the team's offense in a way few other players could. His career numbers and performance at the plate were not just impressive but historic. He was a bona fide star with the potential to achieve immortal fame in the Big Apple. Moreover, the trade was an adrenaline shot into the arms of Mets fans across the tri-state area. Piazza gave them a reason to want to go to Shea. It was not just about the team's now newfound ability to win games but also about seeing the man himself come to bat and launch prolific home runs to left and right-center fields. "I think when Gary Carter came, he was a great player," said Wilpon. "But not of this magnitude. Keith Hernandez was a great player but he wasn't well known. This town is ready and waiting for Mike. Mike Piazza is going to be a tremendous force in this town. He has a chance to be a Willie Mays, a Mickey Mantle."[30]

On Saturday, May 23, Piazza played his first game as a Met. It drew over thirty-two thousand fans, the largest crowd at Shea in a month. When Piazza came to bat in the first inning, he received a long, loud standing ovation from the fans. In the fifth, after starting 0-for-2, Piazza lined a run-scoring double to right field. The fans went nuts, bathing the catcher in adulation they had not showered on any player in years.

The Mets won that day, 3–0, their third win in a row. They did not lose again for another nine days. Piazza recorded a hit in each of his first nine games with the team. Returning to Florida, his home for all of one week, for a two-game series, Piazza went 6-for-10. The offense, meanwhile, came alive, scoring fifty-four runs in the first seven games after the trade. Oddly enough, though, Piazza himself only drove in two of those runs, despite hitting .419 during that stretch. It was an issue, or at least a perceived issue, that Mets fans would soon latch onto and not let go of for some time.

That was still weeks away, though. For now the team was basking in the ambience of a nine-game win streak that had given them a one-game lead in the wild card. Trouble lay ahead, though, and despite its being a collective failure of many aspects of the club, Piazza would bear the brunt of the home crowd's wrath over the team's performance.

• • •

In retrospect it seems ludicrous to describe any portion of the Yankees' 1998 season as disastrous. But the first week of the season was about as disastrous as it could get for any team.

When the Yankees got to Anaheim for Opening Day, the offense that was supposed to pummel American League teams was held to just three runs in the first two games of the year, smothered by Angels pitching. Pettitte gave up four runs in the opener, a 4–1 loss, and the bullpen gave up seven runs in the second game, a 10–2 loss. It was the first time in thirteen years that the team had begun the season 0-2. Perhaps more impactful than the losses, in the second game Chili Davis tore a tendon in his right ankle. He missed the next four and a half months of the season.

The Yankees moved on to Oakland, where they encountered rain and a game postponement and, when they finally started the series, another loss. Cone, given a 3–0 lead, yielded seven unanswered runs to the A's as the Yankees again went down to defeat. It was only three games into the year, but the season seemed to be teetering on the brink as panicky fans and a befuddled owner started to wonder just what exactly was going on here. Where they came from, no one knows, but whispers began that Joe Torre's job might be in danger, all before the team even played a single home game. "Joe Torre's job status was the subject of at least 20 minutes of one of the talk shows on WFAN," noted Dan Castellano of the *Star-Ledger* after the slow start.[31]

It sounded ludicrous, but in the world of George Steinbrenner, nothing was ludicrous. He'd fired Bob Lemon, fresh off a World Series appearance, just fourteen games into the 1982 season, and he'd fired Yogi Berra, a beloved team icon, just sixteen games into the 1985 season. Maybe there was no real threat, but with the team 0-3 in the face of gigantic expectations, maybe there was. "What are you going to say? I don't care about being fired? You lose two or three in a row and it's irritating to hear. It's not something you're thrilled about hearing," said Torre in response to numerous questions about his job status that first week.[32]

Whether the whispers were real or imagined, it certainly felt like the Yankees needed a win to calm everyone down. Instead, in the season's fourth game, they blew a one-run lead in the eighth, and then, with two outs in the ninth and a two-run lead, Graeme Lloyd allowed a two-run home run to Jason Giambi to tie the game. In the moment, it felt calamitous. Two runs in the tenth, though, managed to salvage the game and give the team its first win of the year. "We all knew we had a great team," said Nelson, who got the victory in that game. "We were wondering what the heck was going on. When we finally won, I was like, 'Hey, we won the World Series. Let's pop some champagne.'"[33]

Torre had the entire team sign the lineup card so that he could present it to Cashman, a memento for his first win as general manager. Cashman would have been there in person to receive it, but after the team's third loss, Steinbrenner had told him to leave the team and head back to New York. It served no purpose other than as punishment for the slow start.

That win, however, was tempered by bad news when Mariano Rivera landed on the disabled list. The problem had started during the last series of spring training, a set of games played at the San Diego State University campus against the Padres. Rivera had stepped into a hole near the mound and felt a little tweak in his groin. He did not think much of it at the time. Since the Yankees were getting beaten so badly, Rivera was not needed in the first three games of the year. When he finally appeared against Oakland, he blew the save in the eighth inning. Given the lead back, he was one strike away from closing out the team's first win of the year. But Posada and Torre both noticed Rivera in discomfort, and Torre removed him from the game. "Every time I threw the ball, I felt a kind of stretching," said Rivera. "I was feeling it the whole time. But I'll tell you the truth, if the manager doesn't come out, I would have kept throwing. That's how I am. It's stupid, but that's how it is. I didn't want to give him the ball, but he was right. You can't do that in the beginning of the year. It's too early."[34]

Now utilizing a closer by committee, the Yankees arrived at the Kingdome, host of various nightmares for them over the past few years. They mustered only three hits against Jamie Moyer in an 8–0 drubbing by the Mariners. Moyer, whose fastball couldn't break an egg, struck out eleven Yankees, the first time he had reached double-digit strikeouts in a game in nine years. "There's no excuse for it," said O'Neill. "We're terrible right now. There's not too many people in the locker room who don't feel the same way, pitchers and hitters."[35]

It seemed unimaginable: 1-4. "A week into the 1998 season one thing is certain: Everyone can put away the magic carpets," wrote the *New York Post*'s Joel Sherman about the expectations that the team would roll over the opposition en route to a championship.[36]

Even if it was just five games into the season, the players were starting to recognize and feel that something just was not right. Their play, even in the game they managed to win, had been off. The offense had not gelled in any manner. The pitchers had been largely unable to keep them in a game or, the few times they'd been given one, maintain a lead. Something had to change.

It can be debated whether team meetings have any impact on the game that follows. Sometimes speeches are made, tempers flare, objects are thrown, and a team then wins. Sometimes all of that happens, and then it loses. No one really knows the impact. What is known for certain, though, is that before their sixth game of the year, the Yankees held a meeting in the clubhouse.

Torre spoke calmly, as he often did, about staying focused. Other players were more direct, referencing how O'Neill had been thrown at the night before, a common occurrence when it came to the Mariners. Lou Piniella, the team's manager, had skippered O'Neill in Cincinnati and was frustrated by the outfielder's unwillingness to try and hit more home runs. He respected his talent, but ever since O'Neill had come to the American League, it just so happened that Mariners pitchers constantly threw him up and in. It had led to a brawl in 1996, but more often than not, Piniella and his team got away with it. Some Yankees had had enough of that.

Cone, meanwhile, talked about his having figuratively left his arm on the Kingdome mound after throwing 147 pitches in Game Five of the 1995 ALDS. He hated this place, and he wanted his teammates to hate it too.

The Yankees then went out and did what they would do for most of the remaining 157 games: they ran over the opposition. As if to punctuate the frustration and anger many of his teammates felt, Knoblauch hit the second pitch of the game over the left-field fence for his first home run as a Yankee. Two doubles, a single, a Strawberry home run, and a Posada home run later, New York had jumped out to a 6–0 lead en route to scoring thirteen runs behind a Wells win.

In the final game of the series, teammates and the fanbase collectively held their breath as Hideki Irabu took the mound for the first time that year. Which Irabu would they get? The one who looked magical on that July night against Detroit or the one who gave up nine runs to Baltimore in September? What they got were five solid innings of one-run ball as Irabu struck out seven, including Alex Rodriguez, Ken Griffey Jr., and Edgar Martinez. The game, however, came down to the ninth, where, with New York protecting a two-run lead, Mike Stanton was in trouble. Pressed into closer duty because of Rivera's injury, Stanton allowed a leadoff home run and then back-to-back singles, with Griffey and Martinez coming to bat. Both had a long, well-established history of crushing New York hearts through late-inning big hits. What would happen next felt almost inevitable. Instead of heartbreak, though, Stanton induced Griffey to fly out weakly and then got Martinez to hit into a game-ending double play. The Yankees, heading back to New York, had taken the series and would not lose another one until mid-June.

Returning to the Bronx, the Yankees played one of the most bizarre and memorable home openers in franchise history. Cone, battered in his first start in Oakland, now gave up five runs to the A's in the second inning. It felt like the game could turn into a laugher. Instead the Yankees scored two in the second and five in the third to take the lead. After they added on five more in the fourth, it appeared the Yankees would be the ones who would win this game in a laugher. Instead Oakland put together seven singles, a double, and a hit-by pitch to regain the lead in the fifth, 13–12. Cone left before the inning was over, having allowed nine runs. For the season his ERA stood at 14.90.

The Yankees responded with four singles, a double, and two walks to score four runs and retake the lead in the fifth. From the top of the second to the top of the sixth, twenty-nine runs scored against seven different pitches. It was even more amazing that from there, the offense all but stopped. Only one more run crossed the plate as the Yankees won, 17–13, a record for most runs scored in a home opener. More important, it got the team back to .500. "I think our pitching staff is great," said Martinez. "I don't think we'll have to score that many runs too many times."[37]

Steinbrenner might have disagreed. Rather than bask in the strange win, he sounded off on the team's bullpen. In particular, he set his sights on Darren Holmes, a middle reliever signed from the Rockies in the off-season. "We can't just turn to [Jeff] Nelson and [Mike] Stanton every game," said the Boss. "We have to have it from the young man from Colorado [the Rockies]. He has to start showing something. They say he was throwing 95 miles per hour all the time. I don't see it."[38]

The Yankees swept the A's and were ready to welcome the Angels to the Bronx. Then their seventy-five-year-old stadium dropped a hint that it might be in need of repair.

• • •

The crash reverberated through a mostly empty Yankee Stadium. The game that night was still hours away, thankfully, because if what had just occurred had taken place during the game, there almost certainly would have been loss of life.

At around 2 p.m. on April 14, 1998, a 350-pound steel support beam fell through a ceiling and demolished a seat in the mezzanine level of the stadium. The Yankees postponed their games that night and the following night against the Angels while a thorough check of the rest of the stadium was done. The examination showed no further structural damage, though there was cosmetic damage to the outer part of the stadium caused by seeping water that had frozen and then melted. "This is incredibly bizarre," said Cone at the time. "Most of the players are stunned. The majority of players are also thankful it didn't happen on Opening Day at three o'clock."[39]

The postponements were the first non-weather- or work-stoppage-related game cancellations at Yankee Stadium since 1968, when Opening Day was postponed due to the funeral of Martin Luther King Jr. For years Steinbrenner had been arguing that the Yankees needed a new facility in which to play. The whole ordeal only seemed to strengthen his argument. New York City mayor Rudy Giuliani appeared to agree. "As the mayor and a fan, I want the Yankees to play in New York," he noted after arriving at the stadium to view the damage. "It does indicate that the stadium is old."[40]

Since the Yankees did not want to lose out on all three games of the series—or, more likely, they did not want to have to make up three games later in the season—a fun resolution was devised for the sight of what would have been the third and final game of the series. The two teams moved from the Bronx to Queens, and for the first time in twenty-three years, the Yankees played a regular-season home game at Shea Stadium. "We called Fred Wilpon, the Mets owner, the mayor, the commissioner's office. Everyone cooperated on this," noted Lonn Trost, the Yankees' executive vice president and general counsel.[41]

On a chilly, overcast Wednesday afternoon, over forty thousand fans came out to Flushing to see the novelty in person. The Yankees were already up 5–0 in the fifth when Strawberry, who had hit more home runs at Shea Stadium than any player in history to that date, sent an outside pitch over the wall in left-center field. The famous Big Apple, which popped up behind the center-field wall any time someone from the home team homered, began to rise but stopped just before the Mets logo could be exposed, a playful acknowledgement of the situation. "I've seen that rise a few times," said Strawberry, who had started the year with four home runs and nine RBIS in eleven games. "The only thing is that it had Mets [on it]. It didn't go up all the way, so that was good. I'm a Yankee now."[42]

The Yankees won the game, their sixth in a row since the team meeting in Seattle. The Mets and Cubs played at Shea later that day, marking the first time in the twentieth century that four different teams played in the same ballpark on the same day. After their Shea experience, instead of hosting the Tigers, the Yankees headed to Detroit for three games. They took two of three, swept the Blue Jays, and then returned to Yankee Stadium for the first time since the beam had fallen from the sky. In a stroke of public relations genius, none other than George Steinbrenner himself sat down in loge section 22, box A, seat 7—the very seat that had been pulverized by the beam and was now reconstructed—to watch the game. The move showed fans that it was, in fact, safe to sit in that seat, or any seat, in Yankee

Stadium. When Strawberry sent a moonshot into the upper deck in right field in the first inning, the Boss could be seen enthusiastically cheering the former Met as he rounded the bases. New York took five of six on the home stand, including a dramatic final game against Seattle that saw Raines tie it in the ninth with a home run and Martinez win it in the tenth with a single.

The win put the Yankees record at 17-6. Amazingly, they had done this without getting a single home run from O'Neill or Williams in April, a streak that went on so long that the two made a bet about who would homer first (O'Neill won). Since being three-hit by Jamie Moyer in the Kingdome, they had won sixteen of eighteen games, outscoring their opponents by forty-nine runs. Most important, the walk-off win against Seattle put the Yankees a half game ahead in the American League East, the first time all year they had been in first place. They would never leave the top spot for the rest of the season. Meanwhile, May would bring about one of the biggest headaches of the season, along with one of its most remarkable moments. And one man was responsible for both.

• • •

Joe Torre and David Wells were simply destined to never get along. Wells was loud, crude, in your face, opinionated. He wanted you to know he was in the room. Some, particularly Yankees fans, ate it up. Wells reminded a lot of them of themselves: an average Joe who loved to guzzle beer, run his mouth, and just happened to have an overpowering fastball and a devastating curveball. Torre was no prude, but he didn't need you to know he was in the room. He was not loud, even when angry, nor did he feel the need to share every thought or opinion. As a manager, Torre did not want or need a team full of individuals. He wanted a single unit, with all players abiding by both the organization's rules and the unwritten rules and etiquette of the game. Torre, in essence, just did not want his players to be assholes.

Wells had no desire to follow anyone's rules—not necessarily because he disagreed with them but because he just could not abide being forced to follow someone else's edicts. Wells would do what he wanted to do when he wanted to do it. That included stretching and working out. He and Torre had coexisted for just over one season through a highly delicate balance. Torre did not try to smother Wells, while Wells continued to provide Torre quality innings, giving his team a chance to win.

This uneasy détente broke on May 6 during a sweltering, unreasonably hot night in Arlington, Texas. Thanks to an onslaught of hits, which included the team's collectively hitting for the cycle over the course of five batters, the Yankees jumped out to a 9–0 lead over the Rangers heading into the bottom of the third. Wells recorded the first out of the inning, then allowed one run to score while getting a second out with runners on second and third. Boomer looked like he might escape without further harm when Juan González lined a ball toward second base into the glove of Knoblauch. But the ball ricocheted right out of the glove and into the outfield, allowing both runners to score. The play was originally scored a base hit, then changed to an error, much to the anger of González, who spent the rest of the game pointing at the official scorer every time he reached base. Eventually the play was changed back to a hit, a move that ultimately inflated Wells's ERA that year from 3.23 to 3.49 because the Rangers scored four more runs that inning, making it a 9–7 game. Wells departed before the third was over, handing Torre the ball without looking at his manager.

The Yankees made it 13–7 before Texas tied it at 13. Eventually the Yankees won the game, but the story afterward was Torre's obvious unhappiness with his starting pitcher. He noted that Wells "looked like he [had run] out of gas. Maybe he's out of shape."[43] "I wasn't mad at him personally," added Stottlemyre. "I was disappointed. Whenever you give a pitcher that kind of lead and you feel he shortchanged himself, you get disappointed."[44]

The idea that Wells's weight or that his inability to man up had led to his poor performance infuriated him to no end. If Greg Maddux had a bad outing, nobody questioned his physical fitness or stamina. Why should Wells be treated any differently? The pitcher fumed over the comments and pouted in the clubhouse. After three days, Wells, Torre, and Stottlemyre met to clear the air. It appeared to work, at least in the short term.

In his next start Wells tossed eight innings of two-run ball, striking out nine Royals in a 3–2 win. It was Wells's next start, however, that would give him some measure of flexibility with Torre for the rest of the year. Claiming to be hung over, if not still buzzed from a night out drinking with *Saturday Night Live*'s Jimmy Fallon, Wells began his start against the Twins by retiring hitter after hitter after hitter with relative ease. It came as something of a shock to Posada, who recalled watching the last few minutes of Wells's pregame warmup. "David was everywhere with those pitches—he had no command at all," said Posada.[45]

Wells struck out the side in the third, two out of three in the fifth, and two out of three in the sixth, all while not allowing a single runner to reach base. The fans, many of whom had come to receive a free beanie baby as part of a promotional giveaway, realized early just what Wells was attempting to do. With each proceeding out, they got louder and louder. Wells's teammates knew what was going on too.

Posada refused to sit next to him, even though Wells wanted to talk to him about pitch selection. When Wells went to sit down next to Strawberry, the former Met stood up and walked to another part of the dugout. "They were killing me, man," said Wells.[46]

Wells came close to walking Paul Molitor with two out in the seventh, recovering to strike out the future Hall of Famer and send the crowd into a frenzy. The Twins went three up and three down in the eighth, setting the stage for a ninth inning to remember. After a pop fly and a strikeout, Wells got one strike on Twins shortstop Pat Meares before Meares lifted a lazy fly ball to right field. O'Neill camped under it and squeezed his glove tight for the final out of the Yankees' first perfect game since Don Larsen's achievement in Game Five of the 1956 World Series.

David Wells, who just ten days earlier was being chided for his weight and seemingly imperfect body, was carried off the field by his teammates as he absorbed the adulation of nearly fifty thousand screaming fans. "Nobody can take this away from me, no matter what happens," said Wells afterward. "I'm just going to cherish this for the rest of my life."[47] "When he went 3-1 on Molitor, that's the one memory I'll take from this game. Once he got Molly out, he was going to pitch a no-hitter, a perfect game. That's being tested big-time when you're 3-1 on that kind of hitter and still get away," said Torre.[48]

Steinbrenner sent Wells several bottles of champagne, and the pitcher had a cigar in Torre's office. Wells's season changed after the dustup with his manager. Go figure. After his start on that hot night in Texas, he went 15-3 the rest of the year with a 2.90 ERA, throwing eight complete games and a league-leading five shutouts. If not for the incredible season of Roger Clemens, who garnered all first-place votes, Wells might have taken home the Cy Young Award that year.

Wells's perfect game was the defining moment of the season until the Yankees played their next game, a home affair against the Orioles. The defending AL East champs, who, it was expected, would again be contending with the Yankees for first, were struggling as they headed into the Bronx. Several key players, including Brady Anderson, Rafael Palmeiro, and Cal Ripken, had gotten off to slow starts. Injuries would ultimately force them to use fourteen different starting pitchers. The Orioles came into New York already eleven games behind the Yankees. If there was any chance for them to make a run for first, this series was it. When the Orioles jumped out to a 5–1 lead in the first game, it looked like they might, in fact, be making progress.

After scoring two runs in the seventh, the Yankees put two runners on with two out in the eighth, and Bernie Williams stepped up to the plate, his team down 5–4. On the mound for Baltimore stood Armando Benitez, who was about to take part in the first of many incidents that would embed him in the memories of Yankees and Mets fans for years to come. Benitez had pitched largely in middle relief for Baltimore over the last three seasons. His fastball could be devastating, hitting speeds of nearly one hundred miles per hour. In 1997 he had averaged thirteen strikeouts per nine innings. While Benitez gave up few hits, his problem was frequent bouts with lack of control. His fastball would tail, and he would walk batter after batter.

Benitez had to get Williams out to preserve the lead. Instead he left a splitter over the plate, and Williams drilled it into the upper deck in right field. It was an exhilarating moment, one that had escaped the team against the Orioles at any point the previous season. The crowd was still standing and applauding, perhaps trying to coax Williams out of the dugout for a curtain call, when Benitez hit Tino Martinez square in the back with a fastball. It was a purpose pitch so blatant that home plate umpire Drew Coble immediately ejected Benitez from the game.

Ejection was not good enough for many of the Yankees. The team had become a close-knit unit in the first month and a half of the year. Winning has that effect. But this team was especially noteworthy for its lack of ego. No one was complaining about playing time or how much a teammate earned. The Yankees had become a team in every sense of the word. Now someone had deliberately tried to hurt one of them, coming dangerously close to beaning a teammate in the head.

Players were not just angry; they wanted retribution. They wanted vigilante-style justice. And the one Yankee determined above all others to provide it was Darryl Strawberry. From the moment the ball dented Martinez's back, Strawberry decided that, no matter what obstacle might fall in his way, he was *going* to get to Benitez.

As the crowd howled in anger, the Yankees collectively ascended the top step of the dugout and began marching toward the mound. Benitez dropped his glove and gestured toward the quickly approaching players, as if daring them to come and get him. Strawberry immediately accepted the offer, charging toward him. Before Strawberry could get to Benitez, several players from both teams and the umpiring crew got between them. It looked like this would be a standard baseball fight: a lot of shoving and yelling but little actual fighting. Then, seemingly out of nowhere, Jeff Nelson and Graeme Lloyd, having rushed in from the bullpen, charged at Benitez, desperately attempting to get a punch in. Lloyd initially grabbed the pitcher around the head with both hands before the pushing and shoving of other Orioles loosened his grip. What proceeded was a windmill of thrown punches met by swirling arms trying to block them. Lloyd tried to land several blows but kept getting his fists stopped by other Orioles, whose grabbing at Lloyd became so frantic they inadvertently ripped his warmup jacket right off.

Nelson's and Lloyd's attempts kinetically drove the fight toward the Baltimore dugout, as all players, coaches, and managers now shifted in that direction. As they did, several players stumbled and fell over one another. This allowed Benitez to square off directly with Brosius, one-on-one, right in front of the top step of the Orioles' dugout. Brosius, recognizing he was alone for that moment, backed off as reinforcements came in. At this point, Strawberry reemerged and smacked Benitez on the side of the face, sending the pitcher into the dugout. Brosius then tackled Harold Baines, and individual skirmishes broke out everywhere. Baltimore coach Elrod Hendricks grabbed Joe Girardi. Jimmy Key held back David Wells.

Martinez then began pushing and shoving his way toward the dugout, gesturing with his fingers that this was now the second time that Benitez had hit him. Martinez was correct. On June 7, 1995, while he was still with the Mariners, Benitez had plunked Tino in the back after giving up a grand slam to Edgar Martinez. Tino had not forgotten, even three years later.

It appeared that the worst was over until Benitez, who had reemerged, was inexplicably left all alone in front of the dugout. Nelson looked to take advantage and began approaching. Benitez decided to act first, swinging violently as his teammate, Sidney Ponson, tried to grab Nelson and hold him back. This new development reignited the brawl because, as players gathered around Nelson and Ponson to prevent more fighting, a clear lane was left open to Benitez. Strawberry immediately saw his opportunity and seized it, rushing toward Benitez and cocking his left arm to deliver a hay-maker. Darryl hit Benitez on the side of the face, not quite fully connecting but lunging with enough force to send Strawberry into the dugout. From there a wave of players flooded in, including Benitez, with bodies strewn about everywhere as teammates attempted to stop whatever kind of violence they could. Strawberry was still trying to get at Benitez while Baltimore's Alan Mills started hitting Strawberry. Umpires and stadium security simply stood around the parameter of the dugout, acknowledging that there was nothing they could do to end this. Eventually Torre convinced Strawberry to leave the dugout. As the manager escorted him across the field, fans thunderously applauded Strawberry.

After nearly ten minutes, order was restored, and the game resumed with Tim Raines hitting a home run on the first post-brawl pitch. The Yankees went on to win the game. Afterward Steinbrenner grew emotional when asked how he felt about his team's performance. "We took it right to 'em. I feel very proud of them. All of them. I guess if you can't win ballgames you gotta try and win fights. I guess that's what it is. That's the worst I've seen in 25 years in the game."[49]

Some may have mocked the Boss for his near-tears response, but the brawl itself was a signature moment for the team. The Yankees had been beating up on opponents on the field, now both literally and figuratively. It solidified the team as a cohesive unit for whom little else mattered but winning and protecting one another.

The Yankees swept the series, unofficially eliminating Baltimore from the division race in the process. They finished May at 37-13, with a seven-and-a-half-game lead over the Red Sox for first. If there was any reason to believe they could not continue to perform at this rate, they eliminated all doubt by winning the first nine games of June. The winning streak featured several notably moments.

In early June, Cone was petting his mother's four-month-old Jack Russell terrier, Veronica. The puppy, who had "teeth like little hypodermic needles," according to Cone, bit the Yankees' pitcher on his right hand.[50] The bite was not severe, but it was enough to keep Cone from making his next scheduled start. The Yankees brought up someone initially meant to be just a temporary replacement until Cone's next scheduled start: Orlando Hernández. He was a twenty-eight-year-old rookie, or at least that's what he told people.

Hernández had been a top player in Cuba, but the Castro regime's iron grip prevented him from truly becoming a star. His brother, Levan, defected in 1995. Orlando paid the price. He was banned from the Cuban national team in 1996 and came under stricter scrutiny as fear within the Castro regime grew that he too would defect. On the morning of December 26, 1997, that's exactly what Hernández did. He and seven others, including his wife, sailed from Cuba, leaving behind two kids and his parents. After ten hours at sea he and his group landed on a deserted spit of land called Anguilla Cay. After several days there, they were finally rescued by a U.S. Coast Guard helicopter and transported to an immigration center in the Bahamas. There, rather than accept a U.S. visa, Hernández declared himself a political refugee. Doing so ensured that he would be a free agent rather than having to enter the amateur draft, meaning he could negotiate with any team for his services.

The offers rolled in. The Yankees blew them all away, giving him $6.6 million over four years, a far larger sum than anything anyone else had proposed. Part of the hesitancy from other clubs to go that high was that no one believed Hernández when he said he was twenty-eight. Most thought he was in his early thirties, a belief backed up by an old Cuban baseball card that listed him as being thirty-two. The Yankees didn't particularly care which number was right. They saw an All-Star pitcher either way.

El Duque, a nickname first given to his father but then bestowed on Hernández, started off in the Minors. The plan was to have him slowly and methodically work his way through the system before coming to the big leagues. The Yankees wanted him to adjust to baseball in the United States. But Hernández did not need to adjust. He dominated the Minor Leagues, going 7-1 and averaging nearly thirteen strikeouts per nine innings. That dominance, mixed with Veronica's sharp teeth, got Hernández to the big leagues faster than anyone had anticipated.

Hernández stood out immediately as he took the mound at Yankee Stadium on June 3. He wore his socks pulled up and over his pants, giving him the look of an old-time ballplayer. When Hernández pitched, he jerked his left leg way up, but not in the kicking style of a Juan Marichal or Warren Spahn. Instead he lifted inward toward his chest, bending his leg with his knee nearly hitting him in the chin. After that, he threw from any of several arm angles, including three-quarters and side-arm. The switch in angles made it even harder for hitters to pick up the ball. What truly differentiated

Hernández, however, was his pitch selection. He would often start hitters off with a curveball, then retire them with his fastball. This was a switch. Most pitchers used their fastball to set up their off-speed pitches.

The result was a dominating Major League debut. Hernández struck out the first hitter he faced, en route to giving up just five hits and a single run in seven innings. "He did have a funky delivery, but there was nothing unusual about his pitches," said Quinton McCracken, the first hitter to face Hernández that night. "He just did an excellent job of keeping us off balance."[51]

Hernández was only going to be a temporary member of the starting rotation. In fact, the day after his debut, some media outlets noted that he was about to be sent back down to Triple A Columbus. Instead he made his next start, taking the mound at Olympic Stadium in Montreal and pitching a shutout into the ninth. He lost the shutout eventually but ended up with a complete game, nine-strikeout win in just his second Major League start. He was leaving the Yankees no choice. They had to keep him in the rotation.

The day after Hernández beat the Expos, Raines achieved history when he stole his eight hundredth career base. He was only the fifth player to achieve the feat, and doing it in the ballpark he had called home for the first twelve years of his career was especially satisfying.

Raines's stolen base came in a Yankees 6–2 victory, with the win in that game going to Hideki Irabu. In a season that had, so far, featured a perfect game, a legendary brawl, and the remarkable story of a Cuban refugee, Irabu was easily overshadowed. These events, combined with future developments, would cloud the memory of many players, reporters, and fans who long forgot this indisputable fact: the Yankees' best pitcher for the first two and a half months of 1998 was Hideki Irabu.

It began with his start against the Mariners in Seattle, where Irabu allowed only one run. At no point from that start until June 21, a span of eleven appearances, would Irabu's ERA rise above 2.00. In his first five starts of the year, he gave up just four total runs. Only a surprising lack of run support kept his record at 2-0. After giving up more than one run for the first time that season, he came back on May 25 and tossed a six-hit shutout in Chicago. He won AL Pitcher of the Month for May.

Everything was working for Irabu. His fastball, so lifeless in 1997, was moving with a sharpness that made hitters look wildly overmatched. His split-finger, his moneymaker, was falling off a cliff as hitters, one after another, flailed at it. The result was that in no start before June 21 did Irabu yield more hits than innings pitched. Though his movement also led to a good deal of walks, it resulted in plenty of strikeouts as well. For two and a half months in 1998, Irabu truly was the Japanese Nolan Ryan.

Irabu was 6-1 with a 1.59 ERA after his win against Montreal. It was not out of the question to imagine him starting that year's All-Star game in Colorado. He lost his next start in Baltimore when the Yankees failed to provide him any runs. From there his numbers began to fade. A series of poor starts to end June probably cost him a chance at making the All-Star team. His performance in the second half would fluctuate between brutal (as when he allowed eight runs to Seattle on August 30) to dominant (as when he held the Tigers to five hits and no runs on July 15). But by season's end Torre had lost confidence in Irabu, never sure which version of the pitcher would show up. He ended the year 13-9 and did not appear once in the postseason. Still, from Opening Day until June 21, he was everything the Yankees had dreamed of.

The Yankees, meanwhile, did not stop winning. From early April to mid-June they tied a Major League record by winning or tying twenty-four series in a row. They then took ten of eleven games heading into the break. The wins included a dramatic victory on July 2, when, down three with two outs in the ninth, Martinez launched a ball into the upper deck to tie the game. They walked it off in the eleventh. They achieved another walk-off win the next night and finished the first half by shutting out the Orioles, 1–0. Their record stood at 61-20, and they had an eleven-game lead in the division. It was a performance that had not been seen since that of the 1907 Chicago Cubs.

The question of whether the Yankees could keep up their pace in the second half of the year was answered affirmatively in July. Out of the break, they swept the Devil Rays and lost only one series the entire month. As the July 31 trade deadline approached, rumors swirled that the Yankees would acquire left-handed pitcher Randy Johnson from the Mariners. The tall, dominating lefty was going to be a free agent after the season, and it was unlikely that Seattle would be able to resign him. A debate ensued among fans and insiders about whether a team with a sixteen-game lead and seemingly unassailable chemistry should risk messing that up by traded for the cantankerous pitcher.

Cashman and Seattle GM Woody Woodward discussed the parameters of a deal: Irabu, highly touted prospect Mike Lowell, and one other Minor Leaguer in exchange for Johnson. Just how close it came to happening is speculation because ultimately Cashman opted to do nothing. The Yankees, who were actually in Seattle as the deadline approached, had no visible holes, and while Johnson was a future Hall of Famer, there appeared to be no reason to acquire him other than just because he was available. The Yankees made no deals and breathed a sigh of relief when Johnson was shipped out of the American League and to the Houston Astros, where he won ten of his eleven starts.

Pressing on sans Johnson, the team headed to Oakland, where more history awaited.

• • •

On June 1, the Mets were 31-20. They had weathered a string of injuries and a staggeringly inefficient offense to now lead the wild-card race. Their last game at Shea had drawn a crowd of over forty-seven thousand, the third largest of the season so far. They were coming off their first road series sweep in two years, their first sweep in Philadelphia in three, and their longest winning streak in eight. And then, just like that, the momentum slowed. It was not as if the team had begun to play overly poorly. There was no repeat of the mid-1990s performances and seemingly never-ending pileup of losses. The Mets were just mediocre. And it lasted for two months.

It started with a three-game sweep at the hands of the Pirates in the first three days of June. After that they went 7-8. It was not horrible but not great either. The bullpen, however, became a point of weakness after having performed solidly for much of the first two months of the year. In a four-game series in Florida, Turk Wendell and Mel Rojas give up eighth-inning leads in two of the games, both of which the team lost in extra innings. Then in Montreal, Rojas gave up two more runs in a 5–4 walk-off loss.

Perhaps coincidentally the bullpen's struggles came shortly after the Mets traded Greg McMichael to the Dodgers along with Dave Mlicki. McMichael had been a rock in the team's bullpen the previous year, logging nearly eighty-eight innings and winning seven games. His numbers in 1998 were not nearly as solid, but he'd still been a largely reliable option. Brad Clontz replaced him in the pen. Clontz had experienced some success with the Braves in previous seasons but had struggled mightily in Los Angeles, pitching to a 5.66 ERA in eighteen games. Ultimately Clontz pitched just two games with the Mets, spending most of his time in the Minors before leaving as a free agent.

The trade with the Dodgers also featured an exchange of starting pitchers. Mlicki had been unable to match his performances of 1997, instead struggling to keep runners off base. His 1.63 WHIP (Walks and Hits per Innings Pitched) was among the worst of his career. Mlicki went to Los Angeles in exchange for Hideo Nomo. Two years earlier the deal would have elicited the same kind of attention as the Piazza trade had. Nomo had been a star pitcher in Japan who had come over to the Dodgers in 1995 and had taken the city, the league, and the country by storm. Equipped with a herky-jerky pitching motion that was typical of Japanese pitchers but relatively unseen in Major League Baseball, Nomo first raised his clasped hands above his head, held his set for a moment, then dropped the hands down to his waist and then above his left shoulder as he pivoted his body so that his entire back faced toward home plate, allowing a batter to see his whole jersey number. Then his body began to sink as he spun and hurled the ball toward home plate.

Nomo's delivery helped conceal the ball from batters and disrupt their timing mechanisms. But more than his motion, it was his split-fingered fastball that really confounded batters. For many, the downward drop was unlike anything they had ever seen, and the hype around Nomo in spring training that year was intense. He did not disappoint, helping get the Dodgers back to the postseason for the first time in seven years after going 13-6 and leading the league in shutouts, strikeouts, and strikeouts per nine innings. Batters hit just .182 off Nomo as he took home Rookie of the Year honors.

Fans began mimicking his delivery, and the Dodgers used Nomo to cultivate a larger following among the Japanese community, as they had done with Fernando Valenzuela and the Mexican community in the early 1980s. Nomomania had now replaced Fernandomania.

Nomo followed up his rookie season with another strong performance in 1996, helping the team win the wild card as he finished fourth in Cy Young voting. His numbers were strong again in 1997, but a closer look revealed that National League hitters had begun to figure Nomo out. His walks had increased every year. Batters learned to lay off his breaking pitches as they realized that he often did not throw them for strikes. Hitters had batted a collective .182 against him in 1995, then .218 in 1996, and .243 in 1997. These were still excellent numbers but a clear indication that players were catching up to him. Moreover, after the 1997 season was over, Nomo had surgery on his pitching elbow.

This combination of factors led to a rough start in 1998. Though there were signs of the dominate Nomo, he also got battered in games in Chicago and Florida. On May 30, at home against Cincinnati, he gave up six runs and was booed after being removed from the game in the fourth inning. Nomomania seemed to have ended, a point made clearer when he expressed his displeasure with the team's trading Piazza to the Marlins and asked to be traded himself. In response, on June 1 the Dodgers did the seemingly unthinkable and designated him for assignment. The Mets came swooping in.

Nomo appeared to find his stride in Queens, allowing only nineteen runs in just over fifty innings while striking out fifty-nine in his first nine starts with the team. It was not enough to get the Mets out of their funk, though. They looked desperate when, on June 20, they signed former Yankee Rubén Sierra to a Minor League deal.

"Some of the guys on the staff thought [signing Sierra] was worth considering," said Phillips.[52] Valentine did not appear to be one of those guys. "Slim," he responded, when asked about Sierra's chances of making the big-league club.[53] Sierra stayed in the Minors the rest of the year. He did not appear in the Majors again until 2000. In late June the bullpen's struggles were exposed in the worst way possible: in the first game of that year's interleague Subway Series.

The series was held at Shea for the first time as over fifty-three thousand fans showed up on a Friday night to watch Al Leiter face off against Hideki Irabu. The game was a seesaw affair, the teams trading leads multiple times in the first six innings. In the top of the seventh, with the Mets up 4–3, Leiter walked Knoblauch before badly jamming Jeter on an inside fastball. Jeter was able to meekly shoot the ball the other way toward Olerud. In his rush to get over to first base, Leiter reached to tag Jeter and immediately felt a pull in his knee. He attempted a warm-up pitch, but he could not continue. "I took my one throw and I knew there was no way," said Leiter.[54]

Jeter reached base, and Leiter had to leave the game, forcing Rojas to come in with two runners on to face O'Neill. The move was not without controversy. O'Neill was a .360 hitter off right-handed pitchers at that moment and a .273 hitter off lefties. A lefty, Brian Bohanon, who had been warming up, stood on the bullpen mound and watched as O'Neill deposited the right-handed Rojas's first-pitch splitter into the left-field bleachers for a go-ahead three-run home run. "I wasn't surprised to see Rojas in the game," said O'Neill. "I had faced him in the NL a few times without much success [1-for-5]. He hung it a little and I'm glad we played here, because that ball doesn't go out in Yankee Stadium."[55]

The Yankees eventually won the game as Rojas saw his ERA, which had been at 1.69 just seven appearances earlier, rise to 3.86.

The next day it was the Mets' defense that let them down. Errors by Olerud and Ordóñez accounted for four of the Yankees' seven runs as they won, 7–3. The following night the Mets tried to avoid a first-ever subway sweep, but they were flustered by El Duque's array of pitches. In eight innings they managed just two hits and a single run off the Cuban refugee. Fortunately for the Mets, Masato Yoshii was equally as good, giving up only two hits while striking out ten over seven innings. His only blemish was a seventh-inning home run by Brosius. In the bottom of the ninth the Mets took advantage of a leadoff double by Baerga, who accounted for two of the team's three hits, as Luis Lopez drove him in with a walk-off sacrifice fly. The moment was not without a brief second of controversy. McRae, who had been on first base when Lopez hit the fly ball to right field, took off for second. O'Neill, after catching the ball on the run, spun and fired a throw toward home, trying, in vain, to save the game. Lopez scored easily, but Jeter scoped the ball and tossed it to Tino Martinez, who, diving and catching the ball in one motion, fell over the bag before McRae could get back to first. For a split second the Yankees thought they had salvaged the tie and sent the game into extra innings. Home plate umpire Frank Pulli ruled, however, that the force out of McRae had occurred after Baerga had touched home plate. Per Major League Baseball rule 2.00, that meant the run counted and the game was over. "That was kind of crazy," said Baerga. "But it was nice to come back and win."[56]

It was an exhilarating win for the Mets but did little to jump-start the team. Over the next two plus weeks they lost ten of thirteen games, including a three-game sweep in Atlanta that ended any hope the team had of vying for the division title. If the Mets were going to make the postseason, it would have to be via the wild card. Even that felt like it was starting to slip away. On July 16, after a 4–2 loss to the Phillies, the Mets were four and a half games behind in the wild-card race, trailing three other teams and just barely ahead of the Brewers and Dodgers. Their play had gotten so lackluster that they actually traded with the Dodgers to get Greg McMichael back, just five weeks after they had sent him to Los Angeles.

As the team's play failed to pick up, no one caught the brunt of fans' frustration more than Mike Piazza. The boos had started as early as the first week that he was a Met. Expectations were simply too high for what any player, no matter how talented, could provide. In July the booing became more incessant. It became measurably more noticeable in a July 14 loss to the Braves. With the Mets down two, with two runners on and two out in the seventh, Piazza grounded out meekly against the Braves' John Smoltz, and the boos reverberated around every square inch of Shea Stadium.

Piazza then went 0-5 in a 4–2 loss to Philadelphia, and boos cascaded down with each hitless at bat. It did not matter that he would end the month with a hit in twenty-two of his twenty-six July games or that he still managed to drive in sixteen runs. He was barely hitting above .200 with runners in scoring position, a figure that gave the perception that he could not get a hit when it mattered most. Every time he failed to drive in a runner at Shea Stadium, he heard it from the home crowd. "I can't complain," said Piazza as the booing intensified. "They do it to everybody. If you do the job, they cheer. If you don't, they boo. . . . I'm disappointed in myself as much as anybody."[57]

"Less than three months after they gave Piazza a hero's welcome, New York Mets fans are singing the boos," wrote the *Albany Times Union*'s Steve Campbell. "They've rehearsed the tune so often at Shea Stadium, they can spit out their hot dogs in mid-bite and not miss a beat. Piazza pops out weakly with a runner in scoring position. Boooooo!!! Piazza grounds out with a runner in scoring position. Ya bum!!! Piazza strikes out with a runner in scoring position. Get outta here!!!"[58]

The boos would continue for weeks afterward. Meanwhile, the Mets had gone a combined 25-30 in June and July. Their season, which had begun with so much hope and excitement, was on the brink. Something needed to happen and fast, or it was going to be a long, cold winter in Queens.

• • •

It had been a great first two games against Oakland for the Yankees. In the first game, they scored fourteen runs. Then they had battered A's pitching for ten more runs in taking the first game of a doubleheader. "We didn't have a particularly great pitching staff," said A's general manager Billy Beane. "Well, the first game [of the series], poor Mike Oquist was pitching. We knew we had three more games to play [in the series], so we had to leave him out there, otherwise we would have wound up throwing an infielder in the second game."[59]

In the doubleheader nightcap, though, the Yankees were being embarrassed by former Yankee Kenny Rogers, who at one point retired twelve hitters in a row and took a 5–1 lead into the ninth. The first two hitters reached base, and Rogers came out of the game. He'd been robbed of going the distance, but still the shutdown performance against his old team must have been pleasing. Reliever Billy Taylor came in and induced Chad Curtis into hitting a ground ball to third for a sure-thing, rally killing double play. Instead third baseman Mike Blowers booted the ball, and all runners were safe. With Joe Girardi due up as the potential tying run, Torre sent in Strawberry to pinch-hit for him.

Strawberry had been here before. Earlier in the year, in Kansas City, Torre had also sent him to pinch-hit with the bases loaded. The situation had not been as dramatic as this one. The Yankees were already winning. When Strawberry, who had been smoking a cigarette near the bat rack before heading to the plate, proceeded to hit a grand slam, it merely extended their lead on the way to a victory. Still, the moment was part of a resurgent season for Darryl. He was healthy, he was sober, and he was a model teammate. It was not just that he had led the charge in the Benitez incident. The moody, brooding Straw of the Mets' glory days was nowhere to be found. Removed from drugs and surrounded by an owner who adored him, in part because of the feel-good story he presented, Darryl was thriving. Though not a full-time player, he would ultimately appear in more games in 1998 than he had in any season since 1991. The result was more home runs and more RBIs in one year than he had had in any season since then and a higher OPS than he'd had in any season since nearly winning the MVP in 1988.

As Strawberry came to bat now, the Oakland Coliseum might as well have been Yankee Stadium west. Only a few thousand fans out of the announced crowd of over twenty-three thousand remained, and a large contingent of them was cheering for the away team. Many of the Yankees fans had managed to congregate in the lower level of the stadium, filling up several of the rows that led up from the playing field. When Strawberry turned on a 2-2 fastball, the "hometown" crowd actually went nuts as the ball sailed over the center-field fence to tie the game at 5–5. "I knew I hit the ball well, but it was a line drive, and you're never sure if a line drive will go out of the ballpark," said Strawberry.[60]

In hitting his second pinch-hit grand slam of the year, Strawberry tied a Major League record. Rogers sat stunned in the A's dugout as he then watched the Yankees score five more runs and eventually win the game. To that point the Yankees had been ahead at least once in 97 of the team's 107 games.

The Yankees lost the final game to Oakland but returned home and won twelve of their next thirteen. On August 31 they were 98-37, a remarkable sixty-one games above .500. The ninety-eight wins represented more victories than any Yankees team had had in a season since 1980, and all before the month of September began. They had already clinched at least a wild-card berth, the earliest any team had ever clinched a postseason appearance in the twentieth century, and the division title was a foregone conclusion. All that was left was to get through the last month of the season, avoid injury, and gear up for the playoffs. Yet September would provide a series of memorable moments, most for the right reasons. But not all.

• • •

The Mets awoke on August 1 in need of something—anything—to get them started. They were out of the running for first place. All the talk about the Yankees had overshadowed how dominating a year the Braves were having. Their seventy-two wins were only four behind the Yankees, making the NL East title Atlanta's with two months left in the season. That left the wild card, for which, at the start of August, six teams were realistically vying, including the Mets. If the Mets were going to play baseball in October, the club had to start playing better and do so soon.

A few were not going to be a part of that push. While not making any major moves, the Mets did trade away several players at the July 31 deadline. Among them were Bernard Gilkey, who went to the Diamondbacks, and Bill Pulsipher, who went to the Brewers. Gilkey had not been the same since returning from the disabled list in early May, failing to produce anything close to the numbers he had put up in 1996. In twenty-four July games he mustered only three extra-base hits while striking out nearly as many times as he got on base. "There are no indications to make me believe that," said Valentine when talking about whether Gilkey would ever regain his 1996 form.[61]

Hundley felt somewhat responsible for Gilkey's departure since his moving to left field had made his teammate expendable. "It's tough," said

Hundley, while appearing to hold back tears. "You feel responsible for it. I didn't want to come in here and make that situation."[62]

Pulsipher, meanwhile, had returned after two years on the disabled list and battles with anxiety attacks, but he was being used almost entirely in spot bullpen outings. He had no long-term role on the team, and the Mets sent him to Milwaukee. The trade represented the official end of Generation K as Pulsipher was the first of the three pitchers to leave the team.

Replacing Gilkey was Tony Phillips. A utility man extraordinaire who had spent significant time at nearly every position outside of pitcher, catcher, and first base, Phillips was on the downside of his career. Still, he had led the league in walks twice during the 1990s, and he brought a knack for getting on base that the lineup sorely needed. The Mets had attempted to sign him in spring training. The move generated some criticism as Phillips had pleaded guilty to cocaine possession the year before. It was not that, though, that kept the deal from happening. Phillips wanted more money than the team was willing to offer. "He's lived up to every aspect of his after-care program," said Steve Phillips after the trade, looking to calm any doubts among fans and the league.[63]

The Mets had hoped for more at the deadline. Rumors circulated that they were interested in a deal for Red Sox first baseman Mo Vaughn but balked at Boston's demand for, at a minimum, Olerud and Bobby Jones. Jones's name also came up in a possible deal for White Sox third baseman Robin Ventura until Chicago backed away.

Additions and subtractions now made, the Mets' push toward a postseason berth began with a thrilling August 1 win that was reminiscent of what had made the team so exciting the previous year. With the team down 1–0 in the bottom of the ninth, Matt Franco pinch-hit for Ordóñez. It was Franco's sixty-fourth game of the year, in almost all of which he had appeared as a pinch hitter. It was the role Franco was destined to play his entire career. He had done it with some success in 1997 and was performing even better in that role in 1998. One thing that had been missing, however, was power. Having hit five home runs the previous season, Franco was homerless coming into this pinch-hit at bat. On a 1–0 pitch, he hit a fastball deep into the right-field stands to tie the game.

Twelve pitches later Alfonzo doubled home Hundley to win the game. The Mets were off and running with that win. They clubbed former teammate Brian Bohanon (traded in the second McMichael deal) for six runs the next day, ultimately taking two of three from the Dodgers. In the first game of the next series, against San Francisco, the Mets came back from a 4–0 deficit in the seventh to win the game in ten innings. Two days later, having blown a 7–2 lead in the eighth, they pieced together three singles and a walk to score two in the ninth and win, 9–8.

Embarking on a three-city road trip, New York took two of three in each series as Rick Reed and Armando Reynoso picked up a combined four wins. Olerud strung together a twenty-three-game hitting streak, at one point holding a slim lead over the Rockies' Larry Walker for the batting crown. "It's fun to be in this situation," said Jones. "I've been here when we were 20-some games out and it wasn't fun. This is fun. These games are important."[64]

Jones spoke not just for himself but also for teammates who had been with the club for years and for fans who had endured the early and mid-1990s. Ten wins over fifteen games had shot the Mets up the wild-card standings. They led the Cubs by half a game and had three games in hand. They finished August with ten wins in seventeen games. Taking three of four games in Los Angeles to end the month, they and the Cubs switched positions as the wild-card leader, with both being tied for the top spot on September 1. Meanwhile, starting with a doubleheader on August 18, Piazza had gone on an absolute tear, making it hard to argue that he could not drive in runners when it mattered. Over his final fifteen August games, the Mets' catcher hit five home runs while driving in nineteen. On August 22 his grand slam put the team ahead for good against Arizona. His home run against the Dodgers on August 28 sparked a comeback that culminated in a 5–4 extra-innings win. Piazza kept his hot streak going into September, starting the month with home runs in three consecutive games and six RBIs overall.

On September 4 the Mets welcomed the Braves to Shea for a critical four-game series. The division race was long over, but the Mets needed to show they could beat Atlanta, a team that they would likely have to play at some point if they made the postseason and wanted to get to the World Series. Over Labor Day weekend, with crowds averaging over thirty-five thousand a game, New York took three of four. The final game, played on Labor Day, was a thrilling come-from-behind-win that saw Alfonzo hit a two-out, two-run home run in the eighth off Atlanta rookie reliever John Rocker.

The win kept the Mets tied for the wild-card lead with the Cubs, each with an 80-64 record. For both clubs this was a season full of feel-good stories.

The Mets had suffered through years of bad play and on- and-off-the field embarrassments while their crosstown rivals were rising from the ashes to be the game's best team. The Cubs had suffered through nearly a century of bad play, and that included heartbreaking losses and claims of curses. Since winning their last championship in 1908, their postseason appearances could be counted on two hands. Chicago had surprised many in 1998, thanks to rookie pitcher Kerry Wood, whose curveball had dominated hitters all season, and slugger Sammy Sosa, who had come out of nowhere to emerge side-by-side with McGwire as a challenger to the single-season home run record. The two teams were done playing each other for the year, so their paths would be set against other teams. But the math was simple, or at least so it seemed: whichever of the two played better over the final eighteen games of the season was likely going to the postseason.

• • •

It had been a brutal year for Todd Hundley. Reconstructive surgery on his right elbow had kept him out of action until mid-July. While he was out, the Mets, the only organization he had ever known, had traded for the best catcher in baseball. This left Hundley, the all-time single-season home run leader for catchers, without a position to play. Not wanting to keep his bat out of the lineup, the Mets converted Hundley into a left fielder, a position he'd never played. It was a disaster. He looked understandably uncomfortable out there, never appearing to get good reads on even routine fly balls. His five errors in 34 games were more than those of any Mets outfielder that year and as many as Olerud had committed in 157 games at first.

Whether he was not fully recovered from his injury or just suffering from the uncertainty of his role on the team, Hundley's offensive numbers collapsed. It took him twenty-nine games to hit his first home run. By the end of August he had only six extra-base hits in 111 at bats, including just two home runs. The Mets placed him back on the disabled list with a sore right elbow. He'd returned just in time for the team's most crucial road trip of the year: three games in Philadelphia, three in Montreal, and four in Houston.

Hundley largely sat on the bench as the team split the six games in Philadelphia and Montreal. The split cost them a game in the standings, and they now trailed the Cubs by a single game in the wild-card race. In Houston the Mets had clawed back to stay in the race. They were down two runs in the ninth inning of the first game when McRae hit a two-run home run to tie it. Wendell, Cook, McMichael, and Franco combined for five scoreless innings, and the Mets won the game with two runs in the thirteenth.

Carlos Baerga played hero the next night, hitting a two-run home run in the ninth to tie the first game of a rare indoor doubleheader and send it into extra innings. The Mets took the lead in the eleventh, but the bullpen, exhausted from weeks of overuse, could not hold it, and Houston won it in the twelfth. The Mets won the second game, but the loss put them a half game behind the Cubs. The next night proved to be the most exciting game any Mets fan had watched in years.

Hundley sat on the bench and watched as former Met Carl Everett's home run gave Houston a 2–0 lead in the third inning. The game stayed that way until the top of the ninth. With a runner on first, the Mets were down to their last strike as Olerud faced fireballer closer Billy Wagner. His fastball at times reaching over one hundred miles per hour, the left-handed Wagner was in the second of three consecutive years in which he averaged over fourteen strikeouts per nine innings. Olerud was having his greatest season since 1993, batting over .350 and providing the only constant source of offense outside Piazza. With the Mets' season on the brink, Olerud reached out and slashed a 3-2 fastball down the left-field line. The ball handcuffed third baseman Sean Berry, hitting his wrist and deflecting toward the stands. The Mets were still alive.

Up came Piazza. Earlier in the game Piazza had grounded into an inning-ending double play with runners on first and third. The boos from New York could almost be heard in Houston. In fact, to that point he'd come up with runners on base in each of his first four at bats and had not produced a hit. This at bat was primed to be a signature moment for the catcher; this was why the Mets had gotten him.

The count went to 2-2 when Wagner tried to sneak in a high and away fastball. The catcher turned on it and sent the ball on a line into right-center field, where it landed in the Astrodome's flowerbed, planted just behind and above the wall. "It looked like we were about done and we came up with three runs," said Piazza. "It was a great game. It was like the playoffs."[65]

Piazza pumped his fist as he rounded first base. It was his two hundredth career home run and to that point his biggest. Teammates mobbed Piazza as he got back to the dugout, and the Mets appeared on their way to the win. But in the bottom of the inning Cook gave up the lead on a home run, sending yet another game into extra innings.

Todd Hundley watched from the bench, bat in hand, as the Mets failed to score in the top of the tenth. He kept watching from the bench in the bottom of the tenth, when McMichael loaded the bases with two outs, fell behind 3-0 on Ricky Gutiérrez, and then came back to strike him out on a nasty changeup that sent the game to the eleventh. It was there, with two outs, that Bobby Valentine sent Hundley to pinch-hit for McMichael.

Valentine could relate to Hundley's struggles. Valentine's playing career had been cut short by a collision with an outfield wall. That's not to say that Hundley's career was over. But Valentine knew what it was like to be unsure of what one's role and future were as a big leaguer. If anyone was pulling for Todd Hundley in this moment, it was Bobby Valentine.

Even if Hundley wasn't hitting like he had been 1996, pitchers still considered him a threat and threw to him carefully. As he was coming into this at bat, his on-base percentage remained over .100 points higher than his average. As if to prove that point, Houston pitcher Sean Bergman fell behind to Hundley, 2-0. Then he tried to drop in a sinking fastball. Hundley turned on it, sending it, with one hand, over the wall in center field to give the Mets the lead. "He came out early two days for batting practice," said Valentine. "All he wanted to do was hit homers to centerfield. He hit about 20 of them, exactly like that. And wouldn't you know it . . ."[66]

When Hundley got back to the dugout and sat on the bench, he could not stop smiling. Valentine came over to high-five him and pat him on the head. In the bottom of the inning an amped-up Wendell struck out the side. After four hours of stomach-churning baseball, the Mets had come out on top. The win kept them a half game within the wild-card lead because the Cubs also won. "That has to be the most exciting regular-season series . . . ever," said an exhilarated Al Leiter after the win.[67]

New York returned home during an off day while the Cubs picked up a win, putting the wild-card deficit at one game. Each team had eight games left to play. The Mets missed a key opportunity when, during the first game of the home stand, John Franco could not hold a two-run ninth-inning lead to the worst-in-baseball Marlins. The Mets lost a heartbreaker, made worse by Chicago's losing to Cincinnati. The crowd became vicious in its anger, chanting, "Franco sucks" as the Mets' closer gave up the lead. "Bookmark this one," wrote the *Star-Ledger*'s Mike Vaccaro. "Highlight it in red ink (or underline it in black, the color of mourning), and place it carefully alongside all the other times you've had your hopes and your heart shattered by your favorite team. There have been plenty before, no doubt; there will be others to follow. No doubt. But for right now, this morning, there will be no other disappointment to match what you saw last night, what you feel this very instant."[68]

The Mets won the next game, and in the series finale Leiter threw eight shutout innings en route to a 5–0 win. Meanwhile, Cincinnati completed the sweep of Chicago, giving the Mets sole possession of the National League wild card with just a week left in the season.

The stage was set. All the Mets needed was to perform better than the Cubs over the season's final five games, and they were going to the playoffs. When New York took a 3–0 first-inning lead over the Expos in the first of those five games—which included Olerud's reaching base for a National League record-tying fifteenth consecutive plate appearance—fans could imagine their team celebrating a postseason berth later that week. Instead the Mets failed to score for another nineteen innings. The Expos came back and won the game, 5–3. "I don't have a good answer," said Olerud when asked why the Mets, who would go 4-8 that year against Montreal, had trouble beating an Expos team that was among the worst in baseball. "I think you definitely want to beat up on the teams that are under .500. But it's funny how some teams play you real tough."[69]

The Cubs won their game against the Brewers that day, tying the Mets, but gave New York a gift in their second game against Milwaukee. With the Cubs up 7–5 in the bottom of the ninth, the Brewers' Geoff Jenkins batted with two outs and the bases loaded and lifted a lazy fly ball to the outfield. Cubs left fielder Brant Brown settled under it and then dropped the ball, allowing all three base runners to score and giving Milwaukee the game.

The gift went unopened as the Mets failed to score against Montreal, losing 3–0. After the final out of the game, several players sat on the bench staring blankly into space, contemplating how they had failed to take advantage of possibly another historic Cubs collapse. Meanwhile, as the Mets and Cubs were trading losses, the San Francisco Giants had emerged from seemingly out of nowhere to also compete for the wild card. After having consistently stayed around four games out of the final spot for weeks, the Giants had won five of their last six, taking full advantage of any slip by either New York or Chicago. Both of those teams were off the final Thursday of the season, so when the Giants won their game that day, it put them one game behind both clubs.

Three games were left. Three teams were vying for one spot. The Mets and Cubs were tied. The Giants were behind by a game. The Giants had, on paper, the easiest of the three remaining schedules, heading to Colorado to play a Rockies team about to finish a sub .500 season. Chicago headed to Houston to play the hundred-win Astros. The Mets flew to Atlanta to play the second-best team in baseball.

That final weekend series in Atlanta would haunt the Mets for months afterward. In the first game, they fell behind in the first inning, 2–0, then scratched and clawed their way through the rest of the game but always fell short of taking the lead. With the tying run on third base in the ninth, Pratt struck out to end the game. The Cubs lost while the Giants overcame a 5–3 deficit in the sixth inning to win.

Two games were left. Three teams were vying for one spot. The Mets, Cubs, and Giants were tied. The Giants won yet again. The Cubs held off a ninth-inning rally to beat the Astros. Al Leiter held the Braves off as long as he could, but in the sixth, Atlanta scored three. The offense couldn't connect against Tom Glavine. The Mets lost, 4–0, and no one tried to hide the obvious consequences of the loss. "The mood?" asked Leiter after the game. "It's not good. You would think having the opportunity to get into the post-season would excite you. That alone should get you up. And we've been kind of flat. How do you explain it? I don't know."[70]

One game was left. Three teams were still vying for one spot. The Cubs and Giants were tied. The Mets were behind by a game. The Mets needed a small miracle. At best they would end up in a three-way tie for the wild card. In that scenario they would play the Giants at Shea the day after the regular season ended. If they won, they would then play the Cubs the following day to see who made the postseason. But for that to happen, they had to win their remaining game, and both the Giants and Cubs had to lose. All three games were starting at different times, each an hour apart. The Mets were going first, so at least if they could win, they would be able to put pressure on the two other teams and perhaps force them to make decisions that would impact them in any one-game playoff scenario.

Valentine could have started Nomo in this final game. There was one problem: Nomo did not want the ball. It was not because he was afraid of the pressure. It was because he did not believe he was the Mets' best option. In his previous two starts, although they had come weeks earlier, he had gotten shelled: twelve runs in just under seven innings with only three strikeouts. "Hideo had been pitching very poorly, and in his eyes, he felt he didn't deserve [the start]. I think Hideo was saying, 'Look, for the good of the team, I stink right now. Give it to Armando,'" said Leiter.[71]

Given Nomo's reluctance, the Mets entrusted their season to Armando Reynoso. Injured for the entire first half due to issues with his right elbow, Reynoso had returned and had been lights out, winning his first five starts while not giving up a run in three of them. A rough outing against the Giants distorted his numbers somewhat, but an argument could have been made that Reynoso was the best pitcher to put on the mound in this situation.

Reynoso did not have it, though. He allowed a first-inning run, then four more in the second before exiting the game with two outs in the inning. The Mets attempted a comeback, bringing Piazza up as the tying run with one out in the seventh. He struck out looking on a questionable call. Ultimately Piazza left fifteen men on base in the series, a stat that illogically spurred fans to gripe anew throughout the off-season about his inability to get big hits. The Mets' lost, 7–2, officially ending their season before they knew the outcome of the Cubs' or Giants' games. "I think we ran out of energy as much as anything else. If we had won another, would it end differently? . . . I don't know. I just know it was a bad ending," said Piazza.[72]

Valentine was crestfallen, immediately wondering what, if anything, he could have done differently to salvage the season. "There must have been something I could have done to win a game in the last week," said Valentine. "My frustration is I didn't do anything about it. I should have done something. I should have done something."[73]

The outcome would be even more devastating later that afternoon. The Cubs blew a late lead to Houston. The Giants, who at one point held a 7–0 lead in the game, blew that lead as well. "They're both going to lose. Aren't they?" said a dejected Steve Phillips watching the games from the clubhouse.[74] He was right. The Cubs lost to Houston in extra innings. Just moments after the Astros won, the Giants lost in the ninth to the Rockies. The two played a tie-breaker playoff game the next day, with the Cubs emerging victorious.

The flight back to New York was funereal. Little was said. There was no music, no cards, no hint of cheer. The next day, players went to Shea to clean out their belongings. Some found T-shirts in their lockers that read "1998 Wild Card New York Mets." The organization had been sent several, and someone likely had forgotten to remove them from the lockers after the

Atlanta series. Reed rolled one into a ball and threw it on the ground. "It's hard to believe it's over. I won't watch another game until next year. That's how bad it is," said the pitcher.[75]

Failing to maintain the wild card with five games constituted the Mets' biggest collapse up to that time. A single win in any of the last five games of the season would have changed the Mets' fortunes. It would have given them, at minimum, a chance to advance to the Division Series. Instead Steve Phillips, Bobby Valentine, the players, and the fans were left to stew during a winter of discontent.

• • •

The Yankees officially won the division with a 7–5 win at Boston on September 9. The celebration was subdued, despite what the team had accomplished. The goal was not a division title. It was a championship. Two days later, with the Blue Jays in town, the fightin' Yanks emerged again. In the bottom of the fourth inning, just after rookie Ricky Ledée nearly hit a home run off him, Toronto pitcher Roger Clemens nailed Brosius with a fastball in the middle of his back. Clemens had a well-established history of head hunting, and his conflicts with the Yankees went back years. In one memorable episode in 1991, catcher Matt Nokes, after being hit in the side by Clemens's fastball, fired the ball back at the pitcher before shouting at him after reaching first base. That animosity had not left the organization, even if almost everyone from that team had retired by now. The current Yankees disliked Clemens just as much, if not more.

Brosius had some words for Clemens as he walked to first. Chad Curtis stood on the top step of the dugout, screaming at Clemens. Torre went out to argue with the umpiring crew. Earlier in June the same crew had umpired a game between the Yankees and Orioles and thrown Mike Stanton out of the game after Stanton had allowed a home run to Rafael Palmeiro and then hit Eric Davis with the next pitch. They then declared that, for the rest of the year, they would toss any pitcher who gave up a home run and then hit the next batter.

Clemens had not given up a home run, but Torre felt this was close enough. He wanted the umps to at least issue a warning. They did not, and Torre was the one ejected from the game. "I said yesterday Roger Clemens gets away with things that get other people thrown out of games," Torre said after the game. "This is a perfect example of that."[76]

With his first pitch of the next inning, Hideki Irabu threw a fastball right into the elbow of Shannon Stewart. With pain now shooting through his arm, Stewart began talking to Irabu as Girardi held him back. Rather than wait for whatever might happen next, Irabu sprinted from the mound and directly charged at Stewart, like a bull headed for the matador. Irabu was even more mad than Stewart, upset that Clemens had hit one of his team-mates, and he had to be forcibly picked up by Stanton and removed from the action. Meanwhile, players began pushing and shoving one another as several Yankees, including Curtis and Strawberry, tried to track down Clemens, who had been directed back into the dugout by the umpires so as not to further escalate the situation. Eventually a gaggle of players fell to the ground near the Blue Jays' dugout. When they got up, Strawberry broke free and landed a punch on Toronto reliever Bill Risley.

Stewart got his revenge when he later homered off Irabu for the eventual game-winning run. The loss itself began a streak of games in which the Yankees played their poorest ball of the year, worse than their 1-4 start. They lost three to Toronto, split a series with Boston, and then went to Tampa and were shutout by the Rays, 7–0, in an ugly loss that made Torre erupt afterward. "We stunk tonight, top to bottom," Torre said. "Nobody can just turn it on. Nobody can, when you beat yourself, pitching or outfield play or at-bats. We didn't have good at-bats tonight."[77]

Torre was concerned that his team had perhaps been too successful and was now coasting when in fact it needed to get ready for the postseason. The message seemed to get through. After the embarrassing defeat to Tampa, the Yankees finished the year by winning ten of their final twelve games. Not all credit could be given to Torre's outburst, though. After a season in which one player after another seemed to contribute, the team found yet one more player to do so.

It had been the longest of roads to the Majors for Shane Spencer. Taken in the twenty-eighth round of the 1990 draft, he toiled for years in the Yankees' Minor League system. It was not necessarily without good reason, at least not in the beginning. In his first 618 professional at bats over three years, he mustered only three home runs. He stayed at Single A ball for years, watching as former teammates of his like Jeter, Rivera, Pettitte, and Posada all made it to the big leagues. In 1996, at Double A Norwich, Spencer finally exploded, hitting twenty-nine home runs. Spending 1997 at Triple A Columbus, he was even better, hitting thirty home runs and thirty-four doubles. Having spent parts of eight seasons in the Minors, Spencer now figured his chance to play in the big leagues had arrived. Instead he was gravely disappointed when, in 1998, the team broke from spring training without him. When Davis went down to injury, Spencer got the call. It was only temporary, but the career Minor Leaguer made his debut on April 10 and got his first start on April 17, driving in a run.

Spencer was up and down throughout the summer, playing in a handful of games. On August 7, at home against the Royals, he had a night to remember, going 5-for-5 with two home runs. Spencer's mother, who was in the crowd that night, cried with joy over her son's performance. "I haven't stopped smiling," Spencer said after the game. "I've never had five hits. Not even in Little League."[78]

It was a great moment, but no one imagined what was to come in September. Once the team clinched a postseason spot, Spencer found himself with more chances to play.

He homered in Chicago on September 4.

He hit a grand slam in Baltimore on September 18.

Then three more home runs against Cleveland on September 22 and 23.

Another grand slam against Tampa on September 24.

A solo shot against Tampa on September 26.

Then, on the regular season's final day, against Tampa, he hit another grand slam.

Over forty-seven at bats between August 7 and September 27, Spencer hit ten home runs, including a rookie-record three grand slams. He ended the year with a 1.321 OPS. After the season's final game Spencer was called into Torre's office. When he walked in, Steinbrenner was standing there. "We've got some bad news for you," the owner said, though he could not hide his smile as he said it. The "bad news" was that Spencer had been named to the team's postseason roster.[79]

Spencer's performance had forced Torre to include him, not as an afterthought but as the team's possible starting left fielder. "I hit three grand slams in my career, and he hit three in nine or 10 days," said Torre after the roster was announced.[80] Moreover, Spencer had won over New York, becoming an immediate sensation and earning the nickname "Roy Hobbs," the main character from the movie *The Natural* who does nothing but hit home runs. "All the guys I've played with in the minors, they're living through me right now," said Spencer, referencing the years he had spent toiling in the team's system. "They say now they know that the average guy can make it."[81]

The final regular season numbers for the Yankees seemed illusory. Their 114 wins (against 48 losses) were the most ever by an American League team to that time. Their worst month of the year was September, where they still posted a .593 winning percentage. They outscored their opponents by over three hundred runs and had a losing record against only one team, the Angels. In interleague play they went 13-3. Against the three other American League teams that made the postseason, they went 22-12, and they lost only one of twenty-one games played against the Rays and Royals. They did all this despite the fact that no one on the team hit more than twenty-eight home runs. Instead they did it collectively, as ten players had double-digit home runs and six players stole at least ten bases while hitting at least ten home runs, numbers that would have been even higher if the designated hitter stats of Strawberry and Raines had been combined. Bernie Williams, who missed a month of play after sliding awkwardly into third base at Montreal, took home the batting title. Jeter had the first of his eight seasons in which he had more than two hundred hits. Remarkably the team leaders in batting average, total bases, home runs, hits, and walks were all different players.

On the pitching side the numbers were just as impressive. Six different pitchers won at least ten games. Cone led the way with twenty, his second twenty-win season; in doing so, he set a big-league record for most years between twenty-win seasons, ten. Wells won eighteen while leading the league in win percentage and shutouts. Irabu won thirteen, and El Duque, despite not having made his big-league debut until the first week of June, won twelve. Out of the bullpen Mariano Rivera showed no indication of being rattled by the Alomar home run from 1997. He posted a 1.91 ERA and saved thirty-six, a seemingly low number that had more to do with the team's margins of victory than with his blowing saves. Mendoza, when not starting, was the team's durable long reliever, winning ten games and tossing over 130 innings for the year. Graeme Lloyd, who had long since made fans forget about their vitriol toward him in 1996, was a dominant lefty out of the pen, posting a WHIP of just 0.850.

All of these, though—the records, the achievements, the feel-good moments—would be for not if the team did not win it all. It would be even worse if the team was bounced from the playoffs in the Division Series again. The Yankees simply could not allow that to happen.

• • •

The Yankees' previous three postseasons had been tension-filled, heart-stopping, and heartbreaking affairs. Their 1995 and 1997 seasons had ended after they were mere outs from advancing to the ALCS. Their championship run in '96 included six come-from-behind victories, and two of the remaining five wins were accomplished with the opposition's having put the winning or go-ahead runs on base. There were few, if any, October moments in those three years that occurred without some semblance of stomach queasiness.

That string ended in 1998. While there were a few moments that gave the team and its fans pause, largely the Yankees dominated their opponents on the way to their twenty-fourth title. It began with a three-game sweep of the Rangers in the Division Series. New York pitching held the Rangers, who had scored the second-most runs in baseball behind the Yankees, to just a single run over three games. After trailing constantly in their '96 ALDS match-up, the Yankees never trailed once in the series. Meanwhile, Shane Spencer's dream season continued. In his first-ever postseason at bat in Game Two, he hit another home run. In Game Three, with the Yankees holding a 1–0 lead in the sixth, he hit an Aaron Sele curveball into the left-field stands, giving the team a 4–0 lead. All told, Spencer hit .500 in the three-game sweep with a video-game-like 2.000 OPS. He drove in four of the team's nine runs in the series.

Brosius, who batted .300 with ninety-eight RBIs during the regular season and made the All-Star team, continued his magical year by driving in three of the other runs. Wells shut the Rangers down for eight innings in Game One, Pettitte held them to just three hits in Game Two, and Cone allowed just two hits and no runs in Game Three. In six and a third innings, the bullpen allowed just five base runners, none of whom scored. Never before had a team allowed only a single run in a postseason series of any kind.

The joy of the sweep, however, was diminished by some shocking off-the-field news: Darryl Strawberry had started to feel unwell during the summer. Something about his abdomen just did not seem right. "I was always a big eater, but that summer my appetite disappeared," said Strawberry. "It was like my stomach was empty and growling, but my brain was not interested in food. My brain was telling me something was wrong with my body. I couldn't eat a normal meal."[82]

Strawberry began experiencing excruciating stomach cramps. Then he started seeing blood in his stool. He did not say a word to anyone, though. Not until the team was in Baltimore in mid-September did Strawberry explain his symptoms to his friend, Orioles outfielder Eric Davis. Just the previous year, Davis had been diagnosed with colon cancer. He had successfully undergone surgery and chemotherapy to remove the cancer, and now what his friend told him scared him. Go to a doctor, Davis told Strawberry.

Taking his friend's advice, Strawberry went to get checked out. Just as the series with Texas began, doctors discovered a walnut-sized cancerous tumor in his colon. Torre informed the team before their off-day workout in Texas, after they'd won the first two games of the series. Some cried at the news. This was not the Darryl Strawberry of the 1980s Mets, who had come to be loathed by his teammates for his attitude and standoffish behavior. This Darryl Strawberry was adored by his teammates, many of whom saw him as a mentor. "He has been an inspiration to a lot of the young players in the organization," said Ledée. "He spent a lot of time talking to me and giving me advice in spring training and when I was with the Yankees during the year. He's a good man."[83]

The Yankees then went out to the field for their workout. The mood was somber, with little noise outside the crack of the bat during batting practice. "Darryl is going to have a lot of confusion, and he is going to be scared," said Cone, who, among members of the '98 squad, had been teammates with Strawberry the longest. "We are all scared. But the prognosis is good."[84]

Strawberry underwent surgery while the team was in Texas. Steinbrenner sat with Darryl's wife, Charisse, for four hours while Strawberry was under the knife. The surgery was successful, though Strawberry still had months of recovery time ahead of him.

• • •

Up next was a rematch against the Indians, and it presented an opportunity for the Yankees to exact some vengeance. They appeared to do just that in Game One, starting the series off with four straight singles against Jaret Wright, whose performance in 1997 had led Cleveland to their Division Series win. Wright did not make it out of the first, with New York plating five runs and eventually winning, 7–2. The next night, tied at 1–1 in the top of the twelfth, Cleveland's Travis Fryman attempted to move Enrique Wilson to second with a sacrifice bunt. Tino Martinez fielded the bunt, whirled, and fired the ball into Fryman's back, where it hit the ground and began slowly rolling along the dirt and toward right field. Knoblauch, covering first, immediately pointed to the spot where the ball and Fryman had connected, telepathizing that he felt Fryman had been outside of the basepath. As Knoblauch pointed, the ball kept rolling, and play continued. "I'm saying, 'Get the ball, get the ball, get ball!" said Posada. "They called him safe, and the ball is just laying around."[85]

Fryman immediately ran toward second, and Wilson began a mad dash around the bases. Brosius and Jeter, along with thousands of fans in the crowd, began pointing at the ball and screaming at Knoblauch to run and grab it. He seemingly did not hear any of it until finally realizing that the play was still live. Wilson, stumbling as he did so, sprinted toward home and slid in safely just ahead of Knoblauch's throw. The Indians went on to win, 4–1.

After the game there were dozens of opinions about whether Fryman had run out of the base path, all of them interpreting the rules of the game differently. Steinbrenner was eventually fined for his hard criticisms of the umpiring crew. "They gave me some kind of reasoning, that he had to get back, in other words, he had to get out of those restraining lines to touch the base, which I agree with, except he was never within those restraining lines," said Torre after the game, referring to the explanation the umpiring crew gave him for why Fryman was not called out. "He was on the grass, he was so blatant. I don't know what to say."[86]

It mattered little. All anyone wanted to talk about was why Knoblauch, who was booed loudly by the hometown crowd when he batted in the bottom of the twelfth, had not gone after the ball. Knoblauch himself seemed oblivious to the moment, at least immediately after Game Two. "I thought he should have been called out," said Knoblauch, referencing Fryman. "He was running on the grass the whole way. He was running straight toward me. I thought it was a no-doubter. It's a shame the game is decided like that."[87]

Knoblauch claimed he did not actually know where the ball was, and by the time he did, it was too late. That explanation did not hold water for a lot of people, though. The reason he didn't know where the ball was, they countered, was because he did not bother to look where it was.

Only the next day did Knoblauch fully grasp just how much of the blame he was getting for the loss. He apologized for his inaction. When he was introduced before Game Three in Cleveland, Indians' fans gave him a standing ovation.

Once Game Three got underway, Andy Pettitte was shellacked for four home runs in a 6–1 loss. Feelings of doubt started to creep in. Could it be possible that this team, which had won 114 games, would only be remembered for collapsing in the postseason? And how would George Steinbrenner respond to this club's being bounced by the Indians once again? In order to save their season, the Yankees turned to the one man on the team who, perhaps more than any other, would not feel the slightest bit of pressure in this situation: Orlando Hernández.

On the morning of Game Four, Orlando Hernández had been busing tables at the team's hotel cafe. The fact that he was about to start in the Yankees' biggest game of the year phased him not in the slightest. An hour before game time Steinbrenner told reporters, "We're going to win. I'm telling you, take it to the bank. This team will battle. We're not done. Anybody that writes us off is doing it too soon."[88]

Another pitcher might have found such a bold statement from the team's owner unnerving. Not Hernández. El Duque got some breathing room in Game Four when O'Neill homered off a Dwight Gooden curveball in the top of the first. The 1–0 lead, however, did not seem like nearly enough when Jim Thome came to bat with two runners on in the bottom of the inning. Thome had crushed two home runs off Pettitte the night before, and the moment seemed primed for another home run off Hernández. When Thome hit a 3-2 pitch deep to right, hearts sank across New York. But the ball died on the warning track, preserving a lead El Duque would never relent. He pitched seven scoreless innings, and the Yankees won, 4–0, evening the series at two. "I had pressure, but I had no fear," said Hernández. "I've been through many difficult times in my life, and I knew I would be able to handle it."[89] "What can I say?" asked the Boss. "It was one of the greatest performances I've ever seen in 25 years."[90]

In Game Five Chili Davis took his turn as hero by driving in three runs, while Wells, on his way to winning the series' MVP award, struck out eleven in a 5–3 win.

Despite nearly blowing a 6–0 lead in Game Six, the Yankees held on for a 9–5 victory, clinching the pennant at home. Afterward players took turns speaking to Strawberry on the phone. Jeter, spotting the Boss in the clubhouse, walked toward the owner. "Hold on," yelled Jeter. "Hold on.

Somebody's dry around here."[91] He then poured a bottle of champagne over Steinbrenner's head.

Knoblauch was especially thankful for the ALCS triumph. "If we hadn't won this series, we all know whose fault it would have been. I came to the Yankees because I wanted to get to the World Series. I wouldn't want to have stood in the way of that," he said.[92]

In some ways the World Series felt like a formality. The San Diego Padres had upset the Braves in the National League Championship Series (NLCS) to reach their second Fall Classic in franchise history. There was some surprise when they took a 5–2 lead off Wells in Game One. The moment did not last. Knoblauch, achieving forgiveness from the New York fans, tied the game in the seventh with a three-run home run. Five batters later, Martinez, himself struggling through three largely suboptimal postseasons with the Yankees, hit a grand slam into the right-field upper deck. To that point, Martinez was just 20-for-107, a .187 batting average, with one home run and four RBIs as a Yankee in the postseason. "I knew he had to throw a strike," said Martinez, referring to pitcher Mark Langston when the count got to 3-2. "I was looking for a fastball, and he got it up in the strike zone."[93] "I just remember our dugout and our clubhouse being like, wow, these guys are destined," recalled Jim Leyritz, who was a member of the Padres during the series.[94]

The Yankees went on to win Game One and took Game Two in a runaway. Back in San Diego for Game Three, Brosius put the cherry on top of the greatest single season of his career when, with the team down a run in the eighth inning, he hit a three-run home run off a ninety-one-miles-per-hour fastball from future Hall of Famer Trevor Hoffman. The Padres' closer had blown only one save all year, converting fifty-three of fifty-four opportunities. Ultimately it was a pitch earlier in the at bat that Hoffman would regret. "It was a slider and I didn't throw it where I wanted it," said Hoffman, referring to a 1-1 pitch he threw Brosius that ended up being a ball. "I bounced it in the dirt. I wasn't aggressive in the zone with it. It was a bigger pitch than the ball he hit out. It put him in a hitter's count, 2-1 instead of 1-2."[95]

The count went 2-2, and rather than throw a splitter and risk going 3-2, Hoffman threw a fastball that Brosius hit over the center-field fence. "This is the type of thing you dream about as a kid," said Brosius. "I've done it in my backyard a hundred times. You don't know if you'll ever have the opportunity. I just feel really fortunate to be part of this."[96]

Brosius rounded first and, as the ball disappeared over the fence, screamed out with both arms up. "That's the cover of *Sports Illustrated* right there," Torre turned and said to bench coach Don Zimmer, and in fact, that was the image the magazine used in its World Series edition.[97]

The Yankees completed the World Series sweep the next night. Exemplifying the team concept that had gotten them 114 regular wins, eight different players drove in a run, and ten different players scored a run in the World Series, despite its being only four games. The team collectively batted .309, with a .398 on base percentage. The rookie Ledée became just the third player in history to bat .600 or higher in a World Series in which he played every game. Brosius, who hit .471 with two home runs and recorded an assist on the final play of the year, was the Series MVP. He also became only the second player in history, and the first since Babe Ruth, to hit home runs in consecutive World Series games after the fifth inning. After Game Four the Hall of Fame took his bat.

The Yankees had completed arguably the greatest season in baseball history by going 125-50, more wins than any team had ever compiled in a single year. "Right now, you would have to call them the greatest team ever," said Steinbrenner during the clubhouse celebration. "Based on the record, that's what they are."[98]

They were on top of the baseball world and remained the undisputed kings of New York baseball. But as they stood on top of the world, the Yankees were about to be challenged for the heart of New York and would possibly endure that challenge without the reigning American League batting champion.

5   "I Play Baseball"

It had not been an easy road to the first-ever Mets-Yankees game for Dave Mlicki. After his big-league debut in September 1992, he made a few more starts but ended up tearing his labrum. He missed most of 1993. In 1994 he was healthy, but the Indians were loaded with talent at the big-league level. He spent the entire season in the Minors. That October he and Annie tied the knot. The two had met through a mutual friend while Mlicki was in the Minors and Annie was a senior in college. The first time they met, Annie asked him what he did.

"I play baseball," he said.

"Oh, that's cool. I play tennis. But what do you do for a job?" she replied.[1]

Shortly after returning from their honeymoon, they were at Mlicki's in-laws' home in Chicago, sitting in the living room, when the phone rang. The caller informed Mlicki that he had been traded to the New York Mets. It was a life-altering moment, not just because it meant pitching in the largest market in the country but also because it meant pitching, period. The Mets had plans for Mlicki and not in the Minors.

The first time he walked into the clubhouse, Mlicki was blown away by the players he saw. Guys like Bret Saberhagen and John Franco. "At the time, they didn't know if I was going to start or relieve and [Franco] really took me under his wing immediately and just helped me a ton," said Mlicki.

In 1995 Mlicki was largely a starter and pitched fairly well, a good pitcher on a not-so-great team. The next year, though, he was the odd man out in a rotation that had more than five starters. He ended up in the bullpen. While willing to accept the role, Mlicki found working out of the pen harder than starting. The change in mindset—not knowing when he got to the park on any given day if he was going to pitch—was a difficult adjustment for him. Still, his numbers were impressive, and when 1997 came around, a solid spring landed him in the rotation.

A strong beginning of the year yielded to a difficult run of appearances. In four consecutive starts in late April and early May, Mlicki gave up eighteen runs in seventeen innings. The Mets went winless in his first ten starts of the year. "I had great stuff. I just couldn't get the out when I needed it, or I gave up a hit here and there and I wouldn't get a win," said Mlicki.

There were calls from fans and the press to remove Mlicki from the starting rotation. Mets manager Bobby Valentine ignored them. Instead he put even more faith in Mlicki, allowing the pitcher to go back out to the mound in the eighth inning of a June 4 game against the Marlins so that he could potentially get a win. "I can't tell you how much that meant to me," said Mlicki.

Now, on June 16, 1997, the Yankees decided by the sixth inning that their swing-early approach against Mlicki was not working. Yes, it had produced a few hits over the first five innings. In the fourth, with one out, Fielder had driven a fastball—the same pitch on which he'd struck out in the first—down the right-field line for a double. He never left second base. Through four innings Mlicki had thrown just forty-three pitches, two-thirds of them for strikes. In the fifth Whiten and Curtis had gone down on just four pitches before Girardi lined a fastball down the left-field line for a hit. Jeter could not drive him in. Mlicki threw just eight pitches in the inning.

Fortunately for the Yankees, Andy Pettitte had kept the Mets in check since the first inning. The game remained 3–0. But the Yankees were starting to run out of chances, and their plate approach had largely just resulted in unproductive outs. Of course, that did not mean that taking pitches would result in a better outcome. But it was worth a try.

Pat Kelly began the change in approach with a six-pitch at bat that ended in a questionable strike three check-swing call. O'Neill followed suit with a five-pitch walk, the Yankees' first of the game. The crowd started to stir. When Mlicki threw two balls to Fielder to begin the at bat, a feeling started to grow in the ballpark. This was it. This was the start of the comeback. Fielder would crack one here and drive in a run, maybe even two, and then the momentum would all shift to the home team.

Fielder could not imagine that Mlicki would throw a curveball in this situation. No matter how good it had been moving the first five innings, the Mets' pitcher could not risk running the count to 3–0. But that's just what he did, delivering a devastating breaking ball that Fielder swung over for strike one.

No big deal. Surely a fastball was coming now. Nope. Another breaking ball—this one on the outside corner—that Fielder lunged for and swung over. Cecil walked away from the plate, his exasperation evident. He had been fooled on curves all night and was getting tired of throwing his massive body behind huge swings that missed so badly.

The count now 2-2, Hundley set up on the outside corner. Mlicki came to his set, stepped, and delivered the ball. But it wasn't a curve. It was a slider, and it was not nearly as sharp as the curves he had thrown that night. The slider did not break as hard, staying up in the zone instead of breaking across the plate toward the other batter's box. Worse still, it was nowhere near the outside corner behind which Hundley had set up. Instead it was drifting toward the inner half of the plate. This was Mlicki's first mistake of the night.

BOOM!

The sound off the bat was unmistakable. It was the crisp, pleasant sound of wood meeting the ball just right. It was the kind of sound, if you had not been paying attention but heard it, you would have immediately turned to see how far the ball was going. "He just killed it," recalled Mlicki. The crowd stood up as a buzz went through the stadium.

Tschida sprung out from behind home plate to follow the flight of the ball in case he had to determine if it was fair or foul. He did not have to. It quickly became clear that Fielder's drive was going foul. It landed several rows high in the upper deck, significantly to the left of the foul pole. Cecil had guessed right but was a millisecond too quick. Mlicki had gotten away with his mistake.

Conventional wisdom might have said that Fielder should now be thrown a fastball, given what he had just done. Perhaps his reaction time would be even slower after the series of curveballs he'd just seen. Hundley, however, had a perfect sense throughout the night of what the Yankees were and were not expecting. And Fielder would not be expecting yet another curveball here. So Hundley went right back to the outer part of the plate. This time Mlicki's curve was so good that even Hundley seemed to temporarily flinch as it dropped over the plate.

Called strike three.

Fielder could not believe it. He cursed as he stepped toward the dugout, his hands, still clinched around the bat, momentarily coming upward as if he planned to slam his bat into the ground in frustration. The Mets fans in attendance, approximately 30 percent of the crowd, were elated. The Yankees fans, defeated. Tino Martinez popped up to end the inning. The Yankees had made Mlicki throw twenty-one pitches, the most he had tossed in any inning so far, and they had nothing to show for it except a loud foul ball. Time was running out for the Yankees. They did not know it yet, but the game was about to be put out of reach.

6

Mr. Mojo Risin'

No story loomed larger over the Yankees' post-1998 off-season than whether Bernie Williams was coming back to the team. At their championship celebration in front of New York City Hall, Williams had shrewdly put the pressure on George Steinbrenner by pointing to the owner and telling assembled fans, "You've got to talk to this guy here."[1]

Negotiations were not going well, though. Williams was represented by Scott Boras, the most well-known sports agent in history. Boras had a habit of publicly putting out incredibly high demands for his clients, and more often than not, he ended up getting the better of the deal. With Williams, Boras was demanding a seven-year contract at around $15 million a year, and the Yankees wanted no part of it. They were willing to go only as high as $12 million a year for five years. Negotiations stalled, with neither side willing to budge.

Recognizing that they might lose their center fielder, and perhaps as a scare tactic, the Yankees began having serious discussions about free agent Albert Belle. The reigning leader in slugging percentage, OPS, and total bases, Belle was in contention for the game's most dangerous hitter of the 1990s. He had hit 313 home runs during the decade, including 49 in 1997 while playing for the White Sox.

No one doubted Belle's immense talent. It was his personality that was a concern. Belle had once chased down teenagers who had egged his house and bumped one of them with his car. He had lost thousands in gambling on other sports, though never baseball. From 1991 to 1994 he had been suspended four times: "twice for charging the mound (three games each in 1992 and 1993), once for throwing a ball at a fan in the stands (one week in 1991) and once for having cork in his bat (10 days reduced to 6 days and 7 games in 1994)."[2] He was suspended again in 1996 after he laid a forearm into Brewers second baseman Fernando Viña while attempting to break up a double play. He detested the media, and teammates often shied away from his explosive personality. Belle was . . . a lot.

Trying to get a sense of what he might be in for, Torre played a round of golf with Belle and felt afterward that there would not be an issue. He could keep Belle from creating animosity within the clubhouse. After a meeting of the team's top brass, the Yankees made Belle an offer, roughly the same contract they were offering Williams. Belle was remarkably close to becoming a Yankee—or at least that's what the team thought.

Williams, perhaps coincidentally, perhaps not, called Cashman at the same time Belle was reviewing the contract offer. Bernie was devastated that the team was in fact ready to move on without him. He had substantial offers on the table: one from the Red Sox, at $13 million a season for seven years, and a $100 million offer from the Diamondbacks, a move that offered a chance to be reunited with his former manager, Buck Showalter.

These offers were everything Bernie wanted in a contract, expect one thing: they were not with the Yankees. Williams just did not want to leave New York. He phoned Cashman and, with Steinbrenner listening, implored them to make a counter offer. Bernie was quiet and somewhat aloof, but he was not dumb. Nor was he without feelings. He had been tormented in his younger Yankees years by teammates like Mel Hall, the now-convicted sex offender who had mocked Williams at every opportunity. He had not only put up big numbers with the Yankees, but he had also suffered through years of mental torment. Yes, he wanted a big contract, but really what he wanted was for the Yankees to show they truly appreciated all he had done for them since 1991. "I'm not asking you to top that offer," said Williams, referring to the Red Sox's proposal. "I just need to feel you want to keep me by coming after me with the kind of offer you make to free agents from other teams that have never done anything for the Yankees."[3]

Williams's pleading might not have been enough. Then something happened, another one of those incredible pieces of luck that befell the Yankees in the late 1990s: Belle decided to sign with the Orioles. He had likely been using the Yankees the entire time to leverage a better deal out of Baltimore. Cashman heard the news from Belle's agent and was furious. Not only had the Yankees lost out on Belle, but they might also have lost out on Williams, who, for all Cashman knew, could have already signed on the dotted line with Boston. After Cashman called Steinbrenner—a call in which the Boss lit into Cashman for the whole situation—Steinbrenner decided they would have to up their offer to Williams and sign him or face a torrent of humiliation. In the end Williams signed a seven-year deal for slightly less than Boston had offered. The biggest question mark of the Yankees' off-season was answered and in a way that delighted teammates and fans alike.

Belle, meanwhile, hit sixty home runs and drove in 220 runs over two seasons with Baltimore before a degenerative hip condition forced him to retire at age thirty-four. With Williams settled, the Yankees stayed quiet the rest of the postseason. After all, what steps were really necessary to improve arguably the greatest team in baseball history? The team reported to spring training still basking in the glow of the previous year's accomplishments. David Wells walked into the complex at Tampa all smiles. He was coming off the best year of his career and pitching in a city that adored him, wrinkles and all.

Before he could even throw a warm up pitch, Torre summoned Wells into his office. "What did I do now? It's just the first day of spring," thought Wells as he walked in and took a seat in front of Torre's desk. Boomer, you've been traded to the Toronto Blue Jays for Roger Clemens, he was told. Wells walked back into the clubhouse in shock. Never, for a second, had he imagined this scenario. "Give me a couple days. It's a little rough right now," he told reporters with tears in his eyes.[4] "I've never seen anyone so stunned by a trade," said Cone, who visited Wells at his home shortly after the pitcher left the Yankees' complex and found him inconsolable.[5]

Departing with Wells were Graeme Lloyd and Homer Bush—all told, three key contributors during the championship year whom fans had grown to love for various reasons: Wells because he *was* New York; Lloyd because he never seemed to give up a run in the postseason; Bush because he shined coming off the bench, hitting .380 while stealing six bases in just seventy-eight plate appearances. All three were now headed north of the border.

The most shocking part was not that any one of the three was leaving New York; it was for whom they had been traded. Few active players were more despised in the Big Apple than Roger Clemens. The pitcher, sitting on 233 career wins and five Cy Young Awards (including the last two given out in the American League), had a league-wide reputation as a headhunter who at times could not control his emotions. He had hit countless Yankees over the years. Willie Randolph recalled an August 1993 game in which Clemens had plunked Bernie Williams. "We scored four times in the top of the first," said Randolph. "The big hit was a two-run single that Bernie ripped to center off Clemens. Roger was getting outpitched by soft-tossing

Jimmy Key and wasn't too pleased about that. Bernie's next time up Clemens beaned him. That's the way the man did business."⁶

Most recently Clemens had beaned Jeter in spring training in 1998, then Brosius in the September game that sparked a brawl. There were pitchers who protected both the plate and teammates, even if that mentality was slowly fading from the game. Many players, however, viewed Clemens differently. They felt he got away with such behavior because he himself—having played his entire career in the American League with its designated hitter—never had had to step into the batter's box to face his comeuppance. It didn't take much courage to hit a guy when you threw ninety-eight miles per hour but never had to suffer any repercussions from your actions.

Clemens, however, had been unhappy in Toronto. The team had faltered in 1997 and had been only mildly competitive in 1998. The Rocket, who had never been on a championship team, was running out of chances to win his first title. Toronto, meanwhile, had gambled not on Clemens's performance, but on the idea that it could actually afford the four-year $31.1 million contract for which he had signed. It turns out that as the team continued to struggle, it couldn't. Clemens, as was his right under the deal, requested a trade.

Cashman and Blue Jays general manager Gordon Ash had been talking about a possible trade all winter. The Blue Jays wanted too much, though, asking for Hernández, Mendoza, pitching prospect Ryan Bradley, Bush, and highly touted infield prospect Alfonso Soriano. There was no way that was happening, responded the Yankees. The start of spring training gave Toronto a sense of urgency, though. Management did not want the Clemens saga disrupting the clubhouse. Their demands lessened until, finally, Ash told Cashman they could do the deal for Wells, Lloyd, and Bush.

Cashman, who could not believe the trade could be had within those parameters, brought the offer to team leadership for a vote. They met at a local Tampa restaurant and discussed the situation for hours. Steinbrenner was torn. He had wanted Clemens two years earlier and had lost out. Now was a chance at redemption. But it would come at the cost of Wells, whom Steinbrenner adored. He could not bring himself to vote on the deal. "You guys all know how I feel about Wells," he told the assembled group. "That's why I'm not going to cast a vote on this. At the same time, though, if everyone in the room is in favor of this deal, I won't stand in the way."⁷

Everyone else, in fact, was in favor of the deal. It was not just about getting Clemens. Wells had worn out his welcome with too many of those who now had a vote. There was no disputing his remarkable ability to pitch in big game situations. But the fights. And the gout. And the Babe Ruth hat. And his seemingly giving up when his team needed him. There was even the time in September 1998, when, with Wells on the mound, a pop-up dropped among Jeter, Ledée, and Curtis, and Wells threw his arms up in disgust. Jeter, eleven years Wells's junior, had to set him straight between innings. The Yankees don't show each other up like that, Jeter said. Wells apologized, but it was just one more thing to add to the list. Now, as the brass sat and made a decision, there were already rumors that Wells was going to basically extort a contract extension out of the club. If the Yankees did not give him what he wanted, he was going to get even more out of shape than usual.

The vote took place. It was unanimous. At 11:42 p.m. on February 18, Cashman finalized the deal with Ash. Clemens was on his way to New York. One Boston TV station, Channel 7, broke into regular programming to announce the trade as if it was breaking news of the Kennedy assassination. From there, all of Boston bemoaned the deal.

The Bostonians were not the only ones. To many fans the transaction seemed ludicrous. A team that had just won 114 games and the World Series had now acquired the reigning AL Cy Young Award winner.

It only furthered the perception that big-market teams like the Yankees were competing on an uneven playing field that allowed them, with their enormous revenue streams, to gobble up the best players in the game while small-market teams watched their talent leave year after year. In spring training '98 the Yankees had traded for arguably the best second baseman in the game. Now in spring training '99 they had traded for arguably the best pitcher of this generation. Where did it end?

Not all Yankees fans were pleased either. While many certainly celebrated the acquisition, others were leery of Clemens, a man they had come to loathe, slipping his way into pinstripes simply so that he could leech on to a championship team. Clemens had had his chance two years earlier to be a Yankee and had passed. Why should he get a chance now simply because the Blue Jays had not panned out to his liking? "Clemens is a great pitcher, but Wells is very, very popular. David Wells delivered the goods, day in and day out, and Graeme Lloyd always went out and did what he was told. So let me get over losing them first before I think about Clemens coming to New York," said Bronx borough president Fernando Ferrer.[8]

Ultimately the biggest question would be how Clemens's new teammates would receive him. Many had expressed their distaste for the man, if not on the record with reporters, then in private grumblings within the clubhouse. Could they really accept a guy they felt put careers in jeopardy with his head-high fastballs? "I know I've had good battles with those guys," said Clemens. "I know I've plunked a lot of guys, but I've also taken line drives off my shins. I'm glad to be teammates with them now. I hope they won't think I'm too crazy."[9]

The answers came a week later. Clemens took the mound to throw against his own team during one of the spring's many exercises to prepare for the season. When he looked up, Knoblauch had stepped into the batting cage, decked out in catcher's gear. Clemens grinned, then fired a pitch behind his new second baseman. Jeter came up next, wearing the same attire plus an elbow guard. Clemens grinned again, then fired a pitch behind Jeter too. Any tension about Clemens's fitting in had been lifted away. "I knew something was eventually going to be up," said Clemens. "I thought it was a good move by them. And to make them feel right at home, I had to throw those ones behind them."[10]

Clemens also immediately impressed with his work ethic. "He came to camp in great shape and his arm in midseason condition," said Posada. "He'd have a pitch count during a spring game, reach it, then go down into the bullpen until he'd thrown a total of 100 pitches. He'd sneak in a workout in between innings when he was pitching spring games. He'd practice pickoff moves, do 40 sit-ups, and then do 40 sets of pick-ups, moving side to side to field balls rolled to him."[11]

Ultimately the hubbub around Clemens gave way to more serious news. In February Torre had undergone blood work as part of the team's annual spring-training physical. The results scared doctors enough that they ordered a biopsy. On March 9, one day after Yankees legend Joe DiMaggio died of lung cancer, the results came back: Torre had prostate cancer. Fortunately it had been found early, and his prognosis was positive. Torre himself did not feel sick, though the initial blood test results and the impending biopsy result had made him noticeably more reserved during the early weeks of spring.

Torre called Steinbrenner after getting the biopsy results, then shared the news with former general manager Bob Watson, himself a cancer survivor.

The Yankees had a split squad the next day, meaning their team was divided into two groups that played games in different locations in Florida. Torre shared the news with Girardi and O'Neill and asked them to share with the two groups. The news was not only shocking, but it also came the same day Darryl Strawberry returned to camp after his battle with colon cancer. "It was a big shock," said Chili Davis. "None of us knew what was going on until O'Neill said it."[12] "It's been a rough week," said Steinbrenner. "The organization is a strong organization. The players are strong. It's going to be fine."[13]

Torre would be out several weeks as he received treatment. Bench coach Don Zimmer served as interim manager in his absence.

As the team dealt with its skipper's health scare, controversy emerged in the form of Hideki Irabu. The starting pitcher had shown up to camp seemingly invigorated after putting in a subpar second half of the 1998 season. Mimicking Clemens's workout routines, he lost ten pounds in the early going of spring training. When he took the mound, though, hitters were teeing off. As his spring performances worsened, Irabu gained all the weight back and appeared to be phoning it in on the mound. Things came to a head on March 27 in Clearwater. After the team jumped out to a 9–1 lead over the Phillies, Irabu gave most of it back, allowing six runs and thirteen hits over five innings. Throughout the game he appeared to pay no attention to runners on base, and when he did, he lobbed over attempted pick-off throws. Then, in the fourth, he failed to cover first base when Marlon Anderson hit a ground ball to first baseman Luis Sojo. It was a fairly routine play, one pitchers practiced often in spring training.

Irabu's teammates had had enough. Posada openly grumbled about the pitcher's performance. "You saw it," he angrily told reporters when asked what he thought of the day's events.[14] "I am not concerned but he needs a kick in the ass, no doubt about it," Cashman told reporters.[15]

Two days later the Yankees lined up their pitchers to perform fielding drills and then do some running. "How do I think he did in the drills today?" Stottlemyre asked. "I'm not quite sure he understood [why they were doing them]."[16] While his teammates fumed, Irabu was oblivious to it all. He did not think he had done anything wrong.

Steinbrenner was not fully ready to give up on his big investment, but he was getting close. The tipping point nearly came in Irabu's next spring appearance. Pitching in relief in the ninth inning, he again failed to cover first base on a routine play. Steinbrenner was livid. "He looks like a fat, pussy [rhymes with 'fussy'] toad out there," barked the Boss. When word of Steinbrenner's comments got back to Irabu, he did not understand the context. But when it was explained that the Boss had a history of giving out uncomplimentary monikers, he was devastated. "I can't understand all the stuff that is being said to me these days," Irabu said. "Whether I don't have any guts or I don't have any fight in me. I still feel like people are judging me on a play-by-play basis rather than my overall play."[17]

Irabu, who was in line to be the team's fifth starter, asked that the team leave him behind in Tampa for extended spring training. He did not want to accompany the club to Oakland for the start of the season, certainly not if he was going to be harangued about his weight or effort. After several discussions with management, Irabu did join the club in Oakland, but he pitched out of the bullpen all of April, not joining the rotation until May 2.

The decision not to have Irabu in the rotation was made by Zimmer in direct contradiction to Steinbrenner's wishes. The Boss, despite his anger over Irabu's perceived lack of hustle, still wanted his big signing on the mound. What else was he paying him for? As far as Don Zimmer was concerned, though, he would make the on-the-field decisions about the team. The idea that the owner would dictate to him who would pitch and when was the antithesis of everything Zimmer was about. It was even more crazy to Zimmer given that it was Steinbrenner who had lambasted Irabu in the papers. "Who called him a fat pig, or a fat plum?" Zimmer said after announcing that, no, Irabu would not be in the starting rotation to start the year. "Me? Who called him that? Who started it all? Nothing would've been said if [Steinbrenner] didn't come in there ranting and raving."[18]

Zimmer was an old-school baseball lifer. He felt clubhouse issues could be handled internally. If someone needed a kick in the ass, Zimmer would administer it his way, not through quotes in the press. Zimmer just wanted to be left alone to captain the Yankees until Torre got back. But he would have to deal with Steinbrenner well past Opening Day.

Meanwhile, as the Yankees broke from Tampa, the team decided Strawberry would stay behind. Strawberry had been swinging the bat well in spring training, but he was still undergoing chemotherapy. Management felt it would be better for him to remain in Tampa, finish out his treatments, and then meet up with the team after. For Strawberry the decision was heartbreaking. Once the team left, he felt isolated and alone. He was also angry that the Yankees had not figured him into their Opening Day plans.

The man who had once been considered among the worst teammates in baseball was now desperate to be around his teammates. That, mixed with the physical and psychological toll of the chemo, pushed him to the edge.

Sober for four years, on April 14 Strawberry came home from treatment and had a thought. "It was the notion that there was only one way in the world to ease my pain, one way to quiet the voice of doubt and despair in my head."[19]

He went to a local dive bar in Tampa and had a drink. Then another. Then another. Eventually he scored cocaine off one of the patrons. Then, intoxicated and carrying coke, he drove to a seedy section of Tampa where police alleged he solicited an undercover cop posing as a prostitute. Strawberry was pulled over by a cop who happened to be a transplanted New Yorker and Mets fan. He was arrested for possession and put in a Tampa jail cell.

It did not take long for the story to break as Tampa police released the details just hours after the arrest. The news brought a feeling that with another suspension pending from the Commissioner's Office, Strawberry's career might be over. Selig suspended Strawberry indefinitely, then in June set the suspension at 120 days, retroactive from April 14, the day of Strawberry's arrest. The Yankees decided to keep Strawberry on the team in the hopes that he could return late in the year, healthy and sober.

These numerous distractions aside, the Yankees headed out west to start the season with expectations high—unfairly so. "What do you get when you add a pitcher with five Cy Young trophies to baseball's winningest team since 1906?" the *Philadelphia Inquirer*'s Jason Stark asked. "You get the scariest team of modern times. That's what."[20] "You know how much the Yankees won by last year, the distance is now further with the competition. Believe me, Roger Clemens is so good that in the AL East, the wild-card race has begun for everyone except the Yankees," one scout told the *New York Post*'s Joel Sherman.[21]

The previous year had been the result of so many things going right, all at the same time. It would be ridiculous to think the Yankees could repeat those results. Yet, to some degree, it could have been argued that they were expected to do even better. They had Clemens now. They had El Duque for a full season. Chili Davis was healthy. Ricky Ledée and Shane Spencer were expected to contribute full seasons. There seemed little doubt that the Yankees were headed again to the postseason. The only question appeared to be how closely this team would match the '98 team.

• • •

It had been ten years since the Mets had played with purpose in their final game of the season. That should have made 1998 feel like a season of accomplishment. It did not. Instead it left a bitter taste with players, personnel, and fans. A single win in one of the final five games of the year would have at least gotten them to a one-game playoff. That single win hung over the franchise as the off-season began.

Lingering perhaps just as large as that one (non-)win was a single player: Mike Piazza. Would he return to Flushing? Years later it would be hard to imagine that his return was ever in question. But Piazza's first year with the Mets had been no love affair. Fans had attached unrealistic expectations to him, thinking he would be the equivalent of Gary Carter: the final piece of a championship puzzle, or at a minimum a postseason piece. Carter, however, had joined a team stacked with talent at nearly every position. The 1998 Mets had holes at several positions, a fact they would ultimately have to address in the off-season. But Piazza came first.

There would be no drama in the negotiations. They would not play out like those of Bernie Williams and the Yankees. Instead the day after the Yankees enjoyed their victory parade in 1998, the Mets and Piazza quickly agreed to a deal: seven years, $91 million. It was the largest contract in baseball history. In spite of all the booing he had endured, when Piazza headed to Hawaii after the season ended, he found himself longing to be back at Shea. "I missed the electricity," said Piazza.[22] He added that after arriving in New York, "You sort of just get infected with the attitude. Going somewhere else now—with no offense to any other place—would just be a letdown. It wouldn't be the same, the same electricity wouldn't be there."[23]

Piazza was now a Met well into the next decade, so the team set about addressing the remaining holes in both the lineup and on the mound. But it would get complicated. Just as the annual general managers' meeting commenced in Florida, the Mets announced that Steve Phillips was taking a leave of absence. A former team employee had accused the GM of sexual harassment. Phillips, a married man who had found out about the allegations a week earlier, admitted to team leadership that he had had a sexual relationship with the woman in question but that it had been consensual. He also admitted to other extramarital affairs. All sides agreed it was best for Phillips to take time to deal with his personal life. "While the Mets' organization does not condone Phillips' behavior, we are confident he can put his personal life back in order," said Dave Howard, the Mets' senior vice president for business and legal affairs.[24] Weeks later the matter was resolved through a settlement that avoided litigation.

In Phillips's absence Frank Cashen ran point at that year's winter meetings. The Mets' former GM, who had helped build the championship team of 1986 only to slowly break it apart, had remained with the club for years as an adviser. Now the Mets needed him to get them through the off-season and assemble the missing pieces for success in 1999.

Edgardo Alfonzo had been a serviceable third baseman, but the team was moving him to second to replace Baerga. The Mets wanted a younger option in that position, as well as someone who hit with more power. Alfonzo's move across the diamond meant the team needed a new third baseman. Outfield depth was a problem as well. Hundley was simply not meant to be in the outfield, and Tony Phillips was not being brought back either. Last, the bullpen needed help. Franco, Wendell, and Cook had been the only reliable forces out of the pen, causing Valentine to call on them constantly throughout the past season's final weeks as no one else had been a viable alternative. Moreover, Franco was entering his fifteenth season, and while he was still effective, there were questions about whether he could remain the team's closer.

On November 11 the Mets took the first and what would ultimately be the most well-remembered step to address these shortcomings. They sent Mel Rojas, who had struggled through most of the season's last four months, to the Los Angeles Dodgers in return for outfielder Bobby Bonilla.

Bonilla, born and raised in the Bronx, was no stranger to New York. After establishing himself as an All-Star and perennial MVP candidate with the Pirates, he had signed a five-year, $27.5 million deal with the Mets, the largest contract in team history, after the 1991 season. The signing was a coup for the Mets because they had acquired the most coveted free agent on the market as part of creating a pennant winner after the disappointing 1991 season. It had the added bonus of showing up the Yankees, who had been largely quiet that off-season. Facing increased pressure to make a splash of their own, the Yankees decided, seemingly out of nowhere, to offer Danny Tartabull a contract, something they probably would not have ever done if Bonilla had not come to New York.

Ultimately Bonilla's stats with New York were overshadowed by many factors, but he put up solid numbers in his first go-around with the Mets.

He established career season highs for home runs, slugging percentage, and OPS in his time there and went to two All-Star games. But the teams on which he played were terrible, and numerous off-the-field distractions forever tainted how he would be perceived. Bonilla got into two separate spats with reporters, both caught on film, in which he threatened or implied violence against them. Attempting to drown out crowd noise so he could remain focused at the plate, he wore earplugs during games at Shea, a practice that was immediately caught on camera. True or not, people assumed he wore them so he did not have to hear the fans booing him after he got off to a slow start that first year. He once had Mets PR director Jay Horwitz call the official scorer to complain about his having been given an error on a play in a game where his team had been trailing substantially. The incident angered his teammates, and Bonilla made the situation worse by lying about it to reporters afterward.

In the midst of a fire sale, the Mets dealt Bonilla to the Orioles at the trade deadline in 1995. Bonilla helped lead Baltimore to the ALCS in 1996, then played a key role in the Marlins' winning the World Series in 1997. He had endured a rough '98 season, seeing a sharp decline in his numbers across the board. The Mets were hoping he could provide some outfield depth and that a second chance with the team would erase bitter memories of the first go-around.

Three weeks later, on December 1, the Mets made a series of moves that ultimately impacted the club over the next two years like few others. They addressed their needs at third base, in the outfield, and in the bullpen all within the space of twenty-four hours. The team traded Todd Hundley to the Dodgers in a move that was mutually agreeable for both sides. Hundley simply did not have a position with the team anymore, and though he loved his time in New York, he still wanted to be a full-time catcher. "It's a bittersweet day in Mets history with Todd Hundley leaving the organization," said Phillips in announcing the deal.[25]

In return the Mets picked up Roger Cedeño and Charles Johnson. Cedeño was a speedy outfielder who had yet to really shine on the big-league stage, but he also had not been given a chance as a full-time player. The Mets were willing to give him that opportunity and hope it paid off. "He has an unlimited ceiling," one club official said after the trade.[26]

Johnson was a catcher with power who had been on the Marlins' championship team. He had been part of the deal that had sent Piazza to Florida for a week. Acquiring a catcher for a catcher when a team already had the best catcher in baseball made little sense at first glance—that is, until Steve Phillips, back in control after his brief leave of absence, immediately turned around and sent Johnson to the Orioles for Armando Benitez. "It became clear that there was a basis for a three-way deal to be made," said Phillips, who had been discussing the idea with the Dodgers and Orioles for two weeks before pulling the trigger. "For us one of the key things we wanted to do is look at bringing in a quality pitcher, either a front-line starter or power arm for the bullpen who could set up or possibly close."[27]

In Benitez the Mets had that power arm for the bullpen. The right-hander was known largely for the brawl he had helped start against the Yankees the previous May, but Benitez was more than that. He was a flame thrower, his fastball reaching a hundred miles per hour; such speed, when matched with a splitter, made him incredibly hard to hit. During the previous three seasons the league had failed to hit better than .200 against him. His strike-out rates, which had never been below 10.6 strikeouts per nine innings in any season, were among the best in baseball. There was a red flag, though. Benitez was prone to giving up home runs and untimely hits. In just over twelve postseason innings with Baltimore, he had allowed six home runs, including what ultimately became the deciding moment of the 1997 ALCS. The Orioles had already decided that Benitez could not handle the role of closer, having signed Mike Timlin to perform that role the previous month. Still, it was a huge bullpen upgrade for New York.

Last, the Mets signed Robin Ventura to play third base. The team had been eyeing Ventura for some time and with good reason. For nearly a decade Ventura had quietly become one of the best all-around third basemen in baseball. A five-time Gold Glover, he had averaged, minus one injury-filled season, twenty-one home runs and ninety-five RBIs a year since 1991. New York offered him a four-year deal worth $28 million. The Orioles countered by offering Ventura four years for $30 million. The Mets, after courting B. J. Surhoff as a Plan B, upped their offer by $2 million, sealing the deal. Given the team's thirty-six-year struggle to find a long-term, permanent player at the position, it could have been argued that Ventura was the best third baseman the Mets had ever acquired.

The events of that December 1 showed that the Mets were serious about taking the next step in 1999. They were not going to leave any stone unturned to fill holes in the roster. There was tension brewing, though. When Valentine went to Shea to welcome Phillips back after he resumed his general manager duties, Phillips greeted him coldly. Someone had told the general manager that Valentine had angled for his job while he was out, a rumor that Valentine vehemently denied. The damage was done, though. Phillips would never truly trust Valentine after that, and the relationship was strained for the remainder of both of their tenures with the team.

Phillips carried on, and before the end of the year the Mets made another splash when they signed soon-to-be-forty-year-old Rickey Henderson to a two-year, $2 million deal. Henderson was arguably among the top ten greatest baseball players who had ever lived. He had already broken the single-season and all-time stolen base records and was steadily climbing toward the all-time runs-scored and base-on-balls record, along with reaching three thousand hits. In fact, Rickey's pursuit of those records nearly derailed his deal with New York. As detailed in Howard Bryant's thorough biography of the man, *Rickey*, Henderson wanted a fully loaded Winnebago—the kind in which football analyst John Madden drove across the country—for breaking these records. Phillips said the Mets could not offer that, especially not to a player who had accomplished almost all those walks, runs, and hits for other teams.[28]

Though not the same player as in his heyday, even at thirty-nine, while playing for the A's the year before, Henderson had led the American League in stolen bases and walks. In fact, he had become the first player in sixty years to score over one hundred runs while batting as low as he had that year, .236.

There was baggage too, though. Rickey had left behind a trail of disappointed teammates and fans wherever he went. One common complaint was that Henderson did not play when he did not feel like playing or that he sometimes milked injuries. Such a complaint was not necessarily backed up by the facts. If the strike-shortened 1981 season and the 1987 season, where he missed significant time to injury, are removed, Henderson averaged 148 games played a year during the 1980s. This was a remarkable number given the wear and tear that playing the outfield and stealing all those bases had put on his body.

Another common complaint was that Henderson, if he was unhappy, would not give his all on the field. His career numbers would put that in dispute, but the complaint was not totally bogus. Henderson had been traded from the A's to the Yankees before the 1985 season, and he put together several solid years in New York. Some would argue that he, and not Don Mattingly, should have won the MVP in 1985. By 1989, however, Rickey had had enough of the Bronx. He was upset with complaints about his perceived lack of hustle and just the generally unpleasant aura around the team. On June 20, after sixty-five games that year, he was batting .247, with just three home runs and twenty-five stolen bases. Those numbers would have easily been among his worst if played out over a full year. The next day the Yankees traded him back to Oakland, where, in eighty-five games with the A's that year, he hit .294 with nine home runs and fifty-two stolen bases. The stark differences in those numbers were circumstantial evidence at best, but they seemed to indicate that once Rickey had had enough of the Bronx, he phoned it in.

The ink was barely dry on Henderson's Mets' contract when he stepped into controversy. It began when he made a bold statement. "Right now, I would probably say the Mets are going to win it," Rickey answered when asked who would win the NL East. "The Yankees have been cheering up the fans for a while, so I would say it's time for the Mets to take over."[29] It had been a long time since someone associated with the Mets had talked that way. While it raised some eyebrows, Mets fans were glad to hear someone speak with confidence for a change.

The Mets then announced they would be giving Rickey the number 24 to wear on his jersey. That had been Willie Mays's number, and even though he had made his name as a Giant and spent only his final two seasons in baseball with the Mets, Mays did not think anyone else should wear it. In fact, Mays said, he had been promised no one else would wear it by Joan Payson, the team's former owner. "When I came to New York, she told me this number will be retired on the wall. I think it should be. If it had been any other city than New York, I never would have kept playing," Mays said.[30] But Rickey kept the number.

Phillips still had more moves to make. He signed pitcher Pat Mahomes, a starter turned reliever who had struggled throughout most of his eight-year career, particularly with giving up home runs. Just before the start of spring training Phillips took a chance and signed seven-year career Minor Leaguer Melvin Mora. Confined to late-game replacement duty much of the year, Mora would ultimately play a large role for the team down the stretch that year.

There were even rumors that winter that the Mets were quietly trying to strike a deal with the Blue Jays for Clemens. A potential package proposal, which would have included Alfonzo, began making the rounds. Alfonzo was not pleased, but ultimately it came to nothing more than talk.

Clemens or not, it was an impressive off-season for the Mets. "On the field, they couldn't make it to the playoffs in 1998," wrote the *Bergen Record*'s T. J. Quinn. "But in the battle for off-season headlines and airtime, they have trounced the world champion Yankees."[31]

The Mets headed into spring training a confident team, looking to remove the stench of last season's final week. Even with all the changes they had made in the off-season, as Opening Day approached, they made one more.

It started when the team decided to release Hideo Nomo. The pitcher just had not worked out as the Mets had hoped in 1998. Valentine lobbied hard to resign him that off-season, and the team did. But Nomo had not pitched well in spring training and was not going to make the team. Valentine, who adored Nomo, was heartbroken when Phillips told him that Nomo would be sent to the Minors instead of staying with the club. Rather than accept his demotion, Nomo opted for his release from the team.

Replacing Nomo was someone who, just a decade earlier, it would have seemed improbable would one day be pitching for the Mets: Orel Hershiser. Hershiser, a lanky right-hander who looked more like he might do your taxes than throw a fastball, had been one of baseball's best pitchers in the mid- to late 1980s. He had helped the Dodgers reach the postseason, including in 1988, when he had put in one of the best stretches of any pitcher in history. In the season's final weeks and into his last game of the year, Hershiser set the MLB record by throwing fifty-nine consecutive scoreless innings. His domination continued into the playoffs, where, against the Mets in the NLCS, he left Game One with a 2–1 lead, left Game Three with a 4–3 lead, saved Game Four, and pitched a complete game shutout in the deciding Game Seven. Hershiser easily won NLCS MVP, went on to win World Series MVP when the Dodgers swept the A's, and also won the Cy Young Award that year.

Given how many innings Hershiser had put in during the 1980s, it felt inevitable that arm injuries would happen. They did in 1990, necessitating a shoulder reconstruction that essentially wiped out his whole season. When he returned, he was still a good pitcher but not the dominating guy of 1988. He averaged fifteen wins a year for Cleveland from 1995 to 1997, helping it reach the World Series twice and winning the 1995 ALCS MVP. Hershiser played with the Giants in 1998, again pitching well but not dominating, helping them overtake the Mets and reach their one-game playoff with Chicago.

Hershiser had signed a Minor League deal that spring with the Indians. The terms of the deal allowed him to negotiate with other teams. With a hole now in their rotation, the Mets swooped in and signed him just as the Cubs were about to potentially grab him. A ground ball pitcher, Hershiser was thrilled at the idea of pitching for a team with perhaps the best infielders in baseball. He was also a fan of the ambience of Shea and the creativity of New York fans that he had experienced as an opposing player. "There are a lot of things you can do with the name 'Orel,'" joked Hershiser.[32] "As down as I was yesterday over losing a player that I had a lot of sweat equity in and I was pulling for to do well, I'm even higher than that today knowing that one of the greatest competitors and one of the best pitchers I've ever seen is lined up on our team," said Valentine about releasing Nomo but signing Hershiser.[33]

The forty-year-old Hershiser immediately stepped in and, a day after signing, started in place of Nomo during the team's spring training game against the Expos. "I didn't get hurt, I got my work in and I didn't embarrass myself or the Mets," said Hershiser of his performance that day. "I didn't want to give anybody any material to say, 'Why did they sign some 40-year-old?'"[34]

With these changes the New York Mets headed to Miami to start their season against the Marlins. If "hope" had been the word heading into the 1998 season, "expectations" was the word heading into the 1999 season. And expectations were high for the Mets.

• • •

Roger Clemens's Yankees debut did not go as planned. Getting the ball on Opening Night in Oakland, Clemens held a 2–0 lead into the fifth and a 3–2 lead into the seventh without being able to maintain either. He was good but not great, a performance that could be written off as just an early season hiccup. Even though the Yankees lost the rain-shortened game, expectations for Clemens were still astronomical. After all, if he could win twenty games with the Blue Jays, he could conceivably win thirty with the core of a 114-win team still largely together.

The loss was a temporary setback, though, as the team won its next seven games, including a memorable home opener that saw the return of Yankees legend Yogi Berra. A Hall of Famer who had won three MVPs and a record ten World Series rings as a member of the Yankees from 1946 to

1963, Berra was a nationally beloved figure thanks to his head-scratching remarks (known as Yogisms) and as the face of the popular chocolate drink Yoo-hoo. After retiring, he'd become a coach and eventually managed the Mets to the pennant in 1973. In 1985, during his second year of managing the Yankees, Berra was fired by Steinbrenner after the team started the year 6-10. At first somewhat indifferent, if not relieved, by his firing, Berra became bitter that Steinbrenner himself had not dismissed him, having instead sent general manager Clyde King to wield the axe. Spurred on by his wife, Carmen, Berra made a vow never to return to Yankee Stadium as long as Steinbrenner was running the team. For nearly a decade and a half he had kept that vow, despite countless attempts from former teammates and friends to have him reconsider it. "The longest vacation I ever had from baseball was after George fired me," said Berra.[35]

In the winter of 1999, Yankees broadcaster Suzyn Waldman approached Steinbrenner with the idea of offering an apology to Berra for his actions in 1985. The Boss, growing increasingly sentimental and reflective as he aged, was drawn to the idea immediately. After the two reconciled, on a rainy home opening day, Berra returned to Yankee Stadium. The Yankees responded by pounding the Tigers, 12–3. "It was cold, it was wet, it was muddy but we won," said Chili Davis.[36]

The next day Clemens looked more like the Cy Young Award winner of 1998 when he held Detroit to just three hits and no runs before leaving the game in the eighth. After a minor skid the Yankees won seven of their last nine games in April to finish the month 14-7, only one game worse than their record through twenty-one games in 1998.

The team's record was due, in large part, to the performances of one hitter and one pitcher: Davis and Mendoza. Thirty-nine-year-old Chili Davis began the year with a torrid start, taking advantage of now being the team's full-time DH. Healthy and in what he knew would be the last year of his career, Davis homered on Opening Day and drove the Yankees' offense from there. He recorded a hit in eighteen of the team's twenty-one April games, reaching base in all but one of them. By month's end he was hitting .356 while slugging .630, with five home runs and twenty RBIs. Davis had never really had an off year, outside of injury, but this still seemed like a resurgence. Moreover, Davis, who had learned as a rookie with the Giants at the feet of Hall of Famer Joe Morgan, played a leadership role in the clubhouse. "Having him has been huge," said

Cone that May. "Not only from a production standpoint but from his leadership. He is like having a second hitting coach. A lot of our hitters go to him to talk about hitting."[37]

Davis continued to lead the offensive charge in May, adding on eight multi-hit games and leading the team in home runs and RBIs before starting to slow down in June. Still, the frequency with which he was getting on base was a nice surprise in the early goings of the season.

On the pitching side Ramiro Mendoza emerged as a dependable starter, having replaced Irabu in the rotation at the beginning the year. Mendoza had been, and would largely remain, an unsung hero of the club. Splitting his time between the rotation and the bullpen in 1998, he'd come away with a 10-2 record, throwing mostly a sinking fastball that was nearly unhittable when working right. He'd given up just a single run in five and a third innings of relief in the postseason, earning the win in Game Three of the World Series. Pressed into the rotation to start 1999, he responded by shutting out the A's over eight innings in his first start, then allowed two unearned runs in his next one. Ultimately Mendoza ended April 3-1, with a 2.40 ERA, walking just five hitters in five appearances.

It felt like the team was on pace to match, maybe even exceed, the pace from a year before. Yet May would bring some rude awakenings, potentially souring the return of the team's manager.

• • •

Opening Day did not go as planned for the Mets. Facing off against his old team, Al Leiter gave up three runs to the Marlins before the end of the first inning. Florida won, 6–2. The Mets saved the real fun for the second and third games of the season. Their first win of the year was a 12–3 blowout in which every starter, minus pitcher Rick Reed, had at least one hit and one run scored. The third game was the Rickey Henderson Show. Henderson led off the game with a walk, then in the third hit his first home run of the season. The shot came complete with a Rickey bat flip, a backstep shuffle, and a tug at the jersey. He added another home run and two doubles before the night was over, leading the Mets to a 6–0 win.

In Montreal next, Piazza set the pace with a five-RBI game as New York won three of four. For the home opener at Shea, a supercharged crowd of over fifty-two thousand watched as Bobby Jones held Florida to just one hit over seven innings while also clubbing his first—and only—career home run.

New York reeled off five wins in a row and, after a minor stumble, finished the month with three straight wins against the Padres to go 14-9 in April.

The Mets' record put them in second place, and they were more than keeping up with the Braves in the division. Moreover, their fourteen wins were the same as the Yankees had, so they were also keeping pace with the world champions and possibly playing more interesting ball in the process. Henderson was causing havoc at the leadoff spot, reaching base in nearly 50 percent of his plate appearances while also slugging .500. Piazza had suffered a right-knee sprain a week into the season and had missed two weeks. Still, in ten April games he drove in eleven runs, two of which came when he homered off Trevor Hoffman in the ninth inning on April 27 to give the Mets a come-from-behind walk-off win. The home run and RBI totals helped to begin eliminating, once and for all, the notion that he could not drive in runners in big situations.

While Piazza had sat on the disabled list, his backup, Todd Pratt, had stepped into the void. "Backup" was a phrase Pratt knew well. First drafted by the Red Sox in 1985 and then drafted by the Indians in 1987, only to be returned to Boston months later, Pratt's path to being a full-time big-league player always seemed to be blocked. In Boston it was John Marzano who had stood in his way. When Pratt landed in Philadelphia in 1992, Darren Daulton was the full-time catcher, and he was not going anywhere.

Pratt played a handful of games throughout the 1992–95 seasons, getting his hits and home runs here and there. But in the spring of 1996, just two months after the Mariners signed him, they released him a week before the season opened. Pratt, seemingly out of options, went to work as an instructor at Bucky Dent's Baseball School in Florida. To make ends meet Pratt managed a Domino's Pizza franchise. "A thousand orders in a three-hour period," he said, recalling Super Bowl Sunday in 1997. "I was supervising a full crew and I sweated harder than I ever did in my life."[38]

Pratt's work teaching kids at Dent's school gave him a renewed appreciation for baseball. He realized that he did not know everything and should be more open to hearing feedback that could improve his game. Pratt ended up with the Mets in 1997. Now, filling in for the greatest offensive catcher in baseball, the backup hit three home runs and drove in eleven runs while accumulating a .953 OPS.

The starting pitching had held strong, but it was the bullpen that had really shined in the first month of the year. Benitez emerged as a set-up man in the bullpen, amassing six holds while allowing six hits in just under twelve innings. Cook won four games in the month, more than any pitcher on the team, while allowing just two runs over ten appearances. Wendell appeared in more than half of the team's games in April, allowing only two runs while picking up a win, a save, and five holds.

Even with all of these numbers and solid performances, the feel-good story out of the Mets bullpen in April was John Franco. The senior Met, Franco had endured rough patches the previous season, going 0-8 and posting one of the highest ERAs of his career. He had been through all the ups and downs of the Mets during the '90s and was heartbroken by the team's having fallen just short of the postseason the previous year. Perhaps emboldened by the presence of Benitez, who threatened his closer's job, Franco was lights out in April. Over nine and a third innings, he allowed only six hits, with three of those coming in one game, while striking out ten. His ERA was a microscopic 0.96. On April 14, at home against Florida, he struck out the side to achieve the four hundredth save of his career. To that point he was only the second pitcher to save that many games. "If anyone ever counted John Franco out, they don't have a clue about what they're talking about," said Valentine. "John Franco is what he is and has done what he's done because he's a very special athlete and an integral part of this team."[39]

Franco converted all eight save opportunities in April as the Mets seemed poised to give the Braves a run throughout the rest of the season. But May would be a month of reckoning, and when it was over, Steve Phillips would decide that some people were no longer going to be a part of the organization.

• • •

The Mets did not exactly play poorly in May. It was not the most impressive month, but certainly they had had worse performances in the history of the franchise. Still, the overall output was lackluster. In other years a 13-15 performance would not have been reason to necessarily panic. But these were not the Mets of 1979 or 1993. Expectations were high, so when the team did flounder in the season's second month, it was not going to be shrugged aside. Heads were going to roll.

The bullpen remained strong. It was the starting pitching that had become a disaster, with the offense not far behind. After a decent start, the rotation had gotten blistered throughout May. Leiter, the ace of the staff, was 2-5 with a 6.39 ERA; Yoshi, 4-5, with a 4.94 ERA; Hershiser, 4-4, with a 5.63 ERA;

Bobby Jones, 3-3, with a 5.81 ERA before tendinitis in his right shoulder sidelined him in late May. Jones did not pitch again until September. The poor performances forced Valentine to overtax his bullpen, a dangerous proposition with four months still left in the season.

Meanwhile, despite leading the National League in on-base percentage, the Mets were only middle of the pack in terms of runs scored. They led all of baseball in runners left on base. Piazza, Olerud, and Ventura were producing at a strong clip, with each on pace to drive in over or near to one hundred runs. In fact, Ventura had set a Major League record when, on May 20, he had hit grand slams during both games of a doubleheader against Milwaukee. Everyone else, however, was lagging.

As the Mets' mediocre May continued, pressure began to mount on Valentine. He and Phillips had never been particularly close, and the weak performance strained the relationship further. Valentine, however, was beloved by Fred Wilpon, making it difficult, if not impossible, for Phillips to outright dismiss him. Instead, in a move out of the 1980s George Steinbrenner playbook, Phillips set his sights on three Mets coaches to whom Valentine was closest: pitching coach Bob Apodaca, hitting coach Tom Robson, and bullpen coach Randy Niemann. These were people Valentine knew and trusted. They had been part of his staff since essentially the beginning of his managerial run. That fact, grouped with the team's performance and Wilpon's protecting of Valentine, meant they were vulnerable. After the team closed out the month with a 5–3 loss to the Reds, Phillips decided it was time for executive action.

That bit of news he kept to himself as the Mets strolled into Yankee Stadium on Friday, June 4, just a game over .500. This year the schedule had been adjusted so that the two teams would play six games against each other, three at Yankee Stadium and three at Shea Stadium. The additional match-ups were not necessarily appreciated by the players, many of whom felt there was too much pressure applied to these regular-season games. How much pressure? Consider that for most games during the year, the Yankees reviewed written scouting reports. But for the Mets, the report was delivered orally, in the clubhouse, by advance scouts Bob Didier and Wade Taylor, along with Gene Michael. "Joe [Torre] just said, point blank, 'I'm sick of this. I don't want it go on like this anymore,'" said Valentine. "And I agree. It was three weeks leading up to it [interleague play between the Yankees and Mets] and three weeks after it that the town would be consumed with it. Maybe even longer."[40]

The fans, however, loved everything about the extended interleague play. The more games, the merrier, as far as they were concerned. The 56,175 fans who showed up to Yankee Stadium that night were evidence enough of that.

What they saw was a nailbiter of a game, with the lead changing hands four times. "It felt like a post-season game, completely draining on every pitch," said Cone, who started the game for the Yankees. "I was completely drained when I left the game."[41]

Ultimately the Yankees ended up on top thanks to a seventh-inning double by Brosius. As if to prove the point of what Phillips was about to do, the Mets left nine runners on base, and Reed, the starting pitcher that night, gave up four runs, raising his ERA to 5.33. The following day, as if to again give Phillips all the ammunition he needed to support his impending move, the Mets went 1-10 with runners in scoring position while leaving nine runners on base, and Yoshi gave up six runs in four innings. The Mets lost, 6–3. Ventura and McRae had tried to lighten the mood of the clubhouse beforehand, suggesting the team wear its pant legs higher. Some did. Some didn't. The team's ERA was now nearly 5.00, among the worst in the National League.

The game's most memorable moment came in the second inning, when Rey Ordóñez, with a runner on third, hit a sharp one-hopper up the middle that Orlando Hernández, lunging quickly to his right, was able to snag. The ball got stuck in the webbing of his glove, though, and rather than waste time trying to pry it loose, Hernández threw his glove, with the ball still stuck in it, over to Tino Martinez at first to record the out and prevent the runner from advancing home.

It was a moment of levity, though ultimately the Mets were not laughing. The loss dropped them a game below .500 and six out of first. "The very idea that those Mets and these Yankees might meet to compare talents and pay-rolls in October never looked more unlikely than it did yesterday," wrote the Star-Ledger's Tim Brown.[42] "Although the gimmick of interleague baseball has brought them together in each of the past three seasons, it has not been able to narrow the gap in performance between the city's major-league franchises," noted Newsday's Joe Gergen. "Indeed, after the residents of Flushing spent and spent over the winter, it can be argued that they are farther than ever from emulating the reigning world champions in the Bronx."[43]

That same day, hours after the game had ended, Phillips informed Valentine that he had decided to fire Apodaca, Robson, and Niemann. An argument that lasted nearly an hour ensued. Afterward Phillips called Apodaca, Robson, and Niemann in one by one to inform them they were fired "as Valentine sat in the room and watched like a stunned hostage."[44]

Phillips then publicly announced his decision. Dave Wallace would take over as pitching coach, Mickey Brantley as hitting coach, and Al Jackson as bullpen coach. Jackson, a coach in the Mets' Minor League system, found out he was getting promoted while watching TV. The news broke during halftime of the Knicks game. "This was a tough evening for the organization," said Phillips. "We are one-third of the way through the season and that is enough time to make an evaluation. There is still enough time to get the ship righted."[45]

It was the most dramatic personnel decision that either New York team had made in recent memory. Valentine was outraged and considered quitting and just being done with it all. One club official even told a reporter that Phillips had specifically targeted Apodaca and Robson in the hopes it would make Valentine quit. Valentine ultimately decided to stay, believing the Mets were on the cusp of righting themselves. But he could not hide his disgust over what had happened. "I don't think it could be worse, personally," said Valentine of the timing of the firings.[46]

• • •

Their new coaching staff in place, the Mets now had to avoid being swept out of the Bronx during an ESPN Sunday night game. It was more than that, though. The season was bordering on life support. A turnaround was not going to be made by personnel decisions alone. Players were going to have to step up to get this team back on track. On a nationally broadcast game, Mike Piazza and Al Leiter did just that.

Piazza began the game's scoring with a double in the second as the Mets plated four runs off Clemens. Then in the third he drilled a Clemens splitter over the wall in left-center field. Meanwhile, Leiter kept the Yankees' bats at bay, allowing just a single run in seven innings. The Mets avoided the sweep with a 7–2 win, in the process ending Clemens's American League record twenty-consecutive-wins streak. Clemens was booed off the field after he was removed from the game.

The win did more than just avoid the sweep. Whether the change in coaches had created a ripple wake-up effect within the clubhouse can be debated but never truly known. What is known for certain is that after June

6 the Mets completely altered the course of their season, becoming one of the best and most consistently victorious teams in baseball. They won fifteen of their next eighteen games, reclaiming second place in the process. For the rest of the year they never fell below second.

It felt like all on the team had hit their stride at the same time. After his home run against Clemens, Piazza hit six more in June, driving in fourteen runs for the month. Edgardo Alfonzo, who had gone back and forth between hot and cold early in the season, took off. After the win against the Yankees he collected ten multi-hit games in June, driving in twenty-one runs in the process. Henderson, after spending most of May on the disabled list, was nearly unstoppable in June. He hit .312 and, after being somewhat hesitant to run in his first two months with the team, stole thirteen bases in sixteen attempts. Roger Cedeño, finally given a chance to be an everyday player, was a revelation. He hit .347 in June and stole fourteen bases. Between them, Cedeño and Henderson stole nearly half as many bases in the month as the Mets had done during the entire 1998 season.

One of the best stories to emerge from the Mets' rebirth, however, was that of Benny Agbayani. Like Sid Fernandez, the professional-wrestling-loving Mets pitcher of the 1980s and early 1990s, Agbayani hailed from Hawaii—Aiea, Hawaii, to be exact. A mix of Filipino, Samoan, Portuguese, Spanish, and German and the son of a ballroom-dance-instructing father, Agbayani learned the game of baseball in part from his aunt. He grew up idolizing Rickey Henderson. That was exactly the kind of player he wanted to be. Like Rickey, Agbayani was an exceptional athlete, excelling in baseball, football, and soccer. After his college baseball career, which saw him set several records at Hawaii Pacific University, the Mets selected him in the thirtieth round of the 1993 amateur draft.

Agbayani made his way through the Mets' system, where he caught the eye of Valentine in Triple A Norfolk. Despite his size—he looked more like a football player than an outfielder—Agbayani did not hit with as much power as Valentine felt he could. He worked with Agbayani on a leg kick meant to better help him drive the ball. The result was more doubles and home runs in Agbayani's 1997 season with Norfolk and the possibility of making the big-league club in 1998. An injury derailed that, though he did have a few cups of coffee with the team that year.

Now, when both Henderson and Bonilla were down with injuries, Agbayani got the call to join the team in mid-May. He proceeded to take fans by storm. He homered in his first game of the season, hit two more a week later, and recorded six multi-hit games in his first ten games of the year. Toward the end of May he homered in three consecutive games. The day after the Mets had avoided being swept by the Yankees, Agbayani hit two home runs against the Blue Jays, giving him eight for the year. His OPS was an unworldly 1.390. On June 13 Agbayani's fifth-inning home run off Boston's Mark Portugal made history. He reached ten home runs in the fewest career at bats—seventy-three—of any Mets player ever. "He's swinging the bat as well as anyone I've ever seen swing the bat over that length of time," said McRae.[47]

Agbayani remained modest about his success. "I just go up to the plate and hit," he said. "Whatever they throw, I've got to hit it, right?"[48]

Agbayani's numbers trailed off as the year went along, and pitchers finally made adjustments that kept the Hawaiian in the ballpark. His initial run had been remarkable, though, helping spur the Mets on.

On June 15 at Cincinnati the team tied a franchise record by hitting six home runs in a game. The offense was clicking on all cylinders, but it was the starting pitching that had made a complete 180-degree turn. Leiter, who had given up at least five runs in every single start in May, went 5-0 in June while pitching to a 2.62 ERA. After giving up nine home runs in his first ten starts, he didn't allow a single homer through the month. By the time the All-Star break came around, Leiter, who had started the year 1-4, was 8-6. He attributed the turnaround to something new coaches Wallace and Jackson had told him. "Really, the wakeup call was, 'Look, get back to being aggressive. Forget about everything else.' It's more in-the-head stuff. Yeah, absolutely, Wally and Al helped me with that."[49]

Hershiser, whose ERA stood at 5.77 the day of the firings, won four games the rest of the month. During his final three starts of June he channeled his inner-1988 self by pitching nineteen and a third innings while allowing only twelve hits and two runs. Yoshi, whose June 5 performance against the Yankees had bloated his ERA to 5.52, closed out the month by allowing only seven runs in four starts. Reed, the team's most reliable starter over the previous two years, won three of his final four starts in the month.

Everything was working right for the Mets. Moreover, they were having fun for the first time since April. On June 9 they trailed the Blue Jays by three runs with two out in the bottom of the ninth. After Ventura lined a two-run single off David Wells, Toronto closer Billy Koch, whose fastball topped out at nearly one hundred miles per hour, entered the game. McRae went with an outside fastball and tied the game with a double. In the top of the twelfth, after Shannon Stewart had singled with one out, he then attempted to steal second. The Mets called for a pitchout. Piazza stood up and stepped forward to catch the pitch, then heaved the ball toward second. Stewart was safe, but home-plate umpire Randy Marsh ruled that Piazza had stepped too far out into the batter's box, possibly interfering with the batter's ability to hit the ball. The batter, Craig Grebeck, was awarded first. Valentine came out to argue and was promptly ejected from the game.

A short time later television cameras panned to the Mets' dugout, where a familiar face sat at the end of the bench. Donning a non-Mets cap, glasses, and an eye-black painted-on mustache in the style of Groucho Marx, Valentine had returned to oversee the final innings.

"Robin [Ventura] said something to the effect that I had to get back to the dugout because the coaches don't even know the players in the bullpen," said Valentine, referring to the new coaches' unfamiliarity with some of the players. Normally when a manager is ejected from a game, the team will employee someone who can run instructions from the manager, sitting in the clubhouse, back to the acting manager in the dugout. In this case Hershiser had volunteered to be the runner. "When I got thrown out prior to that, the runners never really worked. It was always too much of a delay," added Valentine. So instead of using Hershiser, Ventura handed Valentine glasses and a hat, told him to take off his uniform, and to go out there himself. "I went into the trainer's room and saw the stickers that go underneath your eye to keep out the glare," Valentine continued. "I put them underneath my nose and looked in the mirror and looked at them [Ventura and Hershiser], and they said, 'No one will ever know.' So I decided to go out where I could just yell down the dugout anything I wanted the acting manager to do."[50]

Valentine was quickly and easily captured on camera. Players, commentators, and even fans were amused by the silly act that seemed to say, "Hey, it's only a game; let's have some fun." Major League Baseball was not amused. It fined the Mets' manager $5,000 and suspended him two games. Valentine's cheap-disguise moment become a part of baseball history and revealed a Mets club that was now, finally, having a good time. Even more important, they won that game in the fourteenth inning.

After having fallen below .500, the team finished out June at 44-34, just three games behind the Braves. On July 2 John Franco strained a tendon in his left middle finger throwing a fastball, marring the start of the month. He did not pitch again until September. Benitez stepped into his place. While it was not known at the time, it was a changing of the guard. Franco, the longest-serving closer in team history, having been in the position since joining the team in 1990, would save games again in the future. But never again would he don the role of team closer. For the rest of 1999 and into 2000 Benitez took over that responsibility. Benitez responded by saving eight games in July, striking out twenty-one in ten and two-thirds innings.

Everyone was hitting. Everyone was pitching lights out. And the manager was playing practical jokes. It was a fun time to be a Met. Then the Yankees came to town. The result would be one of the most memorable games in the two teams' interleague history.

• • •

The crowd at Fenway Park stood and applauded as a man in a gray uniform with a navy blue "6" stitched on the back approached home plate. He exchanged lineup cards with the umpires and the opposing team, then turned and doffed his cap. It was a heartwarming scene. Over thirty-three thousand fans, many of them eternally hostile to that gray uniform and anyone wearing it, had turned up on May 18 and were cheering on Joe Torre's triumphant return to the dugout. Torre, two months to the day after surgery to remove his prostrate, was back and cancer-free. He had surprised the team by flying up to Boston, walking into the clubhouse, and announcing he was back.

Torre returned to a team that was struggling. The Yankees had lost eight of the previous thirteen games, including a brutal sweep at home by the Angels that saw them get shut out in back-to-back games. The White Sox came in and battered them for twenty runs over two losses. Clemens spent the skid on the disabled list, hampered by a hamstring that had made his first month in pinstripes less than storybook. After his dominant performance against the Tigers, Clemens was tagged for seven runs by the Orioles in just three innings and ended the month by giving up five more in just two innings against the Rangers. His ERA stood at 5.47, and he had allowed an astounding forty-three base runners in just over twenty-six innings.

Torre's return was blunted when the team blew a 2–0 lead and lost to Pedro Martinez. The defeat dropped them out of first place for the first time in nearly a month. The next day Boston starter Brian Rose, who entered the game with a 7.38 career ERA, shut them out for seven innings in another defeat.

All told, the Yankees' 15-13 May was their least successful month since April 1997. During this time a familiar face joined the lineup: Tony Tarasco. Tarasco had been in right field for Baltimore during Game One of the 1996 ALCS when twelve-year-old Jeffrey Maier reached over the top of the wall to deflect a Derek Jeter fly ball and turn it into a home run. Tarasco spent a month with the team but limited success and playing availability resulted in his being sent down to the Minors for the rest of the season.

That same month another issue began to emerge, one familiar to the Yankees and the Mets: the yips. The term almost sounds too cute to be taken seriously. Like something one might say to an infant who drops a pacifier. In sports, though, and baseball in particular, "the yips" is no laughing matter. It has wrecked careers and unfairly brought scorn to those afflicted by it.

In its simplest terms, the yips is a condition where a player cannot make the most routine of throws, be he a pitcher, an infielder, or an outfielder. Often the throws themselves will miss the intended target by several feet. It tends to happen without warning. A player will be totally fine one day, overcome by the yips the next. While recent data suggest the yips could in fact be a neurological condition, it was long accepted that it was a mental issue. The Mayo Clinic notes that "some athletes become so anxious and self-focused—overthinking to the point of distraction—that their ability to perform a skill . . . is impaired."[51]

Steve Blass was a lights out pitcher for the Pirates in the late '60s and early '70s. In 1971 he finished the year 19-8, placing second in the National League Cy Young voting. The next season he developed the yips, unable to throw the ball for a strike. He walked eighty-four batters in eighty-eight innings and led the league in hit batsmen despite pitching only those eighty-eight innings. He made one more start in baseball before his career was over.

Former Mets catch Mackey Sasser was afflicted with the yips, possibly after a home-plate collision. While Sasser could still gun runners out who were attempting to steal, he could not make the basic throw back to the mound after a pitch. He started triple- and quadruple-clutching the ball before releasing throws that would fall either too short of the pitcher or sail over his head. Former Yankee Steve Sax became a victim too. For Chuck Knoblauch it started in 1998.

Knoblauch, who had always been sure-handed in Minnesota, began throwing differently in spring training, particularly on plays in which he had time to stop and set himself before throwing. It looked like he was trying to aim his throws to first rather than just go through his natural throwing motion. In the fourth inning of the Yankees' third game of the year, Knoblauch fielded a ground ball by the A's Matt Stairs toward the hole near first base. Stairs was not fleet of foot, giving Knoblauch enough time to stop and set himself. Then, rather than throw the ball to Martinez, Knoblauch flung it toward him, like a college kid tossing a ping pong ball in beer pong. Knoblauch's throw sailed over Martinez's head, and it would have gone all the way to the backstop had Girardi not been backing up the play.

There would be more of those throws throughout the year—enough to make people notice but not enough to create overt concern. Overt concern emerged in 1999. Knoblauch already had fifteen errors by July, on his way to committing twenty-six, far eclipsing his previous season high. Knoblauch was fully enmeshed in the yips. His throws became more erratic, to the point that on routine ground balls hit to him, the Yankee Stadium crowd would hold its breath.

Psychology could certainly have been a part of it. Knoblauch had gotten divorced in 1998, and in 1999 his father was in the midst of a battle with Alzheimer's. His offensive performance, while a catalyst for the lineup, was not on par with his performances in Minnesota. And every error brought more scrutiny from fans, who could not understand how a player could not just throw the ball. Knoblauch worked extensively with third-base coach Willie Randolph on his throwing, but the issue was not mechanical, even if Knoblauch's mechanics were causing these errant throws. It was a psychological—or a neurological—issue that could not be fixed with more infield practice. Knoblauch's struggles would continue.

The Yankees, meanwhile, despite playing mostly .500 ball over the course of a month, were able to retake first place on June 9. They would not relinquish it the rest of the year, though they came close over the next several weeks. They won ten out of eleven at one point, though the Red Sox largely kept pace during this time. The Yankees then headed to Shea for the second half of their interleague match-up. What ultimately happened at Shea would be remembered for years to come, happily by Mets fans, bitterly by Yankees fans.

• • •

Focused laser-like in the direction of home plate, 53,792 people collectively held their breath for one second. Mariano Rivera, who had just delivered a fastball down the lower middle of the plate to Matt Franco, stared in at home plate umpire Jeff Kellogg, waiting for him to call strike three. Such a call would have ended the game and given the Yankees the second game of the 1999 Subway Series at Shea. Instead Kellogg called a ball, moving the count to 1-2. From the Yankees' dugout, an incensed Joe Torre screamed toward Kellogg, "That fucking ball's not low. That's NOT low."[52] Franco, pinch-hitting with the bases loaded, two out, and his team down 8–7 in the bottom of the ninth, would get another chance. "My heart skipped a beat because it was close," said Franco.[53]

The non-strike call seemed appropriate for this Saturday afternoon game, which, even before what happened next, was already the greatest of the first eleven interleague match-ups between the New York clubs. On an overcast yet humid July day, the two teams battled back and forth during the nationally broadcast game, with the lead having already changed hands five times. O'Neill started the game with a two-run home run in the first. The Mets punched and punctured Pettitte for four runs to take the lead heading into the fifth. In that inning home runs by Ledée and Posada tied the game. O'Neill, who did not consider himself a home run hitter but possessed a ball signed by both Babe Ruth and Henry Aaron (then the career leaders in home runs) hit another home run to give the Yankees the lead back in the seventh.

In the bottom of the seventh, his team down by two runs, Piazza sat on a 2-1 sinker from Mendoza and hit it 482 feet away, the longest home run by a Met that year. He capped it off with an epic bat flip before bat flips became an overplayed trademark of the game. The ball left the playing field of Shea, crashing into the top of the blue-and-white-striped tent that had been set up just beyond the visitors' bullpen. Chad Curtis, playing left field, did not move a single step in pursuit of the ball. Jeff Manto, a utility player in the midst of a month's stretch with the Yankees, watched from the bench in awe of Piazza's blast. "I don't usually watch the other team's homers," said Manto. "But that sounded so hard."[54]

It was Piazza's second go-ahead three-run home run in as many days. The night before, he had drilled a Clemens split-finger fastball into the left-field stands, giving the Mets a 5–2 lead. It was a big moment for Piazza, who, yet again, was coming under fire from the fans for failure to provide big hits. "I don't think he needed to, but it was a nice spot to do it," said Ventura of the Piazza shot. "People feel like he has the extra responsibility of doing some things, which he doesn't. But for him to do that was great."[55]

It was little noted at the time, but Clemens threw the next pitch nearly into the gut of Robin Ventura. The Yankees brought the tying run to the plate in the ninth, but Benitez blew a howitzer fastball past Davis to end the game.

Piazza was on pace to play the hero for the second day in a row. Then, in the top of the eighth, Posada hit his second home run of the day, the Yankees' sixth of the game, and it put them up, 8–7. The score remained that way into the bottom of the ninth, when, with one out, Rivera made the mistake of walking Rickey Henderson. Alfonzo then lifted a fly ball to deep center field that Bernie Williams normally would have tracked down. But Bernie misjudged how close he was to the wall; he leapt when he didn't have to, and the ball deflected off his glove. Generously ruled a double, it put runners on second and third. After a quick out that failed to advance either runner, the Yankees opted to intentionally walk Piazza— who almost certainly would have found a way to win the game based on how badly he was crushing the Yankees—and the Mets sent Franco up to pinch-hit.

Matt Franco had baseball—and Hollywood—in his blood. His father, Larry, was a film producer, while his uncle, Kurt Russell, was not just a famous actor but a pretty good baseball player as well. Russell had played Minor League ball in the early 1970s before an injury had forced him into retirement. His nephew, Matt, was not a bad player himself, having been drafted by the Cubs in 1987 at age seventeen. The left-handed Franco toiled in the Minors for eight seasons before making it to the Majors in 1995. Traded to the Mets in 1996, he became a pinch hitter extraordinaire. Now he stood in the box for what, to that moment, was the biggest at bat of his life.

Franco had had a good swing at the first pitch, fouling it back. But on the second, he expected a cut fastball and instead got a sinking one, and he swung right through it. He wasn't sure what to expect next. He got the exact same pitch and watched as it slammed into Posada's glove. Not wanting to give the Yankees any help, Franco immediately swept away the dirt in front of him in the batter's box, as if to convey that he knew the pitch was a ball and had never for a second thought that Kellogg would call it otherwise.

The crowd was still buzzing from the ball one call when Rivera tried the exact same pitch for a third straight time. This time, though, he left it too high over the plate. Franco swatted at it, making solid contact and sending the ball into right field for a hit. Henderson scored easily to tie the game. Even with two outs, it was, for a moment, uncertain if Alfonzo would make it home. Franco had hit the ball on a rope, and it had reached O'Neill on just two bounces. But O'Neill hesitated for a split second, trying not to have to field the ball on a short hop and instead grab it on a clean bounce to his glove. He fired a strong throw to the plate, but the moment's hesitation may have cost him, as Alfonzo slid in safely before Posada could turn and apply the tag.

Shea Stadium erupted. Most of the players turned their attention to Franco, whom they mobbed out near second base. The reaction was that of a team that had just won the pennant, and in a sense it felt that way for the Mets. The win put them in a tie with Cincinnati for the wild card. Moreover, Franco's hit ensured that, for the first time since interleague play began, the Mets were going to take a series from the Yankees.

"To get the game-winning hit, at Shea Stadium, playing the Yankees, with 55,000 people in the stands, bases loaded, down by a run, bottom of the ninth," said Franco. "I don't know how I'm going to do any better than that. It's a dream come true."[56]

"That was the most fun I've ever seen guys have," said Valentine. "That was a very dramatic game heightened by the fact of where we were and who we were playing. It was a game to watch by the fireside in the winter. Just put in the tape and watch the game."[57]

"Of the 11 games the Yankees and Mets have played now over their three seasons of interleague confrontations, this was the best. By far. By any definition of what baseball is about," wrote the New York Times' Dave Anderson.[58]

All that stood between the Mets and a first-ever interleague sweep between the two teams was Hideki Irabu. When Irabu gave up two early runs, it looked like that sweep might happen. Instead the Yankees fought back against Hershiser, tagging him for six runs by the end of the fifth inning. Given a lead, Irabu settled down, retiring the last nine hitters he faced, five of them by strikeout.

The win put the Yankees four games up in first place going into the All-Star break. The Mets, meanwhile, had weathered the storm to keep their season alive. The Braves' strong performance had kept them from gaining much ground, but their 50-39 record keep them in the hunt for first and, if nothing else, in strong contention for the wild card. Meanwhile, having finally won their first series against their crosstown rivals, they had sent a strong message going into the break: this town is up for grabs, and we have every intention of taking it.

The Mets emerged from the All-Star break just as hot, if not hotter, than they'd been in June. Out of the break they won their first seven series, rolling over teams one by one as they climbed the division standings. Octavio Dotel, called up in late June, became a pleasant surprise for the team. Outside of an outing in which the Cubs roughed him up, he pitched four out of five games allowing only a single run while pitching at least seven innings. Ultimately Dotel finished the year 8-3.

On July 22 in Montreal, Hershiser won his two hundredth career game, an impressive achievement given his injuries earlier in the decade. A week later in Chicago, the Mets trailed the Cubs, 7–2, before pulling out a 10–9 win. The victory put them a half game ahead of the Braves in the division, the latest the Mets had been in possession of first since 1990. Outside of the stellar pitching and hitting, there was another factor that was contributing to the Mets' amazing play: defense.

Defense had always been a valued part of the game but generally never put higher than pitching or hitting. Years after the 1999 Mets' infielders fielded their last ground ball, when an analytical revolution took over the game of baseball, statistics were developed showing just how important defense is to a successful baseball team. Such figures did not exist, or at least they were not widely used, before the turn of the century. Still, there was little doubt at the time just how good the Mets were defensively, especially their infield.

By 1999, the league knew how talented Rey Ordóñez was. His diving, sliding, throwing from his back, tumbling over bases, and flying-over-baserunners plays had graced ESPN's *SportsCenter* for years. His performance in 1999, however, took it to another level. It was not just that Ordóñez was making the spectacular plays but that, after June 13, he was also almost literally making every play. On that day, in the eighth inning against Boston, Ordóñez flubbed a throw on a ground ball by Boston's Jeff Frye. It was not an easy play, but the error given to him on it was not unreasonable. It was his fourth error of the year. It was also his last. He played one hundred more games that season without committing another error, breaking the

Major League record for shortstops. The streak, which was later eclipsed, ultimately reached 101 errorless games, a testament to Ordóñez's ability to do the big things and the little things at short.

Standing to Ordóñez's right on the infield, Ventura was nearly as good at the hot corner. His nine errors were the fewest committed during a full season in his career. Both Ventura and Ordóñez would go on to win Gold Gloves for their work that season. Yet it was Alfonzo who may have had the most impressive season of any Mets infielder ever. Playing second base full time, Alfonzo committed just five errors, none of which occurred by his mishandling of a ground ball. It was the first time in the recorded history of baseball that any infielder had gone a full season without committing an error by misfielding a grounder.

In the end, the infield committed only 33 errors that year. The team committed just sixty-eight, easily breaking the Major League record for fewest in a season. The Mets allowed twenty unearned runs, also easily breaking the record for fewest unearned runs allowed in a season. How good were the Mets defensively? Piazza—the catcher!—led the team in errors with eleven. Such a thing was nearly unheard of. Because of the sheer number of opportunities almost all teams see their third baseman or second baseman or shortstop lead in errors. Not the 1999 Mets.

Was the 1999 Mets infield the greatest defensive foursome ever put together? *Sports Illustrated* certainly hinted at it. A cover from that year's September 6 edition shows Ordóñez, Olerud, and Alfonzo standing behind a seated Ventura while Olerud has Ventura in a playful headlock. The headline reads, "The Best Infield Ever?" Inside was a full-length cover story by Tom Verducci that discussed in great detail how Ventura's acquisition had changed the makeup of the team and shored up the infield to a level rarely seen in the game's history.

Greatest infield or not, the Mets kept winning and winning. They rolled over the Padres and the Giants and the Cardinals and the Astros in mid-August, winning eleven of fifteen games. On August 18 their 9–1 win over San Diego gave them possession of first place by one game. At 74-48, they were keeping pace with the Yankees, who had the same record through as many games. Not fully satisfied with the roster, Phillips had made a series of moves before the July 31 trade deadline. In three separate deals he acquired Kenny Rogers, Shawon Dunston, and Darryl Hamilton. All three began paying immediate dividends.

Rogers, the disgruntled former Yankee castaway, had worn out his welcome as a member of the A's. Unhappy with the distance between Oakland and his Florida-based family, as well as the team's play, Rogers had wanted desperately to get out of the Bay Area. "Kenny never really wanted to be here," said A's general manager Billy Beane. "At times, this became a distraction. I had hoped the continued improvement of the team would help rope him into the momentum, but that didn't happen."[59]

Rejuvenated and happy to be back with Valentine, his first big-league manager, Rogers joined the Mets rotation and won his first five decisions. "When I heard we got Kenny Rogers, I thought, 'Great, we needed somebody to sing the national anthem,'" joked Hershiser. "Then somebody said something about chicken. Then I thought the Kenny we really got is probably tired of all these jokes, so we better back off."[60]

Hamilton joined the outfield full time and hit .410 in his first month as a Met. Dunston gave additional outfield depth and hit .309. Everything was working for New York. Fans, now giddy over the prospect of their team returning to the postseason, began chanting, "M-V-P!" when Ventura came to bat. The city as a whole was falling in love with this team. The Mets were thrilling to watch: a mix of wily veterans, top-tier talent, and young up-and-comers who made Shea the place to be in New York again. Ventura had even introduced a theme song for the team: The Doors' "L.A. Woman." The song's bridge features the repeated lyric "Mr. Mojo Risin'," a phrase that caught on quickly within the clubhouse as a sort of rallying cry. Soon the Mets had shirts featuring the phrase and were playing it in the clubhouse immediately after a win.

The Mets were cruising as August ended. They were still in the hunt for first but even if that fell short, they were three games ahead in the wild card. All they had to do was play consistent good baseball in September and a postseason berth was theirs. The team did even better than that, going 12-5 to start the month. With two weeks left to play, the Mets were just a game out of first and four ahead in the wild card. They flew out for a six-game road trip, with the first three games in Atlanta and a chance to take over the division and even, perhaps, clinch a playoff berth during the trip. It all felt so hopeful and joyous. It ended up almost destroying everything the team had accomplished.

• • •

On the morning of Sunday, July 18, it could have been said that the oddest thing about that day's game between the Yankees and Expos was that it was the first of the series. Regular-season series did not begin on a Sunday. Ever. They started on Mondays or Thursdays or Fridays or Tuesdays. Maybe even on a Wednesday every now and then. But a Sunday? No, that simply did not happen. Yet because of the All-Star break and the nature of interleague play, here the two teams were, beginning a three-game series at Yankee Stadium on a Sunday. Nearly forty-two thousand fans had come to the ballpark on this sweltering day, many of them to witness "Yogi Berra Day" at Yankee Stadium.

Berra was showered with gifts and words of praise. He was then joined by his former teammate Don Larsen, the battery mate with whom he had shared the only perfect game in World Series history in 1956. Larsen threw out the game's first pitch, with Berra on the receiving end.

After the pomp and ceremony, the game began. It was clear, from the start, that David Cone had a great feel for the ball. Cone, who sometimes seemingly threw a month's worth of pitches in a single start, needed just nine to retire the Expos in order in the first. In the second, he needed just eleven more. When the Yankees scored five runs in the bottom of the inning, there was curiosity over how Cone would react to sitting on the bench during that long inning in near 100-degree heat. He responded by striking out the side in the third, getting each batter on just four pitches. At this point people started to notice: hey, something might be going on here. Cone's pitches had an incredible amount of movement, and Montreal hitters could not lay off them. They were swinging at pitches that, to viewers at home, looked a foot out of the strike zone. To Expos hitters, though, those pitches looked like strikes until they didn't.

Nine up, nine down. Then, Mother Nature nearly put an end to the magic. In the bottom of the third, the skies opened up, and a thirty-three-minute rain delay ensued. Cone, who had been changing undershirts every inning because of the copious amount of sweat pouring out of him, kept loose by playing catch with a Yankees batboy inside the tunnel outside the clubhouse. Had the delay gone on much longer, it's doubtful that Torre would have allowed Cone to continue in the game. History was neat. Protecting your ace pitcher's arm for the playoffs was better.

When Cone went back out to the mound in the fourth it was clear the delay had no impact. He retired the side in order on just seven pitches. In the fifth, it took eleven. In the sixth, five more. By now fans at the ballpark knew full well what was happening. They were on their feet with every two-strike count and held their collective breath any time an Expo made contact. Cone struck out two more in the seventh, throwing fifteen pitches in the process, the most he would need in any one inning during this game. Twenty-one up, twenty-one down.

Yogi Berra had left the stadium but Don Larson remained in the owner's box, peering down at the field as he shared a nervous energy with those nearly forty-two thousand others. It took Cone seven pitches to get out of the eighth, the only minor scare occurring when Knoblauch had to go up the middle to field a ground ball. Some Expos had already discussed the idea of hitting the ball to the second baseman in the hope that he would commit an error. The crowd now watched, some in horror, waiting to see if Knoblauch would yip his throw. Instead, with no time to think about the play, Knoblauch turned, set himself, and fired a bullet strike to Tino Martinez for the out.

The stage was set for the ninth. Cone, coming into the inning have thrown just seventy-seven pitches—60 percent of the number he'd thrown in just six innings two starts earlier—began with a strikeout. The crowd was now on its feet, cheering with every pitch and booing home plate umpire Ted Barrett any time he called a ball. With one out, Cone threw a sharp breaking ball to pinch hitter Ryan McGuire, who inside-outed the ball toward left field. Ricky Ledée charged in and appeared to have a read on it. Then, in a split second, he lost sight of the ball, either in the glare of the sun or the shirts of the crowd or both. It was a scenario he had fretted about earlier, telling Sojo he was having trouble seeing the ball off the bat. Ledée, whose glove had been facing outward, appeared to involuntarily reset his glove to face inward, almost as though a spasm had occurred. As he did so, the ball dropped into it for the twenty-sixth out. Ledée had not actually watched the ball go into his glove. It was part reaction, part luck. "Oh boy. Oh boy," said a tense Tim McCarver, calling the game for the Yankees on FOX and no doubt echoing the sentiment of fans watching on television who had nearly had a coronary at the sight of Ledée's losing the ball and almost dropping it.

The last out was not nearly as stressful. Orlando Cabrera realized in the eighth inning how it was going to play out. "If he throws a perfect game," Cabrera told teammates, "I'm going to be the last out."[61] Cabrera was correct. In a self-fulfilling prophecy, he hit a Cone breaking ball for a weak pop-up in foul territory, where Brosius charged in and squeezed the ball for the twenty-seventh and final out. Cone, who had come close to throwing a no-hitter on several occasions, had now thrown the sixteenth perfect game in baseball history. He dropped to his knees, put his hands on his head, then embraced Girardi. "I just put a bear hug on him and took him down," said Cone. "I didn't want to let go. Somebody dragged me off him. I wasn't going to let go."[62]

Cone's perfect game acted as an adrenaline shot for the club. The Yankees took two of three from Montreal, swept the Devil Rays, and then made a statement by sweeping the Indians at home by a combined score of 32–10, most of which was driven by a 21–1 route in the second game of the series. The winner of that game was Irabu, who had solidified himself as part of the rotation after his early season troubles. He had begun the month by throwing his second career shutout, then had won two of his next four starts, pitching well enough in each to win. His performance against the Indians, who featured perhaps the game's best offense, was especially impressive: just one run and seven strikeouts over seven innings. Irabu finished July with a complete game win over Boston at Fenway Park. All told, he went 4-0 in July with a 2.64 ERA, easily the team's most reliable starter during that period. He won AL Pitcher of the Month for the second time in his career. He even showed a humorous side: for Steinbrenner's birthday, on July 4, Irabu got him a mechanical toad that could ribbit, a reference to the Boss's toad remark from spring training. Irabu's performances would falter starting in August, as he gave up a smattering of five- and six-run efforts that eroded Joe Torre's confidence in him. He made the postseason roster but would not appear in any meaningful innings.

The Cleveland series also showcased the team's shortstop. Derek Jeter had accomplished in three short years what most players—actually most human beings—did not accomplish in a lifetime. He had won two world championships, collected over two hundred hits in a season, won the Rookie of the Year award, finished in the top three in MVP voting, achieved nationwide notoriety as a matinee idol–type, and had dated Mariah Carey—and all before the age of twenty-five. There wasn't much more for him to prove.

Jeter was not satisfied with all those accomplishments. He wanted to keep winning and winning until he'd eclipsed Berra's record of ten World Series rings, and even then he'd keep going. In 1999 Jeter's performance reached another level, ultimately the best season of his career. It started with three hits and a home run on Opening Day. There were three more hits the next day and ultimately nine multi-hit games in April. More than just the hits, Jeter was hitting for power at a clip unmatched in his career. He belted five home runs in April, half as many as he had hit in 1996 and 1997. In May he recorded at least one hit in twenty-five of twenty-eight games, adding eleven more multi-hit games and four home runs. Jeter made the All-Star team for the second consecutive year, and by the break he was hitting .371 with a 1.065 OPS. He started the second half with an eleven-game hitting streak, which culminated in a weekend series against Cleveland. In the first game he delivered a two-out, bases-loaded hit in the bottom of the tenth inning that turned an 8–7 deficit into a 9–8 win. In the concluding game he hit his fourteenth home run of the season.

Jeter was producing numbers that no Yankees shortstop had ever put up. He was also establishing the credibility within the clubhouse that would ultimately lead to his being named captain in 2003. Two weeks after the Cleveland series, the Yankees were in Seattle when a bench-clearing brawl ensued. It began in the eighth, when, after giving up a three-run home run to Alex Rodriguez, Jason Grimsley hit the next batter, Edgar Martinez. Grimsley was ejected immediately. In the top of the ninth inning, with one out, Mariners pitcher Frankie Rodriguez plunked Knoblauch in the waist. The home plate umpire warned Rodriguez but did not eject him. Mariners manager Lou Piniella came out to remove the pitcher anyway. As he did, an irate Yankees bench collectively jawed at Rodriguez and Piniella. The Seattle manager had a history of throwing at Yankees, especially O'Neill, and the team had tired of it.

Rodriguez walked toward the Seattle dugout, yelling back at several Yankees. Suddenly, Girardi emerged, and the two began hustling toward each other for a direct confrontation. In a flash both benches emptied, with fights breaking out at home plate, along the foul line, and near the Mariners' dugout. Players were tossed everywhere, some too hurt initially to get back up. Chili Davis had Seattle coach Steve Smith in a choke hold. Williams had tossed Seattle catcher Dan Wilson to the ground, where he remained for nearly a minute before finally being able to get up.

It was a total melee. And as it all happened, Jeter stood on the outside of the pile with his friend, Alex Rodriguez, smiling and joking around. The scene angered Chad Curtis. After order had been restored, he confronted Jeter in the dugout, where everyone, including TV cameras, could see. He wanted to know why, as his teammates lay bruised and battered on the field, he had been putzing around and not in the middle of the scrum. Curtis even went so far as to tell Jeter, "You are a good player but you don't know how to play the game."[63] The confrontation continued after the game in the locker room, in front of reporters, before Sojo broke the two up.

Maybe Curtis was right to do what he did. Maybe he was wrong. It did not matter though. People loved Jeter. Curtis, on the other hand, not so much. Curtis had always been somewhat of a polarizing figure, or at least as close to one as was possible in the Yankees' clubhouse in those years. Sporting a rigid buzz cut that would make a marine drill sergeant proud, Curtis gave every appearance of a straight-shooting do-gooder. His overt religiousness made some teammates uncomfortable. He would bicker with Jeter over the shortstop's choice of clubhouse music, recoiling over any song that included profanity in it. Even the way he hurled himself into the air on the follow-through of his throws from the outfield just seemed a bit . . . unnecessary.

Now Curtis had gone a step too far. His criticisms irked both teammates and the front office. It spoke volumes of Curtis's standing in the clubhouse that the organization stood by a still relatively young player who had not engaged in a brawl over an eight-year veteran who had been in the thick of one. The team did not take immediate action, but Curtis's days were numbered; there was no way he would be back in pinstripes in 2000. He was traded to Texas that off-season, where he would tell teammates that if they did not accept Jesus Christ as their savoir, they would go to hell. After retirement Curtis was convicted of several counts of criminal sexual conduct with minors. He served nearly seven years in prison before being paroled.

The Seattle brawl took place during the Yankees' first-ever visit to Safeco Field. The $517 million facility, which opened in the middle of the season, would not have been possible without the Yankees. Their Game Five, extra-inning loss to the Mariners in the 1995 ALDS had created enough momentum for the state legislature to configure a funding structure to make the stadium a reality and keep the team in Seattle. The ballpark was, in one way, a blessing for New York, as the Kingdome had felt like a house of horrors throughout most of the 1990s, with the team going just 25-32 there, including the postseason. So the Yankees were not sad to see the Kingdome go. The feeling might have grown stronger after New York swept its first series at Safeco. The sweep put the Yankees seven and a half games over Boston in the division, and while the Red Sox would make it close in mid-September, the race for first was essentially over.

August and September would play out with the Yankees largely looking ahead to the defending their title in the postseason. There were just a few problems, specifically with their two Texan pitchers who were supposed to make the rotation nearly unbeatable: Clemens and Pettitte.

Roger Clemens was supposed to run away with another Cy Young Award, maybe even became the first pitcher in over thirty years to win at least thirty games in a season. The Yankees had been so good in 1998, and he'd been so dominant in Toronto that those both seemed like real possibilities. Instead he struggled all season long. After his stint on the disabled list in May, his performances got seemingly better. He won four games in June, his implosion against the Mets at Yankee Stadium the only blemish. But outside of a shutout performance against the Tigers, he never really looked like the Clemens who seemed destined for the Hall of Fame. His strikeouts per nine innings was among the worst of his career, and he was allowing more base runners than he ever had. While he still allowed fewer home runs than most pitchers, he was allowing an average of one per game, something he'd only done once before. He looked like the rotation's fourth or fifth starter, not the ace.

After getting hit hard by the Mets again in early July, Clemens got shelled by the Braves. He stood at 8-4 with a 4.98 ERA, easily on pace to be the worst of his career. On the last day of the month he made his first start at Fenway Park as a Yankee. He slogged through five long innings, giving up four runs and striking out only two in a no-decision. There was no big moment, no dominating performance like he'd had in 1997 with the Blue Jays, when he had returned to Fenway and struck out sixteen.

Fans could not understand it and they were starting to tire of Clemens's performances. David Wells had pitched shockingly poorly in Toronto but in July had been firm, tossing a shutout and giving up just thirteen runs over five starts in the month. Was it possible the Yankees would have been better off having never made the deal for the reigning AL Cy Young Award winner?

August was an even more perplexing month for the Rocket. He was battered for nine total runs against the Mariners and A's, then came within one out of a shutout against the Twins, even though he struck out only two batters. Five days later, against those same Twins, he struck out seven but gave up five runs and got the loss. In his last start of the month, the same

Mariners who had gotten him for four runs in Seattle were overmatched, striking out nine times as Clemens held them scoreless over eight innings. Yet even then Clemens seemed to labor, needing 138 pitches to get through the performance.

Then came September. Six starts. Four losses. Three starts in which he gave up at least five runs. There was just no consistency whatsoever to his appearances. He ended the year 14-10, posting the highest ERA and worst WHIP and strikeouts-to-walks ratio of his career. It had been a baffling season, so much so that there were serious questions about whether the Yankees could rely on Clemens in the postseason, especially if their paths crossed with Boston, where Clemens's emotions might get the better of him, or with the Mets, who had tortured him over the last few seasons of interleague play.

If Clemens's season had been baffling, Andy Pettitte's had been disastrous. The lefty, despite being in just his fifth season, was in some ways the rock of the team's rotation. While Cone had dealt with injuries, Irabu with moodiness, and Wells with stubbornness over the last few years, Pettitte had always been steady and reliable. His 1997 season was arguably better than his performance in 1996, when he had finished second in Cy Young voting. His 1998 season had also been solid, with his winning sixteen games. But as the team hit a skid in September, Pettitte endured a rough stretch where he allowed thirty-seven base runners and eighteen runs over twenty-one innings. His ALCS start, in which the Indians hit four home runs off him, did not help alleviate concern that something might be wrong with the lefty. He silenced those critics with his shutout performance in the clinching game of the World Series. Still, within the organization there was worry that the pitcher might have already surpassed his peak in New York.

Pettitte did not squelch those fears during the first months of the '99 season. The Royals got him for seven runs in his last start of April. Two starts later, the Angels got him for six more. In three of his June starts he yielded at least six runs or more, including against the Marlins and Tigers, two of the worst teams in the league. While he was walking batters at a normal clip for him and while he'd never been a strikeout pitcher in the mold of Cone or Clemens, his strikeout numbers were down, and hitters were making more and better contact against him. Even when Pettitte pitched well, he found himself struggling to get further than the sixth inning.

A July 5 loss to the Orioles put Pettitte at 5-7 with a 5.56 ERA, by far the worst numbers of any starter on the club. He won two of his next three starts, despite giving up thirty base runners in seventeen and two-thirds innings, pitching just well enough to win. It was not enough, though, to please George Steinbrenner.

The Boss, for whatever reason, never warmed up to Pettitte. It was odd, given Pettitte's level of success in both the regular season and the playoffs. But Steinbrenner did not feel the same way about the lefty as he did about a David Cone or a Paul O'Neill. After the 1996 season, in which Pettitte went 21-8 and came within just a few votes of winning the Cy Young Award, Steinbrenner nixed a proposed three-year, multi-million-dollar contract extension. The excuse was concern over Pettitte's elbow. Pettitte responded by having arguably the best season of his career in 1997.

Money was in the equation again in 1999, as Pettitte was eligible for arbitration after the season. Steinbrenner was already apoplectic over the Yankees' having lost their arbitration cases to Jeter and Rivera before the start of the year. He pinned those perceived failures brutally on Cashman, using them as an excuse to withhold a portion of Cashman's 1998 World Series bonus money. He did not want to take the risk that Pettitte would also win more money out of him, no matter how bad his numbers were. Steinbrenner told Cashman to find someone to take Pettitte off the Yankees' hands.

While the GM put out feelers, Pettitte hit his low point of the season in his next start, a July 28 appearance in Chicago against the White Sox. Trying to maintain a 2–2 tie in the bottom of the fourth, Pettitte faced Chris Singleton with runners on second and third and one out. Pettitte quickly moved the count to 0-2. Then he did something he almost never did. With two strikes on a batter, Cone had a habit of dropping down in his pitching motion and releasing the ball from a sidearm delivery. The Laredo, it was called. The idea was that if the pitcher changed the arm angle, the hitter would be thrown off and would be more likely to swing and miss or look at a called strike three. El Duque threw from a variety of angles too, though he did it all the time, not just on two strikes. Still, these guys were known for it. Even David Wells had done it every now and then.

Andy Pettitte never did it though. He always threw over the top—same motion, same delivery. Every time. But here, going through the worst season of his life, desperate to keep his team in the game, and pitching under the pressure of an owner who had made it clear he no longer wanted him on the team, Pettitte dropped down and threw his 0-2 pitch from the side. Singleton lined it into right field for a single, giving the White Sox the lead. Torre was incredulous and angry. He did not understand what Pettitte thought he would accomplish by trying such a move. That was enough for the Yankees' manager. He took Andy out of the game immediately.

A clearly befuddled Pettitte could not explain his thinking afterward. "I tried to make up something," he told reporters. "I've been working in my bullpen sessions on dropping down against left-handed batters because they've been leaning over the plate against me. It was a bad decision on my part."[64]

There were three days left before the trade deadline, and Cashman had a deal in place with the Phillies. New York would get pitcher Adam Eaton and center fielder Reggie Taylor plus a Minor Leaguer. But neither Cashman nor Torre had their hearts in the deal. They believed in Pettitte and felt eventually he would come around, probably just in time for the postseason. Stottlemyre, meanwhile, was dumbfounded. "I can't believe you would even consider doing [the trade]," he told Steinbrenner on a conference call, hours before the deadline, that included Cashman and Torre.[65]

The trade never went through. Steinbrenner made clear that if Pettitte continued to falter, it would be on Cashman's and Torre's heads. "Our manager seems to think things are all right," Steinbrenner said after no deal was made. "I have great confidence in our manager."[66]

While Pettitte made it past the non-waiver trade deadline, the threat still loomed that Steinbrenner would force his exile before August 31, when another trade deadline approached allowing teams to move players who had cleared through the waiver process first. With that threat still in the air, Pettitte proceeded to have possibly the best month of his career. Over six starts he allowed just nine earned runs, including two outings in which he yielded no runs at all. He won five of those six starts, his only loss coming courtesy of a single unearned run against the Royals, a game played under swirling rumors that Pettitte's time in New York was about to end. Having not made it past seven-plus innings all season, he pitched eight innings in four of the starts. In the process he lowered his ERA from 5.65 to 4.49. The second trade deadline came and went with Pettitte still a Yankee. While he ultimately finished the season with some of his worst career numbers, Pettitte's August performance salvaged the year. If he could come up big in the postseason, it would almost all be forgotten.

That postseason became official when the team clinched a playoff spot during the final week of the year. The Yankees ended the season with a loss in Tampa, finishing at 98-64. It wasn't the '98 Yankees, but it really never could have been. That was a once-in-a-lifetime team. The '99 Yankees were nothing to be ashamed of, though. Derek Jeter and Bernie Williams each had career years. Williams, after nearly leaving during the off-season, hit a career high .342 and had set additional career highs in runs scored, walks, RBIS, on-base percentage, and total bases. In just about any other season, Jeter might have won the MVP award. But with so many players also having career years, he finished sixth, despite setting career highs in runs scored, hits, triples, home runs, RBIS, walks, batting average, on-base percentage, slugging percentage, OPS, and total bases. Chili Davis could not maintain his torrid start but still managed to hit 19 home runs, giving him a nice round 350 for his career. Davis retired after the end of the postseason.

El Duque established himself as the team's pitching ace, winning seventeen games. Rivera saved forty-five games and posted a 1.83 ERA. The 1999 Yankees had the misfortune of living under the shadow of the previous year's team during the regular season. Now that the postseason was upon them, they would have to deal with those comparisons anew. In addition to the question of whether they could equal the '98 team and win it all, they also had to ask if they'd have to do it under the added pressure of potentially playing the Red Sox and/or the Mets.

• • •

The disappointing ending to the their 1998 season still clung in the air as the Mets looked up at the Turner Field scoreboard on September 23: Mets, 3; Braves, 6.

Three brutal days in Atlanta were now over. It was not supposed to have gone down like this. The Mets had come into the Peach State on a wave of good energy and great playing. Taking two out of three games would have meant a tie for first with just nine games remaining. Even just one of three would have kept the deficit to two games. It would be difficult but certainly not impossible to make up in nine games.

Instead everything seemed to go wrong. In the first game Reed and John Smoltz duked it out into the seventh inning, each allowing only a run. Inning after inning the Mets put runners on base only to fall short of the big hit needed to drive in a run. In the bottom of the eighth, Braves third baseman Chipper Jones hit his second solo home run of the game, giving Atlanta the lead. It was an especially sweet moment for Jones, who reveled in besting the Mets and taunting a New York fan base that had been brutal to him over the years. The fans' anger came not just from Jones's brashness but also because, often, he was finding ways to beat the Mets. His four home runs in that series were proof enough. Mets fans pushed back over the years by yelling a string of obscenities. A particular fan favorite was to refer to Jones by his given first name, Larry. Maybe it irked Jones; maybe it didn't. Either way, the result was the same: he tended to win more battles against the Mets than he lost.

Down a run in the ninth, New York faced Braves closer John Rocker, who was in the midst of a dominating season. The lefty averaged nearly thirteen strikeouts per nine innings, with opponents hitting a meager .180 off him. Rocker struck out Ventura, Dunston, and Agbayani, all caught looking, to end the game.

The next night the Mets battled back from an early 2–0 deficit when Piazza homered off Tom Glavine to tie the game in the fourth. Hershiser kept the game tied until the seventh before allowing a run. In the eighth, the Mets loaded the bases with one out for Bonilla.

It had been a difficult return to New York for Bonilla. Early in spring training he had suffered a partial ligament tear in his knee. He never truly recovered and got off to a slow start, his average falling below .200, the Mendoza line, on April 16 and never going over it again the rest of the year. He also feuded with Valentine over playing time. On June 8 Bonilla told the Mets he was unavailable to pinch-hit. The next day, before the game, Bonilla and Valentine got into a heated exchange in the dugout. Afterward Valentine decided to take a jab at Bonilla by yelling to the rest of the team, "Way to go, you guys. We've got the best 24-man roster in the league."[67] Bonilla refused again that night to pinch-hit. The Mets even placed him on waivers, hoping someone—anyone—would take him off their hands. No one did.

Injuries limited Bonilla's playing until July, when he went back on the disabled list because of his knee. Even the seemingly simply act of placing him on the DL caused an issue. Valentine told reporters he had heard that Bonilla had asked to be placed on the disabled list. "Bobby said that?" Bonilla asked reporters when told of Valentine's comments. "That's funny. He didn't talk to me."[68] It then became a three-way game of telephone among Valentine, Bonilla, and Phillips over who had told whom what and when.

When Bonilla returned from the disabled list, it was strictly in the role of pinch hitter or late-game replacement. Now, in the biggest moment of the year, the Mets had put him up to bat to replace Ordóñez. Bonilla struck out swinging, and the Mets failed to score. Atlanta tacked on two more in the eighth, and Rocker closed out the game again.

Jones struck again the next night, hitting a three-run home run in the fifth to erase a 2–1 Mets lead. The home run gave him seven for the year against the Mets, along with fourteen RBIs in just twenty-nine at bats. The lead could have been 3–1, but in the fifth, Henderson, proceeding gingerly on a double by Alfonzo, ran through third-base coach Cookie Rojas's stop sign and was thrown out at the plate. This time the Mets put up a fight in the ninth, bringing the tying run to the plate with one out. In desperate need of a big hit, they never got one. The Braves completed the sweep, and as they congratulated one another after the game, many Mets players sat on the bench in disbelief. "Let's face it, we got our butts kicked," said Piazza. "They outpitched us, outhit us, outhustled us. We can't be looking at the wild card or the division. We have to look at ourselves and admit we played some pretty bad baseball."[69]

"If this is the moment of truth for the Mets, then here is the real truth. . . . They better hope somebody else beats the Braves in the playoffs," wrote Lupica. "The Mets never do. They couldn't beat the Braves last season when all the money was on the table. They couldn't beat them this week in Atlanta. In just about every big moment, the Mets played small."[70]

Hoping to rebound against a subpar Phillies team, the Mets found more misery in Philadelphia. They carried a 2–1 lead into the bottom of the eighth of the first game with two outs and a runner on. Lefty Bobby Abreu was due up, but rather than go to John Franco, Valentine brought in Benitez, a move that was widely second-guessed afterward. Abreu lined a game-tying double, then scored on a single. The Mets lost, 3–2. Not only was the division race all but officially over, but now the Reds had also climbed all the way back to within a game of tying New York for the wild card.

Philadelphia won again the next day, after which Valentine told reporters that if the Mets failed to make the playoffs, he should be fired. In the series finale, after the Phillies took a 3–0 lead going into the sixth inning, the guy who selected music for Veterans Stadium played "Taps." The Mets trailed 3–2 in the ninth, when they loaded the bases with one out. To this point nothing had gone right in the last week for New York. There had been no big, timely hits. Starters threw perfectly until one mistake cost them two or maybe three runs. Relievers gave up untimely hits when it looked like they were going to escape jams. Valentine's moves all seemed to backfire. No scintilla of luck appeared to be on their side. The previous day Agbayani had lined a ball up the middle in the eighth for a certain hit. It would have brought the Mets within a run and put the tying run on third. Instead Philly second baseman David Doster, playing in the final week of his two-year Major League career, reached up with every inch of his 5-foot-10 frame and snared it, then flipped to second for the double play. Brutal.

Now here were the Mets, in need of a win like possibly never before in their regular season history, with the bases loaded in the ninth and the fastest man in the history of the game at the plate: Rickey Henderson. It was the perfect setup for a perfect moment. Instead Henderson reached for a breaking ball and hit a flare that short-hopped right to Doster at second. The Phillies easily turned the 4–6–3 double play to end the game. Frustration boiled over in the dugout as Ordóñez kicked at objects and other players stared out blankly at the Veterans Stadium playing field. "Rickey's got nothing to say about this crazy stuff going on," said Henderson afterward. "Ride it out. Ride it out."[71] Ordóñez, sitting in front of his locker looking as if someone had run over his dog, used a Cuban expression to sum up what was happening to the team. "So much swimming, only to die on the shore," said Ordóñez.[72]

The loss had officially eliminated the Mets from the division race, and more jarringly, it had put them a game out of the wild-card spot with just six games to play. It was the first time since July 21 that the team was not leading either the division or the wild-card race. It was an unbelievable scenario that only got worse. The next day, an off day for the Mets, they lost another half game when the Reds won again. New York then began a three-game series with the Braves. Just a week earlier this series would possibly have decided the division winner. Now it was mathematically possible that it would result in the elimination of the Mets from postseason contention.

That scenario grew disturbingly closer when the Braves shellacked the Mets in the first game, 9–3, while the Reds beat the Astros. Hershiser lasted just twenty-four pitches in the shortest outing of his career, leaving the game with one out in the first. "They beat the hell out of us again," said Piazza in a quiet clubhouse afterward.[73]

Chipper Jones could not help but point out the collapse of his division rival. "A little bit surprised but it just goes to show you how when one team is going good and one team is going bad how quickly things can get away from you, how quickly things can snowball," said Jones. "We certainly expected a team the quality of the Mets to play us game for game."[74]

The Mets had lost seven in a row and were now two and a half games out. They finally beat the Braves in the second game, thanks in part to an Olerud grand slam. But even with a Cincinnati loss, it felt like too little, too late. The following night, in an incredible game played before more than forty-eight thousand fans on a September Thursday night, the Mets lost a heartbreaker in eleven innings. Valentine, arguing a called strike in the ninth, perhaps out of sheer frustration over his team's collapse, was ejected from the game.

Jones again expressed his delight in the Mets' misfortune. "We weren't going to let anyone slip in the back door of the playoffs by beating the Atlanta Braves. Mission accomplished," said Jones.[75] He then, with much glee, added, "This is the next-best thing to winning the World Series."[76]

A season that had been so full of hope was all but over. The Mets were now two games behind the Reds and Astros for the wild-card spot with three games left. All it would take was a single win by both the Reds and Astros and a single Mets' loss, and the 1999 season would be forever marred by the complete collapse of the team in the final two weeks. "Oh, the Mets are still mathematically breathing, if you see much hope in being two games out with three to go," wrote the *Bergen Record*'s Bob Klapisch. "But Thursday night's 4–3 loss to the Braves all but flipped the calendar to the new millennium at Shea, where, for the second time in two seasons, the Mets have thrown away a wild-card berth."[77]

As fans headed out of the ballpark that night and players headed back to the clubhouse, few, if they were being honest, thought the Mets could pull it off. It just wasn't in the cards that year. New York was going to be eliminated from contention that weekend. The sooner everyone accepted that, the better off they were going to be.

• • •

Friday night, October 1, 1999. Top of the eighth. Shea Stadium. Infield single by Warren Morris ties the game at 2–2. Bases loaded. Two outs. John Franco goes 3-0 on Adrian Brown.

That was the moment when it felt like the Mets' season would end. They had just blown a 2–0 lead to the Pirates in the course of seven batters. As Franco ran the count to 3-0, fans at Shea hung their heads, then looked up at the out-of-town scoreboard to see that while the Astros were losing, the Reds were beating the Brewers in Milwaukee. The end was near.

Then, after two weeks of everything going wrong, something went right for the New York Mets. Franco came back with three straight strikes, two of them probably out of the strike zone. But the umpire gave him both calls and with it a strikeout to end the inning. In Milwaukee the Brewers staged a late-inning comeback, tying the game and sending it to extra innings.

Back at Shea, the game also reached extra innings. In the eleventh, as "Believe" signs flashed across the stadium, Ventura lined a single to win the game. Not much later Marquis Grissom made a two-out diving catch in the tenth to prevent the Reds from scoring the go-ahead runs. In the bottom of the inning, Milwaukee won the game. The Astros lost as well.

The Mets were still alive, and their good fortune continued into the next day. Scoreless into the sixth, they plated two runs off an error and put the game away in the eighth when Piazza hit his fortieth home run of the year. Meanwhile, though the Astros won, the Brewers pounded the Reds for fourteen hits and ten runs. In less than twenty-four hours, the Mets had gone from pull-the-plug status to now being tied for the wild-card spot. They were the Miracle Mets again.

It came down to the final day of the season. Though they were tied for the wild card, the Reds were now also a game behind the Houston Astros for the division lead, and the Mets were also just a game behind the Astros. Should Houston lose that Sunday and both New York and Cincinnati win, the Mets would win the wild card, while the Reds and Astros would play a one-game playoff for the division. If all three teams won, or if the Mets and Reds both lost, the two teams would play a one-game playoff in Cincinnati. If the Mets won and Cincinnati lost, the Mets would win the wild card.

These were crazy scenarios, made all the crazier by how close the Mets were to elimination on Friday night. With their season on the brink and fifty thousand exuberant fans at Shea, Valentine gave the ball to Orel Hershiser. Bulldog did not disappoint, allowing a run in the first but shutting down the Pirates from there before turning the ball over to the bullpen in the sixth. A Hamilton double tied the game in the fourth, and then it became a matter of which bullpen would blink first. The combination of Cook, Mahomes, Wendell, and Benitez pitched three and two-thirds scoreless innings, getting the game into the bottom of the ninth tied at 1–1. After one-out singles by Mora and Alfonzo, Pittsburgh intentionally walked Olerud to face Piazza.

Normally a team would not want to walk the bases loaded for Piazza, but the catcher was leading the league that year in grounding into double plays.

Former Met Brad Clontz entered the game in a nearly impossible scenario. While there was no way to pitch around Piazza, he essentially did just that. His first pitch sailed outside the zone and bounced in the left-handed batter's box, caroming up and over the catcher to the backstop. "I knew he was going to throw some pitch in the dirt to try to get a double play," said Mora, the last player the Mets had cut in spring training but who had been brought up later in the year. "[Third-base coach] Cookie Rojas told me to be ready for him to throw a pitch in the dirt and he did."[78]

Mora scored easily to win the game, and his teammates came flying out of the dugout to smother him. Valentine ran up to player after player, putting his index finger up and yelling, "One more game. We've got one more game."[79]

The Mets did not know what to do next. They had guaranteed themselves at least one more game that year, but where it would be was still unknown. The Astros had plated four runs in the first inning of their game and never looked back, so a three-way tie was not going to happen. But the Reds game in Milwaukee, which was supposed to start at 4 p.m. EST, was in a rain delay that was not going to end any time soon. If the Reds lost that game, the Mets would head for Phoenix to face the Arizona Diamondbacks in the National League Division Series. If the Reds won, the Mets would go to Cincinnati that night for a one-game playoff to be played the next day. "The big controversy was whether or not we should be allowed to celebrate if we win the game, because we haven't won anything," recalled Valentine. "So I don't think that team ever took a picture together because I guess whoever it was in the front office decided that it wouldn't be proper to celebrate."[80]

And so the Mets waited. And waited. And waited. Finally, at 8:45 p.m., with the Reds' game still in a delay, they boarded buses, went to the airport, and flew to Cincinnati. If the Reds lost, they'd simply get back in the air and head to Phoenix.

After a five-hour, forty-five-minute rain delay, the Brewers and Reds finally began play around 10 p.m. EST. In 40-degree weather with, at best, a few hundred fans in the stands, most of them Reds fans, Cincinnati jumped out to a 5–0 lead in the third inning and coasted to a 7–1 win. The game ended at 12:35 a.m. Five minutes later the Mets arrived at their hotel in Cincinnati. Some players, fueled by adrenaline and hunger, stayed in the hotel lobby and ate pizza. Others went to bed, hoping to somehow get a good night's sleep before the most important game the Mets had played in over a decade.

• • •

Several Mets had banner years in 1999. Piazza had the second-best year of his Hall of Fame career, tying career highs with forty home runs and 124 RBIS. Ventura had definitively the best year of his career, setting career highs in base hits, RBIS, batting average, and Wins above Replacement (WAR). Cedeño, under the tutelage of Henderson, broke the team's single-season stolen base record when he swiped sixty-six bags. Henderson achieved his highest batting and on-base percentages in six years. Olerud led the team in on-base percentage. Leiter, Hershiser, Yoshi, and Reed rebounded from horrible starts to the season by being rocks from June until September, collectively winning forty-nine games, almost all of them coming after June 6. The bullpen had been even better, with Cook winning ten games and Franco and Benitez combining for forty-one saves and 169 strikeouts in 118⅔ innings.

There were so many big performances that had gotten the Mets to this one-game playoff at Riverfront Stadium. Yet it was Edgardo Alfonzo who many considered the MVP of the team. Alfonzo had had good seasons in 1997 and 1998, but the Mets had been hoping for more. They felt Edgardo could hit with greater power, which, in turn, would change the dynamic of the lineup with his hitting in front of Piazza. In 1999 Alfonzo rewarded them for their patience, hitting a career-high twenty-seven home runs and driving in a career high 108 runs while also establishing a career high with 315 total bases. He had been a pest to pitchers before 1999. Now he was dangerous.

All year Alfonzo had set the tone. That is why it hardly could have been surprising when, as the second batter of the wild-card game in Cincinnati, he drilled a two-run home run to center field. The stadium fell quiet as Mets spilled out of the dugout, screaming in exuberance. Just six pitches into the game, the Mets had put the Reds in a seemingly insurmountable hole. From there on out, it was the Al Leiter show.

After allowing a one-out single in the second, Leiter did not give up another hit until the ninth inning. "I don't know if he's ever pitched a better game," said Valentine. "He had this look in his eye. When his mind is right, his arm is right."[81]

All the while, the Mets gradually expanded their lead: a walk by Ventura for a run; a home run by Henderson for another; a double by Alfonzo for the last one. With that the Mets had a 5–0 lead in the ninth. Leiter allowed two base runners before inducing a line out to, appropriately, Alfonzo, who caught it for the game's final out. "I really wanted to experience being on the field as one of the nine when it ended," said Leiter.[82]

A cathartic celebration ensued in the Mets' clubhouse. "Here's to the front-runners who counted us out," yelled Todd Pratt. "You know who you are."[83] His comments were directed at members of the media. "This is one of the unspeakable indignities sportswriters endure, suffering insults of backup catchers," wrote the *Daily News*'s Mark Kriegel in response.[84]

Bobby Valentine took the moment in. No one had managed more games since divisional play had begun in 1969 and not made the postseason than Valentine. That streak was over. "I'm drained, I'm excited, I'm elated," said Valentine, drenched in champagne. "I'm thankful. It's a lot of emotions. I don't know if I'm smart enough to tell you all of them."[85]

At 97-66, the Mets had achieved their best regular season since 1988. The late September falter, which could have gone down as the biggest collapse in team history, was relegated to a mere stumbling block. It also marked the first time that the Mets and Yankees had ever reached the playoffs in the same year. Now, given the sudden turnaround in the Mets' fortunes, talk of a subway series was everywhere in the city. First, though, both teams had to win their Division Series match-ups and get past their League Championship Series. The Mets, after celebrating their miraculous ride to the postseason, headed straight for Phoenix and a showdown with the Diamondbacks.

• • •

A mixture of loud boos and inauthentic cheers greeted Roger Clemens as he walked off the mound at Fenway Park, the autumn sun gradually setting on New England during the mid-fall day. It was not supposed to go this way. Game Three of the ALCS was supposed to be one of the greatest postseason pitching match-ups in history: Clemens versus Pedro Martinez. It had the added drama of Clemens taking the mound in the place he had called home for thirteen seasons, with a normally unfriendly crowd even more hostile toward a man they considered a traitor to Boston. Instead of rising to the moment, Clemens pitched as he had for much of that season.

Two hitters into the game, Boston led, 2–0. It took the Red Sox just one turn through the order before they were hitting for a team cycle. With the Yankees already down 4–0, Torre removed Clemens from the game with no outs in the third and a runner on base. The Rocket had faced fifteen batters, allowing eight of them to reach base.

When Torre replaced Clemens with Irabu, who had yet to pitch in the postseason in his career, the manager seemed to acknowledge that this game was a lost cause. Irabu gave up a home run to the first batter he faced. Martinez then took over the game, mixing his changeup and curveball to dominate the Yankees over seven innings of two-hit ball. It was not surprising. Pedro had just completed one of the greatest regular-season pitching performances ever, finishing the year 23-4 with 313 strikeouts. A month earlier at Yankee Stadium, he had given up only a single hit, a Chili Davis home run, while striking out seventeen Yankees. Pedro's sheer dominance over them that year had players and fans hoping that they would not have to face him in a Game Seven. "Certainly, we don't want to see it go seven," said Cone. "That's for sure."[86]

The Game Three loss shook the seemingly invincible nature of the Yankees' postseason run. They had steamrolled through the Rangers in the Division Series, sweeping them for a second consecutive year. Just as in '98, the Yankees pitching staff held Texas to a single run in the whole series. Bernie Williams led the team's offense in Game One, driving in six. In Game Three, Darryl Strawberry, who had returned from his drug suspension to play the last month of the season, hit a three-run home run for the game's only scoring. "I tried something different in this batting practice," said Strawberry, referring to his session before Game Three. "I tried to hit the ball the other way a lot. I figured that's the way I've been getting pitched. I basically went up there with an idea."[87]

The Yankees celebrated the sweep with non-alcoholic champagne so that Strawberry could participate. "We voted and it took three seconds for a unanimous decision," said Curtis.[88]

The Red Sox, meanwhile, had come back from a 2–0 deficit against the Indians to launch themselves into the ALCS, the two rivals now facing off in the postseason for the first time ever. With a supercharged atmosphere at Yankee Stadium for Game One, Boston quickly jumped out to a 3–0 lead. Eventually the Yankees tied it, sending the game to extra innings. In the top of the tenth, with a runner on first, Brosius fielded a ground ball and threw to Knoblauch to start a double play. Knoblauch dropped the ball, but the second-base umpire ruled, incorrectly, that he'd had control of the ball and dropped it on the transfer. The Yankees caught a break and kept the game tied headed into the bottom of the inning. Leading off, Bernie Williams sent a Rod Beck fastball over the center-field wall for a game-winning home run. "He hit the crap out of it. What can I say? I tip my hat to him," said Beck.[89]

A blown call by the ump and a walk-off home run by Bernie in an ALCS Game One: the Yankees had seen this before. "I feel like we stole this one," said Jeter.[90]

Timely hitting and big strikeouts by Mendoza and Rivera had given the Yankees a 3–2 win in Game Two, setting the stage for the Clemens-Martinez match-up. The resulting 13–1 loss was their worst ever in the postseason. Boston set an ALCS record for hits, total bases, extra-base hits, and margin of victory in a single game. The Yankees now needed the old Andy Pettitte to show up in Game Four. Strawberry provided support when, with the crowd chanting, "Just say no" (a reference to the anti-drug slogan of the 1980s), he drilled a home run off the foul pole in right field. Pettitte, meanwhile kept the Sox in check, allowing just two runs into the eighth inning. He departed with a 3–2 lead when Rivera entered with a runner on first and one out. John Valentin sent a ground ball toward Knoblauch, who fielded it, made a phantom tag on the runner headed to second, and threw to first for the inning-ending double play. Replays showed that Knoblauch had missed the runner by several inches, but the Yankees still got the call, their second favorable missed call of the series. In the ninth, a Ledée grand slam put the game out of reach. Red Sox fans, fed up with missed calls, began tossing debris onto the field.

Game Five felt like a formality. Boston, still in the midst of the Curse, seemed resolved to the outcome after the breaks had all gone New York's way. As if to try and feebly push back on the bad karma, the Sox had Babe Ruth's daughter throw out the first pitch. As Bucky Dent took in the game from the stands, Jeter hit a two-run home run in the first inning, and the Yankees never looked back. With George Steinbrenner, dressed in a parka and wearing thick gloves to protect against a bitter cold night, watching on, the Yankees won, 6–1, to take the pennant. El Duque, 1-0 with a 1.80 ERA and thirteen strikeouts over two starts, won MVP honors.

Now the Yankees headed back to New York to see if, ultimately, they were going to be flying to Atlanta later that week or staying right there in the Big Apple for the biggest battle the city had seen in four decades.

• • •

No team had gotten to the postseason faster than the Arizona Diamondbacks. Brought into the National League in 1998, they had suffered through the typical expansion-team woes in their initial season. Owner Jerry Colangelo, however, had no desire to go through a prolonged period of slow growth before his team became competitive. Instead he stacked the roster with veteran outfielders like Steve Finley and Luis Gonzalez, who joined infielders Matt Williams and Jay Bell. Then he signed Randy Johnson and former Met Armando Reynoso to bolster a starting rotation that already had Andy Benes. All four proved to be stellar additions, particularly Johnson, who struck out 364 batters while winning the Cy Young Award.

Led by former Yankees manager Buck Showalter, the Diamondbacks won one hundred games in their second season, taking the NL West Division. Their playoff appearance after only two seasons shattered the previous record of eight set by the Mets. The unusualness of that quick rise created an odd situation: the Diamondbacks became the first team in the history of North American sports to draw fewer fans finishing first than they had drawn when finishing last the previous year. Unlike New York, the Diamondbacks had coasted to the playoffs, allowing them to set their rotation as they wanted heading into the National League Division Series (NLDS). That meant that Randy Johnson, who had struck out an insane 34 percent of all batters he had faced in the regular season, would start Game One.

The Mets, on almost no sleep and still riding the adrenaline rush of their one-game playoff win, did not care about any of that. The last five days had shown them anything was possible, so starting the playoffs against the game's best pitcher, three time zones behind their normally scheduled games, was no worry. They immediately showed just how little it all bothered them.

Henderson, the first Met to bat in a postseason game since Howard Johnson in 1988, flew out to start things off. Then Alfonzo walloped an 0-2 fastball over the center-field fence for a 1–0 lead. For the second day in a row, Edgardo had homered in the first inning to give the Mets the lead. Bank One Ballpark, the squarish-shaped home of Arizona, immediately lost crowd energy. Two innings later, Olerud became the first left-handed batter in two years to homer off Johnson, giving the Mets a 3–0 lead.

Eventually up 4–1, New York looked on pace to take Game One and steal momentum in the series. But Yoshii gave the lead back on a Gonzalez home run, and the game moved to the ninth tied at 4–4. In that inning the Mets managed to load the bases with just one out when Henderson sent a shot into the third-base hole. Williams dove, snatched the ball, and threw to home for the force out. It was a deflating moment . . . until Alfonzo hit a 3–1 pitch for a grand slam.

Alfonzo's grand slam gave the Mets Game One and handed Johnson his sixth straight postseason loss, a Major League record. The Diamondbacks fought back to win Game Two, tagging Rogers for four runs and the bullpen for three more in a 7–1 win. Perhaps just as disconcerting, Piazza injured his left thumb during the game, then had a negative reaction to a cortisone injection, causing the thumb to swell. He was in too much pain to play and missed the rest of the series. Backup catcher Todd Pratt had to start in his place. Meanwhile, Mets fans were annoyed that both games had started at 11 p.m. EST, thus either keeping them up well into the early hours of the morning or causing them to fall asleep before the games were done. Alfonzo's grand slam occurred after 1 a.m. in New York. Blame fell on Colangelo, who had picked the start times. It wasn't entirely his fault, though. Major League Baseball had given him a menu of start times from which to pick. "I would have preferred our usual time (6:30 p.m.) but that wasn't one of the choices. It was 1, 4 or 8. I said 8 because of our workers and the parking downtown," he explained.[91]

The two teams headed to Shea for Games Three and Four and more bearable start times. On a Friday night in Queens, over fifty-six thousand fans jammed into the ballpark, creating an electric atmosphere that was the culmination of more than a decade of pent-up frustration. Mets fans had stood by and watched the dynasty that never was fall apart in the late 1980s, the failed attempts to rebuild it in the early 1990s, the numerous preposterous off-the-field player issues in the mid-1990s, and the oh-so-close efforts of the last three years. This night was a moment for them seemingly as much as for the team itself. They got their money's worth.

Clinging to a 3–2 lead in the sixth, the Mets cobbled together three walks and four singles and batted around to extend the lead to 9–2. In the top of the ninth, Hershiser, the last pitcher to face the Mets in the postseason before this series, closed the game out. It was their first playoff win at Shea since Game Three of the 1988 NLCS.

The moment was temporarily sidetracked when the next edition of *Sports Illustrated* hit the stands. It featured an on-the-mark story about Valentine and his season managing the club. It noted the ups and downs, his foibles, and his having the last laugh by finally making it to the postseason. It also discussed his conflicts with certain players, and that was where the trouble lay. In late September, when the team was free-falling, the players held a players-only meeting while the team was in Philadelphia. *Sports Illustrated* just happened to be there, with Valentine, as the meeting was going on. Perhaps thinking he would no longer be manager when the story came out, or maybe just not caring what he said any more, Valentine unloaded. "You're not dealing with real professionals in the clubhouse," Valentine told *Sports Illustrated*'s S. L. Price. "You're not dealing with real intelligent guys for the most part. A lot can swim, but most of them are just floating along, looking for something to hold on to. That's why, I'm sure, they're having a players-only meeting. Because there's about five guys in there right now who basically are losers who are seeing if they can recruit."[92]

Valentine did not disclose which players he was specifically referencing, although Bonilla was widely assumed to be one of them. When the magazine article came out, reporters rushed to ask Valentine about his comments, which also included references to Dave Wallace having played a role in the June 6 coach firings. Valentine said that pieces of the story were flat out wrong, including the Wallace section. But he did not deny the comments about the players. In fact, he doubled down on them. "If a shoe fits, you should always wear it," he told the press. "If it fits, I think a guy should try it on for size."[93]

The controversy died down, if for no other reason than that the Mets were in the middle of a postseason run. But Phillips, Wilpon, and Doubleday were starting to wonder how much more of Valentine's act they could take.

Leiter took the mound for Game Four with a chance to do something only three Mets pitchers had ever done before: advance the team to the next round of the postseason. The game was crucial for all the obvious reasons. The Mets did not want to risk a Game Five, and they certainly did not want to have to travel back to Arizona. The biggest factor, though, was Randy Johnson, who would get the ball for the Diamondbacks in Game

Five. They may have gotten to him in Game One, but no Met was looking forward to having to face the Big Unit again in a winner-take-all scenario.

After Alfonzo hit his third home run of the series to give the Mets a 1–0 lead in the fourth, Leiter gave it up in the next inning. The game stayed tied until the bottom of the sixth, when New York regained the lead. Leiter cruised through seven innings, allowing only two hits. With two outs in the eighth, it looked like he might be in store to mimic his appearance five days earlier against the Reds. But a walk and a single derailed his momentum, forcing Valentine to remove him for Benitez. The Mets' closer promptly gave up a double, giving Arizona a 3–2 lead.

The Mets were six outs from a Game Five when fortune shined their way. After a lead-off walk to Alfonzo, Olerud lifted a high fly ball to deep right-center field. Off the bat Shea Stadium went crazy, thinking Olerud had just given the Mets the lead with a home run. It soon became clear, though, that the ball was not leaving the yard. Instead Tony Womack, who had just been moved from shortstop to right field that inning, drifted back toward the wall, settled under it, and promptly dropped the ball. Alfonzo went to third and Olerud to second, and the former scored on a sacrifice fly. Three batters later Hamilton came up with two runners on and slashed a ball down the left-field line for what appeared to be the go-ahead hit. The ball struck the ground and bounded over the fence. Mets fans along the line began frantically pointing to indicate that Hamilton's hit had been a fair ball. Luis Gonzalez, not sure what to think, turned and looked at left-field umpire Charlie Williams, who signaled foul ball.

Hamilton did not put up an argument, but Cookie Rojas began emphatically yelling at Williams until the two were nose to nose. Valentine came out to break it up, and as he tried to get between the two of them, Williams nudged Rojas to move away. An enraged Rojas shoved Williams and then shoved Valentine. "The argument's flying back and forth and he calls me [an SOB]," said Rojas. "I don't think any umpire, or any man in the world, can call me that without me saying something back."[94]

Rojas was ejected and ultimately suspended five games and fined $500. Valentine spent the rest of the inning coaching at third base. Replays showed that while the ball had come about as close as was possibly to hitting the line, it indeed had been foul. Play resumed, Hamilton walked to load the bases, and Ordóñez then struck out. Eventually the game moved to the tenth inning.

It was there, with one out in the bottom half of the inning, that Pratt came to the plate. Filling in for the injured Piazza, Pratt had yet to make a mark in the series. He'd gone hitless the day before, though he had drawn two walks, and he was 0-4 in this game. In the eighth, he had come up with runners on first and third, one out, and the game tied. It was a golden opportunity for Pratt to be a lifelong hero in New York. Instead he hit one back to the pitcher, who threw the runner out at home.

Diamondbacks reliever Matt Mantei, who had averaged over fifteen strikeouts per nine innings in the regular season, threw Pratt a 1-0 fastball over the heart of the plate. Pratt swung and sent the ball deep to center. Mantei immediately threw his arm down in disgust. No one else seemed to know in that moment what Mantei already knew. Center fielder Steve Finley raced to the wall and, once he got to the warning track, began shuffling as he watched the ball, checked for the wall, turned to watch the ball again, then turned to check the wall again. Meanwhile, 56,177 fans and both teams stood on their toes tracking the flight of the ball and wondering what would happen next. Just as he got to the fence, Finley stretched out with his glove hand. On television and for most of the people in the ballpark, the ball disappeared, but at that moment Finley brought his glove back down and looked into it, as if to confirm he had caught the ball. Then, as he recognized that he in fact had not made the catch, he turned and stared confusingly back toward the infield diamond, as if to say, "Where the hell did the ball go?" "When he [Pratt] hit the ball, everyone thought there's a chance except we had seen Steve Finley make these spectacular catches every time he went to the wall against us in the past," said Valentine. "When he went to the wall and he went up and he came down, I actually thought he had caught it."[95]

Pratt's shot, which would have been a home run anyway, had tipped off Finley's glove and shot back behind the fence and into the players' parking lot. Once everyone realized what Finley now knew, pandemonium broke out. The Mets scrambled onto the field as Pratt, who had stopped between first and second because he could not tell if Finley had caught the ball, circled the bases, emphatically waving his arms.

John Franco, the winning pitcher in the first postseason advancing clincher for the Mets since Game Six of the 1986 NLCS, raised both arms in the air and began high-step prancing like a show horse walking by the judges. The reliever had not won a game in over two years. "Finally," he said of breaking the winless streak. "It would have to be me. Yeah, I'm pumped up with adrenaline."[96] After the game, with tears in his eyes, Franco embraced Wilpon.

"L.A. Woman" blared through the clubhouse as teammates hugged one another, poured champagne on each other, and just took in the joy of the moment. Pratt refused to take all the glory. "To be honest with you, it's just like another game. Don't get me wrong, I'm very happy I gave my team a chance to go to the NLCS, but I'm one guy in the mix. I could have easily been the goat today."[97]

Shortly after Pratt's series-ending shot, about 1,600 miles away from Shea, John Rocker got Ken Caminiti to fly out to center field, ending Game Four of the Braves-Astros NLDS and finishing the series. It was official. The Braves, many of whom had taken significant joy in crushing the Mets' spirits and nearly ruining their season in the final weeks of September, would play host to the Mets in Game One of the NLCS. Certainly the Mets had to feel a little anxious. They had won only three of twelve regular-season match-ups against the Braves. Atlanta featured three future Hall of Famers, all still in their prime, in their rotation, and it had a lights-out closer in Rocker, who fed off negative energy and had already grown to detest New York City and Mets fans in particular. Two weeks prior, after having been hit with a variety of objects at Shea, Rocker told the *New York Post* that he "fucking hated Mets fans."[98]

Chipper Jones was about to win the MVP award after a monster season that included a .633 slugging percentage. The Braves featured five players with twenty or more home runs and six with at least ten steals. They could beat teams in just about any way, and that was why they had won a Major League best 103 games in the regular season.

That didn't stop Valentine from throwing down the gauntlet. "It's going to take a good effort to stop us," he told reporters during the post–Game Four celebration. "The next team we are playing is going to be playing against some ghosts because they said we were dead. I don't know if they have ever played against people who have come back from the grave before."[99]

The Mets were going to need all their skills—and a little luck—if they were to triumph over the Braves—and possibly meet up with the Yankees in the World Series.

• • •

Ryan Klesko turned on a Rick Reed fastball and brutalized it. It looked like the kind of home run hit in a wiffle ball game: the ball just obliterated and clearly about to travel a great distance. As Klesko's shot landed to the left of the Mets' bullpen, the crowd at Shea Stadium fell deathly quiet. In the span of three pitches, Atlanta had taken a 2–1 lead in the eighth inning of NLCS Game Four. Just as it had felt over two weeks earlier against Pittsburgh, so now the Mets' dream of getting to the World Series appeared dead. Over the past four days they had endured one soul-crushing loss after another. It had started with Game One, when they had brought the tying or go-ahead run to the plate in every inning from the sixth to the ninth without scoring. Atlanta won, 4–2.

In Game Two the Mets held a 2–0 lead after five innings, thanks in part to a Melvin Mora home run. Mora became just the second non-pitcher in history to hit a home run in the postseason before hitting one in the regular season. It didn't hold up, though. Rogers gave up two two-run home runs in the sixth. New York lost, 4–3.

Game Three was especially cruel. The Mets had not committed more than one error in an inning all season. Then errors by Leiter and Piazza led to an unearned run in the first, the only run Atlanta would score. New York put at least one runner on base in each of the first seven innings but failed to score. The lead-off hitter reached to start the bottom of the ninth and never left first base. It was the fourth time the Braves had shut out the Mets that year. All other teams had done it twice combined. The 1–0 loss put the Mets in a 3–0 deficit, one from which no team in baseball history had ever come back at that point.

The inevitability of it all felt clear to everyone in Game Four. Still, the Mets would not give in. Smoltz and Reed engaged in a pitchers' duel that saw Smoltz blink first, allowing a home run to Olerud in the sixth. Reed, meanwhile, had been untouchable, allowing only a single hit through seven innings. Then came the eighth: a home run by Brian Jordan to start; the bomb by Klesko right after. Braves, 2–1. "If there was a tunnel from the mound to the dugout, I would have crawled through it," said Reed. "To be honest, I thought the season was over."[100]

With their season six outs from being over, the Mets staged a comeback in the bottom of the inning. With two outs, a double steal by Cedeño and Mora put runners on second and third for Olerud. Batting against Rocker, against whom he was 0-9 coming into the at bat, Olerud ground a high hopper up the middle for a single, giving the Mets a 3–2 lead. After the inning Rocker walked back to the dugout and absorbed the abuse fans where hurling at him. A few days earlier, after Atlanta had taken Game Two, Rocker had gleefully exclaimed, "To hell with New York fans, they're a bunch of stupid asses anyway."[101] He also referred to them as "less than human."[102] Now, while Mets fans screamed at him, he raised his left hand, stuck up three fingers, then made the zero sign, all while mouthing, "3–0." There would be more of that to come.

Benitez closed out the game, and the Mets were still alive. "At least we can say we weren't swept, which is better than nothing," said Piazza.[103]

What happened after Game Four would be twenty-six of the greatest, most dramatic innings in the history of Major League Baseball. The Mets and Braves engaged in a battle in which both teams refused to cede any ground. It was replete with knock-out pitching, clutch hitting, defensive gems, lead changes, unbelievable comebacks, and crushing miscues.

It started at 4:11 p.m. EST on Sunday, October 17. The day was dreary as the threat of rain hung in the air all afternoon. Yet winning Game Four had rejuvenated the fan base and implanted in the minds of the team a "Why not us?" attitude. Olerud exemplified that when, in the first inning, he hit a two-run home run off Maddux to give the Mets the lead.

In the top of the fourth, Yoshii gave up a lead-off double, then two more hits and a walk, allowing the Braves to tie the game. Valentine, not wanting things to slip away, called in Hershiser. The Bulldog responded with three and a third innings of scoreless relief, striking out five. That included getting out of a bases-loaded, one-out jam in the sixth, when he struck out Maddux on an attempted suicide squeeze, and the Mets were able to tag the runner out to end the inning. Maddux got out of a similar jam in the bottom half when he induced Ordóñez, just 1-12 in the series, to hit into an inning-ending double play.

Atlanta had the bases loaded in the seventh and put two runners on in the eighth. Both times the Mets' bullpen shut them down before the Braves could take the lead. With darkness now having fallen over Shea, inning after inning went by without either team scoring. Valentine cycled through nearly every pitcher he had available in order to keep the season alive. After Yoshii and Hershiser, it was Wendell. Then Cook. Then Mahomes. Then Franco. Then Benitez. Then Rogers. None of the Mets relievers yielded a run. The team used more pitchers in Game Five than it had ever used in a single game in its history. "I don't think there could be more moves than this," said Valentine.[104]

By the thirteenth, Valentine had essentially run out of options and handed the ball to Dotel, who was going to have to pitch for as long as the game lasted. It almost lasted just another inning. With two outs and a runner on first, Chipper Jones lined a double down the right-field line. It was a horrid sight for fans. The idea that Jones, of all people, would be responsible for ending the team's season was too much to bear.

Mora, playing deep in right field for this exact scenario, rushed toward the line and cut the ball off before it reached the wall. He turned and fired to Alfonzo, who pivoted and hurled the ball toward home. The throw took something of a short-hop bounce, but Piazza, back behind the plate for this series, was able to catch it cleanly, turn, and block home. The runner, Keith Lockhart, was out by ten steps.

The Mets failed to score in the bottom of the inning, which ended with Rocker's striking out Piazza. As Rocker walked off the field, he looked at a group of fans sitting behind the Braves' dugout who had been yelling at him, and he shouted, "Hey, what are you talking about? I just struck out your best hitter."[105]

After fans enjoyed a fourteenth-inning stretch, the Mets put the winning run on second in the fourteenth but could not drive him in. In the fifteenth, with two outs and a runner on, Lockhart lined a ball into the right-center field gap. Dunston, unsure whether to dive or not, remained upright as the ball fell in and then shot past him toward the fence. Atlanta took the lead, 3–2.

Dunston, agonizing over the ball that had fallen in front of him, led off the bottom of the inning. It had been raining intermittently throughout the game. Now rain was falling faster and faster. Facing Kevin McGlinchy, Dunston worked the count full. Then he fouled off a pitch. Then another. Then another. Then another. Then another. Then one more—six all together with the count full. On the seventh full-count pitch, he grounded the ball up the middle for a base hit. All told, Dunston's at bat lasted six minutes, and it breathed life into the dugout and stadium.

Reflecting on the gravity of the moment, Valentine allowed Dotel to step into the batter's box. Dotel was, almost certainly, going to attempt a sacrifice bunt to move Dunston over. After Dotel got to the plate, however, Valentine changed his mind. There was no guarantee Dotel could deliver the bunt or do so in a way that would move Dunston over. It was not worth sacrificing an out for potentially no reason. Instead Valentine sent Matt Franco to bat, one of two remaining position players.

Franco walked, and Alfonzo sacrificed the runners over to second and third. The Braves intentionally walked Olerud, loading the bases and giving Pratt the opportunity to play hero once more.

"A 32-year-old who, to call him a journeyman, would be kind, at least prior to the last few weeks," was how NBC's Bob Costas introduced Pratt as he came to the plate. The fans were in an absolute frenzy, as if they could will the tying and winning runs in by raising their cheers to ear-shattering levels. When McGlinchy threw three straight balls to start the count, Mets players emerged from the dugout and prompted the crowd to grow even louder. After a gimme strike, Pratt took a pitch outside for ball four. Shea erupted. Dunston crossed home plate to tie the game, a big smile on his face as if the memory of Lock-hart's triple had been washed away. Journey's "Don't Stop Believin'" blasted over the speakers across the ballpark. "The Mets will not die," remarked Hall of Famer Joe Morgan, doing the color analysis with Costas.

Up next came Ventura, who had set a Mets single-season record that year by hitting three grand slams. Ventura, however, was mired in a postseason slump. Coming into the at bat, he was just 1-18 in the series, that one hit having come earlier in Game Five. Before that single, Ventura had failed to hit a fair ball out of the infield through Games Three through Five.

"They're 90 feet from Game 6," remarked Costas as the count went to 2-1. Not wanting to walk Ventura and having trouble gripping the wet baseball, McGlinchy threw a fastball down the middle. Ventura swung and drove the ball into history. The Braves immediately began walking off the field, even before Ventura's shot landed over the 371-foot sign in right-center. "A drive to right . . . BACK TO GEORGIA," exclaimed Costas as a wall of sound exploded from Shea Stadium.

Ventura rounded first and, looking to his left, immediately saw that Pratt and Olerud, the two runners in front of him, had stopped rounding the bases and were headed toward him. Ventura motioned for them to keep going and touch home plate. They ignored him. Before he could get to second, Pratt ran straight at Ventura, causing Ventura to leap to avoid a collision, at which point Pratt caught him, giving Ventura an elevated bear hug. Ordóñez followed suit, then Yoshii, then player after player. "Mr. Mojo Risin'" began blaring from the speakers.

The Mets, drenched with rain, embraced one another in short center field, a moment that out of context would have looked like a championship celebration. For the umpteenth time in three weeks, they had come back from the dead to play another game. A fired-up Valentine began pointing his finger across the Shea Stadium crowd, yelling, "THANK YOU!" "It was the only time, and I played, coached and managed in Shea Stadium, that I actually saw that second tier rocking. We were so worried for a second that it might actually even collapse," said Valentine. "It was exhausting. I remember at the end of the game, and I didn't play for a second in it, but I stood for all fifteen innings in the same spot, except to go to the water cooler, and I was exhausted."[106]

It was a remarkable scene at Shea. It was 9:55 at night, just short of six hours since Game Five had begun. The scoreboard showed fifteen innings of baseball and a final score of Mets 7, Braves 3. Shortly after the game, because Ventura had made it only to first base and had never touched any other bag, his hit was recorded as a single, and the score was changed to 4–3. That did not really matter though. What mattered was that the Mets were alive. "As long as we won, it's fine with me," said Ventura about his grand slam single. "I knew it went over. But it didn't matter. I didn't want to run that far anyway. I was tired."[107]

The fact that the series had been 3–0 two days earlier was now irrelevant. It was just another Game Six in which one team had three wins and another had two. How either had gotten there no longer mattered. What mattered was that the Mets were headed back to Atlanta and had their ace pitcher, Al Leiter, ready to take the mound and force a Game Seven.

• • •

It would have been hard to imagine, as Ventura was getting swamped by his teammates, that the 1999 NLCS could have produced a better, more intense game than Game Five. Yet, some way, somehow, it did with Game Six.

What would turn out to be an October classic certainly did not feel that way in the bottom of the first. Leiter, who had stopped the Reds and the Diamondbacks and had kept the Braves at bay in Game Three, was a mess. Pitching on three days' rest for just the second time in his career, he hit the lead-off batter, walked the next hitter, allowed a double steal where a run scored on a Piazza throwing error, and then hit the next batter. No pitcher had ever hit two batters in a single Championship Series inning before. Two singles later, it was 4–0 Braves, and Leiter's night was done. "I stunk," said Leiter. "What can you say? I couldn't throw a strike. I let my team down."[108]

For only the second time in his career, Leiter had started a game and failed to record an out. "He threw 25 pitches, didn't retire a batter, and now may have all fall and winter to rest," said Costas, calling Game Six for NBC, as Leiter walked off the field. Atlanta added another run to make it 5–0.

That lead held up for five innings as the Mets failed to chip away at the five-run deficit. Then in the sixth, they showed signs of life, plating three runs and bringing the go-ahead run to the plate in Ordóñez. But Ordóñez continued his postseason struggles, lining into an inning-ending double play. The double play hurt that much more when the Braves made it a 7–3 game in the bottom of the inning. His team now nine outs away from the World Series, Braves manager Bobby Cox wanted to put his foot on the Mets' throat. He brought in Game Four starter Smoltz to start the seventh. It went about as well as Leiter's start had.

Franco doubled. Henderson doubled him in. Alfonzo came within a few feet of a home run. Olerud singled Henderson in. In the previous two innings the Mets had collected more hits with runners in scoring position than they had in the first five games combined. It was a 7–5 game, with Piazza coming to the plate. The Mets catcher, hampered by his injured thumb, had been overmatched for much of the playoffs. He had driven in only two runs and had yet to collect an extra-base hit. Piazza had largely been a nonentity during the team's run.

The entire Mets bench stood on the top step of the dugout, leaning over the railing. The tension inside Turner Field was palpable. Braves fans, given what had occurred over the last three days, could almost sense what was about to happen.

"They deserve a pat on the back no matter what happens," said Morgan, doing the Game Six color commentary for NBC, about the Mets. "I mean, they were left for dead by the Braves with three games to go. They were two out with three games to go and they bounced back, beat the Reds, beat the Diamondbacks and they will not die here against the Atlanta Braves."

Four seconds after Morgan finished his succinct summary of the Mets' last three weeks, Smoltz attempted to sneak an outside fastball by Piazza. The pitch was flat, and Piazza turned on it. The sound of the bat hitting the ball was perfect—reminiscent of a sound effect used in a baseball movie. Everyone knew it was gone, but the initial reaction was partially subdued because no one could believe what was happening. It was a textbook Piazza home run, traveling to right-center field. He rounded the bases without revealing his feelings in the moment, even keeping his head down as he reached the dugout. The rest of the Mets, however, could not contain their joy. After the ball landed beyond the fence, Leiter wrapped his arm around the neck of a teammate and planted a kiss on his cheek.

After the Mets had calmed down, Turner Field grew still. The crowd was in shock, and Smoltz had been removed for Mike Remlinger when Ventura sent one to the wall in right. It came within a few feet of giving the Mets the lead.

Hershiser kept the Braves scoreless in the seventh. In the top of the eighth, Mora came to bat with a runner on second and one out. If the Mets did manage to come back and win the series, Mora was making a case for MVP. He had a .429 OBP, three runs scored, and two outfield assists, including a crucial one in Game Five that may have saved the Mets' season. Against Remlinger now, Mora strengthened his case by lining a single to center. The Mets had actually taken the lead. No team in baseball history had ever forced a Game Seven after being down 3–0. New York was just six outs away from becoming the first to do so.

John Franco could not hold the lead in the eighth, though, and the game went to the tenth inning tied at 8–8. Mora played hero again in the tenth, singling with a runner on first to put runners on the corners with one out. At exactly midnight, a Pratt sacrifice fly put the lead back in New York's hands. Benitez could not hold it. He allowed a one-out single to Ozzie Guillén that tied the game. The single could also have led to the end of the Mets' season had Mora not unleashed a laser-like throw to third base to nail the runner.

New York failed to muster a run in the top of the eleventh. In the bottom of the inning, the Braves loaded the bases with one out against Rogers, the Mets' eighth pitcher of the game. The Mets' season all came down to a single pitch after Andruw Jones worked the count full. Needing to throw a strike, Rogers reared back, threw as hard as he could, and delivered a pitch well outside the strike zone for ball four.

Valentine watched in horror as Rogers delivered ball four. He slammed his hands on the railing, screaming, "NO! NO!" at the reality that it had all ended on a walk. "I was sure that Jones was gonna swing. Walking wasn't his forte. I felt the ball was gonna be put in play somewhere. So when he took, the 'NO!' was that he didn't swing. I couldn't believe that he didn't swing."[109]

The heartbreak was clear in Valentine's face. He then paced the top step of the dugout as half the Mets filed into the clubhouse. The other half stayed, staring at the celebration before them. Leiter, who had nearly thrown his arm off getting the Mets to and through the playoffs, stood with his arms crossed over the dugout railing.

Just like that, the Mets' magical 1999 season was over.

• • •

In a way, the World Series match-up was a letdown, at least for New Yorkers. A subway series would have been the perfect ending to twentieth-century baseball. Moreover, the Mets had their best team in over a decade, maybe one of their best ever. It would have been an incredible match-up, full of dozens of side stories. Instead baseball fans got a rematch of the 1996 World Series. That in itself was a bit of intrigue. Even more intriguing was the argument that this World Series would determine the team of the decade. The Braves had won the championship in 1995 and the pennant five times, along with making the postseason in eight straight seasons (not including the strike-cancelled postseason of 1994). The Yankees were two-time world champions in the decade, having made the playoffs five times. Both teams started the decade as bottom dwellers, with clubhouses full of misery and eccentric owners at the top. Both had rebuilt their organizations through a bevy of young talent, mixed with shrewd trades and free-agent signings. Now they faced off one more time in the World Series to claim not just the title of world champions but also that of team of the decade.

El Duque, fresh off his ALCS MVP, made a statement in the first inning by striking out the side. It was clear from the start that Hernández was on his game. His fastball, though not fast by elite standards, was overpowering the Braves as they had trouble differentiating between it and his off-speed pitches. His varying arm angles made it all the more difficult. Hernández struck out eight of the first eleven batters he faced, not allowing a hit. In the fourth, he made his only mistake of the game, leaving a fastball out over the plate that Chipper Jones sent deep into the right-field stands at Turner Field. El Duque was unfazed, retiring the next eight hitters in a row and leaving after the seventh, having allowed only the hit to Jones. "You don't see performances like that everyday," said Torre.[110]

In the top of the eighth, a single, a walk, and an error brought Jeter up with the bases loaded against Greg Maddux and his team down 1–0. Jeter, who led the Major Leagues in hits that year, lined a Maddux fastball into left to tie the game. Maddux left for Rocker, who entered the game yielding just a .140 average to left-handed batters on the year. He faced Paul O'Neill, who had come to New York in 1993 with a reputation for being unable to hit lefties, no matter how hard or soft they threw. It annoyed him to no end. He had spent the last seven seasons proving his doubters wrong. Earlier that year he had collected his first career hit in eighteen at bats against lefty Jesse Orosco, hitting a home run that also drove in career RBIS 999, 1,000, and 1,001. "The fans gave me a curtain call for reaching 1,000 RBIS, but maybe it should have been a curtain call for collecting a hit off the invincible Orosco," said O'Neill.[111]

Years earlier it was unlikely that O'Neill would have gotten the chance to hit in this situation. Even now he had batted just .190 off lefties during the regular season, the worst average among full-time players. Torre left him in. O'Neill approached the at bat with one thing in mind: make contact. He turned just enough on an inside fastball to send a base hit into right field, scoring the go-ahead runs. "I'm as happy as anybody, believe me," said O'Neill of the hit. "Your job as a hitter there is to put the ball in play. I did the job."[112] A walk later, the Yankees were up 4–1. They had scored four runs without lifting a single ball into the air. A combination of singles, walks, and errors ultimately gave them Game One.

The idea of momentum in sports has been largely debunked. Yet after the Yankees' Game One victory, it just felt like the momentum was all on New York's side. Not relenting after the comeback win, the Yankees scored three runs in the first inning of Game Two, effectively ending the game before the Braves sent a batter to the plate. Cone threw seven innings of no-run ball, holding the Braves to just one hit, as Hernández had done. The Yankees won, 7–2.

Game Three was going the Braves' way. At Yankee Stadium, Atlanta collected ten hits and five runs in less than four innings off Pettitte, a bitter way for the lefty to end his season. Down 5–1, the Yankees slowly began chipping away until Knoblauch came up as the tying run in the eighth inning. The Yankees had gotten to where they were based largely on the talent they had accumulated over the years. But no team wins that many games without things breaking its way. The Yankees had caught breaks in 1996, 1998, and in the 1999 ALCS against Boston. Now, in Game Three, they caught another. Knoblauch sent an outside pitch by Glavine deep to right field. Braves outfielder Brian Jordan tracked the ball to the wall, leapt, extended his glove above the fence and then . . . the ball went into and out of his glove, ricocheting into the stands for a two-run, game-tying home run. "I knew I hit it pretty good," said Knoblauch. "Jordan, who's a great outfielder, jumped and I prayed, 'Come on.' I got a break."[113]

Two innings later Curtis ended the game with a solo home run. "I can't say I ever felt that way before. I was rounding the bases and I was kind of tingling. I've heard people talk about it," said Curtis.[114]

Even in this joyous moment, Curtis could not avoid controversy. Days earlier, before the Game Two ceremony, Major League Baseball had honored the hundred greatest players in baseball history as voted by the fans. One of them was Pete Rose, the all-time hits leader who had been banished from baseball for making bets on the game while he was manager of the Reds. At the time, Rose was still denying he had bet on baseball, even in the face of overwhelming evidence of his guilt. Present at Turner Field for the celebration, Rose gave a live interview to NBC's Jim Gray. At one point Gray asked Rose if he wanted to admit that he'd bet on the game. Rose refused, and Gray continued to push, causing Rose to ask why Gray would ruin the moment like this.

Others, including players and fans, felt the same way. The pushback against Gray was intense, including threats of violence left on his voicemail. It grew so strong that Gray and NBC felt they had no choice but to address it before the start of Game Three. Gray explained: "[I] thought it was important to ask Pete Rose if this was the right moment for him to make an apology. If in doing so the interview went on too long, and took some of the joy of the occasion, then I want to say to baseball fans everywhere that I am very sorry about this."[115]

Apparently it was not enough for the players—or at least not for Curtis. After Curtis crossed home plate with the winning run, Gray pulled him aside for a live interview. Curtis refused to answer Gray's questions. "As a team we kinda decided that . . . because of what happened with Pete we're not gonna talk out here on the field," said Curtis, before adding a shoutout to his grandmother and walking back into the clubhouse.

It would be disputed as to whether such an agreement had been made among the players or if Curtis had acted on his own. Either way Gray was embarrassed, though he was ultimately vindicated when years later Rose, trying to soften opposition to his being elected to the Baseball Hall of Fame, admitted what had long been obvious: he'd bet on the game.

Curtis's home run and controversy aside, the Yankees were now just one game away from their second consecutive World Series sweep. "They just have a certain aura about them right now," said Chipper Jones, almost conceding the series after Game Three. "It seems that no matter how far they're down, or what the situation is, they're not out of it."[116]

The Yankees asked Clemens to bring them the win in Game Four. This was, in fact, the exact kind of moment Clemens had wanted when he had demanded the trade from Toronto. Here he was, taking the mound in a position to give his team a championship, something he'd been able to do only once before. That game had ended with an infamous groundball by Mookie Wilson, helping his now crosstown rivals to ultimately win their last championship.

There would be no such misfortune on Clemens's second attempt. Though not overpowering, Clemens did just enough to keep the Braves off balance, holding them to two hits through seven innings. The Yankees pieced together three runs in the third, and it looked like Clemens might even be able to go the distance and throw the last out of the World Series. That was so until, with two outs in the eighth, Walt Weiss stepped on Clemens's leg as he attempted to cover first base on an infield hit. Clemens tried to get the next batter out but couldn't, walking off the mound to a loud ovation. His regular season had been his worst ever, and his ALCS performance had been a dud. Yet all it took to win over New Yorkers was a big game performance in a World Series clincher.

All that was left was for Mariano Rivera to get the final three outs. Before he could do that, though, Jim Leyritz added another notch to his postseason heroics belt. The Yankees did not really have a spot for Leyritz when they reacquired him in a trade with the Padres that summer. But Leyritz had gotten word to Steinbrenner that he would like to return to New York, and the Boss could not help himself. He loved that Leyritz always seemed to come through when it mattered. There was one big problem, though, outside of Leyritz's having no spot. He could not hit the ball with any power. "I ended up breaking my hand on June 22," said Leyritz. "Chan Ho Park hit me with a pitch and broke my hand." The King had not played in a game since, and even though he could swing the bat, his hand had not fully healed. "I could barely hit the ball out in batting practice. Knoblauch and Jeter would give me crap about it. I said, 'Guys, relax. I'll hit one when it counts.'"[117]

Leyritz had not homered since June 5. His slugging percentage since his return to New York was lower than his on-base percentage. Yet pinch-hitting for Strawberry in the eighth inning of Game Four, Leyritz hit a 3-2 pitch over the wall in left for his eighth career postseason home run in just sixty-one at bats. That was a home run every 7.6 at bats in the playoffs, compared to every 28 at bats in his regular-season career. It was the first pinch-hit World Series home run in seven years and the last home run of the twentieth century. Moreover, Leyritz's second career World Series home run created amazing similarities with his first. Both were hit in the eighth inning of a Game Four against the Braves. Both came in Leyritz's first at bat of the night. Both came against pitchers, Mark Wohlers and Terry Mulholland, who pitched for the Yankees at some point in their careers, and both were hit over the heads of left fielders, Andruw Jones and Gerald Williams, who played for the Yankees at some point in their careers.

The King had his moment. Now Rivera had his, setting the Braves down in order in the ninth to close out the World Series and give New York its twenty-fifth title. Cameras panned to Clemens as he sprinted toward the mound in celebration. "It's just been wonderful to play with these guys," said Clemens during the victory celebration. "I think I kind of feel what it's like to be a Yankee."[118] The Rocket later emerged from the clubhouse celebration to dose fans in champagne and high-five them along the dugout. It was a surreal scene for any fan who had watched baseball over the last fifteen years.

Clemens had his title, and the Yankees, as Costas noted after the final out, were the team of the decade. By going 12-1, the Yankees had actually performed a game better than the 1998 team in the postseason. These teams were no longer the America's sweetheart version of 1996, though. Fans outside of New York were already leery of the Yankees' continued winning ways in an age of rising salaries. Even though many of the players were home-grown and many of the key trades did not involve marquee players (outside of Clemens, of course), resentment grew far and wide. Just how much longer were the Yankees going to continue to push teams around with their millions and millions of dollars? The answer nearly came sooner than a lot people would have thought because 2000 was not going to be a walk in the park for the New York Yankees.

7

Smell of the Stadium

The first Mets series against the Yankees had popped out immediately to Dave Mlicki when he saw the 1997 team schedule. He wanted to be a part of it. He wanted to pitch in that series so badly that he thought about it constantly for months. Then, a week before it was set to begin, he realized his turn in the rotation would line up exactly with the first game. Valentine then confirmed it: Mlicki would get the ball for the first-ever regular season match-up between the Mets and Yankees.

That day Mlicki had gotten to Yankee Stadium early. He'd never been able to walk around it before. He strolled through Monument Park and took in the sights of one of the most famous sports venues in the world. He could not believe how lucky he was to be a part of the series—to be *the* guy starting the first game. Looking back years later, he could still remember minute details about the day, including the smell of the stadium as the game went along.

Mlicki took the mound in the bottom of the seventh in a much more comfortable position. In the top of the inning, Matt Franco and Luis Lopez had cobbled together back-to-back seeing-eye singles off Pettitte before the lefty had loaded the bases with two outs for John Olerud. Pettitte could not have picked a worse hitter for whom to load the bases. Olerud was batting .441 with runners in scoring position. Pettitte tried to throw a pitch low and away, one of the few places where Olerud was vulnerable, but he missed his spot. The ball tailed over the plate, and Olerud sliced it through the hole into left field. Two runs scored. The Mets were up, 5–0.

Gifted a much larger lead, Mlicki did what he had done most of the game: he allowed a Yankee to get on base. Charlie Hayes walked to start the inning. The crowd, at least the Yankees fans, had largely been taken out of the game by Olerud's single. Now they began to sit up again. Another hit mixed with a home run, and their team would be right back in it.

Except their team could not figure out Mlicki. Again trying to avoid deep counts, the next two batters both swung at the first pitch with nothing to show for it. Mark Whiten popped up to second. Chad Curtis flew out to right.

Two hitters.

Two first-pitch fastballs.

Two outs.

Sure enough, the next batter, Joe Girardi, swung at the first pitch. This time Mlicki fooled him with a curve, which Girardi swung right over. No more fastballs after that kind of swing. Mlicki delivered two more curves before Girardi hit a chopper back to him for an easy third out.

The Mets went quietly in the top of the eighth. Perhaps the most entertaining aspect was a television ad that appeared between innings featuring Alex Rodriguez. The budding star told kids to avoid dipping tobacco and just "play the game." Viewers could appreciate the irony only in retrospect.

With the score still 5–0 and the Yankees down to their last six outs, many fans began to head toward the exits. Some may have regretted it when, with one out, Mlicki gave up back-to-back singles to Kelly and O'Neill. That brought Fielder up, yet again in a big spot. Just as they had done for inning after inning, Yankees fans began to stir. Here was one more, and perhaps the final, opportunity to get back in the game. Among those rising to their feet along the first-base line was Jesse Jackson, the civil rights leader and former candidate for president who was sporting a Yankees cap.

Hundley, sensing the need to slow things down a little, went to the mound to talk to Mlicki. It was a veteran move. There really was not much to tell his pitcher at this moment. Hundley just wanted to give all the players a minute to catch their breath while fifty thousand people rose and cheered all around them.

Fielder had buried a slider foul into the upper deck two innings before. No one would have blamed Mlicki for hesitating to throw a curve in this situation. But Mlicki and Hundley had been throwing against conventional wisdom all night. There was no reason to change now. Fielder watched as a first-pitch curveball sailed outside for a ball. Mlicki and Hundley switched back to a fastball, perhaps hoping to fool Fielder. This time the pitch sailed inside for a ball.

The crowd grew even louder. There were few better counts for a hitter than 2-0, especially with two runners already on base. Fielder had to assume that Mlicki would want to throw him a strike. Even if Fielder hit it into Monument Park, the Mets would still be up two runs. Better that, in theory anyway, than loading the bases for Yankees' home run leader Tino Martinez.

But what, exactly, would Mlicki throw to get that strike? Fielder could not know. Conventional wisdom said fastball. But, again, conventional wisdom had no part in this game. That is why Mlicki threw a 2-0 curve. Fielder was out on top of the pitch, grounding it to third, where Franco temporarily had trouble getting it out of his glove. He finally tossed it to second for the out.

The crowd fell silent, except for Mets fans. Even when the next batter, Martinez, went to a full count, Yankees fans remained subdued. They were cautiously optimistic but also not willing to get fooled again. Mlicki buried a fastball inside on Martinez, who lifted a weak fly out to center. Many Yankees fans in the crowd, on the bat's contact with the ball, had jumped up, desperately hoping for something to celebrate. Tino knew better, though, cursing himself as soon as the ball left the bat.

Mlicki allowed himself a small fist pump on the mound before heading toward the dugout. He had put himself in precarious positions all night, only to escape by throwing curveballs when he should have thrown fastballs and vice versa. The result was that the Yankees were 0-10 with runners in scoring position and Mlicki was pitching a shutout through eight innings.

The game was effectively over. The only question now was whether Mlicki would come out in the ninth and finish the job.

8

Until Someone Beats Us

The Mets were filing into the clubhouse at Turner Field after watching Kenny Rogers walk in the end of their 1999 season. Players were already in a dour mood, some on the verge of tears, when a bizarre scene greeted them. There, in the middle of the locker room, were Bobby Bonilla and Rickey Henderson, playing cards and even laughing.

Henderson, a notorious card player who often won more money off his teammates than he lost, had been upset at Valentine over the previous few days. It started with Valentine's removing him from Game Four of the NLCS in the middle of an inning, a move that Henderson found embarrassing. He was so upset about the perceived slight that he reportedly left the stadium that night without knowing that the Mets had won. "Someone had to run up to Rickey in the tunnel and tell him we won. All he said was, 'Oh.' And kept walking," one team source told the *Bergen Record*.[1]

Then Valentine removed Henderson from Game Six during a late-inning double switch. Why be in the dugout if his manager did not care to have him in the game? It was inevitable that the two clashed. Valentine had even poked fun at Henderson's card playing just two weeks earlier. Henderson had been laid up with a hamstring strain, causing Valentine to remove him from the Pirates' game on the season's final day. The next day Rickey started in left field. "You know, it wasn't affecting his card game," said Valentine, when asked if Henderson was good to start the game despite the hamstring issue. "If he can play cards, he can play ball."[2]

Valentine was strong-willed and did not shy from confrontation when necessary. Rickey had no use for authority, and while he wanted to win, he did not believe in the rah-rah classic clichés that permeated most sports teams. So with the season on the line, and with so many of their teammates having given their blood, sweat, tears, and even possibly their careers to advancing through that postseason, Rickey and Bonilla played cards in the clubhouse as though they were in the middle of a spring-training rain delay.

There is some dispute as to how much the scene angered their teammates. One thing is certain: it angered someone enough that the person leaked it to the *Bergen Record*'s Bob Klapisch. "There were players crying and screaming in the dugout after Rogers walked home the winning run. Then they walk in the clubhouse and see that?" said one source to Klapisch.[3]

In some ways it was appropriate. Bonilla, in his first go-around with the team, had threatened Klapisch in front of rolling cameras six years earlier, unhappy about Klapisch and John Harper's book detailing the Mets' nightmarish 1992 season.

"These guys were just gutted," said Klapisch. "They had the worst loss of the year, ended their seasons, and these two fucking guys were laughing and playing cards. There were guys who wanted to bash their heads in with baseball bats. And it was a big 'fuck you' to the manager."[4] "Can you believe Bonilla and Henderson did that?" one Yankees player told the *Daily News*. "But we shouldn't be surprised, I guess."[5]

That was the end for Bonilla in New York. His second go-around as a Met had been a failure. Hampered by injuries and eclipsed by younger players, he had turned in the worst year of his career. Now this card-playing incident officially sealed his fate. As if to make matters worse, in December Bonilla threatened to be a clubhouse issue unless he became an everyday player in 2000. The Mets released him shortly after the New Year. "It makes sense for everybody to where we can now part company," said Phillips in announcing the move. "It gives Bobby an opportunity to go somewhere else and play and relieves us of having to deal with what we felt would've been an issue needing daily attention and daily addressing."[6] Phillips refused to disparage Bonilla. He, and the club, just wanted to be done with him.

"Like many players, Bobby was the last to know that his career was over," said Valentine in his autobiography. "And like many players, he became a real pain in the ass. Bobby was bigger than most, and his problems were bigger than most."[7]

Bonilla was not done with the Mets, though. As part of his release, New York agreed to buy out the remaining $5.9 million on his contract. Rather than pay him that full amount at the time, however, the Mets wanted to use that money to improve the team for the 2000 season. They decided they would pay Bonilla $1.2 million annually for twenty-five years, starting on July 1, 2011. Because of the structure of the deal and the buyout, those freed up dollars did not count against the team's payroll, meaning the league could not tax those dollars. Also the Mets held part of an annuity with a securities investor that they believed would pay huge dividends in the future. The investor was Bernie Madoff, later convicted of perpetrating the largest Ponzi scheme in human history. The Mets were financially crushed by the scheme. Starting in 2011, July 1 became "Bobby Bonilla Day," an unofficial holiday Mets fans celebrated mockingly.

Henderson was not far behind Bonilla. He did what he had done in nearly every clubhouse in which he had ever played: he had worn out his welcome, at least with management. Valentine told Phillips to get rid of him, and it would happen soon enough.

The Bonilla-Henderson Cardgate affair only added more bitterness to the season's end. The Mets had come so close to making history: forcing a seventh game after being down 3–0 in a seven-game series. Had they won Game Six, who knows what would have gone down in a Game Seven where both teams had depleted bullpens mixed with a string of hot hitters. Moreover, the Mets had to then watch as the Yankees came in and swept Atlanta right out of the World Series.

A long winter set in. However, the Mets had proven themselves to be a team to be reckoned with. Their infield was among the greatest ever assembled; their catcher was offensively the best at his position in history; their outfield was filled with a cadre of young, impressive talent; and their pitching staff had stood tall after a horrid start to the season. For the first time in a long time, the Mets were not in need of numerous upgrades in the off-season.

That did not stop them from trying to make the ultimate upgrade. Ken Griffey Jr. was the greatest player in baseball. From the moment he had made his debut with the Mariners in 1989, he was a bona fide star. McGwire and Sosa hit more home runs, but it was not as if Griffey was a Punch-and-Judy hitter. He had led the American League in home runs over the last three seasons, averaging fifty-three a year during that time, along with 142 RBIS. His slugging percentage was always hovering near .600, and he was the most highlight-reel producing center fielder since Willie Mays. No one made use of the five baseball tools—hitting, hitting with power, running, fielding, and throwing—like Junior.

Griffey was set to become a free agent after the 2000 season. There was almost no chance Seattle would resign him due to the size of his expected contract. Thus in early November 1999 he asked to be traded. Having been in the Majors for ten years and with the same team for at least five, Griffey had the right to decline a trade to any team to which he did not wish to go. The Mets wanted in.

Phillips reached out to Seattle GM Pat Gillick during the December winter meetings in Anaheim. They began working out the structure of a deal. There was just one problem: Griffey wanted no part of New York. He had come to resent the Yankees due to their treatment of him and his father, Ken Sr., when his dad played for New York in the 1980s. That resentment may have spilled over into all aspects of the city. Instead Griffey would accept a trade only to the Cincinnati Reds, where there was a chance his father would one day manage.

Griffey's refusal to come to New York was no secret as Phillips and Gillick worked out a deal. It did not matter to Phillips. Perhaps Junior would change his mind when the proposal officially came his way. On December 13 Seattle and New York reached an agreement. Griffey would go to the Mets in exchange for Benitez, Cedeño, and Dotel. "If either the Mets or the Mariners think Junior's going to change his mind, it looks like they're going to be wrong," said one NL executive.[8] Sure enough, when presented with the deal, Griffey said no. It was a soul-crushing rejection for Mets fans, who resented Griffey for years to come because of it. There was also the question of why the Mets would even pursue such a possibility, and anger the players in the proposed deal, if they knew it would not happen anyway. "I don't feel like we were wasting time," said Phillips. "I think it was a worthy effort to pursue, and an exciting one to pursue."[9]

The Griffey deal now officially dead, New York offered Hamilton and Wendell to Baltimore for outfielder B. J. Surhoff. That deal did not work out either, in part because Surhoff did not want to leave Baltimore for family reasons. Discussions of a deal for the Indians' Manny Ramirez went nowhere as well.

Their pursuit of a big-name outfielder stymied, the Mets moved on to their next goal: adding at least one more starting pitcher. The rotation had needed solidifying even before Hershiser left that off-season as a free agent to pitch one last season in Los Angeles. Two days before Christmas, they found their man. Mike Hampton had been lights out for the Astros in 1999, going 22-4 and allowing the fewest home runs per nine innings of any pitcher. He finished second in the Cy Young voting. His sinker, which helped induce a league-leading thirty-eight double plays, would be perfect for the best fielding infield in baseball. Hampton was also the best hitting pitcher in the game, having slugged three triples and driven in ten runs while batting .311 in 1999.

The deal came about after both teams had lost out during the winter meetings. While the Mets had not landed Griffey, the Astros had not been able to snag a catcher or trade away some of the team's outfielders, of which there were many. The two teams had not discussed a Hampton deal yet because the Mets did not have what the Astros wanted in return. Over the next two weeks the Astros moved outfielders and got some pieces they needed from other teams. That provided more wiggle room for the two sides to make a deal. Houston wanted, at a minimum, a young pitcher and would be willing to take an outfielder too. The Mets offered Cedeño, Dotel, and a Minor League hurler. That was enough to get the deal done, with the Astros giving up Hampton and outfielder Derek Bell. "We've waited for the opportunity for a long time to secure a starter of Mike Hampton's ilk," said Phillips. "We had to step up and do this. This transaction certainly catapults us beyond the team that won 97 games last year."[10]

Hampton's demeanor also seemed perfect for a team looking to take the next step. Nicknamed "Bulldog," he had a fierce drive to succeed. "I go out there with intensity and competitiveness to do what it takes to win," said Hampton. "I just think in New York it's probably going to bring it out in me even more."[11]

Cedeño had been a sparkplug for the Mets, giving them speed that they had never had before. Their outfield, however, had an abundance of talent, making him expendable. Moreover, there were concerns about his defensive abilities and his decision making. "Word got around the team that Cedeño had purposely slowed down on the base paths, passing up chances to steal so he wouldn't create excessive expectations for himself in the future," noted the *Bergen Record*'s T. J. Quinn.[12]

Dotel showed promise, but the Mets were betting that ultimately he would not pan out as hoped. Still, Valentine was not thrilled. He had been kept out of the decision-making process that off-season and could not understand why the team was dealing Cedeño. He thought Cedeño was on the cusp of becoming something really special. He also was not thrilled with getting Bell. The outfielder had a reputation as being a bit of an eccentric and not in an endearing way. When he arrived for spring training, Bell told Valentine and the assembled coaches that they would never see him wearing the same outfit twice. Ever. He was as good as his word, wearing a different outfit every single day of the season. Some were amused. Others thought it a waste of money. Valentine wondered how Bell would fit in a clubhouse that already had a few players he considered problems.

The trade put the Mets front and center of that off-season. It gave them enough credibility that some believed this could be the year they would overtake the Braves in the NL East. Even losing Olerud, who had signed with the Mariners, had not been as big a possible blow because the team had inked Todd Zeile to a contract to play first. Zeile was coming off one of his best seasons, having slugged forty-one doubles and twenty-four home runs as a member of the Rangers. He was not a first baseman, having only played a few dozen games at that position in his career. That fact angered Valentine, who felt that if the Mets had allowed him to speak to Olerud, he could have convinced him not to sign with Seattle. Valentine was kept out, Olerud left, and Zeile would have to learn to play first.

The Hampton, Bell, and Zeile deals were the major moves of the off-season but not the only ones. The Mets also made transactions that involved three notable players returning to New York, two of whom would not make it to the regular season and one of whom lasted just two games. On December 10 they traded for Jesse Orosco. The lefty reliever, who happened to also be the last Met to throw a pitch in the World Series, was entering his fourth decade in Major League Baseball. Orosco had been a reliable specialist out of the Orioles bullpen for years until injuries hampered his 1999 season. His second go-around with the Mets lasted three months. In March 2000 he was traded to St. Louis during spring training for infielder Joe McEwing. Orosco had gotten battered in the spring, going 0-1 with a 9.00 ERA and was likely not going to make the team's Opening Day roster. "Disappointed," replied Orosco, when asked about the trade, "but it's better than a pink slip."[13]

Two days after trading Orosco away, the Mets released Charlie Hayes. The former Yankee had signed on with the club in January and produced in spring training, batting .386. But there was not enough room on the roster for him, not with Melvin Mora and Kurt Abbott on the team. "I think Charlie Hayes could play in the major leagues," said Phillips. "If we had a 26-man roster, then he would probably be on our team."[14]

Not long after they had signed Orosco, the Mets traded Luis Lopez to Milwaukee to reacquire Bill Pulsipher. Part of the vaunted Generation K that never materialized, Pulsipher had pitched through a season and a half of injuries with the Brewers. He had yet to regain the form that had made him one of the Mets' top prospects earlier in the decade. Unlike Orosco and Hayes, Pulsipher got past Opening Day, making two May starts. He was hit hard in both of them and traded away shortly thereafter.

Their roster now largely set, the Mets assembled in Port St. Lucie with expectations similar to those of their late 1980s heydays. They had arguably only gotten stronger in both pitching and hitting, now looking at full seasons out of potential stars like Mora and Agbayani. Fred Wilpon set the tone on day one when he declared that he expected the Mets to get to the World Series.

"The Mets are about as good as last year when they won 97 games," said Andrew Marchand of the *New York Post*. "Although the Braves' lineup is improved, their pitching is weaker. Thus, the Mets will win the NL East and win the NLDS, but lose to the wild-card Braves in the NLCS, leaving Valentine and the organization with a decision-filled winter." "I don't know if the Mets are good enough to play with the Yankees yet, or if they ever will be. But I am reasonably sure they will be more fun to cover, and perhaps even more fun to watch," wrote the *Post*'s Wallace Matthews.[15]

New York left Florida for the start of the season. It would be no ordinary Opening Day, though. In fact, there had not been one like it in the history of Major League Baseball.

• • •

The Mets had made their mark in the off-season. The Yankees, on the other hand, were staying quiet. They were two-time defending champions, and the majority of their team was under contract through at least 2000. Clemens and Pettitte, somehow the two biggest question marks in the rotation, were not going anywhere. The few moves the Yankees did make were largely addition by subtraction. Two weeks before Christmas they unloaded Chad Curtis on the Texas Rangers, receiving two pitchers who collectively played twelve games with the Yankees. Nine days later they dealt Irabu to the Expos.

Hideki Irabu's numbers with the Yankees were ultimately better than would be remembered. He was the team's best pitcher for long stretches of the 1998 and 1999 seasons, and he could have made the All-Star team if not for so many other dominating pitching performances in the first half of 1998. At times his split-fingered fastball was unhittable, matching the hype that had followed him from Japan. Still, his inability to pitch consistently well over a full season distorted his numbers. More important, though, at least to his legacy, was his inability to ever feel comfortable in the United States or even in his own skin. Irabu's deeper psychological issues made him ill equipped to handle the pressure of New York. That was how he'd be remembered. Irabu spent three more years in the big leagues between the Expos and the Rangers. He tried pitching in Japan again and even played in independent leagues for a bit. But he never found true happiness. His drinking, which had been an issue during his playing days, grew worse. His wife left with their two young children. On July 27, 2011, Irabu hanged himself inside his California home.

The Curtis and Irabu trades were the biggest moves the Yankees made in the off-season, highlighting just how little they felt they needed to improve the team. Still, whatever his attitude, Curtis had been a serviceable option in left when needed. Chili Davis retired, utility man extraordinaire Luis Sojo was allowed to leave via free agency, and the team was uncertain if Shane Spencer or Ricky Ledée were going to pan out. The Yankees needed depth, and they knew it. To get it, they turned to two familiar faces: Roberto Kelly and Tim Raines. Kelly, an outfielder from Panama, had come up in the Yankees' system and, during the club's darkest years, been one of their few offensive bright spots. He was the team's lone representative at the 1992 All-Star Game. But Kelly's habit of swinging at just about everything did not align with Gene Michael's philosophy of rebuilding the club through getting on base. He dealt Kelly to Cincinnati for Paul O'Neill, a risky deal at the time but one that eventually became among the most celebrated in club history.

Kelly had bounced around with seven different teams since the trade. He had played well everywhere he went but could never establish roots in any one organization. He was coming off a year in which he had posted one of his highest career on-base percentages, so the Yankees decided to bring him home to the Bronx.

A week later, the Yankees also brought back Tim Raines. The future Hall of Famer had been a key contributor to the team's '96 and '98 championship teams and was universally loved in the clubhouse. With no spot for him in 1999, he signed with Oakland. In a show of how much they adored their former teammate, when Raines returned to Yankee Stadium with the A's, the Yankees pranked him by giving him an empty box that was supposed to contain his '98 championship ring. Raines's season ended in July, when he was diagnosed with lupus. Healthy thanks to medication that controlled his kidney inflammation, Raines was now back in New York. Kelly and Raines would not be the last former Yankees to rejoin the team that year.

• • •

There was little to be determined for the Yankees in spring training other than who might win the starting job in left field: Spencer or Ledée. The rotation was set. The starting infield was without question. Posada was now officially the team's full-time catcher. Girardi had left after four seasons in which he'd won three titles and been a mentor to a future star catcher—not bad for a guy who had been booed by the hometown crowd the first time he appeared at Yankee Stadium. All the Yankees needed to do was get through spring training without injury or drama so they could begin the march for a third straight title. That idea lasted all of a few hours.

The night before the team's first full workout, news broke that Darryl Strawberry had failed another drug test. The test was from a month earlier and Acting Commissioner Selig had met with Strawberry the same day the story broke to explain the failed test and to say that Strawberry would face a yet-to-be-determined punishment. Selig made clear, or at least he thought he did, that Strawberry was to go home and await the commissioner's ruling. Instead, the next morning, Strawberry inexplicably tried to join the team as if nothing had happened. He met with Torre in the manager's office, then made a statement while standing in the dugout. "I'm not running and hiding. You guys know I've always been forward," he told reporters.[16]

Strawberry had informed the club that he was allowed to be there. Suspecting otherwise, reporters tipped Selig off when they called the commissioner's office to confirm if that was true. It was not. As Strawberry was out shagging fly balls, Minor League coach Rob Thompson came out and informed him he had to leave the facility. It was the last on-the-field act Strawberry performed as a Major Leaguer.

Steinbrenner had once been the epitome of 1980s "just say no" drug rhetoric. The years, however, had softened him on the issue, and he chose compassion in his comments about Strawberry. "I am getting a different side now from medical experts, people who really know that this is something," Steinbrenner said on the same day Strawberry was forced to leave spring training. "I'm going to stand by him. I'm going to try to see that he rights his life. If it's in baseball, fine. It it's outside baseball, fine. That's up to Bud [Selig]."[17]

Selig made his ruling four days later. "In the end, I could not ignore Darryl's past infractions and concluded that each of us must be held accountable for his or her actions," said Selig in announcing a one-year suspension.[18] That would take Strawberry through his final contract year with the Yankees. The implications were obvious, even to those who did not want to say so out loud: Strawberry's playing days were over. No one was going to take another chance on him. He finished his career with 335 home runs, a thousand RBIs, and four World Series rings.

The feel-good story of Raines returning did not last either. The outfielder performed better than expected, batting .292 in spring, but something just was not right for him. Possibly drained by the medical treatments he had received in the off-season, Raines found himself having to mentally prepare for games in ways he had never previously had to do. He also knew age was catching up with him. In a mid-March game against the Pirates, he fouled off a belt-high fastball rather than lining it somewhere for a hit. That was a clear sign for him. The next day Torre asked him if he wanted to pinch-hit in the ninth inning of a game against Toronto. He declined. "For me to turn down the at-bat, something had to be wrong," Raines acknowledged.[19]

Raines announced his retirement two days later, content in knowing he would be spending more time with his family. A year later he came out of retirement to play for the Expos, the team with which he had spent the majority of his career. In the last week of the season, he was traded to the Orioles so that he could play with his son, Tim Jr. After playing with Florida in 2002, Raines retired for good.

As the Yankees broke camp, they felt they needed a little more speed in the lineup and signed Lance Johnson. The former Met, who had set the franchise record for most hits in a season, had not played a full season in four years but could provide additional depth in the outfield.

For the fourth consecutive year, the Yankees began the season on the West Coast. Unlike in the previous three years, though, they won on Opening Night. Hernández, the team's fourth different Opening Day starter in four years, held the Angels in check while a two-run home run by O'Neill and solo shot by Spencer cemented the win.

With that win the Yankees were off and running. An eight-game winning streak in the middle of April took them into first place. They ended the month 15-8 and in sole possession of first place. Hernández performed even better than he had the year before, picking up four wins in April and giving up just six runs over his first four starts of the year. Clemens showed flashes of his former Cy Young Award self, going at least six innings in each of his six April starts while yielding two runs or fewer in four of them. Jeter, O'Neill, and Posada carried the offense, each hitting above .300 and each sporting an OPS above .900. The team was firing on nearly all cylinders. There were issues, though.

Pettitte strained a muscle in his back, the result of ducking out of the way of a broken bat during spring training. He thought he could pitch through the discomfort, but in his first start of the year he allowed five runs in five innings and looked uncomfortable on the mound. Though he insisted he could make his next start, Torre decided not to chance it. Pettitte went on the DL.

While Pettitte was injured, no one had any idea what was wrong with David Cone. The ace righty had gotten shelled for eight runs in his first start of the year, though it was not uncommon for Cone's first performance of a season to be a bad one. He had started badly in 1998 and had gone on to win twenty games. But he got hit again in his next start, and in his fourth game of the year, he gave up seven runs to the Blue Jays. Nothing Cone threw was working, evidenced by the paltry number of strikeouts he was getting in each game. A solid start at month's end gave reason for hope, but in April Cone still went 1-2, with a 7.66 ERA and, for him at least, a startlingly low six strikeouts per nine innings.

For the offense left field and DH were not producing as hoped. Spencer and Ledée were barely hitting over .200, with Ledée having produced only four extra-base hits the entire month. Roberto Kelly began to feel pain in his elbow early in the month before landing on the disabled list. He needed Tommy John surgery and never played again. Lance Johnson performed well in sporadic duty, but the Yankees had misjudged just how much they would want his speed over someone else's power, and they released him at the end of May.

Those issues aside, the team was still in first place, and no ballclub goes an entire season without some tales of woe. So long as the Yankees kept winning, they could afford not to have offensive production from the left fielder or even the designated hitter. As the calendar turned to May, though, those holes in the lineup became glaring.

• • •

Mark McGwire did not want to fly all the way to Japan to play baseball. He could appreciate that the commissioner's office was trying to expand appeal to the game by proposing that the 2000 season start in Tokyo. He just didn't want his team to be part of the appeal. When Major League Baseball came to McGwire's Cardinals and the Mets in August 1999 with this proposal, the Mets agreed, though players like Henderson and Piazza had concerns about the travel. The Cardinals did not, though. "Major league baseball belongs in the United States," said McGwire, shortsightedly as it would turn out. "The Japanese have Japanese baseball, so there's no reason for us to go over there."[20] Cardinals players voted the idea down. It was then brought to the Cubs, thanks largely to the appeal in Japan of Sammy Sosa, who agreed to go. With that the stage was set for Opening Day on March 29 at the Tokyo Dome, with another game to be played the following day.

For Bobby Valentine the trip was a homecoming of sorts. He had managed the Chiba Lotte Marines in Japan in 1995, leading the club to a surprising second-place finish. Fans had come to adore Valentine and his style of baseball. But Valentine clashed with club leadership and was let go after just one season. He remained popular, though, and fans had even started a drive to bring him back after his sacking.

There was plenty of pomp and circumstance in the lead-up to the game. A welcome reception at the U.S. embassy—the same building in which General Douglas MacArthur had accepted Japan's surrender to end World War II—featured Hall of Famers Hank Aaron, Ernie Banks, Lou Brock, Billy Williams, and Tommy Lasorda. Players were also invited to the imperial palace, along with shopping in the famous Ginza district.

The Mets were listed as the home team for the first game, despite being nearly seven thousand miles from Shea Stadium. Hampton got the start and threw the first official Major League pitch ever outside of North America. It was 7:05 p.m. in Tokyo, or 5:05 a.m. in New York, when Hampton began his Mets' career by walking lead-off hitter Eric Young Sr. Despite the time difference, Mets fans awoke early to watch Opening Day. "By 7 a.m., we had between 20 and 30 people here watching the game," said Doug Horan, a manager for Kelly's Tavern in Neptune City, New Jersey.[21]

The Cubs eventually grabbed the lead, and Hampton, maybe jittery or not fully ready given the abbreviated spring, allowed thirteen base runners in five innings, including a career-high nine walks. Perhaps he was also thrown off by the lack of crowd noise. The Yomiuri Giants, who played their home games in the Dome, had asked that fans not be unruly or do anything that might cause embarrassment. So the fans behaved themselves, and it created an odd atmosphere. "This had a playoff atmosphere at the beginning, like you were watching halftime of the Super Bowl," said Wendell. "Then the game starts and you can hear the umpire going, 'Strike' or 'Ball.'"[22]

Hampton took the loss in the team's 5–3 defeat, which most fans probably heard about on their way to work. Meanwhile, Valentine drew the ire of Cubs manager Don Baylor when, in the ninth inning, the Mets manager protested the game. Valentine argued that the Cubs had illegally made a defensive replacement because a player had been mistakenly left off Baylor's lineup card. The move left Baylor irritated, and that then left Valentine irritated. Baylor saw it more as showboating. "You just have to understand Bobby, which I try to do," he said.[23] Valentine could not understand what the fuss was about. Baylor was the one who had screwed up, Valentine thought. How could he not protest? "It will be huge," Valentine said of the story that would come out of all this. "I was involved in it, so it will be ridiculously huge. The other guy made the mistake and I'll be the idiot."[24]

The second game brought genuine excitement to the Tokyo Dome. Reed was phenomenal as he kept Chicago to a single run over eight innings. The game went to the eleventh inning, where, after two outs, the Mets loaded the bases for Agbayani. The outfielder golfed a 1-0 pitch just over the wall in center field for a grand slam. It was an especially sweet moment for the outfielder. Agbayani had made the team out of spring due to an injury to pitcher Glendon Rusch. Once Rusch returned, Agbayani understood that he would be sent back down. In response, he had asked to be traded.

The Mets' reaction to Agbayani's shot showed just how much the team loved him. Agbayani, who had used an especially high leg kick, reminiscent of Japanese players, to hit the ball, raised both arms in triumph as he rounded first. Pratt was shouting so loudly that it looked like he might blow a gasket. The Mets had their first win on the Asian continent and of the season, making the long flight home much more tolerable.

Given three days to rest from jet lag, the Mets played their unofficial home opener on April 3 in front of over fifty-two thousand fans at Shea. Bell, in his first game as a Met in Queens, played hero, hitting a go-ahead home run in the eighth that ultimately held up. Over the next two weeks, however, the

Mets struggled for cohesion. The pitchers especially had trouble, possibly a consequence of the short spring and travel to the other side of the world. Hampton, in particular, looked unconformable on the mound. While not necessarily known as a strikeout pitcher, his inability to get hitters to swing and miss, combined with his difficulty finding the strike zone, resulted in thirty-three base runners in his first three starts of the year. He lost each of those games, and his seventeen combined walks were the most he had ever given up in that span. "Right now, we basically stink," he said after an 8–5 loss in Philadelphia. "And I'm a big part of it. . . . I've stunk it up. I stink right now."[25] *Newsday* pointed out that Hampton's numbers after three starts were near identical to those of Kenny Rogers from the 1999 postseason, a comparison not meant to be complementary in any fashion.[26]

Hampton won his next two outings but did so largely in spite of his performance, yielding ten total runs. After six starts with the Mets, he was 2-4, with a 6.48 ERA. It did not take long for those numbers to draw the ire of fans.

Meanwhile, Valentine was in the hot seat again, this time for comments he had allegedly made to a group of students at the University of Pennsylvania's Wharton School of Business. Valentine had gone there as a favor to an investor in a dot-com charity that the manager had started. His remarks to the students were nothing out of the ordinary. All was well. Then, as Valentine walked out of the building, a group of students approached him and began asking questions about the team's off-season moves. Valentine, still upset about his lack of a role in all the trades and signings, decided to have a little fun and vent. There was no reason, as far as he was concerned, to think his comments would ever be public.

"Why did you sign Derek Bell?"

"Because we didn't want to give Benny a chance to become a star."

"Why did you give Ordóñez a multi-year contract?"

"Because we wanted to reward him for having the lowest on-base percentage and slugging percentage in the history of baseball."

"Why did you sign Todd Zeile? What happened to John Olerud?"

"Because it would be too easy for us to win and have four Gold Glovers with [Olerud's] playing first base. We needed a challenge."[27]

Valentine left, figuring he would never think about his appearance another day in his life. He was unaware that one of the students had a blog, a fairly new concept on the internet in which any person could simply piece together his or her thoughts on issues of the day or report news as the blogger saw it. That night a blog from someone identified as Brad34 appeared online and reported Valentine's comments. All of a sudden, Brad34 became the most important person in the world to the Mets' organization.

Valentine found out when a reporter called to ask him who Brad34 was and if Valentine had said those things in his speech to the students. "No, who the fuck is Brad34?" replied Valentine.[28] He denied making those remarks in his speech, a response that was technically and shrewdly true. Soon Phillips called Valentine and asked him the same thing. Valentine gave the same response. Phillips did not believe him and told him that if Valentine had in fact said those things, he was going to fire him. The Mets hired an investigator to find Brad34 and confirm what he'd written. Rumors of a tape spread. It turned out there was a tape but of only half of Valentine's speech.

The search for Brad34 continued for hours. Eventually Brad Rosenberg was found. He said Valentine had not said those things in his speech, which was technically true, and that he'd taken some liberties with his blog post. Valentine got away with it, but just barely. The experience led him to try and be more guarded with his interactions moving forward.

A mid-April home series against the Brewers turned out to be just the salve the Mets needed. It started with a 10–7 win punctuated by Ventura's fourteenth career grand slam, tying him for the most of any active player. The next day Reed, who nearly took a comebacker to the face on the fifth pitch of the game, gave up just one run over seven innings, getting the win. In the final game of the series, Mora's first career regular-season home run walked it off in the eleventh. The sweep put the Mets over .500, and they stayed there for the rest of the year.

The Mets continued their strong play, making mincemeat of the Cubs in a three-game sweep where they scored a total of thirty runs. Needing a spot starter for a make-up game against the Dodgers, New York called on Pat Mahomes. Father of the future star quarterback for the Chiefs, Mahomes blanked Los Angeles into the sixth, allowing just two hits. An infield single by Matt Franco in the ninth gave the team its eighth straight win.

The streak reached nine games, with the ninth win coming in especially satisfying fashion for fans. With the Mets clinging to a 6–5 lead against Cincinnati in the ninth, Ken Griffey Jr. came to the plate with the tying and go-ahead runs on base. Still angry over being rejected by him during the off-season, the crowd at Shea had been letting Junior have it all night.

With the game on the line, Benitez struck Griffey out looking as fans giddily rejoiced. The Mets closed out April at 16-10 and in second place.

While Hampton had struggled throughout the month, new Met Derek Bell was nearly unstoppable. After starting the season at just 4-29, Bell then had ten multi-hit games over a twelve-game span. The streak included three three-hit games and two four-hit games. During the sweep of the Cubs, Bell went 10-12, with a home run and six RBIs. In Philadelphia earlier in the year he had made an all-out diving grab of a ball hit in the gap with the bases loaded, a play that made multiple highlight reels throughout the year. After a month in Flushing, Bell was a hit.

Alfonzo performed as if his 1999 season had never ended, driving in nineteen runs before the end of April. In the last series of the month at Colorado, he went 10-13, with eighteen total bases. Piazza was belting the ball, accumulating five home runs and sixteen RBIs. At Pittsburgh on April 14 he had his first career five-hit game, hitting two home runs in the process. When Piazza was not playing, his backup did not miss a beat. In the same Colorado series where Alfonzo had walked over the Rockies, Pratt went 7-11, with three extra-base hits. Ventura hit six home runs and drove in twenty.

All told, April had been a solid month for the Mets. They had accomplished that 16-10 record (one win and one loss had taken place in March) without getting almost any quality performances out of their ace. Imagine what would happen when Hampton started pitching like Hampton again.

That started to happen in May. The lefty put in a string of strong performances, winning four games and allowing only one run over a three-start stretch. Oddly, though, the Mets faltered in May, having their worst month of the season. There was no prolonged losing streak. In fact, after losing the first four games of the month, they never lost more than two in a row the rest of May. There was also no prolonged winning streak, and that was the problem. They lost some; they won some.

There were joyous moments here and there. One came on May 21, when they faced off against Randy Johnson for the first time since the Division Series the previous October. The Mets tagged Johnson for five doubles and three home runs. One of those home runs came off the bat of McEwing, his first of the year. The game went back and forth until Bell won it in the ninth with a line-drive single to right. The win gave the Mets a sweep of Arizona, marking five straight wins against the Diamondbacks going back to the previous year's postseason.

There were also inevitable moments. For example, Rickey Henderson's days as a Met were marked the second he was found playing cards in the clubhouse after Game Six of the NLCS. He had requested a trade just before the start of the season and the Mets would have obliged him, but no one was willing to make a deal. As the Mets struggled, Henderson challenged Valentine's authority as manager, saying Valentine had no plans to turn the team around. Some of this might have been tolerable had Henderson repeated his 1999 performance. But he was struggling mightily at the plate, garnering only a single extra-base hit and five stolen bases through thirty games. The final straw came on May 12 at home against the Marlins. Leading off, Henderson drilled a ball to deep left field. Rickey began his home trot, putting his head down and not watching as the ball hit the wall rather than leave the yard. Henderson ended up on first rather than second. While some players tried to cover for him, saying it was an innocent mistake, Valentine had had enough. He told Phillips he wanted Henderson gone that night. Phillips told Valentine to sleep on it. He did, and it did not change his mind. That same day, Henderson had tried to fight a reporter and then had said, regarding his home run trot on a single, that he would do the same thing again in the same situation. "I hit the ball out and it didn't go out," he explained. "I can't change my home run trot. If I'd looked up and paid attention, I'd know the ball didn't go out and I'd be on second base standing up."[29] That was *exactly* the problem, thought Valentine. It was also enough for Phillips. Henderson was released that day. "The reasons are fairly obvious as to why we've done this," said Phillips. "Earlier I said no matter how talented you are if you continue to say the wrong thing and do the wrong thing, you wear out your welcome."[30]

Valentine, who had come to regret his handling of Rickey, largely because he felt he had compromised too much in dealing with him, did not hold back. "As far as I'm concerned, I didn't think I could compromise my principles anymore," said Valentine. "I'm perceived as an inflexible hard head, but I thought I bent too much and I wasn't really having fun living with myself."[31]

There were also devastating moments. For example, Ordóñez was not having a great year, one of many players struggling in the early goings. His record streak of consecutive errorless games had ended at 101 in Tokyo. After signing a four-year contract extension in the off-season, he was having his worst offensive season yet, batting just .188. Still, his defense could not be beat, and there was hope that his bat would come around eventually—until May 29. Against the Dodgers in Los Angeles, he went to slap a tag on F. P. Santangelo, who was attempting to steal second. Santangelo's helmet made contact with Ordóñez's left arm, breaking the ulna. What the team initially hoped would be a six-week injury ended up ending Ordóñez's season. Teammates tried to put a spin on it. "It's probably a little test for us to realize that if this is a team of destiny and a team that is supposed to go on to some bigger and better things, stuff like this happens," said Leiter.[32]

The end result of all the slumps and mental errors and injuries was a 13-14 month, putting the team seven games out of first and raising questions about whether the Mets were for real in 2000. Come June, the Mets would answer that question with one of the most dramatic and talked about games ever at Shea.

• • •

The Yankees were sputtering out of control. They had started the month of May hot, winning seven of the month's first eight games. That had included a thrilling victory on May 5 that saw them come from two runs down in the ninth to win the game on a Posada three-run walk-off home run. Then it all stopped. It would be another two months before they won at least three games in a row. They were swept out of Detroit mid-month, losses that knocked them into second place. They lost series to Cleveland, Boston, and Oakland, playing just .500 ball in May. June brought even worse play. Nothing seemed to go right. Cone had showed signs of turning things around in mid-May, only to then give up six runs in back-to-back starts. In seven of his first twelve starts of the year, he allowed at least four runs while never striking out more than six batters.

Roger Clemens had spoiled his solid start to the year with a couple of May clunkers in which he had given up six runs in each. He then gave up twelve earned runs in just ten innings to start June before leaving with a strained right groin in his next appearance. He missed two weeks.

Orlando Hernández went down with an elbow strain, missing one start before coming back on July 1. He made two strong starts before the Marlins lit him up for seven runs. Five days later the elbow strain landed him on the DL. He missed nearly a month.

As the injuries mounted, the Yankees were forced to turn to their Minor League system for backup. Jake Westbrook, acquired in the Irabu deal, made his big league debut on June 17 and gave up six runs before he could get past the second inning. In his second start he allowed four more before reaching the third. Ben Ford made a serviceable team debut in Chicago before getting slammed for seven runs in two innings against Detroit. Between the injured Clemens and Hernández and whatever was happening to Cone, the team needed help.

On offense, Tino Martinez was battling through the worst power outage of his career. He hit two home runs in the first week of the season but only five total in May and June. On June 30 his slugging percentage stood at .428 and his OPS at .755, far lower than what he'd accomplished in previous years with New York. The Yankees had even considered trading Martinez to the Braves, though the deal never happened. Ledée had started to heat up toward the end of May, but his power numbers were just not what the Yankees had envisioned.

The bottoming-out moment occurred when the White Sox came to town for a four-game series in mid-June. In the first game Chicago came in and built an early 1–0 lead off Pettitte. Leading off the third inning, Ray Durham hit a hard shot right at Knoblauch. He fielded the ball cleanly and then whipped a throw to first for which Martinez had to lunge off the bag to prevent the ball from sailing into the dugout. Error number one.

In the top of the fifth, with two outs and a runner on third, Carlos Lee hit a ball up the middle that Knoblauch made a nice backhand stab of, but turning to throw, he side-armed the ball, and his throw tailed up the line toward home plate. The only thing that prevented it from going to the dugout was that it hit Lee as he ran toward first. Error number two.

In the next inning, with one out and runners on first and second, Frank Thomas hit what looked like a double-play ground ball to short. Jeter threw to Knoblauch at second for one out, but Knoblauch's throw to first tailed away from Martinez again, this time toward right field. Martinez could not stay on the bag. Error number three.

When Torre came out to the mound for a conference, the entire infield came in except Knoblauch. He remained at his position, holding his glove in his right hand, his other hand on his hip.

"Chuck is fine when he has to make a diving play, then scramble to his feet and throw," recalled Rivera years later. "The yips come when he has time to think about it. I've never been on a team with a player who has had the yips until now, and it's just horrific to watch . . . and probably the worst part—beyond even the embarrassment and humiliation—is the way it sucks every bit of fun out of playing the game."[33]

After the third error, when the inning ended, Knoblauch walked off the field and headed straight for the tunnel leading to the clubhouse. "I'm done," he told Torre as he moved past the manager.[34] Torre followed him to the locker room, where Knoblauch made clear he was serious. He was done with baseball. Torre told him to go home and think about it. The Yankees lost, 12–3.

Knoblauch was distraught, uncertain how things had come to this. Some teammates were worried he might do something more serious than just retire from the game. The pressure was too intense. The team rallied around him, with Jeter chiding the fans for their ridicule. "I've said before that we're not going to win without Chuck, and it's about time the fans got behind him," Jeter told the press after the game against Chicago.[35]

Knoblauch returned the next day and recorded two hits in a 3–1 losing effort. The following day, in the fourth inning, Knoblauch charged a ground ball by Greg Norton and, on the run, fired the ball into the seventh row behind the Yankees' dugout. It struck Marie Olbermann, mother of then Fox Sports anchor and former *SportsCenter* anchor Keith Olbermann. The following day the *Daily News* back page had a picture of Knoblauch with the headline "Look Out!"

Torre was starting to get mad at reporters over their treatment of his second baseman. After the White Sox series, in which the Yankees ended up losing all four games by a combined score of 42–17, he went after Olbermann's former employer. "I don't know who did this," Torre said, referring to a *SportsCenter* anchor. "Somebody doing the late one, but [Houston's] Billy Wagner walked four guys and [the anchor] says, 'Bring in Chuck Knoblauch.' It's just to be cute and that pisses me off."[36]

Whatever Torre's anger, Knoblauch was now too much of a liability for the Yankees to keep putting him out in the field every day. It was clear, no matter what his teammates tried to do, that the Yankees needed help at second base. Just two days after the White Sox series debacle, they sent Jim Leyritz to the Dodgers for infielder José Vizcaino. It was a little-noted deal at the time, but the Yankees knew they could not rely on Knoblauch in the field, especially in the later innings, during the season's stretch run, and if they made the postseason. Vizcaino, a former Met, had made only two errors all year to Knoblauch's thirteen. He could provide defensive relief at second the rest of the season, and if every now and then he managed to get a hit, that would just be a bonus.

Leyritz, meanwhile, was shocked. "I went up to the [hotel] room to the call the babysitter and she said there was a message to call [Yankees GM] Brian Cashman," he said. "I don't know what to think. He told me he knew I wanted to stay and everything, but . . ."[37] Leyritz played forty-one games for the Dodgers that year, the last forty-one of his career.

As the Vizcaino deal developed, the Yankees had something even bigger in mind to help their offense. Hoping to inject star power into the lineup, the team worked out a trade with the Tigers for slugger Juan González. The two-time MVP had hit over forty home runs five times in a season. Over the previous four seasons he had averaged an amazing 140 RBIs a year. González had also terrorized the Yankees, including hitting five home runs against them in the 1996 ALDS. After he had spent the first eleven years of his career with Texas, the Rangers traded González to Detroit before the 2000 season. Whether it was the Tigers' spacious new ballpark, the passage of time, or both, González's numbers that year were not his standard offensive output. It was still better than most, though.

On June 22 the Yankees and Tigers agreed to a deal: González in exchange for Ledée and Minor Leaguers Drew Henson and Randy Keisler. But there was an issue. González would be a free agent after the season. He was willing to go to New York without a contract extension. The Yankees, however, we're not willing to trade for him unless he agreed to an extension in advance. Steinbrenner, unwilling to go more than a year, offered up a one-year deal worth $12.5 million. González rejected that offer, expecting the Yankees would come back with another. Instead they informed the Tigers that if González would not agree to an extension, they wanted to renegotiate who would be part of the trade. "Apparently they went back to Detroit and tried to rework it as a three-month rental," said González's agent, Jim Bronner.[38] With that, on June 26 any chance of González's playing for the Yankees ended.

That same day the Yankees turned their sites from the 1998 American League MVP to the 1998 National League MVP, Sammy Sosa. Sosa had taken the country by storm that year when he had seemingly come out of nowhere to join Mark McGwire in the race to break the single-season home run record. Sosa ended up with sixty-six, then followed that up by hitting sixty-three in 1999. While he wasn't on that kind of pace in 2000, his numbers were still better than were those for anyone on the Yankees: a .313 average with twenty home runs and sixty-six RBIS.

Steinbrenner loved the idea of Sosa's bringing his star power and charisma to New York. The Cubs, not believing they would resign Sosa when his contract ended after the 2001 season, were willing to deal him. The Yankees and Cubs had been having discussions at the same time New York had been trying to deal for González. Once the González trade disintegrated, talks between the two sides intensified. In exchange for Sosa, the Cubs would receive Ledée or Spencer, along with several prospects, including the highly touted Alfonso Soriano. For three days talks continued. At one point someone involved in the negotiations let out that the two sides were "very close."

"Very close" is as close as they would get though. No consensus could be reached on which players to include in the deal. The Yankees reportedly balked when the Cubs insisted that Spencer be part of the trade package. They also did not want to trade away so many prospects, hoping to retain them to make a deal for a pitcher down the line.

After much back and forth, Steinbrenner's advisors decided against making the Sosa deal. Instead they argued that the team should make a different trade. The deal happened almost by accident. Cashman called the Indians' assistant GM Mark Shapiro to find out how he could get a 1999 championship ring to Gary Tuck, who had been the Yankees' catching instructor before heading to Cleveland. During the call Shapiro mentioned that the Indians were willing to trade David Justice, largely to get his contract off the books because it paid him roughly $21 million through 2002. Justice would be a perfect addition to the Yankees. He was not a marquee name like González or Sosa. But he had put up years of solid offensive numbers, and his plate discipline matched with the team's general philosophy. Justice's teams had appeared in the postseason for nine consecutive years. He was no stranger to pressure. Moreover, Justice was in the midst of one of his best offensive seasons ever, having already hit twenty-one home runs. New York would also not have to give up the farm to get him. Cleveland asked for Ledée, pitcher Jake Westbrook, and another Minor Leaguer. That meant the Yankees could still add a pitcher when the time came. They were already looking at possible deals for the Twins' Brad Radke or the Phillies' Curt Schilling.

That was good enough for Steinbrenner, who signed off on the trade the night of June 28. In one week the team had gone from a trade for González to that trade falling apart to a near deal for Sosa to a trade for Justice. "I'm happy, and hopefully this will quiet things down so we can focus on baseball," said a relieved Torre when news of the Justice move reached him.[39]

Justice's first game with the team was a disappointing 6–4 loss that saw the Yankees drop to 38-36 on the season and three games out of first place. They strung a few wins together before heading to Shea Stadium for a series that would be memorable for all the right and, unfortunately, wrong reasons, some of which would resonate into October.

• • •

Mike Piazza mini-hopped a few steps down the first-base line as home plate umpire Gary Cederstrom rushed out from home plate. Both were tracking the flight of the ball that Piazza had just belted down the left-field line. Hit on a rope, the ball appeared to never get higher than thirty or so feet off the ground, and both Cederstrom and Piazza were checking to see if the shot would stay fair. It plunked the blue wall that sat behind the outfield fence, making a mark between the foul pole and Tom Seaver's retired number 37. With that, Shea Stadium collectively lost its mind. Perhaps no midseason home run in Mets history had caused a reaction such as this—and with good reason. The home run, hit on June 30, was the culmination of several separate storylines around the team, which had now been brought together by this moment.

The first storyline was the Mets' torrid path through the month of June, when they lost only a single series. Between June 22 and 28 they won seven games in a row by a combined score of 57–26. Leiter had reestablished himself as the ace of the staff, going 4-0 in the month to improve to 9-1 overall. No one, however, was making more of an impact than the team's catcher. Starting on June 7 at Baltimore, Piazza went on a history-making streak perhaps unmatched by any previous Met. From then until June 30, a span of seventeen games, he hit seven home runs and drove in twenty-seven runs. He recorded a hit in each of those games, ultimately on his way to a twenty-one-game hitting streak. On June 28 he drove in a run against Florida, breaking the previous Mets record of ten consecutive games with an RBI. Piazza, however, had yet to drive in a run coming into his at bat against the Braves on June 30.

Then there were the Braves themselves. New York had been chasing them all season—again—and had managed to narrow the gap between the two teams to just two games when Atlanta came to Shea on June 29. It is remarkable that, just two weeks before the All-Star break, it was the first time the two had played each other all year. The drama of the series, however, was about more than just avenging the previous year's NLCS defeat. The animosity between certain Braves players and New York—the city, not just the Mets—had not abated. In fact, thanks to John Rocker, it had gotten much worse.

Rocker had already been despised in New York due to his comments leading up to and during the NLCS. Things, in theory, should have cooled down in the off-season. Then Rocker spent a day with *Sports Illustrated*'s Jeff Pearlman that would have a lasting impact and consequences.

Pearlman, who described himself as a low-level baseball writer at the time, had been tasked with doing a profile piece on Rocker during the 1999 NLCS. He had spent pockets of time with the reliever over the course of a few days, spoken to his parents, and heard from his teammates. Rocker did not seem all that bad based on their comments. "The story I wrote was a much more positive piece about John Rocker," said Pearlman. "Honestly, the story I wrote, the original piece, was like a redemptive piece. It was, 'He seems like a jerk, but he's not really.'"[40]

That story never ran. The Yankees swept the Braves, and *Sports Illustrated* saw no reason to run a story on someone whose team had just gotten crushed in the World Series. A few weeks later Pearlman was tasked with picking up the story and freshening it up. He arranged to tag along with Rocker for a day down in Atlanta. When Pearlman got into Rocker's car, it was clear that this was going to be a different kind of interview. "There was this moment early on where he starts cursing and talking about Asian women and how they can't drive," said Pearlman, referring to a moment when the two got stuck behind another car. "And the guy driving was a white guy."

Later on, after Rocker referred to his own teammate Randall Simon as a "fat monkey," he then laid out his true view of New York. "Imagine having to take the [Number] 7 train to the ballpark, looking like you're [riding through] Beirut next to some kid with purple hair next to some queer with AIDS right next to some dude who just got out of jail for the fourth time right next to some 20-year-old mom with kids. It's depressing."[41]

Pearlman, at first unsure what to do given how bizarrely the whole day had gone, decided to write the story as he had experienced it. The profile was set to appear in *Sports Illustrated*'s last issue of the century, along with a listing of the top athletes of the twentieth century from all fifty states. Given how huge the task of compiling that list had been, Pearlman was uncertain if anyone would even notice the Rocker piece.

Everyone noticed it. The story, with its incendiary and racist, bigoted, and sexiest remarks, blew up immediately. First Lady Hillary Clinton and New York City mayor Rudy Giuliani, both running for a New York Senate seat, slammed Rocker for his remarks. Even Rocker's hometown mayor chimed in. "Of course he owes an apology to Macon. He owes an apology to Major League Baseball. He owes an apology to America," said Mayor Jack Ellis of Macon, Georgia.[42]

Commissioner Selig called Rocker's comments "reprehensible and completely inexcusable" and ordered him to undergo psychological testing.[43] He fined the pitcher $20,000 and suspended him for seventy-three games, though ultimately the suspension was cut to two weeks and a fine of $500. "We have asked for his termination and still stand by that," said Jeff Graham, executive director of Atlanta's AIDS Survival Project. "This certainly falls short of what we asked for and think is appropriate."[44]

Rocker's comments brought a whole new level of intensity to the Braves-Mets rivalry. The first game between the two teams in 2000 had meaning both literally and figuratively—literally because if the Mets swept, they would be in first place; figuratively because the Mets wanted to provide the ultimate "screw you" to John Rocker. They failed, at least initially.

Rocker entered the first game in the eighth inning to protect a 6–4 lead. The crowd booed incessantly as he entered, as he warmed up, and as he threw to Robin Ventura. The only time they cheered was when Rocker missed the strikeout, a failure that elicited loud, mocking applause. Rocker retired the side in order and walked back to the dugout. This time he did not say a word to the crowd; rather, he looked around with the largest shit-eating grin Shea Stadium had ever seen. The Braves won, making the Mets and their fans even hungrier for some form of revenge.

That led into June 30. The Mets were losing before they even came to the plate and down 8–1 in the bottom of the eighth inning. A loss would drop them four games out of first, but even worse, it would seemingly secure the Braves dominance over them for one more season. Then the comeback, which would be remembered and discussed for decades, started.

It began with a whimper. Ventura grounded out to drive in a run, leaving a runner on base with two outs and the team still down six runs.

Todd Zeile singled; 8–3, Braves.

Jay Payton singled.

Benny Agbayani walked.

Mark Johnson walked; 8–4, Braves.

Melvin Mora walked; 8–5, Braves.

Derek Bell walked; 8–6, Braves.

Edgardo Alfonzo singled; 8–8.

Now Piazza was up. The fans could not believe what they were seeing, nor that the inning had played out so that the hottest hitter in baseball was now at the plate. As he stepped into the batter's box, Piazza thought about how crazy the stadium would get if he got a hit in this situation. He then jumped on the first pitch from former Yankee Terry Mulholland. "The worst pitch I've ever thrown," Mulholland called it.[45] The ball left the yard in just three seconds. "I wasn't sure if it was going to hit the wall or go through the wall," said Zeile.[46]

Piazza pumped his first like he was punching someone in the gut while Pratt leapt out of the dugout like he had jumped off a trampoline. The team and the city had wanted this home run. They needed this home run. "It just seems like we've been falling into that pattern against the Braves during the season," said Piazza, referring to the team's performance in the first seven innings of the game. "We come in tight, we press, we make mistakes, we don't make good pitches. I can't explain it. That's baseball. Hopefully, this will relax us quite a bit."[47]

It was the second-biggest comeback in team history; it gave the Mets the win and extended Piazza's consecutive-games RBI streak, which eventually ended at fifteen, the second most in National League history.

Starting July where June had left off, the Mets torched Greg Maddux for seven runs in two innings, his shortest outing in four years. They won, 9–1, as Leiter's record improved to 10-1. The Mets were two games back of first and two games up in the wild-card standings when the Yankees came to town—sort of.

• • •

Dwight Gooden's career was over. He'd just been released by the lowly Devil Rays, a work-in-progress expansion franchise desperate for players but not desperate enough to maintain Doc's services. After leaving the Yankees in 1997, Gooden signed on with the Indians and, after missing the first two months of the season due to injury, pitched moderately well in 1998. Over the final two months of the year, he went 5-0, providing stability to the back end of Cleveland's rotation. More injuries abounded in 1999, though, as Doc battled through possibly the worst year of his career. A free agent after the season, Gooden was now a thirty-five-year-old pitcher with a history of injuries who could not get anyone out anymore. Houston, coming off a division title, gave him a low-risk, high-reward contract and an opportunity to make the club out of spring training.

Gooden had the distinction of throwing the first pitch ever at Houston's new stadium, then named Enron Field, in an exhibition match-up against the Yankees. A week later he made his first start as a National League pitcher in six years, getting a no-decision. Before he could make his next start, the Astros sent Gooden to the Devil Rays for cash. Since Doc was a Tampa native, there was hope that being close to home could reinvigorate him and get him to show some of the old flash. There was also, of course, the possibility that being so close to home could lead him back to addiction. The year before, Gooden had published his autobiography, *Heat*, in which he talked openly about his problems with drugs and what they had done to his life.

By all accounts Gooden was clean when with the Devil Rays. In his first start he held the Tigers scoreless and picked up the win. It was downhill from there. Gooden was getting battered in start after start, giving up a startling fourteen home runs over seven games. In twenty-one and two-thirds innings in May, he allowed forty-six base runners, failing to win a game. The Rays were 15-30, already twelve games out of first on May 25, and had no one to replace him in the rotation, but they were not going to keep putting Doc out there. They released him that day. Gooden's performance had been so poor that Tampa actually asked him to retire. "He's a warrior and has been through a lot of ups and downs," said Devil Rays general manager Chuck LaMar. "I felt like that his playing days were coming to an end and I wanted him to go out the right way," LaMar continued. "I thought it was time to make a move with Dwight and I gave him that opportunity to retire."[48]

Gooden was 2-3 with a 6.86 ERA for the season. Teams collectively had hit .319 against him with a .645 slugging percentage. There was little reason for anyone to come calling, even if Gooden still wanted to pitch. But Doc believed he had something left. He made a personal appeal to Steinbrenner to give him the chance to prove it. The Yankees, meanwhile, realized that between Cone's head-scratching ineffectiveness and the lingering injuries around Clemens, Pettitte, and Hernández, they needed an insurance policy. After Gooden's small-scale tryout in front of team brass, the Yankees signed him and sent him to their Tampa complex to work on mechanics and a new pitch, a screwball, with long-time coach and Steinbrenner confidant Billy Connors.

Doc worked through his new pitch and his old ones, then started two games for the Gulf Coast team. Even though the team was at the lowest rung of the Minor Leagues, his performance was still impressive: eight innings, three hits, no runs, and twelve strikeouts. At that rate, Gooden was going to get his opportunity with the big club.

On July 8 that opportunity came about in the most unreal of ways. Gooden was going to get the start for the Yankees. But this was not just any start. He'd be taking the mound at Shea Stadium in the first game of a day-night doubleheader that would be played in two different ballparks.

The quirk in scheduling was due to a rainout a month earlier. The first Subway Series of the year at Yankee Stadium was largely forgotten and for good reason. The two teams had traded blowout games, with Piazza hitting another home run off Clemens in the first game and the Yankees tagging Bobby Jones for seven runs in the second. The final game, a Sunday night affair, was at first rain delayed. This produced the most memorable moment of the series when Ventura, wearing a Piazza jersey and a fake mustache, mimicked the star catcher's batting stance, swing, and running gait as he trotted around the tarp-covered field. Ventura ended it with a slip-'n'-slide-like finish into home plate.

The moment provided levity for teammates and fans alike as the game was ultimately postponed. With no ideal off day in the schedule for either team to make up the game, the league decided to do something that had not been done in nearly ninety-seven years: the two teams would play a Saturday, July 8, doubleheader with the first game an afternoon event at Shea and the second an evening event at Yankee Stadium. It was a unique way to resolve the issue of when to play while also injecting some additional intrigue into the games.

In this scenario Gooden took the Shea Stadium mound for the first time since June 24, 1994. Doc's team—his current team that is—had already taken the first game of the series the night before. It was a tense pitchers' duel, with Leiter giving up two first-inning runs and then no more while El Duque held the Mets scoreless into the eighth. The game changed in the bottom of that inning, when, with a runner on third, Bell drilled a Hernández breaking ball to right field. O'Neill raced for it and, his back pressed against the fence and his eyes actually closed, leapt and caught the ball. A run scored, but the catch prevented a game-tying home run. The Yankees won, 2–1.

Elevating some of the pressure on Gooden, the Yankees jumped out to a 2–0 lead off Bobby Jones in the top of the first. Doc, sporting long sleeves in the early July heat, took the mound to a warm ovation. There were few feelings of resentment just because he sported the gray uniform of the crosstown rival. Instead the hometown crowd felt warmth toward the man who had been a crucial part of their last championship. And, in some way, many of them probably wanted Doc to succeed overall.

Gooden quickly threw two strikes to Mora. It was only two pitches, but he already looked like a different pitcher than the guy getting crushed in a Tampa uniform. His pitches had better movement and better location. Gooden retired Mora on the next pitch and got out of the inning unscathed after a Bell single. Doc maintained the Yankees' lead until the fifth, when Bell tied the game with a double. Gooden got through the inning, and Martinez homered in the sixth for the eventual game-winning run. Gooden secured the victory, the 191st of his career and his first at Shea since April 16, 1994. "I was just really happy for him," said Cone of Gooden. "He came right out of the gate throwing strikes, and I knew he'd be fine."[49]

The first game in the books, the teams packed up and got on their buses for the nine-mile drive from Flushing to the Bronx. They hopped on the Grand Central Parkway, over the Triborough Bridge, then onto the Major Deegan Expressway. All the while they had a police escort, and fans everywhere were either following their motorcade or waving from overpasses. "We had a presidential escort today, it seemed like," said Pettitte.[50]

Pratt, wanting to capture the uniqueness of the moment, filmed every minute of the trip from Shea to Yankee Stadium on a camcorder.

The feel-good nature of the first game was quickly eradicated by second-inning events in the second game. With no score, Piazza led off against Clemens. Up to that moment Piazza had owned Clemens like few hitters ever had: 7-12 with three home runs. Not only that, but Clemens overall also had brutal numbers against the Mets: 1-4 with a 9.10 ERA. Clemens couldn't get Piazza out, and he couldn't beat the Mets. Something needed to change.

Up on the count at 0-1, Clemens decided to come up and in with a fastball. Without question Clemens was trying to send a message and make Piazza uncomfortable in the box. It was really all he had left at that point to keep Piazza from hitting another titanic home run off him. What is questionable is whether Clemens deliberately intended what happened next. His fastball sailed directly toward Piazza, striking him in the helmet toward the bill, impacting Piazza's forehead. The ball bounded high up in the air as Piazza immediately fell backward, his helmet falling off and his bat dropping from his hands. Piazza lay flat on his back in the batter's box as Mets training staff rushed to check on him. The catcher's eyes were closed for what felt like an eternity. When they opened, he seemed to stare blankly ahead, as if he could not sense where he was.

Clemens crouched down in front of the mound, watching as Piazza was aided into an upright position. He later claimed that he tried to call Piazza to check on him but that Piazza refused to take the call. As all of this took place, Mets bench coach John Stearns began screaming at home-plate umpire Doug Eddings. That's twice, he yelled, referring to the Mets' belief that Clemens had been headhunting throughout the first few innings of the game, not just with this one pitch to Piazza. "I wasn't catching when Roger hit Mike in the helmet, but I know that Rocket wouldn't go after somebody that high intentionally and that he wasn't trying to hit Piazza at all," recalled Posada in his autobiography.[51]

Piazza, with assistance, was led back to the dugout and removed from the game. The half inning ended uneventfully. With his second pitch of the bottom of the inning, Glendon Rusch plunked Tino Martinez directly on the ass with a fastball. Martinez calmly took his base as Eddings warned both dugouts. An animated Valentine emerged from the dugout under the guise of checking in with his pitcher, only to begin shouting at any umpire he could find. Valentine was already upset with this crew, having been ejected one batter into the first game of the doubleheader for arguing a base-runner interference call. Now he was livid that his team would be punished simply because Roger Clemens had a long history of headhunting. Valentine made his point with the crew and avoided getting thrown out again.

With order now restored, the game went on. The Mets got to Clemens with two two-out runs in the fifth to take the lead. Three singles in the bottom of the inning put Knoblauch up with the go-ahead runs on base. On Rusch's first pitch, Knoblauch sent a fly ball deep to left field. Lenny

Harris went back, leapt, and at first appeared to have made a spectacular catch. But as he descended from his jump, Harris's arm hit the wall, and the ball dropped out of his glove for a three-run home run. "I couldn't tell if he caught it or not. It was so far away," said Knoblauch.[52] The Yankees led, 4–2, and that's how the game ended.

The talk afterward, however, was only about one thing: Clemens hitting Piazza in the head. "My player who's had pretty good success against their pitcher got hit in the head," said a still upset Valentine. "I've seen him [Clemens] hit guys in the head before."[53] Phillips was more direct, stating that Clemens was trying "to hurt one of our players. It's garbage."[54]

"Steve Phillips . . . really escalated things," said Cone. "He was very angry and very aggressive in his postgame comments. He shut down the weight room the next day when we went to Shea Stadium. Yankee players weren't allowed in the Mets' weight room the next day. He just kept it going. He said, 'Keep the players away from each other.'"[55]

The Mets avoided what would have been a Shea series sweep the next day when Hampton shut the Yankees down over seven innings and Benitez stomped out a potential rally in the ninth. But even with the win, the Clemens-Piazza affair was still on people's minds. The rivalry had been intense before, but there had been no real dislike among the teams. That changed. Clemens was now a marked man in the Mets' clubhouse, just as he had been in the Yankees' clubhouse before the trade that brought him to New York. "I hope someday Clemens will pitch in a National League park and we're playing against him," said Valentine in a not-so-veiled threat.[56]

If these two teams were to meet in October—a possibility that was looking increasingly likely—this side story would probably overshadow much of the discussion about the first Subway Series in forty-four years.

On July 9 all was still just conjecture, though. It was possible that both teams would not see each other again until 2001. For now, as they headed into the break, each had to focus on getting to October first. Time would tell if there would be a Clemens-Piazza rematch.

• • •

Dwight Gooden might be a Yankee again, but the team still needed pitching help coming out of the break. El Duque was about to land on the DL with elbow soreness. Clemens had been out with a groin strain. Cone was still struggling, to the point that he figured the Yankees would have no interest in bringing him back after the season. "The last thing I wanted to do was get run out of here, to have them take the uniform away," said Cone, who was 1-8 in mid-July with a 6.63 ERA. From May 14 to August 5 the Yankees lost all thirteen games Cone started. "I wanted to go out in a Yankee uniform with pride. This is my worst nightmare."[57]

Gooden, even with his impressive debut against the Mets, was not seen as reliable enough for the duration of the season. Deciding not to wait until the trade deadline, the Yankees made a major move during the break, trading a slew of prospects to the Reds for starter Denny Neagle. Several other teams had been in pursuit of Neagle, including the Mets, Braves, Diamondbacks, and White Sox, forcing Cashman to include more prospects than he might have wished. "We gave up a lot. I'm not going to hide that," said Cashman about the deal.[58]

The left-hander, who had started Game Four of the 1996 World Series for the Braves against the Yankees, was 8-2 for the Reds and among the best pitchers available on the market. A free agent after the season, he hoped to pitch well enough to secure a long-term deal with New York. Neagle was also known for a spot-on imitation of a train whistle, perhaps the kind of levity the usually stuffy Yankees clubhouse could use. "I know there's been players throughout their careers that don't necessarily like to play in New York, whether they say the fans or the media can be tough on them," said Neagle after the trade. "You've got to have fun with it. That's right up my alley, to go there with some of the most crazy, wildest fans in baseball."[59]

New York was not done yet. Shane Spencer, slugging .460 with nine home runs in half a season of play, tore a ligament in his right knee during the first inning of the final game before the break, ending his season. Spencer, who had finally been given the starting job in left field after a disappointing season in 1999, was so heartbroken by the news that his season was over that he did not speak to reporters after.

David Justice could fill in in left, but that meant the Yankees would need a designated hitter with some power. On July 21 they acquired Glenallen Hill from the Cubs. Hill had been having his best season ever in limited playing time in Chicago, hitting eleven home runs and driving in twenty-nine. He gave the Yankees the pop they wanted from their DH.

Still not pleased with the depth of their bench, the Yankees made more moves. In early August they signed Luis Polonia for a third stint in New York. Polonia, a member of the team from 1989 to 1990 and 1994 to 1995,

UNTIL SOMEONE BEATS US

had drifted across the Majors and even the Mexican League since his last time with the Yankees. He gave them another option in the outfield.

On August 7 the team made two more deals, one noteworthy and one seemingly inconsequential. Utility infielder Luis Sojo had signed with the Pirates in the off-season, hoping to get more playing time with a struggling team. Pittsburgh, however, had been terribly bad and a drastic change in culture for the two-time world champion. The Yankees traded to bring him back to New York, much to his relief. Sojo had been desperate to get back to playing meaningful baseball. He was tired of games in front of small crowds and that had no bearing on the postseason, except for maybe whichever team Pittsburgh was facing. Getting dealt back to New York was like being paroled and given a brand new Corvette and keys to a mansion on the way out of the prison gates.

The same day they reacquired Sojo, the Yankees accidentally claimed José Canseco off waivers from Tampa Bay. The decision had been set in motion before the 2000 season. At the time, July 31 represented the trade deadline, in that any player traded after that date would first have to clear waivers. This allowed all Major League teams a chance to claim a traded player before any deal was finalized. If that happened, that player's current team could decide to pull that player off waivers, negating the proposed trade, or it could allow that player to simply go to the team that claimed him. For the team trying to make the trade, it meant that that player could now not be dealt anywhere. Some teams made claims just for this purpose—that is, to prevent rival teams from acquiring players that could help them down the stretch.

Steinbrenner wanted the Yankees to be doing more of this. In the past few years he had berated Cashman any time a competitor made a post-deadline trade. The year before, he had been especially enraged when the Indians acquired Harold Baines from the Orioles. When the Devil Rays placed Canseco on waivers for the purpose of trading him, Cashman could already hear the Boss shouting in his ear if the former MVP ended up going to the Blue Jays. Besides, Cashman figured, there was no way Tampa Bay was just going to let the Yankees take him.

That, however, is exactly what happened. The Devil Rays had no use anymore for the moody slugger, who after a solid 1999 season had slowed considerably in 2000. GM Chuck Lamar happily allowed the Yankees to take Canseco off his hands. The move shocked everyone, even Cashman, who had not informed Steinbrenner before making the claim. The Yankees had no spot for Canseco to play, nor was anyone thrilled with his $1.4 million salary or the $500,000 they would almost certainly now pay to buy out his contract after the season.

Torre was especially unhappy. He thought the team was going to scoop up former Yankee Mike Stanley, who had been released by Boston. "From what I understand, [Yankees brass] went to the coaches and said, 'Do you want Stano back?' and they said, 'Yeah, get him back.' For whatever reason, that dragged on," recalled Stanley.[60] The Yankees never acted, and Stanley signed with Oakland.

At least Stanley could play first base when Martinez needed a break. "I don't know," Torre brusquely responded when asked how he would get Canseco into the lineup. He really didn't. Even Canseco didn't. "I don't know how I'm going to fit in," he said. "I really don't know what they want me to do."[61] Torre was especially unhappy not just because he had no place to play Canseco but also because he did not need someone of his ilk in the clubhouse.

Canseco had long since worn out his welcome with a lot of people in baseball. The 1988 AL MVP and the first person to steal forty bases and hit forty home runs in a season, Canseco loved the high life and the spotlight. He loved flash. He had also been arrested for reckless driving, carrying a loaded gun in his car, battery, and domestic abuse. Canseco was a lot. People put up with him because he clobbered the ball, hitting forty-six home runs with Toronto in 1998 before hitting thirty-four with Tampa in 1999. One week into August 2000, though, he had only nine home runs.

And there was more. Canseco was not yet the poster child for steroids. That would come a few years later. But by 2000 people had their suspicions, about both him and others. Whispers about performance-enhancing drugs (PEDS) had been rampant for years. Power numbers were up. Player sizes were up. It was, in retrospect, fairly obvious what was going on. But few wanted to question it, either out of naiveté or for fear of ruining what had become an amazing era of baseball. The McGwire/Sosa home run chase of 1998 had revitalized the game and riveted a nation. When Associated Press reporter Steve Wilstein pointed out in 1998 that McGwire had Androstene-dione, a testosterone-producing pill, in his locker, he was ridiculed and vilified for trying to rain on baseball's home-run parade. That off-season, pitcher Rick Helling told a group of assembled player reps and the Major

League Baseball Players Association that steroids were running rampant in the game. Nothing came of it.

Meanwhile, the issue had already come to the Mets' and Yankees' clubhouses, perhaps more so than most other clubs. Kirk Radomski, who became a focal point for steroid distribution in the game, was a Mets clubhouse attendant in the early and mid-1990s. He allegedly provided steroids to the team's former first baseman, David Segui. Radomski claimed that before the 1996 season, he had told Todd Hundley how he could hit more home runs if he used steroids. He then allegedly sold Hundley Deca-Durabolin, and Hundley went on to break the single-season home run record for catchers.

Brian McNamee was a former police officer who had landed a job as the Yankees' bullpen catcher and batting-practice pitcher in 1993. Eventually he joined the Blue Jays, where he met and became close with Clemens. McNamee later alleged that he began injecting Clemens with steroids in 1998. When Clemens was traded to the Yankees, he insisted that McNamee come to New York after his contract with Toronto expired. In 2000 the Yankees brought McNamee on board as the assistant strength and conditioning coach. It raised suspicions among a few players.

"What the fuck are you doing here leading stretching?" Cone barked at McNamee that spring training.[62] Cone was not amused by any of this. He was leery of McNamee's presence around the team and did not love the idea that the Yankees would just give Clemens what he wanted.

McNamee claims that Clemens insisted on continuing to use steroids again in 2000 and that he introduced him to human growth hormones. Clemens long denied all of the allegations.

It is impossible to talk about Major League Baseball from 1997 to 2000 without mentioning PEDs. That period, now known more commonly as the Steroid Era, represents a bittersweet time in the game. Those years are among the most eventful and exciting in the entire history of organized baseball. All of that is marred, though, by the sheer volume of alleged PED use. But therein lies one of the biggest problems. When it comes to PEDs in that era (pre-2001), it is a mix of admissions and allegations. Dozens of players have been accused of using PEDs during that time. Some have admitted to using. Others have denied it. The denials come on varying scales. Some are made in the face of overwhelming evidence of PED use. Others denials are based on hearsay or allegations made by the suppliers.

The Mitchell Report, conducted by former U.S. senator George Mitchell in 2007 to examine PED use in the game, named several Yankees and Mets players of the late 1990s and early 2000s as having used PEDs. Other allegations came from McNamee and Radomski or other sources of reporting. All told, ten Yankees from the 2000 team would be either accused of or admit to using PEDs at some point during their careers: Knoblauch, Neagle, Hill, Justice, Stanton, Canseco, Leyritz, Pettitte, Clemens, and pitcher Jason Grimsley. Matt Franco and Todd Pratt of the 2000 Mets were also named, while several former Mets from the mid-1990s were included as well.

Those revelations were a ways off, but Canseco still represented an element that Torre did not want in his clubhouse. He would have to find a way to deal with it, though.

• • •

The Mets began the second half of the season with a grueling eleven-game road trip through four cities. Their 5-6 record on the trip was nothing to rejoice about, but the return of Piazza was. Forced to missed the All-Star Game after Clemens had hit him in the head, Piazza started the first game after the break and played as if nothing had ever happened. He hit four home runs and drove in nine during the first six games of the second half.

When they finally returned back to Shea, the Mets looked rejuvenated. They swept the Expos and Cardinals and took two of three from the Reds. Their 63-45 record was three games better than that of the defending world champions after their 108th game of the year. New York was talking about the Mets, even wondering if they might be able to overtake the Yankees as the city's team. Attendance had climbed steadily over the past few years. The days of a half-full Shea Stadium during a summer weekend game were over, as evidenced by the nearly 139,000 who came out for the weekend series against St. Louis.

As the trade deadline approached, the Mets knew they weren't perfect. Ordóñez's being lost for the season had created a significant gap at short. Kurt Abbott, signed in the off-season to be a steady infield backup, had been given the starting job in Ordóñez's absence. The Mets were hoping he could repeat his 1995 season in Florida, where he had hit seventeen home runs. But he never found his groove and missed most of July due to a bulging disc in his back. With Abbott down, the Mets turned to Melvin Mora to fill in. Mora was not the answer. Not only was he not a shortstop, but he also had not been hitting the way the team had imagined when he had competed for NLCS MVP honors the year before.

The Mets knew they needed help. As in the off-season, when they had attempted to trade for Griffey, they aimed high. Barry Larkin was among the best shortstops in baseball and possibly the best in the National League. In over a decade with the Reds, Larkin was an eleven-time All-Star, a three-time Gold Glover, and a former MVP. He hit for average, occasionally for power, and he knew how to draw a walk and steal a base. In addition, things had gotten uncomfortable in Cincinnati. The team, one game from a playoff berth the year before, had struggled all season long to find its footing. It barely managed to stay above .500 throughout July. The Mets offered Cincinnati three Minor Leaguers for Larkin, who was a pending free agent after the season. One of them was Alex Escobar, considered to be the Mets' top prospect.

Like Griffey before him, Larkin had a 10/5 ability to veto any trade. He made clear that he would reject any deal that did not include a large contract extension from his new team. The Mets were not going to offer that. They were already paying Ordóñez around $4 million a year for three more years to play short. Moreover, the team was focused on pursuing the Mariners' star shortstop, Alex Rodriguez, also set to become a free agent. Phillips told Reds GM Jim Bowden that no extension would happen. "[Bowden] said, 'Yeah, yeah, don't worry about it,'" Phillips said. "'He'll accept a deal. It might take a little bit of convincing but I think he'll welcome getting out of the negativity of Cincinnati.'"[63]

Larkin did not welcome it. He rejected the deal, as he said he would, and hours later signed a three-year extension with the Reds. Stung but still needing an upgrade at shortstop, on July 28 the team moved Mora and three Minor Leaguers to the Orioles for veteran shortstop Mike Bordick. Brought up in the waning days of the Oakland dynasty that never was, Bordick had been a reliable shortstop throughout the decade. He'd recently gone through a minor power surge, for him at least, after moving over to Baltimore and had already set a career high for home runs that season. "The Bordick trade is so much better than the Larkin deal it almost makes you want to scold Phillips for not doing it in the first place," wrote the *Star-Ledger*'s David Waldstein.[64] That sentiment was due in part to the fact that the Mets did not have to give up Escobar in the deal or sign Bordick, a pending free agent, to an extension.

New York knew Bordick could not completely replicate Ordóñez's play, but he was sure-handed, often among the leaders in fewest errors committed at his position. By all accounts it was an upgrade. That much seemed clear when, on July 29, Bordick homered on the first pitch he saw in a Mets uniform.

While looking to improve at short, the Mets also sought more outfield depth. They acquired Bubba Trammell from Tampa in a deal that moved four players, including Paul Wilson. Like Pulsipher, Wilson had also been a member of Generation K for whom injuries had derailed his career. Wilson had not pitched in the Majors since 1996, and while he was on his way back to the big leagues, the team felt it could not rely on him moving forward. Not to be outdone by Bordick, the day after that shortstop had gone deep, Trammell also homered in his first at bat as a Met.

With those trades done, the Mets had their roster for the rest of the season. Then they went on a tear, winning their first four games of August while allowing only a combined six runs. For the month, they won every series but one. It was not just that they were winning. They were also beating teams that were in direct contention with them for the wild card. Against the Giants, Diamondbacks, and Dodgers, they took nine of thirteen, including beating Randy Johnson twice. Contributions came from everywhere, but Alfonzo continued to make a case for being one of baseball's best players. He began August by notching at least two hits in seven of the first eight games of the month. In the thirteen games against the NL West's top teams, he hit .383 and drove in eight runs. Out of the bullpen, Benitez had fully embraced being the team's official closer. In August he saved eleven games while posting a microscopic 0.61 ERA.

Even potentially devastating moments turned into moments of levity. On August 12, at home against the Giants, with the Mets leading 1–0 in the fourth, Giants batter Bobby Estalella lifted a fly ball to left field with the bases loaded. Benny Agbayani tracked the ball, ran in, and made a nice catch, after which he jogged toward the stands and handed the ball to a young kid. As he did so, fans began screaming and gesturing to him that there were only two outs, not three as Agbayani clearly thought. Quickly realizing what he'd done, Agbayani ran back and took the ball away from the fan, but it was too late. Since he had put the ball out of play, the runners were allowed to advance two bases, resulting in two Giants runs. Zeile ensured the mental error did not cost them the game by hitting a two-run home run in the eighth.

UNTIL SOMEONE BEATS US

When August ended, the Mets were 79-54, not only well ahead in the wild card but also tied for the NL East lead. As September began, fans began to wonder what was in store. The last two years had seen collapses, one fatal and one near fatal. This team appeared too good to let something like that happen. Still, anything was possible, especially with six games remaining against Atlanta.

September's start did not fill fans with confidence as the Mets suffered three straight walk-off defeats in St. Louis, the last loss occurring after Trammell had hit a two-out, two-run home run in the ninth to tie it. They won only one of their first six series of the month, going 7-12 in the process. The sagging play put them out of contention for first place, even though they had held the lead to themselves for a day at the start of the month.

Fortunately, no other team in contention for the wild card was able to take advantage of the team's losses. After all that struggle, the Mets still maintained a five-and-a-half-game lead for it. With a week and a half left in the season, they turned it back on, winning nine of their final eleven games. There would be no end-of-year collapse this season. On September 27 they clinched their second consecutive postseason berth with a 6–2 win over Atlanta. It was the first time in club history they had made the playoffs in back-to-back years. Their game on September 28 was their first in three years that truly had no meaning on the outcome of the season.

Even with the win, the animosity between the Mets and Braves was obvious. "We can do our celebrating inside. We don't have to make a spectacle of it," said Hampton, a not-so-subtle jab at the Braves, who had celebrated winning the division title the night before on the field at Shea.[65] "I'm really proud of this team," said Valentine. "I've heard about all the struggles this team has had and we just won our 90th game."[66]

When the season ended, the Mets were 94-68, ultimately only a single game behind the Braves. Though their record was three games behind that of the 1999 Mets, this team seemed to be in better control throughout the course of the season. There were funks during the year but never any moments of grave concern such as those that had preceded the firing of three coaches or their nearly missing the playoffs the year before. The 2000 Mets were truly a team effort. They set what was then a club record for home runs in a season with 198, with every position racking up double-digit home runs except shortstop and pitcher. Piazza led the way with thirty-eight, while Zeile, Alfonzo, and Ventura collectively hit seventy-one. Piazza and Alfonzo tied for the team lead with a .324 average, creating a dynamic 2-3 punch in the lineup. Jay Payton, a 1994 first-round draft pick, made the Majors for good after only cups of coffee the two previous years. He hit seventeen home runs, the most by a Mets rookie since Darryl Strawberry in 1983, while providing one highlight-reel catch after another in the outfield. His performance earned him third place in the National League Rookie of the Year voting.

Hampton, Leiter, Reed, Bobby Jones, and Rusch stayed relatively healthy throughout the year, starting all but 11 of the team's 162 games. Each reached at least eleven wins, making the Mets one of only three teams to have five pitchers with double-digit victories. Hampton recovered from his bumpy start to go 15-10 and lead the team in innings pitched while also leading the league in fewest home runs allowed per nine innings. Benitez became the first Met to ever save forty games in a season, finishing the year with forty-one.

The Mets felt good, healthy, and strong as they headed into the first-round match with the Giants. San Francisco was no slouch; in fact, it had finished with the best record in baseball. The Giants were one of the two other teams to have five pitchers win double-digit victories, and their lineup featured one of the game's best players, Barry Bonds. At thirty-six, Bonds had set a personal single-season record by hitting forty-nine home runs, and he had also led the league in walks. Joining Bonds was former Met Jeff Kent, who had just finished the best season of his career en route to winning the National League MVP award. This match-up would be no cake walk for the Mets, who headed to the City by the Bay to play the first two games of the series.

• • •

All the Yankees' wheeling and dealing appeared to be paying off. After a June in which they had posted their worst full-month record since May 1995, the team caught fire in July and August, going 36-20. The new acquisitions were a big reason why, starting with David Justice. Since joining the Yankees, he'd been a godsend, providing big hit after big hit. In July, his first full month with the team, he batted .383 with six home runs, nineteen RBIS, and a .479 OBP. He raised his OPS a full .61 points during that time. He was not just getting on base, but he was also hitting for power. He kept it going in August, racking up eight multi-hit games, including six more home runs, the biggest of which occurred on August 8 against the A's at home. With the Yankees down a run in the ninth and facing former Met

Jason Isringhausen, Bernie Williams hit the first pitch of the inning for a game-tying home run. Before the crowd had a chance to sit down, Justice hit the next pitch into the bleachers in right-center, where a fan made a spectacular catch of the ball using a souvenir plastic cup. The win put the Yankees four and a half games up in the division, and Justice was starting to generate talk of MVP votes.

Denny Neagle's first two starts as a Yankee could hardly have gone better. Facing the Phillies and the Twins, he threw seventeen innings of nine-hit, two-run ball, going the distance in his second start as fans gave him a thunderous ovation when he left the field. Torre found spots for Canseco throughout August, and the slugger responded by hitting four home runs, including a moon shot into the upper deck of Yankee Stadium for his first as a Yankee, and driving in eleven runs in his first sixteen games with the team. Polonia hit .333 in his first month back with the club. Sojo was inserted into the lineup as the team's everyday second baseman and responded by hitting .317 in August and even showing some pop when he hit two home runs in a three-game series against Anaheim—as many home runs as he had hit in 1997 and 1999.

No new acquisition, however, made as big a splash upon joining the team as Glenallen Hill. In his first at bat with the Yankees, he hit a home run twenty rows back into the left-field stands in Baltimore. Four days later he hit a grand slam in the ninth inning at the Metrodome. He took off from there.

August 4: A home run against Seattle.

August 7: Another home run against Seattle.

August 10: A home run against Oakland.

August 12: A home run against Anaheim.

August 17: Another home run against Anaheim.

August 18: Two more home runs against Anaheim.

August 20: Another home run against Anaheim.

August 21: A broken-bat home run against Texas.

August 24: Another home run against Texas.

All told, Hill hit .429 with twelve home runs in his first sixty-eight at bats as a Yankee. "He's so locked in, anything over the plate, it doesn't matter what pitch it is, he's just killing it," said Pettitte. "He's making this ballpark look like it's Enron Field or Coors Field."[67]

The contributions from all the new players were undeniable. The Yankees went from being two games out on July 1 to being five up on August 30.

Winning ten of the first thirteen games in September expanded that lead to a season-high nine games on September 13. With just nineteen regular-season games remaining, the Yankees looked all but set to clinch another division title and get back to the postseason. What followed was an excruciatingly bad stretch of baseball that not only made a subway series look impossible but also cast doubt that the team would even make the playoffs at all.

• • •

The last two and a half weeks of the Yankees' 2000 season were among the worst in the history of the franchise. That's not an exaggeration. It's not weighted to account for their being defending champions or leading the division at the time. It simply represents the level at which they played to close out that season.

It began innocuously enough: an extra-inning loss to the Blue Jays at home. The Yankees were still eight games up in first. The next day, however, was indicative of what was coming. Cone gave up six runs, and the bullpen allowed five more during an 11–1 blowout loss to the Indians. Cleveland took three out of four games, outscoring the Yankees by twenty runs and dropping their lead to seven games. The Yankees went to Toronto, where the Blue Jays battered Pettitte for five runs and the bullpen for nine more in an opening game loss. The Jays swept the series.

There was a little over a week to go now, and the Yankees' lead had been reduced to four and a half games. A series split with Detroit provided some solace. But their 6–3 win on Sunday, September 24, was their last of the regular season. They lost their remaining seven games, getting massacred in nearly all of them: 15–4 to the Tigers; 2–1 to the Devil Rays; 11–1 to the Devil Rays; 11–3 to the Devil Rays; 13–2 to the Orioles; 9–1 to the Orioles; 7–3 to the Orioles.

Nearly everyone was guilty of falling apart. Cone, who after working in Tampa with Billy Connors, had actually rebounded in August to pitch fairly well, separated his shoulder diving for a bunt on September 5. "My first thought was just fear. I didn't know how much damage there was in my shoulder," said Cone. "My second thought was that it was a fitting end to a miserable season for me. Any my third thought was that I can still come back, that maybe there is a chance I can do something this year."[68]

Cone was not the same after having allowed twenty-three runs in just under fifteen innings in his last four starts. The love affair with Denny Neagle ended. After his knockout performances in his first two starts, the American League had quickly figured Neagle out in August. In six starts he went 2-4 with a 6.69 ERA, and that included one outing in which he had given up no runs to the Angels. He blamed the issues on poor mechanics, saying he was raising his arm just enough to allow hitters a better look at the ball.

Neagle rebounded in early September, but like Cone, his last four appearances of the year were disastrous: twenty runs allowed in eleven and a third innings. In his September 17 start against the Indians, he gave up eight runs before being yanked in the top of the third. He was booed off the mound. "I was horrible. I would have booed myself," said Neagle.[69] Torre gave an indication of things to come when he showed his annoyance with Neagle's performance. "Bad counts to bad people," said the manager. "Three and-oh to Manny, you saw what happened," added Torre, referring to a Manny Ramirez first-inning home run.[70]

Even Clemens, who was second in the American League in ERA and had started pitching like the Rocket of old, gave up thirteen runs in his last two starts of the year.

The offense disappeared that final week, scoring a total of eleven runs over six games. None of it made sense. With each loss, players pressed harder, but it only seemed to yield worse performances. "It's like every time someone makes an out here, it's the end of the world," said Sojo in the midst of the losing.[71]

The Yankees ended the year going 3-15. Had they not managed to hang on—and they just barely did so—it would have been the worst late-season collapse in baseball history. While all of this was going on, for the third season in a row a member of the team had been afflicted with cancer. This time it was pitching coach Mel Stottlemyre, who had revealed earlier in the year that he had been dealing with bone-marrow cancer. He had remained with the team for most of the season but in mid-September took a leave to receive further treatment.

Despite their performance, the Yankees clinched the division in Baltimore on the third to last day of the year thanks to a Red Sox loss. Players celebrated, as they should have given the accomplishment, but the celebration felt muted. Players grew defensive at the notion that the team had backed into the playoffs, yet that was the perception of fans and possibly other teams. "We're not celebrating tonight's game," said Jeter. "We're not celebrating the last two weeks. We're celebrating a lot of hard work that started last February."[72]

"Once upon time, maybe three weeks ago, the Yankees seemed dangerous and their pursuit of a third straight championship was not doubted," wrote the *New York Times*' Jack Curry on the night they clinched the division. "Instead, the Yankees limped into Camden Yards as an embarrassed team last night and those queasy feelings remained as the Orioles thumped Andy Pettitte, 13–2, and shoved them to their 13th loss in the last 16 games."[73]

The two-time defending champs looked tired and, suddenly, really old. At 87-74, it had been their worst season in eight years. Only four teams in history had won fewer than ninety games in a season and had gone on to win the World Series. Worse still, the Yankees were about to face a young, exciting Oakland A's team that had surprised many by overtaking the Mariners and winning the AL West. The A's could smell blood in the water and had every intention of ruining the subway series that New Yorkers had been dreaming about for so long.

• • •

San Francisco's Pac Bell Park sat on the eastern edge of the city, just south of the I-80 Bay Bridge and abutting San Francisco Bay. The architects of the stadium had chosen to leave the views facing toward the bay unobstructed, creating some of the most remarkable scenery of any ballpark in baseball. Behind the right-field wall lay a small inlet that drew water from San Francisco Bay into the Mission Bay neighborhood of the city. This inlet was renamed McCovey Cove when the stadium opened in 2000, in honor of the legendary Giants Hall of Famer. Because the right-field stands consisted of only a few rows of seats and because all that separated the stadium from the cove was a small walkway, one of the great new aspects of the ballpark was that a home run to right field could land in the water. Watching people plant themselves in a kayak, canoe, or boat in the cove so that they could snag a home run ball quickly became one of the charming features of the place.

McCovey Cove also created another feature. During night games at the park when a ball went to right field, the camera would pan out, and behind the fence would appear a vast, dark emptiness, as if after the stadium ended, there was simply nothingness.

That void was in full view as Mets, Giants, and fans of both teams stared at J. T. Snow's fly ball to right field in the bottom of the ninth of NLDS Game Two. The fate of the entire series seemed to hang with that fly ball. Before

Snow had swung, the Mets had been clinging to a 4–1 lead in a game they desperately needed to win. They had lost Game One after Hampton got hit for five runs, four of them coming in a third-inning rally that put the game out of reach. Looking to save the Mets' season, Leiter had kept the Giants to just a single run in Game Two while New York notched two runs in the second and two more in the ninth on an Alfonzo home run. Alfonzo's home run had seemingly sealed the win and evened the series. But in the bottom of the ninth, San Francisco put the first two runners on; then, after an out, Snow came to bat.

Benitez had entered the game after Valentine had allowed Leiter to face Bonds to start the inning. The Mets' closer had been lights out during the season but had a checkered playoff history. In Game Three of the 1996 ALDS he had allowed the go-ahead grand slam to Albert Belle. Though not his fault, he had been on the mound for Baltimore when Jeffrey Maier had interfered with Jeter's fly ball in the 1996 ALCS. The following year, he had allowed home runs in Games Two and Six of the ALCS that gave Cleveland two wins, including the series clincher. In the 1999 NLCS against the Braves, he had given up the tying run in the tenth inning of Game Six.

Now, with the Mets' season on the brink, Benitez had been entrusted to get New York even in the series. With the count 2-1, he tried to bust Snow in with a fastball. It missed its spot and tailed over the middle of the plate. Snow swung and at first glance appeared to have crushed the ball far into the vast reaches of McCovey Cove's nothingness. Instead the ball hung in the air, seemingly forever, as everyone watching was left to guess if it would stay fair, much less make it over the fence. The ball descended and dropped into the hands of several fans sitting in the first row just to the left of the foul pole, where it dropped, hit the grating atop the right-field brick wall, and fell back onto the field of play.

Tie game.

Giants manager Dusty Baker stomped up and down with the enthusiasm of a ten-year-old as Bonds ran giddily around the bases ahead of Snow. Benitez paced the mound, staring out with a mixed expression of bewilderment, disappointment, and annoyance. The home run, which likely would have been an out or at worst a double in any other National League ballpark, appeared to have crushed the Mets' season. Yes, the game was not over, but there was a palpable feeling that this moment would result in a 2–0 deficit in the series.

Benitez escaped further damage, sending the game to the tenth. There, with two outs, Hamilton, bothered by an arthritic toe, lined a double to center field, and Payton followed with a single to give the Mets the lead back. After Benitez allowed the lead-off hitter to reach in the bottom of the inning, John Franco was tasked with saving the game and, really, the season. Two outs later, he faced off against Bonds, who represented the game-winning run. In a classic confrontation, the count went full before Franco snuck a curveball on the inside corner for a called strike three. "I've been making a living with that pitch for 17 years. No better time to throw it," said Franco.[74] Bonds threw his left arm up in disgust as Franco pumped his fist, pranced off the mound, and rushed to embrace Piazza. The team's all-time saves leader had just come up with the biggest save of them all.

In the Giants' clubhouse former Met Jeff Kent said the Giants were the better team and that once they got to New York, they would "smack" the Mets. His comments did not go unnoticed.[75]

Game Three proved to be just as tense. Back at Shea, the Giants jumped out to an early lead, which they maintained until the bottom of the eighth. There, with two outs and a runner on second, Alfonzo lined a game-tying single. The game remained tied into the thirteenth, as Cook, Wendell, Franco, Benitez, and Rick White managed to pitch seven scoreless innings of relief. In the thirteenth, Agbayani came up with one out.

It had been an odd journey for Agbayani in 2000. On the eve of Opening Day in Japan, he had been set to be sent down to the Minors. Despite his meteoric rise the previous year, there was no spot for him on the roster, and unlike other players, he had options to be sent down to the Minors. Valentine adored Agbayani, but it was simple math. Then Rusch got hurt, and off Agbayani went to the Far East. He went on to set career highs in nearly every major offensive category that year. Moreover, he had drastically improved his batting eye. While his average went up three points, his on-base percentage went up twenty-eight points. He had managed to get on base five times in Games One and Two combined, but he was 0-5 so far in Game Three. The Mets were looking for a hero, and on a 1-0 pitch, Agbayani stepped into the breach. Right as Oakland was stomping the Yankees just a few miles away in their ALDS matchup, Agbayani hit one into the left-center field stands to give the Mets Game Three and the lead in the series. "There's a silence when you're running around the bases . . . and there's a tingling feeling in your head," said Agbayani of what it was like to hit the game-winning home run.[76]

The Mets were one game away from advancing. On the mound for them in Game Four stood Bobby Jones. If one had to pick any of the five Mets' starters to pitch the greatest postseason game in the team's history, Jones probably would not have been the choice. He'd had the worst season of any Mets starter in 2000, posting an ERA of 8.10 after his first ten starts of the year. His performance had been so poor that the team sent him down to the Minors for two weeks in June. While he improved in the second half, his numbers were still less than impressive, especially his twenty-five home runs given up in just under 155 innings. Moreover, he had never appeared in a postseason game before, much less a possible clinching game, much less a possible clinching game against a team that had finished third in the league in home runs and second in slugging percentage.

Valentine had three options for Game Four: Hampton on short rest, Rusch, or Jones. Last on that list was Jones. Valentine was more likely to go with Hampton or even Rusch. But he had not made a decision the night of Game Three, a (non)move that was largely interpreted as gamesmanship and just another Bobby-V-being-Bobby-V moment. In truth Valentine really did not know whom he was going to pitch until he got to the ballpark before Game Four.

As he walked toward the clubhouse, Valentine ran into Jones's wife, Kristi. He was about to tell her that he did not know yet who was pitching. "Pitch Bobby today," Kristi told him before he could say anything. "He's going to pitch the game of his life."[77] Valentine decided to give the ball to her husband.

What happened next defied all expectations. In the late afternoon dusk of fall, Jones retired the Giants in order in the first. Then he did so again in the second. And again in the third. And again in the fourth. Twelve up, twelve down. During that time, only one hitter got the ball out of the infield. Bonds struck out twice. Meanwhile, in the bottom of the first, Ventura's two-run home run had given the Mets all the runs they would need. "At this point, it doesn't matter what I did during the season or what I ate a week ago," said Ventura, referencing his career low .232 batting average during the regular season. "It just matters what I did today and what we do tomorrow."[78]

In the top of the fifth, his perfect game still intact, Jones left a 1-2 fastball over the plate to Kent, who lined it just over the reach of Ventura for San Francisco's first hit of the game. The Giants eventually loaded the bases before Jones escaped without allowing a run. No other Giant reached base as Jones meticulously retired batter after batter in the sixth, seventh, and eighth innings. By the top of the ninth, New York had built a 4–0 lead, enough of a cushion for Valentine to let Jones try and finish out his masterpiece. It took Jones seventy-four seconds from the first to the last out of the inning, getting Bonds on a fly ball to center. "I just felt like I could throw the ball where I wanted to," said Jones of his performance. "I had confidence in all my pitches and there was also some adrenaline, too."[79]

The Mets gathered behind second base in short center field to celebrate, and the talk after was of the performance of the unlikeliest of heroes. "I'm so proud of him," said Leiter about Jones. "To go out and pitch the best game of his life and dismiss all the critics who thought this was a bad decision. . . . He went out and nailed it."[80]

As the celebration went on in the Mets' clubhouse, the Yankees were three thousand miles away, trying to keep hope of a subway series alive. "We want to take care of our own business," said Valentine. "If, in fact, it is a head to head with the Yankees a couple of weeks from now, we'd love to steal their thunder."[81]

. . .

For a few innings in Game One of the ALDS, it looked like the Yankees had gotten past their nearly three weeks of horrific play. They jumped out to an early 2–0 lead, their first lead in sixty-three innings, thanks to timely two-out hitting by Sojo and Brosius. Clemens held it until the fifth inning. A mix of singles, walks, and a wild pitch gave Oakland the lead. Even when the Yankees tied it back up, they gave the lead right back. "The bottom of the order beat our brains out," said Torre of the A's.[82] They went down meekly in the last three innings against former Met Jeff Tam, former Yankee Jim Mecir, and former Met Jason Isringhausen. Suddenly it felt as though the postseason would end just the way the regular season had ended.

The feeling continued into Game Two. For five innings the Yankees could not capitalize off Kevin Appier, a pitcher they had knocked around to a 7.56 ERA during the year. In the fifth, after a leadoff single, Appier struck out the side swinging. New York's saving grace had been Andy Pettitte, who allowed only a single hit through the first five innings. In the sixth, the Yankees broke it open, thanks to hits by mid-year acquisitions Hill and Sojo. The Hill hit, in particular, was a big one. He was 2-14 against Appier in his career coming into the at bat, while Polonia, sitting on the bench, was a career .349 hitter against the pitcher. Torre, playing a feeling and not the odds, let Hill bat, resulting in a run and the lead. "When you make a commitment, we just decided, let's stay with him," said Torre.[83]

Pettitte kept the A's scoreless into the eighth before allowing a double with two outs. The next batter hit a ground ball to Sojo, who, in attempting to throw the ball to first, tripped over his own feet and fell down. "Oh, my god!" exclaimed Torre, who must have felt some sense of dread after all the team had been through in the last few weeks.[84] Rivera came in and held it down for the last outs, giving the Yankees a 4–0 win and life again.

The Yankees won Game Three at home. In Game Four, with the hometown crowd giddy over the thought of watching a series-clinching win, Oakland's Olmedo Sáenz ripped a three-run first-inning home run off a Clemens splitter. Neither the crowd nor the Yankees ever got back into the game. The A's coasted to an 11–1 win, sending the series back to Oakland for a decisive Game Five the next evening.

None of the Yankees wanted to make that six-hour flight. Earlier in the series, Steinbrenner had complained about this very scenario. "This is not right and baseball shouldn't allow it," he said before Game One. "To make both teams fly all night across the country, after a night game, and then play the next night is disgraceful."[85]

Having gotten to their hotel rooms at four o'clock in morning, jet lagged and disappointed over having not taken care of business at home, the Yankees slogged their way through an afternoon workout at the Oakland Coliseum. As they did so, the video scoreboard showed a live press conference in which A's third baseman Eric Chavez was talking to reporters. Chavez was a great young player, enjoying what would be the first of seven consecutive seasons in which he hit at least twenty-two home runs and drove in at least seventy-two runs. Someone asked him his thoughts on potentially ending the Yankees' dynasty with a win that night. "I [wouldn't] mind at all," replied Chavez. "They've won enough times. It's time for some other people to have some glory here. But, no, they've had a great run; they've done a phenomenal job as it is. But it's time. I think tonight, if we can get this game, I think people are going to start looking at this team for years to come as hopefully starting something that they . . . have done the last couple years."[86]

There was nothing at all wrong with Chavez's comments. In fact, he was shocked when, after the game, reporters told him that the Yankees had taken offense at his remarks. It was a little silly, but perhaps tired and annoyed at their own play, the Yankees felt that the A's third baseman had made a mistake by talking as if their run was already over.

Now motivated beyond just the idea of winning the game, the Yankees set out to deliver a message. Leading off Game Five, Knoblauch singled on the first pitch. Jeter walked. O'Neill singled. Williams drove in a run on a sacrifice fly. Justice walked. Martinez hit a sun-aided three-run double. Posada singled.

That was enough to knock A's starter Gil Heredia out of the game after having record only one out. Three singles later, including Knoblauch's second of the inning, the Yankees led, 6–0. The Coliseum went quiet as many could not believe what they had just seen. Yet as they had done all year, the A's fought back. They slowly began chipping away at the lead, dinking Pettitte for a single here and a walk there. A Justice home run in the fourth—the Yankees' only one of the entire series and first in eight games—felt like it put the game out of reach at 7–3. But Oakland scored two in the fourth, knocking Pettitte out as Torre put the game, and the season, in the hands of Mike Stanton. The lefty, who had endured some rough stretches of play that year, responded by retiring the first six batters he faced. Stanton handed the ball off to Nelson, who retired all four batters he faced.

With the Yankees still leading 7–5 in the bottom of the eighth, Torre decided to bring in Game Three starter El Duque for his first-ever big league relief appearance. Hernández struck out a batter before allowing a double. Enter Rivera, who kept the score at 7–5 going into the ninth. After two quick outs, Mariano gave up a single, putting the series-tying run at the plate in the form of none other than Eric Chavez.

The tension in the stadium was gut wrenching. Oakland had been on such a magical run that it seemed fully plausible that Chavez would tie the game with one swing. The Yankees, meanwhile, still had the bad taste of the season's final week in their mouths. Blowing this lead would be fitting.

All the drama, however, ended instantly. Less than five hours after the Mets had eliminated the Giants, Rivera threw a first-pitch cutter in on the hands of Chavez, who lifted a meek pop-up into foul territory along the first-base line. After what felt like an eternity, Tino Martinez caught the ball, raising both arms in triumph. The screams of his teammates could be heard on television while the rest of the ballpark fell silent. This was not like the past Yankees' division-series victories, where teammates calmly congratulated one another while offering bland quotes about now taking the next step. This was a cathartic "See, we-are-not-nearly-done-yet" victory. "People want to say we're done, we're old, our run is over," said Jeter, drenched in champagne. "But until someone beats us, we're still the champs."[87] "We're older, but I don't think we're too old," said Torre. "I like to look at it as experience. And when the postseason comes, we're going to make somebody beat us."[88]

• • •

For the second straight year, the wild-card Mets had bested a team with a better record in four games, including winning every game at Shea and two by walk-off home runs. It was suspected before the postseason started that if the Mets were to beat the Giants, the result would be an NLCS match-up with the Braves. For some, that possibility set shivers down the spine as New York had yet to show an ability to best Atlanta. For others, it presented the perfect chance for revenge. The Braves foiled such a plan, though, when they were surprisingly swept out of their NLDS match-up with the St. Louis Cardinals. There would be no 1999 NLCS rematch.

In many ways the Cardinals mimicked the Giants, only they had perhaps had a stronger overall year despite winning two fewer games. Led by Jim Edmonds and Mark McGwire, they had hit more home runs than the Giants and gotten more wins out of their starting pitchers, including twenty from staff ace Darryl Kile. During the season the Cardinals had taken six of nine games over New York, including a three-game sweep in September in which every game had ended in a walk-off.

The Mets had no intention of repeating their previous year's performance and digging themselves an 0–3 NLCS hole. Out of the gate, they sought to make a statement that this team was different. To do that, they needed Piazza. The Mets' catcher had been largely a nonfactor against the Giants, managing a few hits but never driving in a runner. Known as "the Monster" inside the clubhouse because his talent and ability to hit a baseball were downright scary, Piazza came up in the top of the first inning of Game One and grounded a double down the left-field line to drive in a run.

"The Monster is out of the cage," screamed Mets bench coach John Stearns in the dugout. "The Monster is out of the cage. Let's go!" Before the game, Stearns and others had been talking about how if they could unleash the Monster on the Cardinals, they would really take off. They were right. Piazza's double jump-started the team, which built a 6–0 lead on the way to winning Game One. Hampton, battered in his start against the Giants, made amends by pitching seven shutout innings. "I wanted to be a contributor instead of a liability," said Hampton, who came into the start with an 0-2 record and a 5.87 ERA in four postseason starts. "I just wanted to do my part and help this team win. I didn't do that in the first series."[89]

Game One also created some hostility between the two teams. After Cardinals relief pitcher Mike James allowed two home runs in the top of the ninth inning, he hit Bordick on the right thumb. After the game Phillips said he thought James had hit Bordick on purpose.

"I can't believe he said that. Did he say that?" asked Cardinals manager Tony La Russa. "He ought to be ashamed of himself."

"I'm not ashamed of myself," Phillips responded when told of La Russa's comments.[90]

There was more. Cardinals first-base coach Dave McKay thought the Mets were tipping off hitters about pitch location by whistling from the bench. After Zeile homered in the ninth, McKay confronted him in the bottom half of the inning. Valentine denied the Mets were doing anything, instead turning things back around on St. Louis. "Isn't that something?" said Valentine. "That falls in line with [former Mets catcher] Jerry Grote calling and telling us that he saw Will Clark peeking in on television. I'd just like to say that no one on our traveling party can whistle like that."[91]

The war of words aside, Piazza stayed hot in Game Two, homering to give the Mets a 3-1 lead in the third. The Cardinals fought back, tying the game at 3-3, where it stayed until the eighth. Timo Pérez lined a two-out single to keep the inning alive.

Pérez had been an unexpected and wonderful surprise for the Mets. Although his birth name was Timoniel, he decided to go by Timo to avoid hearing people constantly butcher his name. "The Americans don't pronounce it right," said Pérez after informing reporters and the team's public address announcer about the name abbreviation. "If they said it right, I'd let them, but they don't say it right."[92]

Growing up in the Dominican Republic, Pérez made the unusual choice of heading to Japan to begin his baseball career. Signing with the Hiroshima Toyo Carp as a teenager, he spent four seasons there before Mets assistant general manager Omar Minaya discovered him. He signed with the Mets during spring training in 2000 and made his way up the system by impressing the organization with his ability to hit, particularly to bunt and to wait on breaking balls. What especially impressed the team was his quickness as a center fielder and his ability to read balls off the bat. It was a skill perfected in Japan. Rather than follow the flight of the ball, Pérez moved to the spot where he felt the ball would eventually land. It was a subtle yet big difference in how other members of the team played. "He does some things that our other outfielders don't," said Valentine.[93]

On August 30 the Mets had called Pérez up to the big leagues to ensure that he would be eligible for the postseason. After a slow start, he began hitting toward year's end, becoming the starting center fielder in the playoffs. His three-hit performance had helped the team win Game Two of the NLDS, and his overall play immediately endeared him to Mets fans.

Pérez scored the go-ahead run in Game Two again St. Louis when Alfonzo lined a double to right-center field. The Cardinals fought back, plating two to tie the game at 5–5. In the ninth, Payton delivered again, knocking a single to center to score McEwing with the eventual game-winning run. "No one on the team, maybe no one in the league, has more confidence than Jay Payton," said Valentine. "I'm sure he thought he was the right man for the job."[94] The Mets headed back to Shea in control of the series.

After a blowout loss in Game Three, the Mets started Game Four with four consecutive doubles and added a fifth double later in the inning, the most for a single inning in NLCS history. These resulted in four runs, bringing the team back from an early 2–0 deficit. The Mets tacked on three more an inning later, seemingly putting the game out of reach. But the Cardinals scored three in the fifth and had the tying run at the plate before Rusch, in relief, closed the door on the rally. The Mets won, 10–6, and with the Yankees still battling in the ALCS, it was possible that the Amazin's would clinch a World Series spot before the Bronx Bombers.

Any drama around the Mets advancing ended almost immediately in Game Five. Three singles, a walk, and a ground out put the Cardinals in a 3–0 deficit. That was more than enough for Hampton. The lefty kept St. Louis guessing all game, using his fastball to overpower them and his off-speed pitches to keep them off balance. After a two-out single in the fourth, he didn't allow another hit the rest of the game. The Mets built their lead up to 7–0 and the crowd spent the later innings in heightened anticipation, merely counting the outs until a euphoric celebration could ensue. Team management had brought in new speakers for the series, placing them behind the centerfield fence. They gave off an Iron Maiden–

like sound that shook the ballpark. In the seventh inning, a "Yank-ees suck" chant broke out.

With two down in the ninth, Hampton induced pinch hitter Rick Wilkins to fly out to center. Jumping enthusiastically as he tracked the ball, Pérez made the catch mid-leap, and the celebration began. Ventura rushed to the mound and picked Hampton up by the legs, whereupon the rest of the team engulfed them. After fourteen years—fourteen long years that had seen the dissolution of a near dynasty and some of the worst moments of the club's history—the Mets were National League champions again.

Hampton took home MVP honors, winning both his starts, throwing a complete-game shutout in the clincher, and overall allowing no runs in sixteen innings. The award was well deserved, but he certainly had competition. Rusch had pitched three and two-thirds innings of scoreless relief, getting the win in Game Four. Pérez had hit .304, made several spectacular catches, and scored an NLCS record eight runs in the series. Piazza—the Monster—had truly come out of the cage, hitting .412, reaching base in over half his plate appearances, and notching two home runs. Alfonzo had hit .444 and had driven in four runs. Agbayani had hit .353, including two doubles and three runs driven in. Zeile had homered and had driven in eight of the team's twenty-seven runs in the series.

Now the Amazin's sat back and watched the result of the ALCS. The Mets had been rooting for the Yankees, said Pratt, "but not Sunday night [ALCS Game Five] because we wanted to be the first ones to get in."[95] "I'm rooting for the Yankees, to be perfectly honest," said Zeile, who, as a Ranger, had been eliminated by the Yankees in the previous two postseasons. "I don't see any reason to pull any punches at this point. I'd love to see a Subway Series. I have unfinished business with the Yankees."[96]

The next two days would determine if their World Series appearance would be a cross-country affair with a team they had never faced before or an intercity match-up with a team they knew intimately well and for which the pressure would be unlike anything they had ever experienced.

• • •

Onward the Yankees went to face the Seattle Mariners in the ALCS. Just five years earlier, Seattle had beaten the Yankees in an epic five-game Division Series that had ended the Yankees careers of countless players, staff, and the team's manager. Seattle's win had also created a new stadium for the

Mariners, preventing the team's departure to Tampa. Safeco Field, which the Yankees had inadvertently helped create, would play host to Games Three through Five.

Given the drama of that '95 Division Series and its fallout, there was an attempt by the media to make the 2000 ALCS about the Yankees getting revenge on Seattle. It fell short. Most of the players on the Yankees in 1995, largely because of the team's loss to the Mariners, were no longer Yankees. In fact, three of Seattle's key players—Tino Martinez, Nelson, and Sojo— were now with New York, and Ken Griffey Jr. and Randy Johnson had left Seattle. Moreover, the Yankees had won three championships since.

The idea of this being a revenge match-up was thus lacking in support. But the drama that the outcome of this series could possibly lead to a subway series was in no way made up, even if fans across the country could not give a damn about that concept. Like it or not, it was now the talk of the postseason. "For decades, New York sports fans have dreamed of having the World Series all to themselves again," wrote the *New York Times'* Tyler Kepner. "That could change this year, if the Mets get past the St. Louis Cardinals and the Yankees beat the Seattle Mariners."[97] "Every victory," wrote Mike Lupica, "makes the town giddy these days. Every loss feels like the bottom falling out of the stock market."[98]

"Using the off day between series to gather strength and crow about their teams, Mets and Yankees fans broached all sorts of subjects online, from pitching to predictions, hitting to heartache, and strategy to sentiment," noted the *Bergen Record*'s Daniel Sforza. "In often misspelled and badly punctuated bulletin-board postings and chat-room conversations, they expressed themselves stridently, and behind the cloak of anonymity accorded by the Internet."[99]

The Mets were doing their part against the Cardinals. The Yankees, however, were stymying talks of a series with their performance against Seattle. Over the first sixteen innings of the series, they failed to score a run—not that there weren't opportunities. With runners on first and second and no outs in the third inning of Game One, Brosius hit into a double play. Two innings later, he could not come up with the big two-out hit with runners on first and third. The next inning, the first two runners reached base before O'Neill and Williams struck out and Justice flied out. In the ninth the Yankees put runners on first and second with one out but could not get a run across. Despite a stellar effort from Neagle, they lost, 2–0.

Game Two was more of the same. They loaded the bases in the first inning, then hit into a 2–3 double play and failed to score. Brosius led off the third with a single and was promptly picked off. Two runners got on in the fifth. Two runners were left on base in the fifth. "There was a little tension in the dugout," said Sojo. "Normally, we're joking around on the bench."[100]

Meanwhile, Hernández was keeping the Mariners at bay, allowing just a single run over eight innings as hitters flailed at his mix of fastballs and off-speed pitches.

The Yankees were down to their last six outs in Game Two. Despite all the talent on the team, a feeling was starting to sink in: maybe they just did not have it this year. Maybe the mix of all the new spare parts was not enough to compensate for a team's getting older. They had struggled through the last weeks of the season, and while no one thought they were truly that bad, perhaps their performance in the series was more representative of what this team was.

Then, just like that, the team that could not buy a run for twenty-one consecutive postseason innings exploded. Arthur Rhodes, he of the 3-5 career record and 7.14 ERA against the Yankees, faced Justice, who led off the eighth inning. Justice sent a ball off the wall in left-center field. Williams singled him in to tie it. Two singles later the Yankees had a 3–1 lead. Three hits later Jeter came up and capped the inning off with a two-run home run. All told, it was an ALCS record eight hits in one inning—five singles, two doubles, one home run, and seven runs—over the span of forty-one minutes. The Mariners looked shellshocked as they walked off the field. "Down 2–0 going into Seattle would've been devastating," said Knoblauch. "And right now, we're riding a high."[101]

Tied at 1–1, the series moved to Safeco Field, where the Yankees' bats kept bashing. They took Game Three, 8–2, knocking out thirteen hits. The next night, home runs by Justice and Jeter accounted for all five of the team's runs, but it wasn't the Yankees' offense that people were talking about afterward. That night Roger Clemens turned in possibly the single-most-dominating pitching performance in postseason history.

It started with Clemens striking out the first two batters of the game. Then he came up and in on Alex Rodriguez twice. He was sending a message: "This plate belongs to me." A visibly annoyed Rodriguez stared at Clemens; later Piniella would chirp a string of vulgarities toward the Yankees' bench. "It's puzzling how that can happen when a guy has such good control," said Rodriguez. "It's funny how he never misses up and away. It's always up and in."[102]

It was clear from the beginning that Clemens had different stuff that night. His fastball was alive; it just had a kind of movement that had been absent from that of any other game he had pitched with New York. His splitter was dropping from waist to toes. The Mariners looked vexed as hitter after hitter struck out or was retired meekly. Through five innings Clemens did not allow a hit and struck out six.

After the fifth inning Clemens only got better. He struck out two in the sixth before allowing his first hit, a lead-off seventh-inning double that nicked the top of Martinez's glove before going down the line. "I really didn't focus on that," said Clemens about losing the no-hitter. Then, without a hint of irony given his numerous incidents with hit batters, he added, "I've always felt that I throw too many strikes to throw a no-hitter, because I'm going to give a guy a pretty hittable ball, with something on it. To throw one, I'd have to be fairly wild."[103]

From there Clemens struck out Alex Rodriguez and Edgar Martinez on splitters. A walk brought Mike Cameron up as the tying run. With the count 3-2 and the crowd going ballistic while waving thousands of white towels, Clemens reared back. He had struck out Rodriguez and Martinez on splitters, and Cameron appeared to be expecting the same pitch. Instead Clemens threw him a fastball on the outer half of the plate for a called strike three. As Cameron flipped his bat in disappointment, Clemens bent down on one knee and pumped his fist in front of the mound. It was an exhilarating moment, but more important for the Yankees, it preserved the lead. Clemens struck out two more in the eighth and two more in the ninth before getting Rodriguez to ground out to end the game. "That's the most dominant I've ever caught him. That was very special," said Posada.[104]

All told, Clemens struck out fifteen Mariners and allowed only a single hit while pitching a complete-game shutout. "I think it probably ranks with Bob Gibson and [Don] Larsen as the greatest postseason games I've seen pitched," said Steinbrenner.[105]

The Yankees had a chance to clinch the ALCS and at least hold up their end of a subway series. When they took a 2–1 lead in the fourth inning, it looked like they might be celebrating in Seattle. Yet after scoring those two runs, they had the bases loaded with no outs and failed to plate another. That proved consequential. Seattle plated five in the fifth inning, knocking

Neagle out of the game. A bases-loaded rally in the seventh fell short when Posada and Hill struck out. The Yankees lost, 6–2, the only noteworthy part of the game being Dwight Gooden's last appearance in the Major Leagues. Any celebration would have to wait.

• • •

El Duque was on the mound. The offense had shined in Games Two through Four, and the Mets had already clinched the pennant. The stage was set, and in advance of Game Six of the ALCS, most of the talk centered on what a Yankees' victory would mean for the city in the coming days. Sojo ran into a Mets fan while shopping at White Plains Mall who wished him luck. He wanted a subway series.

"I was on the plane today with this guy from Chicago, a high-roller," said Don Mattingly, who threw out the first pitch before Game Six. "He was asking me if he should stay around for the weekend if it's a Subway Series. And I told him that whatever he had to pay for a couple of tickets, it would be worth it."[106] "I've been hearing about a Subway Series since Nelson [Doubleday] and I bought the team 21 years ago, and for 21 years before that," said Wilpon. "I want New York to be the focus of baseball."[107]

A charged-up Yankee Stadium was quickly silenced when the Mariners took a 2–0 lead four batters into the game. New York could not figure out Seattle starter John Halama and went quietly through the first three innings. When Carlos Guillén crushed a ball into the right-field upper deck, giving Seattle a 4–0 lead in the fourth, Steinbrenner shouted from the press box, "Get him [Hernández] out of there. He's having a bad night. He doesn't have his best stuff."[108] It felt more likely that a Game Seven would be played the following night.

As they had done in Game Two, however, the Yankees climbed back. In the bottom of the fourth, a Posada double plated two, and an O'Neill single added another run to make it a 4–3 game. It stayed that way into the bottom of the seventh. Singles by Vizcaino and Jeter put runners on first and third with one out for Justice. Piniella brought in Rhodes, a questionable move given Justice's .445 batting average with two home runs in his career against the lefty.

Rhodes pitched Justice cautiously. It would be hard for him to keep Justice from tying the game, but he could at least keep him from giving the Yankees the lead. When the count moved to 3-1, Rhodes tried to sneak in a fastball. Justice crushed it, launching an obvious off-the-bat home run into the upper deck in right. "Justice hit a ball that discovered new civilizations, way beyond the right field wall," described the *Seattle Post-Intelligencer*'s John Hickey.[109] Seattle right fielder Raúl Ibañez barely moved an inch in pursuit of the ball.

"Get your tokens ready! You might be boarding the subway," screamed Yankees radio announcer Michael Kay as Justice rounded the bases and the stadium unleashed a crescendo of noise. In the dugout an animated Justice kept pumping his fist and yelling as the crowd cheered him on for a curtain call. "It was just magical, it was unbelievable as I rounded the bases, just to see this place erupt," said Justice.[110]

When O'Neill singled in two more runs and Vizcaino added a sacrifice fly to make it a 9–4 game, fans began chanting, "We want the Mets!"

The Mariners would not go quietly, though. Rodriguez homered off Hernández to start the eighth, and Seattle scored two more runs off Rivera, the first postseason runs he had allowed in thirty-three and a third innings. In the ninth, with two out, Rodriguez mustered an infield hit, getting the tying run to the plate in Edgar Martinez. Yankees fans shuddered. Martinez had not only ended the team's 1995 season with his extra-innings double in Game Five of the ALDS, but he had also battered Rivera like no other hitter: ten hits in twelve at bats.

The concern was all for naught. Martinez grounded out to Jeter, ending the ALCS, igniting a celebration in the stadium, and putting in place the first World Series ever between the New York Yankees and the New York Mets. Justice, appropriately, won ALCS MVP. All anyone wanted to focus on, though, was the match-up now set to begin on Saturday, October 21, at Yankee Stadium.

9   Joy in Metsville

Dave Mlicki had not been thinking about throwing a shutout until about the eighth inning. Before then he was just trying to keep the Mets in the game. Now, at 5–0 in the ninth inning, the first interleague game between the Mets and Yankees was all but over. Thousands of fans, many of them likely Yankees supporters, had already headed home. The only mystery left to this game was whether Mlicki would come back out in the bottom of the ninth and attempt to complete the shutout.

The mystery intensified when the Mets added another run in the top of the ninth. The run came, in part, because of an error by pitcher Graeme Lloyd. "You know the Boss is gonna be on the phone after this game and ordering mandatory PFP (pitchers fielding practice)," remarked FX's Chip Caray. The remark was said in jest, somewhat, yet there was a ring of truth to it. There was no way George Steinbrenner was going to be pleased with this first regular-season game effort against the Mets.[1]

The displeasure could only have grown in the ninth. Mlicki did indeed come out to start the inning. The Yankees, meanwhile, were not going to change their game plan, even if it had not really worked to this point. Hayes led off the inning and swung at a first-pitch fastball, fouling it off. Hayes then committed a baseball sin. He knocked a Mlicki curve down the left-field line for a hit. The ball bounded off the wall and was quickly recovered by Bernard Gilkey. Hayes, his team down six runs, tried to stretch the hit into a double. Gilkey chucked the ball on the fly to second, where Hayes was easily tagged out. It felt fitting for a Mets team where everything on the night had gone right.

Whiten then singled, rubbing salt on Hayes's base-running gaffe. It did not matter to Mlicki. Even with the abundance of base runners, throughout the game it looked as if he and Hundley were merely playing a game of catch. No hitters, no fielders, no umpires. Just the two of them, tossing the ball. "I didn't hear anything. I didn't see anything. It was just Todd and I," said Mlicki.[2]

That continued as Mlicki easily got the second out of the inning on a ground ball. There was just one out to go. That one out was Girardi, who appropriately swung at the first pitch and grounded a single into center field. Despite two runners now being on base, Bobby Valentine had no plans to remove Mlicki. No Mets pitcher had tossed a complete game yet that season. Valentine was giving Mlicki an opportunity to be the first and on the biggest stage of the year so far.

Mlicki, who had been able to shut out the crowd noise all night, now finally did hear something from the stands. A "Let's go Mets" chant had broken out, and with many Yankees fans already on the Major Deegan Expressway or on a subway car, even Mlicki could not zone out that noise.

Reigning American League Rookie of the Year Derek Jeter strode to the plate. Jeter had been one of Mlicki's many victims, looking at a curveball for strike three back in the third. Mlicki set, checked the runners, then delivered a big, looping curveball.

Strike one.

The count eventually went to 2-2. In the Mets' dugout, players sat on the edge of the bench, ready to celebrate. In the stands, what was left of the crowd, almost exclusively Mets fans at this point, stood and cheered. Jeter stepped out and took a few one-handed practice swings, looking as if he was preparing himself for having to fend off an inside pitch. Finally he stepped back in.

Mlicki came set, checked the runners, then delivered, flicking his wrist as he released the pitch. Hundley had set up outside but quickly realized the ball would not be hitting its mark. To Jeter it looked like the ball was going to run right into his body, just as it had appeared in the third inning. But just as it had in the third inning, the ball instead dropped down and right into the strike zone.

Called strike three.

Game over.

Mlicki pumped his fist and then embraced Hundley. "You earned it," said Hundley who flipped Mlicki the ball.[3]

Mlicki *had* earned it. The man who had entered the game 2-5 with a 4.70 ERA, who had never thrown a complete-game shutout, and who had never struck out more than seven batters in a game, had just put in the performance of a lifetime. He had shut out the reigning world champions at Yankee Stadium in the first-ever game between these two intra-city rivals.

Mlicki would never have another game like it in his career. Later, after he was done with the bevy of postgame interviews, Mlicki snuck back out onto the field, lifted the tarp placed over the pitcher's mound, and scooped up a handful of dirt. The dirt and the ball that struck out Jeter to end the game were placed in a prominent position in the basement of Mlicki's home. He also proudly kept his jersey from that night.

Decades later Mlicki opened his mail one day to find the back page of the June 17, 1997, *New York Daily News*. It featured the headline "Joy in Metsville," with a picture of Mlicki celebrating the game's final out. A fan had mailed it hoping Mlicki would sign it and send it back to him. Mlicki, who continued to receive requests like this for years after his shutout performance, happily obliged.

For two hours and forty-four minutes on that June night in 1997, it did not matter who won more championships, who had a better record, or who had more marquee players. All that mattered was that the Mets had been New York's dominate team.

10 Up the Middle

Johnny Kucks had had a remarkable year for the Yankees. In just his second big-league season, the pitcher had won eighteen games and thrown three shoutouts, and he had done all of it by pitching mostly to contact. In 224 plus innings, he had struck out only sixty-seven batters. He went to that year's All-Star Game and even earned MVP votes. Kucks pitched in Games One and Two of the World Series in relief, both games the Yankees lost. He then toed the rubber as the team's Game Seven starter, a risky choice by the manager but one that paid off. The Yankees took an early 2–0 lead and never looked back. In the ninth Kucks worked with a 9–0 advantage as he reared back and fired an 0-2 pitch for strike three. It was Kucks's first and only strikeout of the game; it came against Jackie Robinson, and it ended the 1956 World Series.

Over the next forty-four years no New York teams faced each other again in the Fall Classic. The Brooklyn Dodgers and New York Giants headed to California in 1958, leaving the Yankees alone in the city until the Mets arrived in 1962. The Yankees made the World Series in each of the Mets' first three seasons, but the Amazin's were bottom dwellers. When the Mets won their surprise championship in 1969 and made it to Game Seven of the 1973 World Series, the Yankees were a .500 team at best. In the late 1970s and early 1980s, as the Yankees consistently made the postseason and won two championships, the Mets were among the worst teams in baseball. For a while 1985 was as close as it got as both teams competed until the final weekend of the year to make the playoffs. But the Yankees then fell into irrelevance as the Mets built a near dynasty. The pendulum swung back in the mid-1990s.

At long last the two teams would meet in the ultimate contest of who would truly be New York's team. For the rest of the country's baseball fans, many of whom believed that the media unfairly fixated on all things New York, the match-up was a horror story, a snooze fest, or a little bit of both. "They're both based in New York. They both spend big. Both have obnoxious fans. Both act as if the sun rises and sets between Long Island Sound and the Hudson River," wrote the *Atlanta Journal and Constitution*'s Mark Bradley.[1]

"It feels like all of New York is extending a Statue of Liberty–sized middle finger at the rest of the country while saying, 'The World Series is back in the city that invented it, where it belongs,'" said the *Chicago Tribune*'s Skip Bayless.[2] Patrick Reusse of the *Star Tribune* in Minnesota believed that "folks in the country officially have tired of the Yankees and the idea that baseball championships are now the exclusive property of the game's highest spenders. The non–New York sporting public sees the Mets not as a group of intriguing underdogs who made it here as the National League wild card, but rather as another big-market team that has spent huge dollars to win a pennant."[3]

But within New York City and extending out through Connecticut and New York State, past Pompton Lakes, New Jersey, to the Delaware River and reaching down to Seaside Heights, the Subway Series was all anyone was talking about.

"Every time someone asks me to rate my World Series titles with the Yankees, I sigh and tell them it's like asking me to rate my three children," wrote O'Neill in his autobiography. "I cherish all of those championships equally. But in terms of endless drama, constant excitement, overwhelming hype, and a local rivalry playing out on a national stage, the 2000 World Series against the Mets was a special event."[4]

"I can say this," said Willie Randolph, who grew up in the city and, while he spent most of his playing career with the Yankees, he ended his career as a Met. "I never felt as much pressure to succeed as I did in that Series. I've told people that I would have given up two of my championship rings in order to beat the Mets. As a hometown guy, it would have been tough, maybe even impossible, to show my face anywhere in the city if we had lost the Series."[5] "I had someone drive up to my gate and ring my bell, saying they were big Mets fans and needed some extra tickets," said John Franco.[6]

The drama began after the last out of the ALCS and intensified two days before the Series started. Agbayani sat for an interview with legendary radio personality Howard Stern. Asked for a prediction on the series, Agbayani responded, "I'll say five games. And we're going to win it." He repeated the prediction hours later in an interview with *Live* host Regis Philbin.

It's unlikely that Agbayani's prediction would have been taken seriously had it not been about the Subway Series. Any reasonable person would have seen it for what it was: a playful moment during a few not-meant-to-be-serious interviews. Instead the whole thing blew up. The *New York Post* used it for front-page headline fodder, and the Yankees tacked it up in their clubhouse. Newspapers across the country, looking for something to write about in the days before the Series, ran with the story.

"How could anyone possibly think I was serious?" said Agbayani when asked about his comments later on that day.[7] The whole hubbub was ludicrous, but it exemplified the hysteria surrounding the Series. Eventually, on Saturday, October 21, the two teams got down to business.

Billy Joel, a lifelong Yankees fan who lived in the Mets' stronghold of Long Island, sang the national anthem before the first game. Nearly fifty-six thousand came out to Yankee Stadium, most seemingly Yankees fans, but certainly a large number of Mets fans were in attendance. "You know why there's so many of them?" asked Mets fan Billy Bergmann about all the Yankees fans. "If you leave one alone, he can't do anything right."[8]

Taking the ball for the Mets was, fittingly, a former Yankee: Al Leiter. Leiter had made his big-league debut there thirteen years earlier, electrifying the crowd with strikeout after strikeout. Much had transpired since then, and few would have guessed on that night in 1987 that the young lefty on the mound would be the next Mets pitcher to start a World Series game.

Facing Leiter was another lefty who had made an impression in New York: Andy Pettitte. Pettitte had saved the Yankees during the ALDS against the A's, shutting Oakland down in Game Two. His steadfast performance in Game Three had tilted the ALCS in the Yankees' favor. Now the lefty whom George Steinbrenner had desperately and foolishly wanted to trade a year earlier was starting Game One of arguably the biggest match-up of the Boss's ownership.

In the early goings neither pitcher gave an inch. Through three innings both Leiter and Pettitte stranded runners on base, buckling down to induce weak ground balls and weak pop-ups. Piazza led off the fourth with a seeing-eye single up the middle, the kind of ground ball that Jeter's detractors would say he should have fielded. With Zeile now up and the count 1-1, Pettitte came set. Since he had come up to the big leagues in 1995, no pitcher had picked off more base runners than Pettitte. The difference between his move toward home plate and his move toward first base was miniscule, so miniscule that some base runners did not dare take more than a step or two off the bag. In this instance Piazza was actually initially moving back toward first base as Pettitte began his motion. Piazza then took a step toward second, at which point Pettitte straightened his right leg and threw over to Martinez. Mets first-base coach Mookie Wilson picked up the move quickly, shouting, "Back!" but it was too late. Piazza, who had been not more than four feet off the base, tried to change his momentum before realizing his only chance was to start running toward second. After a toss from Martinez to Jeter, the shortstop applied the tag for the first out.

On the next pitch Zeile pounded a Pettitte curve into the dirt in front of home plate, where it deadened and rolled into foul territory along the third-base line. It so clearly seemed to be a foul ball that FOX, broadcasting the World Series, did not even bother to pan to a view of the ball. Zeile began sprinting down the line toward first and then stopped, also believing the ball to be foul. Trickling along the dirt, though, the ball inexplicably rolled back toward the line into fair territory, where Brosius picked it up and easily threw to first for the out. One inning later Payton drove a ball into the dirt behind home plate, but the backspin carried the ball forward into fair territory. Posada easily tagged out Payton, who had remained in the batter's box. The Mets had made three base-running gaffes in two innings.

Leiter, meanwhile, was dealing. He ended the fourth inning by striking out Williams and Martinez, both swinging, and he began the fifth by doing the same to Posada. The Yankees mustered only two hits through five innings, looking more like the team in the final weeks of September than one that had just pummeled the Mariners. But Leiter needed run support, and in the sixth inning, he came within mere inches of getting it.

Timo Pérez stood on first with two outs as Pettitte delivered an 0-2 curve to Zeile. The Mets' first baseman, who hit Pettitte better than possibly anyone in baseball, went down and gulfed the pitch, sending it high and deep to left field. Yankee Stadium collectively stood still as everyone watched the flight of the ball, wondering if it had enough to get into the stands. Justice sprinted over and back, following the path of the ball as it descended. On television and to many in the ballpark that night, it appeared that the ball had landed in the first row of seats and then had dropped back onto the warning track. The way the ball fell, deadened and weakly, gave every indication that it had hit a fan or a fan had tried to catch it and failed, meaning that it was a home run. Pérez, rounding second as the ball fell, certainly thought that was the case, as did much of the Mets' dugout and many watching the game on television. Zeile raised his fist in triumph as he headed toward first base and put his head down as he began what he thought was a home-run trot.

Several Yankees, however, saw exactly what had happened. The ball had landed at the literal top of the padded wall in left field, just out of the reach of Yankees fan Jack Nelson, who, while later claiming he had wisely avoided touching the ball to prevent a fan-interference call, had actually just not reached far enough to interfere with the play. Instead of deflecting into the stands—as almost any other ball in that situation would certainly have done—it had simply gone limp and dropped onto the playing field. Pérez, believing the ball was a home run, immediately realized that no umpire had signaled as much and began sprinting toward and then around third. Justice quickly scooped the ball up and fired to Jeter, who sprinted across the outfield toward the left-field stands when he caught the ball and, still on the run, fired a one-hop throw to Posada. Pérez was out by a foot. "I saw it hit off the top of the wall and out of the corner of my eye I saw we had a shot at Pérez," said Jeter.[9]

Valentine emerged from the dugout looking confused and signaling with his hand that he thought the ball had left the yard. Stearns emerged yelling, "That's a home run! That's a home run!" The umpiring crew explained that there had been no interference, and Valentine had no choice but to return to the dugout, the game still scoreless. "I was confused by the ball," said Pérez after the game. "I saw the fans put their hands up and I thought it was a home run. I slowed up a little. If I would've run all the way through, I would've scored. I have no excuses about it."[10]

Pérez's hesitation, while in some ways understandable given that many people thought the ball was out, had cost the Mets a run and the lead. It was the team's fourth base-running gaffe of the game. "It has been a disaster for the Mets on the bases tonight. Embarrassing," said FOX broadcaster Tim McCarver as the bottom of the sixth got under way. He then added, "One of the characteristics of this Yankees team over the last five years, they have been very opportunistic. You make mistakes against them and they strike."

Four minutes after McCarver said this, Justice came up with runners on first and second and lined a ball into left-center field. Both runners scored easily as the Yankees became the first team to score in the Subway Series. Yankee Stadium hummed with continuous noise even after Leiter got out of the inning without further damage. The Mets, however, refused to wilt. They loaded the bases with one out in the seventh for Trammell.

Torre had Jeff Nelson warming up in the bullpen, but rather than go for the righty-righty match-up, he kept Pettitte in the game. Trammell, 7-18 with a home run lifetime against Pettitte, lined a 1-1 pitch into left for a game-tying single.

Eventually, with runners on second and third and two out, Alfonzo hit a weak tapper between third base and the pitcher's mound. Brosius, playing back, fielded and threw to first, but it was too late. Alfonzo beat the throw by a step, and the Mets, for all that had gone wrong over the past few innings, now held a 3–2 lead.

Leiter kept the Yankees at bay in the seventh, then yielded to John Franco in the eighth. In the veteran's first World Series appearance, he allowed a lead-off single but no runs to preserve the lead. After failing to get a runner in from third with fewer than two outs in the top of the inning, the Mets handed Benitez the ball for the bottom of the ninth.

Inside Yankee Stadium fans of both teams kept a steady drumbeat of noise throughout the bottom of the inning. Leading off, Posada made the hearts of Mets fans skip a beat when he sent a shot deep into center field. Leiter, watching from the bench, held his breath as Payton flagged the ball down at the warning track. Up stepped Paul O'Neill.

O'Neill, like many Yankees, had struggled during the last month of the year. A hip injury had caused him to miss time, and when he played, his bat looked noticeably slower. "I had a right hip pointer that required a cortisone shot before the series, and I wasn't even sure I would be able to run or play against the Mets," said O'Neill.[11]

In the last sixteen games of the year, O'Neill did not have a single extra-base hit. He was well aware of his performance. The longer he went without being able to drive the ball, the less confident he felt with every at bat. Plus, he had not necessarily been looking forward to a subway series. Just weeks earlier, when the possibility had been raised, O'Neill had responded, "I just couldn't handle that."[12]

Now, against Benitez, O'Neill's bat looked even slower. A series of defensive swings put him in a 1-2 hole, and he appeared to be an easy mark for a strikeout. The Mets had to be aware of O'Neill's sluggish bat. Everyone was. One did not need to be a scout to see it. But Benitez continued to fire pitches away from the plate, and O'Neill continued to foul pitches away, prolonging the at bat. Benitez kept throwing the ball away, away, and away. On the tenth pitch of the at bat, with the count full, O'Neill took ball four outside. "Because it had been such a long at bat, I felt like I had hit a home run when I heard the umpire say, 'Ball four.' If Benitez had known how lost I felt, he would have zoomed three fastballs down the middle and been done with me," said O'Neill.[13]

The walk brought nearly all the fans in the stadium to their feet. Polonia, pinch-hitting, lined a single to right. FOX, meanwhile, began broadcasting a bevy of images and statistics that had to churn the stomach of any Mets fan watching. It started with a statistic showing that no reliever had given up more postseason home runs in baseball history than Benitez. The broadcast next proceeded to show some of the home runs, including shots by Belle, Jeter, Tony Fernández, and Snow. Shortly after, Vizcaino flared a single into left field to load the bases. "José started because his batting average against me was almost .600," said Leiter, who was slightly off (Vizcaino was hitting .526 off him coming into Game One). "Albeit most of the hits couldn't blacken your eye, they were still hits."[14]

A sacrifice fly tied things up, sending Game One into extra innings.

In extra innings the Mets' bullpen continuously walked a tightrope while the offense struggled to make headway. Nine Mets hitters came to the plate between the tenth and twelfth innings. They went 0-9 with five strikeouts. In the bottom of the tenth, the Yankees put runners on second and third with no outs. Rusch, in relief, got out of it thanks to a pop-up and a double play. In the next inning, Rusch put runners on second and third with two out before Wendell came in and escaped the jam. When the Yankees loaded the bases with one out in the twelfth only to watch Sojo pop out, it looked like the Mets would escape one more time. But Vizcaino slapped Wendell's first pitch into left for his fourth hit of the game, giving the Yankees the win. "I was very excited when I came to the Yankees because I thought I'd get a chance to play in the World Series," said Vizcaino. "I never thought I would be a hero in Game 1."[15]

At four hours and fifty-one minutes, it was the longest game in World Series history to that time. "I thought it was a heck of a game," said Valentine. "We gave them a pretty good run for their money, and we just came up a little short."[16]

Game One had been exhausting but thrilling. Game Two would just be flat out bizarre.

• • •

The first inning of Game Two of the 2000 World Series featured one of the oddest moments to ever take place in the Fall Classic. It involved a confluence of events that, had even one of them been missing from the equation, the incident would not have been nearly as memorable. Roger Clemens had to be the pitcher. Mike Piazza had to be the hitter. Both had to move or be in certain positions, and the ball and Piazza's bat both had to go a certain way. If any of those had gone differently, the memories of Game Two would be far different, with the consequences not stretching into the 2002 season.

It happened after Clemens started the game by blowing a ninety-seven-mile-per-hour fastball past Pérez for a strikeout and then dropping a splitter in the dirt against Alfonzo for another swinging strikeout. It was only two batters, but Clemens looked like the same pitcher who had one-hit the Mariners a week earlier. There was also something about Clemens that stuck out, to both his teammates and his opponents that night. He was always amped up when starting a game. It was part of his makeup, and it was what made teammates love him and opposing teams and fans despise him. This was different, though. Clemens's energy level was on another plain. The Mets' bench noticed it, thinking he looked "weird" out on the mound. It would continue through the game, with even Posada motioning to Clemens to turn it down a little after one of his split-fingered fastballs exhibited too much movement.

An already super-amped Clemens then faced Piazza for the first time since hitting him in the head in July. The count went to 1-2 in what seemed like it would now be an anticlimactic event. Clemens threw a fastball hard in. Piazza, at that moment 7-12 with three home runs and nine RBIs lifetime against Clemens, swung as the ball sailed in on his hands. He made contact, with the ball striking the lower half of the bat and shattering it into several pieces. As the ball slowly hopped foul into the Yankees' dugout, the barrel of the bat, now with a jagged edge protruding from it, shot out toward the pitcher's mound. It took one bounce, skidded along the grass for a few feet, then suddenly catapulted up and into the arms of Clemens. The pitcher grabbed the piece of bat with his right hand and, without care for where he was throwing, hurled it toward the Yankees' dugout. Piazza first turned to look at the bat shattering in his hands and then, not fully knowing where the ball had gone, quickly started running down the first-base line before he realized it was a foul ball. Just as he began slowing down, Clemens threw the bat shard within a few feet of him, almost hitting him with it.

Piazza, still carrying the handle of the bat, turned and looked at Clemens with confusion then started to approach the pitcher.

"What's your problem?" asked Piazza.

Clemens did not directly respond. Later he said he could not hear Piazza over the crowd noise.

"It was bizarre," remarked Piazza. "I was trying to figure out if it was intentional or not. . . . I really didn't understand. I was trying to get him to say it was an accident or whatever."[17]

As the two got closer, both benches emptied, though no fights or even any pushing broke out. As is seen on the television broadcast, "I thought it was the ball," shouted Clemens, who seemed oblivious to what he had just done. He could not understand why Piazza was coming toward him or why the umpire was simply not giving him a new ball to pitch with.

After Clemens retired Piazza on a ground ball to end the inning, he approached home-plate umpire Charlie Reliford. "That's my fault," Clemens told him as he patted Reliford's chest.

Clemens was correct. The incident was his fault. He had acted foolishly, throwing what was, in essence, a weapon, in the direction of another human being without any regard for that person's welfare. Also, his claiming that he thought the bat was the ball, though supported by television cameras that caught him saying as much immediately after he chucked the shard, struck many as odd. Even if true, so what? No one was disputing that Clemens had fielded the bat. It was throwing the bat that they could not figure out. Would Clemens, or any pitcher, throw a batted ball in the direction of his own dugout ten feet from home plate? "Throwing [the bat] in the direction of Piazza was a rash reaction," wrote Randolph in his autobiography. "Claiming that he thought it was the ball was probably an even weaker response."[18]

Still, the incident itself would become overblown as players and fan bases coalesced behind their preferred narrative for what had happened. The media immediately seized on it. How could they not? There was already drama behind Clemens and Piazza, not to mention Clemens and the entire Mets team. Before the start of the Series, Pratt had said about the Yankees, "We actually like their team. . . . Well at least 24 of the guys."[19]

And now there was a dangerous flying object between the two teams. On FOX Tim McCarver did not help when, in the moment, he blasted Clemens and implied he had thrown the bat intentionally. Those who hated Clemens used the moment to point out just what an asshole he really was. The constant showing of slowed-down instant replays of the incident certainly made it look like Clemens had deliberately thrown the bat at Piazza.

The truth is likely far less complicated. Clemens, already overly intense, quickly realized the bat was not, in fact, the ball, and immediately tossed it aside, albeit in an inexcusably irresponsible manner. When viewed in real time, it is clear that Clemens never actually looked up to see where Piazza was running. He caught the bat, he turned, and he chucked it off the playing field. "I was fired up and emotional and flung the bat towards the on-deck circle where the batboy was. I had no idea that Mike was running," said Clemens after the game.[20]

Batgate would not disappear. Some Mets players and fans resented that Clemens had thrown a lethal weapon at the team's best player and had not faced any repercussions. "If I was Mike, I would have been thrown out of the game because I would have tried to kick his ass," said Lenny Harris. "I'm from Miami—Liberty City. I've got to throw some hands."[21] Clemens was eventually fined $50,000 for his action. That was not enough, though. People wanted vengeance. The disappointment for the Mets lasted past 2001 since Clemens did not pitch against them that year. In 2002 Mets pitcher Shawn Estes, who was a Giant when the Subway Series took place, threw a pitch behind Clemens in his first at bat at Shea since Batgate.

After the dust settled in Game Two, Hampton went to work for the Mets, hoping to keep his NLCS MVP form. He struggled early with his command, walking two batters in the first and allowing two-out singles to Martinez and Posada, giving the Yankees a 2–0 lead. Brosius added a solo home run in the second, the first home run of the Series and the first home run by any player in a New York subway series since Moose Skowron in 1956.

Hampton struggled throughout the night, though he kept the Yankees from fully blowing the game open. Still, the Yankees added a run here and a run there. O'Neill suddenly found his stroke, something he attributed to a bit of superstition. Before Game One, Yogi Berra had picked up O'Neill's bats and rubbed them for good luck. After O'Neill collected a hit and the famous Benitez walk, he sought out Berra again before Game Two. "Eventually, Yogi arrived and I almost tackled him and dragged him over to work his magic on my bats again," said O'Neill.[22] The result was three more hits in Game Two, including a single that made it 4–0 Yankees. Eventually they built a 6–0 lead.

While the Yankees were building their lead, Rivera ran into Steinbrenner in the clubhouse. Throughout the series the owner was a nervous bundle of energy—some of it good, much of it not. He lived in constant fear that something would go wrong and the Mets would pull it off, a result that he felt would sentence him to a lifetime of utter humiliation. He asked Rivera if the closer thought the Yankees would pull off the World Series win. Rivera was so certain they would that he made Steinbrenner a bet: we win it all, you fly me and my family to Panama on your private jet. We lose, and I take you out to dinner anywhere you want. Steinbrenner took the lopsided bet.[23]

Clemens, meanwhile, was nearly unhittable. He allowed a second-inning single and a seventh-inning single, both to Zeile, but no other hits. The Mets could not catch up to his fastball, which, like in his ALCS outing, showed movement that had been largely missing during his first two years in New York. His splitter, meanwhile, was about as sharp as it would ever be during his Yankees career. Clemens struck out nine Mets that night, all of them swinging.

It was a 6–0 game entering the top of the ninth. Outside of the first inning, it had been a largely uneventful game and one with little drama. Thoughts began to drift to Game Three and how the Mets would have to come back from an 0–2 hole, just as they had done in the 1986 World Series.

Fans were already filing out of Yankee Stadium when Alfonzo lined a single to left field to start the inning. Clemens had left the game, his pitch count too high to let Torre have him complete his second shutout of the playoffs. Jeff Nelson got the ball, in part to prevent the team from having to use Rivera given that it was a non-save situation. The closer had worked two innings in Game One. After Alfonzo's single, Piazza came to bat. A smattering of boos greeted him. Nelson got a quick first strike then tried to come in on Piazza with a fastball, similar to what Clemens had done in the first inning. Rather than shatter his bat, though, Piazza turned on the pitch and, flat footed, drove the ball into the foul pole just above the upper-deck façade in left field. It was his first career World Series home run and the first by a Met since Darryl Strawberry and it put New York on the board. Still, it was a 6–2 game, and there was no immediate cause for alarm for the Yankees—until Ventura, the next hitter, singled.

Nervousness began to creep into the stadium, evidenced by the fans' booing of Nelson after he gave up his third hit of the inning. Second-guessing started as well. While not directly saying so, FOX broadcaster Joe Buck implied that perhaps Clemens should not have been removed from the game.

Torre took no chances. He removed Nelson and brought in Rivera to finish it off. Rivera injected calm when he quickly got ahead of Zeile, 1-2. Zeile, responsible for two of the three hits Clemens had given up over his last seventeen innings, then turned on a fastball. Immediately an "Ohhhhh" went up from the crowd, much of which thought Zeile had just cut the Yankees' lead to two runs. The ball sailed high into deep left field, where Clay Bellinger, a late-inning defensive replacement who had spent ten years in the Minor Leagues before making his big-league debut that April, began tracking it.

Bellinger went back and calmly reached up to catch the ball at the top of the wall. It possibly would have been a home run, though more likely it would have hit the top of the wall. Still, Valentine stared from the top step of the dugout with a bemused smile on his face, as if to convey that he could not believe what had happened. Two nights in a row now Zeile had come within mere inches of a two-run home run.

Order felt restored for the home crowd—until Agbayani singled. Now the Mets had the tying run in the on-deck circle and thoughts of the June 30 game against the Braves running through their heads. After a wild pitch moved the runners to second and third, the Yankees caught a break when the Mets made yet another base-running mistake. Pinch hitter Lenny Harris hit a chopper back to Rivera, who turned and fired to second after Agbayani had gotten too far off the base. Agbayani took off for third, forcing Ventura to head home, where he was easily thrown out.

There were now two outs. The tying run was still in the on-deck circle, but the Mets' rally felt squelched. Moreover, the Yankees had played 107 World Series games in which they had taken a lead into the ninth inning. They had lost exactly one of those games, back in 1947. As Payton came up, the Yankees' fans began to stand, cheering their team on as they awaited the final out. Then Payton did something exactly one player had ever done before and no player would do again: he hit a home run off Mariano Rivera in the postseason. The shot, hit down the line in right field, cut the lead to one run. Cheers erupted from the Mets fans still left at the game while the Mets' dugout felt as if they could actually pull this off. It would be the most incredible comeback in World Series history and a gut punch to the Yankees.

Rivera was unfazed by it all. As if to convey that he had had enough of all this, he quickly delivered three straight strikes to Kurt Abbott, as Abbott looked at the last pitch to end the game. The Yankees had won, yes, but those five runs gave the Mets a sense of hope as they returned to Shea.

After the game all anyone wanted to talk about was Clemens and the splintered bat. "I don't know what's going on in his mind," said a still angry Stearns. "He better check out what's going on [psychologically]. . . . The last time, he drills our guy. This time, he throws a bat at him. At some point in time, you have to decide how much you can tolerate."[24]

Everyone was asked about the incident. Just about everyone agreed it was bizarre. Joe Torre, however, was not befuddled by it at all. He was angry—angry that reporters would not stop asking about it in the postgame press conference; angry that it overshadowed his team's being up 2–0; angry that reporters seemed to imply that Clemens had deliberately thrown the bat at Piazza. "Why would he throw it at him?" Torre angrily retorted in response to one question. "So he could be thrown out in the second game of the World Series? Does that make sense to anybody? Or is that too shitty a story to write?"[25]

No one could recall seeing Torre this publicly combative with the media before. Perhaps Torre really was upset with the line of questioning and could not hide it as well as he'd previously done over four years in New York. Still, Torre's behavior absorbed many of the pointed questions that Clemens would have to face. Torre's responses—angry, incredulous—put reporters on the defensive as Clemens came into the conference room. While he still had to answer for his actions, the tension had been largely removed. Torre had taken most of the blows in defense of his pitcher.

• • •

Shea Stadium was electric. To witness the first World Series game at the stadium since Jesse Orosco had thrown his glove in the air to celebrate a championship, 55,299 fans had come out to Queens. Being down 2–0 in the series did not faze the crowd or its team. The Mets had made a habit of overcoming adversity over the past few seasons, and no team had played better at home that year than they had. There was an energy pulsating through the ballpark as the minutes ticked down to the start of Game Three. Celebrities like Bruce Willis, Jimmy Kimmel, and Billy Baldwin sat in the stands. NSYNC, the world-famous boy band whose *No Strings Attached* album was the biggest selling album of the year and second-biggest of the decade, sang a heavily harmonized version of the national anthem. With that, Game Three got under way.

Rick Reed toed the rubber for the Mets, trying to make up for his performance in Game Three of the NLCS. In that outing he'd allowed five runs before getting hooked in the fourth inning, ultimately taking the team's only loss of the series. Now the Mets were calling on him to save their season. Torre, meanwhile, was stuck without a designated hitter in the National League park and had to adjust his lineup. Knoblauch was the odd man out. That meant Torre needed a new lead-off hitter. He went with Vizcaino, who was batting .400 in the series.

Reed looked great early on. Yankees hitters were unable to pick up which pitches he was throwing, and Reed moved the ball across the plate and changed speeds with precision. Jeter struck out looking on an outside fastball. Williams struck out looking on an inside fastball. Martinez struck out swinging on a high fastball. Posada struck out looking on a two-seam fastball that broke across the plate. Brosius struck out swinging on a two-seam fastball that broke in on his hands. Reed, who had averaged fewer than six strikeouts per nine innings that year, whiffed five of the first six batters he faced. He threw up. He threw down. He threw inside. He threw outside. Each strikeout amplified the noise coming from the crowd. It had the feeling of Bobby Jones's performance against the Giants.

Unfortunately for Reed, Orlando Hernández had all of his pitches working just as well, if not better. El Duque, now 8-0 in his career in the postseason and battling flu-like symptoms, struck out Pérez, Alfonzo, and Piazza in the first, all swinging. Mixing his fastball, his curveball, and his angle of delivery, Hernández kept all three off balance. His first pitch of the second inning, however, was a mistake. He left a fastball over the plate to Ventura, who hit it just beneath the scoreboard in right field for a 1–0 Mets lead. As the Beatles' "Twist and Shout" blared from the loudspeakers, the Mets leapt out of the dugout to celebrate. With the way Reed was pitching, Ventura's home run felt like it could be enough to win the game.

Hernández gave a look on the mound that acknowledged he had made a poor pitch. Then he got right back to work, striking out Zeile, Agbayani, and Payton. Six outs, six strikeouts for El Duque.

It did not take the Yankees long to get back in the game. Though Reed retired the first two hitters in the third quickly, recording his sixth strikeout, he gave up a two-out single to Jeter. Then Justice sent a ground ball just under the glove of Zeile and down the right-field line for a game-tying double. Reed escaped further damage. In the bottom of the inning, the only batter who reached base was Reed, who singled in his first World Series at bat.

In the fourth the Yankees took the lead. With Martinez on first, O'Neill lined a triple into the right-center field gap. It was his first triple since July 1999, his second hit of the game, and a bit of redemption for the hampered right fielder. O'Neill's contract would be up at the end of the year, and his recent struggles to drive the ball had many thinking he would simply retire rather than sign another deal. Now, when it mattered most, O'Neill was turning it back on again.

The Mets avoided allowing another run, thanks to Hernández's coming up in the batting order, and the game moved on with the Yankees leading, 2–1. El Duque worked around a smattering of trouble in the fourth and fifth to preserve the lead, but the Mets finally tied it in the sixth. After they got the first two runners on, Zeile, the team's hottest hitter in the Series, reached out and pulled a breaking ball down just inside the foul line in left field. It brought the tying run in and put runners on second and third with no outs. When Agbayani walked to load the bases, the Mets were posed not only to take the lead but also perhaps to blow Game Three wide open.

Instead Hernández got Payton to reach over a foot outside the strike zone to record his tenth strikeout of the game. Bordick came up next. Hitting 4-30 in the postseason, Buck and McCarver wondered if this situation did not call for a pinch hitter. Bordick was able to work the count full, but the most important pitch of the at bat came when the count was 1-0. With just about everyone expecting a fastball, Hernández dropped in a curveball for strike one. That pitch got Bordick wondering just what combination he would see in the rest of the at bat. It was not out of the question that El Duque would drop a 3-2 curve. Instead Hernández threw a fastball over the plate, which Bordick swung through for strike three. Hernández pumped his fist as the Yankees fans in attendance screamed in celebration. Two pitches later, the inning ended.

A pinch hitter replaced Reed in the sixth, meaning that the game was now in the hands of the Mets' bullpen. Wendell, Cook, and John Franco responded by scattering two walks, a hit, and a hit batter across the seventh and eighth innings. The game remained tied at 2–2 in the bottom of the eighth.

Torre wanted to remove Hernández at this point. El Duque had given the Yankees a chance to win it, and since he was feeling ill, Torre did not want to push him too hard. But El Duque refused to leave the game. Torre kept him in. "He wasn't wishy-washy," said Torre. "And what he has done for us [in the] postseason, it was really tough for me to deny him what he really wanted very badly."[26]

Hernández struck out Ventura to start the inning. The strikeout, his twelfth of the game, established a new World Series single-game record for the Yankees. Then Zeile singled, giving him multi-hit games in each of the first three games of the Series. Hernández, vigorously chewing his gum, faced Agbayani and decided to go full sidearm on a 1-0 fastball. Agbayani lined it so hard into left-center field that the ball appeared as though it would come through the television screen for fans who were watching. It skimmed along the grass all the way to the wall. As Shea went nuts, Zeile rounded the bases and scored without a throw. "As I was rounding first, I said, 'C'mon, Todd, you can do it, you can do it," said Agbayani. "Once he crossed home plate, I was like, 'thank you.'"[27]

Just about the entire Mets bench greeted Zeile as he got to the dugout steps. The Vengaboys' "We Like to Party" blasted into the stadium as fans continued to cheer long after Zeile had crossed home plate. Payton then legged out an infield hit, and that was it for Hernández. He'd allowed twelve base runners while striking out twelve batters, and he left the game with his perfect postseason record on the line. "All we heard was how he won so many times in the postseason and had never lost," said Agbayani. "So, there's always a first time for anyone."[28]

The Mets added another run to take a 4-2 lead into the ninth inning. They handed the ball to Benitez to close it out. Despite everything that had happened in the bottom of the eighth, the crowd was now strikingly subdued. No one was standing, and there were only mild cheers when Benitez started the inning by throwing a first-pitch strike to the pinch-hitting Knoblauch. It was almost as if the crowd refused to exert energy until Benitez could prove that he could close the game out.

Then Knoblauch singled up the middle, and Shea Stadium began to stir. As if to convey the uneasiness emanating from the crowd, FOX displayed a graphic titled "Armed & Dangerous." It noted that Benitez had only converted three of nine save opportunities in his postseason career. "The ugly numbers for Benitez," noted Buck.

Benitez caught a break when he retired Polonia on one pitch. Even after that, the crowd still hesitated to get fully engaged. Part of that may have been the arrival of the next batter. Derek Jeter was hitting .500 in the series and had already established a knack for timely hits. Benitez overwhelmed him, though, striking him out on a nasty slider. It was the twenty-fifth strike out of the game, tying the World Series record. That left it up to Justice. Not only did the Mets want to end the game here for the obvious reason, but also on deck was Bernie Williams, who in his career was 6-7 off Benitez, including the home run in 1998 that started the Orioles-Yankees' brawl. In no way did the Mets want Williams coming up as the go-ahead run.

The crowd allowed itself to get more into the moment as Benitez worked to Justice. The count went to 3-1 when Justice turned on a fastball. At first glance, it looked as though he had crushed the ball. But the noise that followed was the unmistakable sound of a bat cracking. Justice's shot was merely a soft liner that went into the stands down the right-field line. A new piece of timber in hand, Justice sat on a 3-2 fastball and popped it up. Alfonzo settled under it for the catch.

It is fitting that John Franco, who had pitched a scoreless eighth, was credited with the win. At forty, he was the second-oldest pitcher in history to win a World Series game.

The Mets' victory snapped the Yankees' record fourteen-game World Series win streak. More important, it brought the Mets back to life in the Subway Series. They would not roll over and get swept as the Braves and Padres had done before them. They were going to make the Yankees earn it. The game-winning hit was especially sweet for Agbayani after the backlash he had endured for his joke prediction. "I didn't stand up and definitely say we were going to win in five. If I could predict things like that, I wouldn't be playing baseball. I'd be doing something else with my money," said Agbayani.[29]

"It was important to get this out of the way, this aura, all the streaks and all these intangible things they might have against us," said Zeile. "To get one under our belt, especially against a pitcher like El Duque, we're relieved to say the least."[30]

One more win, and it would just be a three-game series. The Mets would turn, as they had in the clincher over the Giants, to Bobby Jones to get them evened up.

• • •

George Steinbrenner blamed the Game Three loss on the clubhouses at Shea. He felt his players could not get comfortable in such ragged accommodations—at least as he saw them. "I want them to feel they're at home. Hell, they *are* at home. Just in the wrong ballpark. This place is a dump," he growled.[31] The Boss ordered staff to go pack up the team's leather chairs and couches from Yankee Stadium and bring them over to Shea. A Ryder truck arrived at 11 a.m. the day of Game Four with the furniture in tow. "It's nice to know we can make the Yankees uncomfortable," said Valentine when hearing the news. "That's encouraging."[32]

It was a prime example of how involved and invested the Boss was during that week. "Mr. Steinbrenner made himself a really big presence in that series," remembered Rick Cerrone, the Yankees PR director at the time. "He wasn't hanging around the clubhouse in Atlanta [in 1999]. He wasn't hanging around the clubhouse in San Diego [in 1998]. But he basically lived in the clubhouse at Shea Stadium."[33]

Steinbrenner could not have been thrilled with the Mets' Game Four pregame entertainment either. The Baha Men had taken the field to amp up the crowd with "Who Let the Dogs Out?" which had become the Mets' anthem during the season. The song was written by Trinidad Soca performer Anselm Douglas and first garnered little attention after its 1998 release, but the Baha Men covered the song, and their version exploded in 2000. By the time the World Series came around, the album containing the song had sold over one million copies, putting the band on the map. In July John Franco and Harris urged the Mets to start playing "Who Let the Dogs Out?" "The guys just said, 'You have to play this one,'" said Vito Vitiello, who oversaw the music selection at Shea Stadium.[34]

The song, with its catchy "Who Let the Dogs Out?" refrain mixed with barking, replaced "L.A. Woman" as the club's anthem. Nelson Doubleday was no fan. "I can't stand that let-out-the-dogs song," he said.[35] That didn't stop it from soon playing before Mets games or when Benitez, who was friends with the band, entered from the bullpen. When the Mets won the pennant, their anthem played over a cheering fan base. "As soon as the game finished, right after the guy caught the ball, it was 'Who Let the Dogs Out?' just blasting out of the system," said Baha Men drummer Mo Grant, a diehard Mets fan. "I was thinking, 'How crazy is this?'"[36]

Grant and his bandmates were now performing the song on the field, at Shea, before a World Series game. As the Baha Men sang and danced, Cone looked across the dugout and found his old teammate, John Franco. Cone could not believe what he was watching before a World Series game. "Are you fucking kidding me?" he mouthed to his ex-teammate, who shrugged his shoulders in a what-can-you-do manner. "It crystallized the difference between the Mets and Yankees because you'd never see that at Yankee Stadium. I remember our whole bench going, 'This is bush,' because we were looking for things to grab onto to use as motivation," said Cone.[37]

The Mets did something a little more traditional when they asked five members of the 1969 Miracle Mets championship team—Tom Seaver, Donn Clendenon, Al Weis, Tommie Agee, and Ron Swoboda—to throw out the first pitch.

Torre, meanwhile, needed someone at leadoff. Because a designated hitter could not be used in the National League ballpark, Knoblauch rode the bench. Vizcaino had played second and hit leadoff in Game Three, but Torre wanted Sojo playing second for Game Four. Torre also felt Sojo was a natural number-two hitter, so someone had to bat in the top spot. He decided to go with Jeter. "Hopefully," Torre said before Game Four, "at the top of the lineup he can get things going. I'd like to see him score a run in the first inning."[38]

The Mets, meanwhile, were on a high. Yes, they still trailed in the Series. But the Game Three win had given them a reason to believe a comeback was possible. Why not? The last two Subway Series—in 1955 and 1956—had also featured teams coming back from a 2–0 deficit. They were also going up against Denny Neagle, with whom they were familiar from his years of pitching in the National League and who had struggled for most of his time with the Yankees. The Mets were feeling good about their chances in Game Four.

Those good feelings lasted all of the time it took for Jones to release his first pitch of the game and Jeter to hit it. Just before Jones wound up, Knoblauch said to no one in particular but loudly enough for others to hear, "First pitch is going out."[39] As flashbulbs popped all around, Jones tried to get a fastball by the Yankees' shortstop, but instead of heaving it on the outside, he left it over the plate. Jeter sent it into the left-field bleachers. One pitch; 1–0, Yankees.

"If Jeter saw a first-pitch fastball that he could smash, he would swing," said O'Neill. "He wasn't looking to work a walk or have an extended at bat.

He could and he would—if that's how the at bat unfolded. But he was ready to do damage from pitch one."[40] "I never expected him to swing," said Jones. "You read the scouting reports, watch them play and see that they work the count and take a lot of pitches. I thought I could get one by him."[41]

Knoblauch emerged from the dugout with his index finger pointed in the air as Vizcaino bear-hugged him from behind. Vizcaino then pointed at Knoblauch, reminding everyone that he had called this moment. They then did a two-handed high five. "It was just a feeling," Knoblauch said afterward. "You say it and you see what happens. You look smart when it happens."[42]

"We win Game 3, we're home for Game 4, and we couldn't even get comfortable in our goddamn chair," said Mets executive Jim Duquette. "To have it go up in smoke like that so fast, it was more deflating than the Timo play."[43]

The buzz from Jeter's home run, the eighth first-at-bat home run in a World Series game in history, persisted for the remainder of the half inning. Yankees fans and Mets fans were incredulous that the game had started that way but for different reasons. Payton and Agbayani, meanwhile, could not believe how loud the stadium had gotten after Jeter made contact. Payton had already expressed concern over how many Yankees fans had been in the crowd during Game Three. "It felt like we're in Yankee Stadium," Payton said to Agbayani as the two got back to the dugout.[44]

Payton was especially irked when he heard "Let's go Yankees" chants at Shea but had not heard "Let's go Mets" chants at Yankee Stadium. "It would be nice to be in our house and not have to hear Yankee fans. But I know that won't happen. They simply have more fans in the city than we do. We're trying to change that," he added.[45] In fact, some Mets fans had tried to start chants at Yankee Stadium but were immediately drowned out by Yankees fans chanting, "Mets suck."

Neagle, meanwhile, looked like Randy Johnson in the first inning, striking out Pérez and Piazza. Then O'Neill looked like Rickey Henderson in the second, legging out his second triple in as many nights after going the entire season without hitting one. O'Neill scored on a sacrifice fly. Leading off the third, with his friend and impending free agent Alex Rodriguez watching from the stands, Jeter hit a triple thanks to an abnormally high bounce of his one-hope fly ball off the center-field wall. Jeter scored on a groundout, making it 3–0, Yankees, in the third inning. It felt like a laugher in progress, with the Yankees continuously adding runs as the game went along. The Mets needed something—anything—before this game got out of hand. They got it in the bottom of the third.

Pérez led off the inning with a single and stood on second base with one out when Piazza came up. Piazza had nearly homered in the first, though Neagle ultimately got him out by staying on the outer part of the strike zone. On a 1-0 pitch, Neagle again tried to stay away. Piazza, swinging largely on his front leg, reached down and gulfed the ball into the left-field stands, not far from where Jeter's home run had landed. It was a shot of pure strength, achieved because Piazza was able to adjust to a changeup and muscle it over the fence.

The Mets were back in the game. Jones kept the Yankees at bay in the fourth and fifth innings, despite allowing three base runners. Neagle was not perfect, but he kept a base runner from scoring in the fourth and retired the first two hitters in the fifth. He was cruising and looked more comfortable on the mound than he had in some time. Torre took no risks, though, with Piazza coming to the plate. Piazza had nearly homered in the first and had actually homered in the third. The Yankees manager just did not feel comfortable with the at bats Piazza was having against Neagle, so he emerged from the dugout and removed him from the game. "Piazza is one of the few players who is in scoring position when he gets in the batter's box," said Torre. "He had a couple of good swings off Neagle, even though I didn't think the home run came on a bad pitch, and I just made up my mind Cone was going to pitch to Piazza at that point."[46]

Neagle's shocked expression when he saw Torre emerge left nothing to interpret. Just one more out away from possibly earning the win in a World Series game, he could not believe he was being removed. As Torre made his way to the mound, Neagle stared out at the scoreboard, as if needing to reconfirm that in fact it was still the fifth inning and he had not qualified for the win yet. Then, while looking down, he handed Torre the ball without ever glancing up at his manager. Neagle walked briskly off the mound, his head facing down at the field. He received congratulations from a handful of teammates and went through the tunnel to the clubhouse. He never pitched another game for the Yankees.

The reaction nearly took away from the new drama playing out on the field. Replacing Neagle was a familiar face to Mets fans, though he had not stepped onto the Shea Stadium mound since August 12, 1992. By every measure David Cone's 2000 season had been a disaster. Torre had put him on the postseason roster largely because there were no better options for that spot. Cone had played almost no role in the team's playoff run so far, pitching a single, largely meaningless inning in Game Five of the ALCS.

Initially there had been some debate over whether Cone might actually get the start for Game Four. That debate irked Neagle, whose public comments about the issue forced him and Torre to meet privately to resolve any uneasiness. But Cone had told Torre that he did not think he would be of much use as a starter. His arm was still aching from the shoulder separation in Kansas City. He could provide some help out of the bullpen if need be, using location and off-speed pitches to get hitters out. But start? For the first time in his career Cone was saying that no, he could not do that.

Torre had gone with Neagle, but now Torre was calling on a veteran he trusted—something he could not say about Neagle—to get one of the biggest outs of the year. "I'm a victim of not having done it long enough for Joe," Neagle later said.[47]

Cone, sporting a long-sleeved undershirt, went to work. Piazza took the first two pitches, as if he was studying this version of Cone to see if there was anything left. With the count 1-1, Cone threw a slider that Piazza swung through. It had late break, the kind of slider Cone would have thrown two years earlier but one that had felt largely absent in 2000. Cone tried the pitch again, and Piazza fared only mildly better, fouling the pitch off to stay alive. Then Cone got lucky. He came in with a fastball that Piazza appeared to be waiting for, but the slugger swung just under the ball, popping up to second base. Cone walked off, giving no indication of the triumph he had just accomplished. He would have come back out to pitch the sixth, but the Yankees got enough runners on base in the top of the inning to bring Cone's spot up in the batting order. Torre pinch-hit Canseco for Cone, and he struck out looking. Like Neagle, when Cone had walked off the mound in the fifth inning of Game Four, it was the last time he pitched for the New York Yankees.

Rusch replaced Jones in the sixth, officially making it a game of the bullpens. What happened over the next four innings was that each bullpen was bending but not breaking. Canseco, having not appeared at all in the postseason and having gone nearly four weeks without an at bat, struck out looking on an inside fastball with two runners on. Zeile continued to impress by leading off the sixth with a single. The Mets ran themselves out of another inning, though, when Agbayani lined a shot up the middle that

Nelson, now in the game, snared for the out. Zeile broke with contact and was easily doubled up.

The Yankees got a runner in scoring position in the seventh when Sojo singled, and then, having stolen only four bases in the last three seasons, he swiped second base. Rusch, however, struck out Williams looking after a long and tense match-up that saw Williams foul off several pitches before being rung up by home plate umpire Tim Welke. The fans delighted in the called third strike as they began to feel, with every passing missed opportunity by the Yankees, that the Mets would come back and win the game.

That comeback did not happen in the seventh or eighth innings. Nelson struck out Payton to start the seventh, then walked Harris. Torre brought in the lefty Stanton with the pitcher due up, and Valentine countered by having Trammell pinch-hit. Trammell struck out. Valentine continued to play chess, having Kurt Abbott pinch-hit for Pérez. Abbott struck out too.

Stanton had faced two hitters and had struck them both out, but Torre wanted to put the dagger in the Mets. He brought Rivera in for the eighth. Alfonzo greeted Rivera by lining a shot to short right field that looked like a lead-off single until O'Neill rushed in and made a sliding catch. It was still early, but between his hitting and now his fielding, O'Neill was starting to make a case for Series MVP. Alfonzo could not say the same. In his first World Series, he was struggling to find a grove, now with just two hits in sixteen at bats. "I picked the wrong time to be in a slump," he said after the game.[48]

O'Neill's catch stung even more when, with two outs, Zeile lined a single to center. Zeile had now achieved multi-hit games in each of the first four games of the Series. That left it up to Ventura. Perhaps not wanting to get behind on the count, or perhaps just looking for the first pitch he could hit, or both, Ventura swung at Rivera's first-pitch fastball. The ball shot straight up in the air, hovering over the infield for what seemed like an eternity until it fell into Jeter's glove for the third out. Ventura cursed himself, starting to slam his bat down in disgust before halting and trotting toward first.

While all of this drama occurred, a different drama played out in the Yankees' clubhouse. A fire had broken out on the third level of Shea Stadium. Firefighters moved to extinguish it by opening a standpipe. This, in turn, caused a pipe just above the Yankees' clubhouse to burst. Enough water poured in to collapse the clubhouse roof, filling the room with putrid water. Steinbrenner, who happened to be in the clubhouse watching the game when this occurred, jumped in to help clear the water out. Then he handed out fifty- and hundred-dollar bills to the firefighters who had come to assist. He also told others in the clubhouse that he was certain the Mets were, somehow, responsible for this. Steinbrenner had long been paranoid that when the Yankees played at Shea, the home team found ways to annoy and spy on his club.

Despite putting two runners on in the top of the ninth, in which Rivera also faked a sacrifice bunt before flying out to right, the Yankees failed to score an insurance run. That kept hope alive for the Mets. Two runs against Rivera was a tall ask, but one run was certainly possible.

Agbayani, Payton, and Matt Franco were due up. All of them had been postseason heroes over the last two years or heroes against the Yankees. If there was ever a moment to have a moment, this was it. Only five teams in history had come back from a 3–1 deficit in the World Series.

Rivera, who hardly walked anyone anyway, went right after Agbayani. On a 1-1 pitch, Agbayani swung at a middle-of-the-plate fastball as if the life of every person at Shea depended on his hitting a home run. He was only able to muster a foul tip into Posada's glove. With the count 1-2, Rivera came back with the same pitch, only a little more inside. Welke called strike three like he was deliberately trying to mimic Leslie Nielsen in *The Naked Gun*.

Payton, his Game Two home run off Rivera still fresh in everyone's mind, put in a solid at bat, working the count full. As fans around the stadium, including some of New York's finest, clasped their hands together, in hope or in prayer, and others sported inside-out, upside-down rally caps, Payton fouled off two pitches. He had Rivera's timing. Finally Payton hit a rope to left. At the first crack off the bat, the crowd began to roar. But the ball did not have enough travel on it, and Bellinger caught it easily for the second out.

Now came Franco. Outside of Dave Mlicki, no one had created a more memorable moment so far between these two teams than Franco. His game-winning hit in July 1999 was the gold standard for Mets fans during the four seasons that the teams had played against one another. FOX made sure to show the hit as he came to bat. Franco set up near the outside of the batter's box. When Rivera fell behind,1-0, Franco sat on a fastball and swung with all the force he could muster, trying to tie the game. He was way ahead of the pitch, though, and sent it far into the right-field stands for a foul ball.

Rivera's 1-1 pitch caught the outside corner. The Yankees were one strike away. Back in that July 1999 game, they had also been a strike away. Rivera had thrown an 0-2 fastball that every Yankee thought should have been called strike three. It was not. The next pitch ended up in right field to end the game. Rivera threw nearly the exact same pitch now in Game Four. It was slightly more outside. In fact, it was arguably less of a strike than the pitch from 1999. Rivera had an advantage this time, though, that he had not had in that 1999 game. He and Posada both realized instantly how far Franco was standing from the plate and that it meant he was expecting a cutter. He was never going to get one. "I thought for sure he was going to come inside," said Franco, explaining why he was standing so far from home plate during the at bat. "He'd done it to me before, and I've seen it on TV a thousand times, just breaking bats with that cutter in. I wasn't going to get beat that way. He made two great pitches and there was basically no chance."[49]

Franco was referring to the 1-1 fastball on the outside corner and the 1-2 fastball, which also hit the outside corner. Not expecting another outside pitch, Franco stood and starred as Welke rung him up, ending the game. Rivera, who rarely showed much emotion on the mound, emphatically pumped his fist. The Yankees, who had gone 0-6 with runners in scoring position and 1-17 with runners on base in Game Four, had found a way to win. As they congratulated each on the field, most of the Mets cleared out of the dugout. Not Mike Piazza, though. Piazza stood and stared, his expression a mix of "How did we get here?" and resolve not to let this Series end at Shea the next day. "We're one win away from where we want to be," said Jeter. "But this Mets team is the best team we've played in the five years I've been here in the postseason. They're not going to give up."[50]

• • •

If the Mets were going to keep their season alive, there wasn't anyone on the mound they would have wanted more than Al Leiter. He had pitched in countless big games before. The pressure would not get to him. The Yankees had historically not hit Leiter particularly well, including in Game One until Justice's double. Moreover, Leiter was a bulldog. He was going to put everything he had into every pitch in Game Five. For Al Leiter, the Yankees were not going to win the World Series because of him.

Up against Leiter that night was Andy Pettitte. He had been in the league only six years at that point, yet Pettitte had pitched a lifetime's worth of big games by then. Not a single season had gone by yet where he had not started a postseason game. Game Five was the fifth time the Yankees were giving him the ball in a potential Series-clincher. They had won three of those previous four, with those wins giving them the 1996 ALCS, the 1998 World Series, and the 2000 ALDS. Clemens, Cone, and Hernández may have had more dominant, more flashy stuff, but there may not have been anyone else on the mound that Yankees fans wanted to see in that moment more than Pettitte.

Oddly, despite how Jeter had begun Game Four, Torre bumped him from the lead-off spot to the second spot. Knoblauch remained on the bench while Vizcaino led off the game. Valentine, meanwhile, loaded his lineup with right-handed batters, except for Leiter and Ventura, the only lefty to homer off Pettitte during the regular season.

Meanwhile, in the Yankees' clubhouse before the game, FOX broadcasters began preparing just in case there was a victory celebration later that night. They placed wires in strategic spots, including underneath a table, presumably to get postgame sound bites. Cone decided to have some fun. He enjoyed pushing the Boss's buttons and got away with more than just about any other player when it came to ribbing the owner. So he fed into Steinbrenner's paranoia that the Mets had indeed bugged the clubhouse. "Boss, there's the microphone," the pitcher told him, pointing it out under the table.[51] Steinbrenner—who was perpetually annoyed by FOX's always trying to set up for a victory celebration before the Yankees had actually won, a move that he considered a jinx—demanded the wire be cut.

Over in the Mets' clubhouse, former Dodgers manager Tommy Lasorda walked into Valentine's office to pump up the club as it faced elimination. "It's been done before, Bobby," said Lasorda, referring to the Mets' need to win three straight games. "I want you to beat the Yankees so bad. I'm telling you, I'm rooting harder for your team than I did in my own games against them."[52]

Haze caused by pregame fireworks settled over the field as Vizcaino dug in to start the game. The fans were somewhat subdued, as if they were waiting for the bottom to fall out while simultaneously keeping hope alive for a Game Six. More than one "Ya' Gotta Believe" sign was visible in Shea Stadium that night. It remained that way even after Vizcaino grounded out. That subduedness turned to elation when Leiter struck Jeter out on a sharp slider. Leiter got through the inning without allowing a base runner. It was the first time in twelve innings that the Yankee had failed to get at least one runner on base.

Pettitte, who had not allowed a home run in twelve starts, including the postseason, sandwiched a Piazza single around three ground-ball outs. A scoreless game moved to the second when Williams led off the inning. It had been a rough World Series for Williams to that point. He had gone hitless in fifteen at bats and had failed to drive in a run, a dramatic turn from his ALCS performance of ten hits in twenty-three at bats. "He's trying to hit the ball into the parking lot instead of hitting it over the fence," said Torre, who felt Williams was too amped for the Series.[53]

Williams fought Leiter off with several foul balls. "I think those swings that he just had are the best swings that Bernie Williams had in the four games that we've had," remarked FOX broadcaster McCarver perceptively as Williams fouled off pitch after pitch. Leiter then came in with a cut fastball that did not cut. Like a knuckleball that spins too much, it was only slightly better than a batting-practice fastball. Williams popped it down the left-field line and into the stands, giving the Yankees a 1–0 lead.

The home run was disheartening but by no means fatal. Leiter got out of the inning without further damage and then did something no one would have predicted: he played a key role with his bat. The Mets put runners on second and third with two out. It felt like a lost opportunity with Leiter due up. Historically most pitchers were terrible hitters. It was just not something they worked at for a variety of reasons, not the least of which was that half of MLB did not require them to bat. Still, even for a pitcher, Leiter was a terrible hitter. In fifty-eight at bats during the regular season he had mustered only three hits while striking out thirty-three times. At that point, he was a career .093 hitter in the regular season who had struck out in 57 percent of his at bats. Leiter just could not hit.

Thus it should not have been surprising—yet somehow it still was—when Leiter laid down the equivalent of a drag bunt. It was perfectly placed, scooting past Pettitte and forcing Martinez to field it. Pettitte ran to cover first, but in his effort to find the bag and catch the ball all at once, he dropped Martinez's toss. Leiter, who had switched bats just before approaching the plate (leading to suspicion afterward that he had a bat specifically for bunting), was safe, and a run scored to tie the game.

On the next pitch, with the crowd still aglow from Leiter's bunt, Agbayani chopped a weak ground ball along the third-base line. Brosius charged and, knowing he did not have time to glove the ball and throw Agbayani out, attempted a bare-hand play. The ball did not bounce as high as he was expecting, though. It eluded his grasp and bounded into short left field. The Mets went ahead, 2–1. A bunt and a single, which, if combined, would have barely made it from home plate past second base, had given the Mets the lead and life in Game Five.

The lead invigorated Leiter. He mowed the Yankees down in the third inning and left Williams stranded on first base in the fourth. Over the course of six pitches in the fifth, Leiter, who at one point paused so he could shoo a moth off the mound before it got stepped on, scattered a base hit over three ground-ball outs.

Pettitte managed to keep the game close despite allowing multiple base runners in the fourth and fifth innings. He eliminated one runner with his second pick-off of the series. A moment of levity occurred in the fourth inning when Abbott broke his bat on a foul ball and the barrel went right to Jeter at short. Jeter reached down, picked it up, and slowly, with a sheepish grin on his face, walked the broken shard over to a batboy.

Game Five remained 2–1, Mets, into the top of the sixth. After a quick out, Leiter squared off against Jeter. Leiter had gotten the better of him in the first inning, striking him out on a down and in slider. In the fourth, Jeter had adjusted, hitting the ball hard to left but not getting enough of it for the ball to carry. In the sixth, on a 2-0 count, Leiter tried to sneak a fastball in. Jeter turned on it. Leiter kicked the dirt on the pitcher's mound before even looking up to see the result. He knew. The ball landed in the visitors' bullpen, Jeter's second home run in as many nights. It also extended his World Series hitting streak to fourteen games, going back to the 1996 match-up against the Braves.

The Mets tried to recapture the lead in the bottom of the inning. Payton and Abbott both singled with one out. Leiter came up next, and Valentine opted not to pinch-hit for him. He firmly believed that Leiter was still his best option to keep the Yankees at two runs. Leiter laid down a sacrifice bunt, this one fielded cleanly for the second out of the inning. The go-ahead runs now in scoring position, Agbayani grounded out to end the inning. The Mets had another chance in the seventh, when Alfonzo led off with a single. They spent the rest of the inning working counts, forcing Pettitte to throw nineteen additional pitches. But they failed to move Alfonzo off first, with Zeile and then Ventura striking out to end the inning.

Neither team could get a run across in the eighth. Game Five moved to the ninth inning tied at 2–2. Pettitte was out, having left after the seventh for Stanton. Leiter remained in. He seemed to be gaining strength as the game went along, pitching almost entirely off pure adrenaline. He struck out Jeter and Williams, the two players to homer off him, in the eighth. To start the ninth, he struck out Martinez swinging on an 0-2 pitch. Then he struck out O'Neill, in what some thought might be his last career at bat, also swinging on an 0-2 pitch. The Mets were one out away from getting the top of their order up in the ninth. Leiter got to a full count on Posada. One more strike to go.

• • •

The biggest rally of the Yankees' dynasty happened so simply. There was no long, crushing drive into the stands or a shot down the line. It happened in a way that, just two decades later, would seem foreign in a game that had come to rely almost entirely on homers to score runs. And that, in part, is what made it so painful for the Mets.

It began with the 3-2 count to Posada. Leiter wound up and delivered a cutting slider that dove down across the plate and in toward Posada's knees. The Yankees' catcher was fooled, likely expecting a fastball. As the pitch broke in, he halted his stance in a crouched position, possibly thinking the ball was about to strike him in the leg. His frozen stance gave the impression that he was trying to will the pitch into being a ball. It broke too far inside, missing the strike zone. Posada removed his shin guard, then took first base.

The crowd began to stir. People had been clasping their hands, others partially covering their eyes, as the Posada at bat played out. Now they began to feel truly nervous. The tension grew when Brosius lined a 1-1 single to left. Runners on first and second, two outs. "After the Posada at-bat, I was upset," said Leiter, who thought he had gotten his team to the bottom of ninth still tied. "I was too excited."[54]

Out in the Mets' bullpen, Franco had been warming up throughout the inning. Valentine was not budging. He was going to sink or swim with Leiter on the mound. Besides, it was not as if Leiter had been getting smacked. He had struck out the last three hitters he had faced before walking Posada. Meanwhile, the next batter, Luis Sojo, was not a long-ball threat. It was not as if he would turn a Leiter mistake into a three-run Yankees lead.

Leiter was at 141 pitches. The Mets' outfielders, knowing Sojo was almost literally no threat to go deep, played shallow in the hopes of throwing a runner out on a base hit. They also had the advantage that Posada, one of the team's slowest runners, was on second. Unless Sojo hit a ball into the gap, Agbayani, Payton, or Trammell were going to ensure there was a play at the plate on a base hit out of the infield.

Leiter got the sign from Piazza, came set, then delivered pitch number 142. It was a fastball that tailed slightly inside. Sojo, using one of Clay Bellinger's bats, swung his awkward, all-limbs swing and hit the ball almost directly into the ground. It hopped just to the right of a sprawling Leiter and kept hoping and hoping up the middle. "All my career, I've never hit Leiter good," said Sojo. "But [first base coach Lee Mazzilli] told me to hit the pitch down the middle and everything would work out for us."[55]

Abbott and Alfonzo both frantically dove, with each barely missing the ball in a moment that would have seemed cartoonish if the outcome had not been so important.

All told, Sojo's ground ball took four hops before making it into center field for a hit. Posada, arms akimbo, raced around third and toward home. Payton, who had been playing incredibly shallow, fielded the ball a mere twenty feet from the infield dirt. "When I saw it, I was hoping one of the infielders could knock it down," he said.[56]

Payton then threw an absolute missile toward home, his momentum so strong that he flew onto his stomach after releasing the ball. Piazza moved to block the plate and stuck his glove out to catch the ball. But the ball and Posada arrived at the same moment. It struck Posada in the left thigh and bounded toward the Mets' dugout. Posada slid across home plate, giving the Yankees the lead. Watching the ball carom away, Posada popped up and immediately began waving Brosius home. He did not have to. The ball had fallen into the Mets' dugout, and since it was thrown from the field of play, Brosius was awarded two bases, giving him home plate automatically. The Yankees led, 4–2. Sojo stood on third, smiling perhaps the biggest smile of his life. The Yankees on the bench had all leapt out of the dugout to follow the ball and then cheered Posada and Brosius home. All except for Mike Stanton, who sat on the bench, calmly drinking a cup of water as if he was merely watching batting practice and not the possibly deciding hit of the World Series.

"It came down to Al or Johnny [Franco] and Johnny on three days in a row," said Valentine about the Sojo at bat. "I decided to go with Al. Striking out those first two guys and the pitches he threw to Posada made me think he had plenty. I was wrong. It was the wrong decision."[57] "I was comfortable with the decision," said Piazza. "Al had pitched his butt off all night. It was his game to win or lose."[58]

Valentine headed to the mound and removed Leiter from the game. The pitcher briskly walked off, despondent. It was not supposed to go like this. He sat on the bench, his cap pulled down so that his eyes were just barely visible, his hand up to his face as if contemplating how this could have happened. "It's the most emotional I ever felt," said Leiter.[59]

John Franco came in and got the last out. As the Mets walked off the field, fans tried to muster enthusiasm for a ninth-inning comeback. But Sojo's seeing-eye single was still too fresh and too shocking. Their effort was subdued.

Meanwhile, in the Yankees' clubhouse, FOX and various other news media wanted to begin preparations for what they assumed would be a postgame victory celebration. Steinbrenner refused to let them in. He wanted no preparation whatsoever. Anything of the kind would jinx his ballclub. So he locked the clubhouse doors and told them all to pound sand. Eventually a representative from the Commissioner's Office worked out a deal with the Boss to allow them in to do their job. As they began pouring in, Steinbrenner warned the commissioner's rep that if the Yankees somehow did not win the game, it was on him.

Out on the field, Rivera, sitting on a streak of seventeen consecutive converted postseason saves, entered for the bottom of the ninth. He had already converted six World Series saves in his career, tied for the most in history with Rollie Fingers.

Darryl Hamilton led off. It was a small sample size, but Hamilton was 2-3 in his career off Rivera, numbers few hitters could boast. Almost the entire crowd stood, Yankees fans in anticipation of a championship, Mets fans in an effort to boost their team's chances of a comeback. Hats were turned backward. Nails were chewed on. Prayers were said.

Rivera quickly went up 0-2, then delivered a cutter that actually missed its spot. But Hamilton swung through it, just barely nicking the ball as it pounded into Posada's glove for strike three. Hamilton turned quickly to check if the ball had gotten loose and, seeing it hadn't, walked head down back to the dugout.

Up came Agbayani. Rivera pitched to him as if facing Babe Ruth. Nothing was close, outside of a 3-0 pitch, and Agbayani walked. The crowd nervously applauded, glad the tying run now was coming up but still nauseous over the possible end of the season. Even the Mets' dugout seemed guarded, many of the players giving away no emotion as Alfonzo came up with a chance to tie it. On a 1-1 pitch, Rivera threw a fastball down the middle. It was a mistake, one few pitchers could have gotten away with. Alfonzo timed it perfectly but swung just under it, fouling it back behind home plate.

The crowd grew louder. Actor Tim Robbins, sporting a Tom Seaver jersey and wearing an upside-down, inside-out rally cap, enthusiastically joined a "Let's go Mets" chant. Rivera threw the same pitch on 1-2, only this time it tailed a little more outside. Alfonzo swung, hitting the ball toward the end of the bat and sending a fly to right that O'Neill easily caught.

After all that had gone on in 2000 between these two teams and all that had transpired with the Mets over the last three seasons, it seemed fitting that the game and the Series came down to Mike Piazza.

The Yankees' infielders quickly gathered around Rivera on the mound as Piazza strode to the box. Jeter led the discussion. "You want to be careful here," he told Rivera. "You know what he can do. Move the ball around and go after him hard."[60]

Through the course of Alfonzo's at bat, Agbayani had managed to get himself to third base. Rivera could now carefully pitch around Piazza if he wanted to take his chances with Todd Zeile. Instead, as Jeter had said, he went after him hard. Rivera hurled a fastball right down the middle for strike one.

Piazza stepped out, banged his bat against the sides of his cleats, then got back into the box. At exactly midnight on October 27, 2000, Rivera delivered another fastball over the plate. Piazza swung, and when he made contact the hearts of millions of Yankees fans stopped momentarily. "Oh no," exclaimed Torre. Shea, meanwhile, let out a burst, as if one of the marquee moments in franchise history was about to unfold. Everyone watching, either at the stadium or on television, thought Piazza had just tied the game.

Off the bat the ball looked like it would travel deep into the left-center-field bleachers or even into the multi-level camera setup that stood just next to dead center field. What happened next will forever make little sense. One can view the moment over and over and over, and each time it still looks like Piazza had just tied the game. "His drive sounded good off the bat, and I remember Joe [Torre] telling me afterward that he jumped up and had a sickening feeling in his stomach," said Posada.[61]

The ball, inexplicably, did not leave the yard. In fact, it did not even make it to the warning track. Williams raced over, caught it, then bent down on one knee before popping up and pumping his fist in celebration. Rivera danced off the mound, arms raised into the air, embracing Posada before the rest of the team engulfed them on the mound. In less than a minute, white hats and gray T-shirts declaring the Yankees champions were passed around to players. A short time later, several Yankees stood in the clubhouse shower singing "Who Let the Dogs Out."

Many of the Mets stood in the dugout watching the celebration unfold. Valentine paced the dugout, arms folded, almost as if he wanted to remember this moment as a lesson so that he never had to repeat it. The Subway Series—a five-game match-up in which the potential tying run had made the last out in four of those games and the other game was Vizcaino's walk-off hit—was over. The oddity of the Clemens bat incident and the rest of the country's seeming indifference to an all–New York match-up sullied the memory of just how intense the Series had really been.

The question of who owned New York's baseball soul was now settled officially. What had started in 1985, the first year that both teams were truly relevant at the same time, and had continued since then through the brutal and embarrassing downfall of both franchises, then their Phoenix-like rising from the ashes, had concluded with the ultimate conquest for the heart of the city.

Notes

2. NOT ANY NASTIER

1. Quoted in Klapisch and Solotaroff, *Inside The Empire*, 57.
2. O'Connor, *The Captain*, 123.
3. Quoted in John M. Goshko and Nancy Reckler, "Yankees Storm through Town in Confetti Blizzard," *Washington Post*, October 29, 1996.
4. Quoted in N. R. Kleinfield, "A Parade of Pride in Yankee Triumph," *New York Times*, October 30, 1996.
5. Quoted in Jon Heyman, "John Is Gone," *Newsday*, December 16, 1996.
6. In 2019 Wetteland was charged with child molestation, but the charges were ultimately dismissed after a mistrial.
7. Quoted in Pessah, *The Game*, 187.
8. Quoted in Madden, *Steinbrenner*, 376.
9. Quoted in Pat Borzi, "Yanks De-Light 'Slim' Wells," *Star-Ledger*, December 20, 1996.
10. Quoted in Thomas Hill, "Yankees Fall into Wells," *New York Daily News*, December 18, 1996.
11. Quoted in David Lennon, "Wells Eager to Join Yankees Rotation," *Newsday*, December 18, 1996.
12. Quoted in Lawrence Rocca, "How to Shatter a Bad Reputation," *Bergen Record*, July 7, 1997.
13. Author's interview with Bobby Valentine, January 31, 2024.
14. Valentine and Golenbock, *Valentine's Way*, 203.
15. Quoted in Kim Rogers, "Reds Opening Pitcher Doesn't Give Up Hope," *Indianapolis News*, April 4, 1995.
16. Quoted in Buster Olney, "Mets Make Reed No. 5 In Starting Rotation," *New York Times*, March 25, 1997.
17. Quoted in Mike Payne, "Big-League Comeback," *St. Petersburg Times*, March 30, 1990.
18. Quoted in Jack O'Connell, "Griffey Takes Care of Yanks," *Hartford Courant*, April 2, 1997.
19. Quoted in Jack Curry, "The Yankees' Encore Folds under Griffey's Bat," *New York Times*, April 2, 1997.

20. Quoted in "Gooden Irked with Yankees' Medical Staff," *Seattle Times*, April 12, 1997.

21. Quoted in Mark Herrmann and David Lennon, "Mattingly Part of 96 Champs, Even If He Wasn't a Yankee," *Newsday*, April 12, 1997.

22. Quoted in Mike Lupica, "Taking Wheel for Ride into Yankee Stadium," *Daily News*, April 12, 1997.

23. Quoted in Pat Borzi, "An Opening Lesson: It's Not '96 Anymore," *Star-Ledger*, April 12, 1997.

24. Jack Curry, "Party-Crashing A's Show Yanks It's a New Season," *New York Times*, April 12 1997.

25. Jack Curry, "Yankee Bullpen Woes Come as Eye-Openers," *New York Times*, April 17, 1997.

26. Jack Curry, "The Latest Misfortune for Rivera? It's Leyritz," *New York Times*, April 16, 1997.

27. Quoted in Bob Klapisch, "Cone a Silver Lining in Bronx Cloud," *Bergen Record*, April 12, 1997.

28. Rivera with Coffey, *The Closer*, 87.

29. Quoted in Borzi, "Opening Lesson."

30. Quoted in Ken Davidoff, "Posada Ditches Monkey," *Bergen Record*, May 5, 1997.

31. Posada with Brozek, *The Journey Home*, 10.

32. Posada with Brozek, *The Journey Home*, 164.

33. Quoted in "Chewing-Tobacco Withdrawal Shakes Harnisch," *New York Times*, April 2, 1997.

34. Rafael Hermoso, "Bullpen Fails against Padres," *Bergen Record*, April 2, 1997.

35. Quoted in Thomas Hill, "Harnisch Reveals Depression," *Daily News*, April 26, 1997.

36. Quoted in Ike Kuhns, "For Openers, Mets Swept by Giants," *Star-Ledger*, April 15, 1997.

37. Quoted in Hal Block, "Baseball Retires No. 42 to Honor Jackie Robinson," Associated Press, April 16, 1997.

38. Quoted in Golenbock, *Amazin'*, 566.

39. Quoted in Ike Kuhns, "Mets Head for Break with Sunny Disposition," *Star-Ledger*, July 7, 1997.

40. Steve Adamek, "Simply Amazing: Mets Still in It," *Bergen Record*, July 7, 1997.

41. Rocca, "How to Shatter a Bad Reputation."

42. Quoted in Jack Curry, "Hayes Offers Apology," *New York Times*, June 11, 1997.

43. Bob Klapisch, "Has Cecil Seen Error of His Ways?" *Bergen Record*, April 2, 1997.

44. Quoted in Murray Chass, "The Cold Reality of Winter Moves," *New York Times*, April 12, 1997.

45. Quoted in Jon Heyman, "Marine Landed," *Newsday*, April 23, 1997.

46. Quoted in Heyman, "Marine Landed."

47. Quoted in Tracy Ringolsby, "Padres Play by Rules and Win Pitcher," *Oklahoman*, January 19, 1997.

48. Quoted in Heyman, "Marine Landed."

49. Quoted in Bob Klapisch, "To Yanks, Irabu Means Trouble," *Bergen Record*, May 28, 1997.

50. Quoted in Bob Klapisch, "Wait Ends for Irabu, Yankees," *Bergen Record*, May 30, 1997.

51. Bob Klapisch, "Boss Gets His Gun," *Bergen Record*, April 23, 1997.

52. Claire Smith, "In This Game, Victory Goes to Losers," *New York Times*, April 24, 1997.

53. Quoted in Jack Curry, "Witness Who Called the Police Describes Wells's Fight," *New York Times*, January 17, 1997.

54. Quoted in Murray Chass, "3 Days after Ejection, Wells Is Redeemed," *New York Times*, June 18, 1997.

55. Quoted in Murray Chass, "Wells Celebrates the Babe's Return, but Cleveland Provides the Fireworks," *New York Times*, June 29, 1997.

56. Quoted in Aditya Deshingkar, "What Really Happened to David Wells' Babe Ruth Hat?" *Essentially Sports*, December 29, 2021.

57. Rivera with Coffey, *The Closer*, 88.

58. Quoted in Kepner, *K*, 269.

59. Rivera with Coffey, *The Closer*, 89.

60. Quoted in Lawrence Rocca, "Mets Beat Tom like a Drum," *Star-Ledger*, July 12, 1999.

61. Quoted in Buster Olney, "Ochoa Blast Caps Mets Rally," *New York Times*, July 14, 1997.

62. Lawrence Rocca, "Dreamy Mets Say: Pinch Us," *Star-Ledger*, July 14, 1997.

63. Quoted in Rafael Hermoso, "Joe Mac Axed," *Bergen Record*, July 17, 1997.

64. Quoted in Mike Lupica, "Mets Decide Joe Must Go," *Daily News*, July 17, 1997.

65. Quoted in Don Burke, "Mets' Move: Shea, It Ain't So, Joe," *Star-Ledger*, 1997.

66. Quoted in Burke, "Mets' Move."

67. Quoted in Rory Costello, Turk Wendell SABR bio, https://sabr.org/bioproj/person/turk-wendell/#sdendnote4sym.

68. Bob Klapisch, "Yankee Debut Draws Full House," *Bergen Record*, July 11, 1997.

69. Quoted in John Giannone, "Irabu Shows Yanks They Have a Rising Gun," *Daily News*, July 11, 1997.

70. Quoted in Joe Gergen, "Irabu Makes Believers Fast," *Newsday*, July 11, 1997.

71. Quoted in Tom Pedulla, "Irabu Saved by 12-Run Support," *USA Today*, July 16, 1997.

72. Quoted in Jack Curry, "After a Major Setback, He's a Minor Leaguer," *New York Times*, July 29, 1997.

73. Quoted in Thomas Boswell, "By George, Yanks Are a Bloody Mess," *Washington Post*, September 6, 1997.

74. Quoted in Don Burke, "Boss Talk," *Star-Ledger*, June 3, 1997.

75. Quoted in Jon Heyman, "Duncan to OF?" *Newsday*, June 3, 1997.

76. Quoted in John Giannone, "Bombers' Unreal Deal," *Daily News*, July 6, 1997.

77. Quoted in Jason Diamos, "Rogers Deal Falls Through," *Dallas Morning News*, July 6, 1997.

78. Quoted in Heyman, "Duncan to OF."

79. Quoted in Jack Curry, "Strawberry Predicts He Will Have Surgery," *New York Times*, June 3, 1997.

80. Quoted in Jon Heyman, "AL Playoffs 97," *Newsday*, September 30, 1997.

81. Quoted in John Giannone, "Duncan, Yanks Feel Relief after Deal to Blue Jays," *Daily News*, July 30, 1997.

82. Quoted in Pat Borzi, "Going, Going Duncan Finally Gone," *Star-Ledger*, July 30, 1997.

83. Quoted in David Lennon, "Duncan Has Wish Fulfilled," *Newsday*, July 30, 1997.

84. Bob Klapisch, "Goose Knows How Wetteland Felt," *Bergen Record*, December 22, 1996.

85. Quoted in Jason Diamos, "Trade Began with a Bang, Finishes a Bust," *New York Times*, July 6, 1997.

86. Quoted in Gerry Fraley, "Boggs' Agent Talks with Rangers about Yankees' Trade for Palmer," *Dallas Morning News*, July 9, 1997.

87. Quoted in Jack Curry, "A Midseason Classic: Irabu Wins His Debut," *New York Times*, July 11, 1997.

88. Quoted in Jack O'Connell, "Now, the Job at Third May Be Boggs' to Lose," *Hartford Courant*, September 12, 1997.

89. Quoted in O'Connor, *The Captain*, 128.

90. Quoted in Bob Klapisch, "Boss, Wells Butted Heads," *Bergen Record*, September 15, 1997.

91. Quoted in David Lennon, "Extra Bases," *Newsday*, September 17, 1997.

92. Quoted in O'Neill and Curry, *Swing and a Hit*, 71.

93. Quoted in John Giannone, "Yanks May Have Place for Boggs After All," *Daily News*, August 20, 1997.

94. Quoted in Rafael Hermoso, "Mets Wild-Card Bid Decked Again," *Bergen Record*, August 18, 1997.

95. Valentine and Golenbock, *Valentine's Way*, 207.

96. Quoted in Buster Olney, "Hum, Machiavelli," *New York Times*, August 21, 1997.

97. Jason Diamos, "Hundley Is Shaking Off Remarks Made by Valentine," *New York Times*, August 22, 1997.

98. Quoted in Thomas Hill, "Cal Rips Pen," *Daily News*, August 30, 1997.

99. Quoted in David Ginsburg, "Mets' Harnisch Put on Assignment," Associated Press, August 30, 1997.

100. Lynette Holloway, "Ruling Could Return Children to Everett," *New York Times*, October 29, 1997.

101. Quoted in Colin Stephenson, "Gilkey's Bat Is Awakening," *Daily News*, August 22, 1997.

102. Quoted in Rob Parker, "Don't Be Fooled by Mets Season," *Newsday*, September 24, 1997.

103. Quoted in Jason Diamos, "End for Team's Dream and Hundley's Season," *New York Times*, September 24, 1997.

104. Mike Celizic, "Denying Mets Magic," *Bergen Record*, September 24, 1997.

105. Ian O'Connor, "Cone-cern Is Now Alarm," *Daily News*, October 1, 1997.

106. Paul Doyle, "Plunk's Collapse in Sixth Inning Takes Fans Back," *Hartford Courant*, October 1, 1997.

107. Quoted in Dennis Manoloff, "Yankees Produce Power in Triplicate," *Cleveland Plain Dealer*, October 1, 1997.

108. Quoted in Bob Klapisch, "Comeback City," *Bergen Record*, October 1, 1997.

109. Quoted in Jack O'Connell, "Who Said the Yankees Couldn't Win a Slugfest?" *Hartford Courant*, October 1, 1997.

110. Quoted in Jon Heyman, "Sandy Does It Again," *Newsday*, October 6, 1997.

111. Quoted in David Lennon, "Indians Take It to the Limit," *Newsday*, October 6, 1997.

112. Rivera with Coffey, *The Closer*, 93.

113. Quoted in Jack O'Connell, "There Was Little Noise in the Yankees Clubhouse," *Hartford Courant*, October 6, 1997.

114. Quoted in Alan Robinson, "Yankees' Bullpen Not Perfect after All," Associated Press, October 6, 1997.

115. Mike Celizic, "Bombers in a State of Disbelief," *Bergen Record*, October 6, 1997.

116. Quoted in David Lennon, "Indians Send Yanks Home," *Newsday*, October 7, 1997.

117. O'Neill and Curry, *Swing and a Hit*, 7.

118. O'Neill and Curry, *Swing and a Hit*, 7.

119. Quoted in Pat Borzi, "Classic Fall for Yankees," *Star-Ledger*, October 7, 1997.

3. SQUARE IN THE BACK

1. All Mlicki quotes in this chapter are from author's interview with Dave Mlicki, August 25, 2023.

2. Quoted in Murray Chass, "The First Brag Belongs to Mlicki and the Mets," *New York Times*, June 17, 1997.

3. Chip Caray on FX, June 16, 1997.

4. A VIABLE MAN

1. Tom Keegan, "Amazin's Land Leiter but Still Want to Make Sheffield Deal," *New York Post*, February 7, 1998.

2. Will Leitch, "The Glass Arm," *New York Magazine*, March 15, 1998.

3. Quoted in Murray Chass, "Leiter's 'Great Future' Will Be as a Jay," *New York Times*, May 1, 1989.

4. Quoted in Golenbock, *Amazin'*, 573.

5. Quoted in Dan Castellano, "Good First Impressions Reunite Olerud, Mets," *Star-Ledger*, November 25, 1997.

6. Quoted in Buster Olney, "Taking Shorter Deal, Olerud Signs with Mets," *New York Times*, November 25, 1997.

7. Quoted in Claire Smith, "Japanese Pitcher Joins the Mets Starting Staff," *New York Times*, January 14, 1998.

8. Quoted in Steve Jacobson, "As the Yankees Turn," *Newsday*, February 4, 1998.

9. Quoted in Mark Fischer, "Pedro Martinez Badly Wanted the Yankees to Trade for Him," *New York Post*, September 24, 2019.

10. Quoted in Dave Anderson, "Sports of The Times; All Together, Applause for Watson," *New York Times*, February 3, 1998.

11. Quoted in Pessah, *The Game*, 221.

12. Quoted in O'Connor, *The Captain*, 129.

13. Quoted in Bob Klapisch, "Watson Out," *Bergen Record*, February 3, 1998.

14. Quoted in David Lennon, "Watson Tells Boss It's Over," *Newsday*, February 3, 1998.

15. Quoted in Buster Olney, "Knoblauch Officially an Irksome Yankee," *New York Times*, February 7, 1998.

16. Quoted in Madden, *Steinbrenner*, 377.

17. Quoted in Jon Heyman, "Introducing Boy Wonder," *Newsday*, February 4, 1998.

18. Quoted in Jacobson, "As the Yankees Turn."

19. Quoted in Tim Brown, "Watson Deals Himself Out," *Star-Ledger*, February 3, 1998.

20. Quoted in Buster Olney, "Yanks Pay Hayes to Play for Giants," *New York Times*, November 12, 1997.

21. Quoted in Buster Olney, "Brosius Gives Yankees a Most Valuable Year," *New York Times*, October 22, 1998.

22. Quoted in Jason Diamos, "A Midsummer Classic in March as Mets Nip Phillies," *New York Times*, April 1, 1998.

23. Quoted in Marty Noble, "Can't Ask for Much More," *Newsday*, April 1, 1998.

24. Quoted in Lawrence Rocca, "Mets Finally Zero in on Victory," *Star-Ledger*, April 1, 1998.

25. Quoted in Joel Sherman, "It Took Incredible Chain of Events to Bring Mike Piazza to Mets," *New York Post*, July 21, 2016.

26. Quoted in Murray Chass, "Doubleday Takes Wheel and Revs up the Mets," *New York Times*, May 31, 1998.

27. Jason Diamos, "Mets Get Piazza's Power at Bat and at the Gate," *New York Times*, May 23, 1998.

28. Bob Klapisch, "The Big Catch," *Bergen Record*, May 23, 1998.

29. Mike Lupica, "Mets Deliver a Hot Piazza," *Daily News*, May 23, 1998.

30. Quoted in Joe Gergen, "Mets Make a Deal," *Newsday*, May 23, 1998.

31. Dan Castellano, "In World Boss Rules, Anything Is Possible," *Star-Ledger*, April 7, 1998.

32. Jack Curry, "Steinbrenner Hushes Whispers about Torre (for Now, Anyway)," *New York Times*, April 11, 1998.

33. Quoted in Curry, *The 1998 Yankees*, 34.

34. Quoted in David Lennon, "No Mo for Joe," *Newsday*, April 7, 1998.

35. Quoted in Tim Brown, "Hitting for the Birds, Yanks Stay Peepless in Seattle," *Star-Ledger*, April 7, 1998.

36. Joel Sherman, "Bombers Aren't Crash-Proof Team," *New York Post*, April 7, 1998.

37. Quoted in Ken Davidoff, "Extreme Game; Yankees Win Wild One," *Bergen Record*, April 11, 1998.

38. Quoted in Peter Botte and Rafael Hermoso, "George: Holmes Clueless," *Daily News*, April 11, 1998.

39. Quoted in Pat Borzi, "Structural Alarm at Yankee Stadium," *Star-Ledger*, April 14, 1998.

40. Quoted in Borzi, "Structural Alarm at Yankee Stadium."

41. Quoted in Paul Rogers and Daniel Sforza, untitled article in *Bergen Record*, April 14, 1998.

42. Quoted in Shawn Powell, "Double Play at Shea," *Newsday*, April 16, 1998.

43. Quoted in Jack O'Connell, "Wells' Performance Weighs on Torre," *Hartford Courant*, May 9, 1998.

44. Quoted in Gregory Shutta, "Mr. Perfect," *Bergen Record*, May 18, 1998.

45. Posada with Brozek, *The Journey Home*, 218.

46. Quoted in Buster Olney, "Rarest Gem for Yankees' Wells: A Perfect Game," *New York Times*, May 18, 1998.

47. Quoted in David Lennon, "David Wells Perfecto," *Newsday*, May 18, 1998.

48. Quoted in Rob Parker, "David Wells Perfecto," *Newsday*, May 18, 1998. Please note that this article and the one cited in note 47 are two different stories with the same title.

49. Quoted during press conference, May 19, 1998; available on YouTube.

50. Buster Olney, "Hernandez Is Everything Yanks Hoped," *New York Times*, June 4, 1998.

51. Quoted in David Lennon, "Duque Debut Is Dazzling," *Newsday*, June 4, 1998.

52. Quoted in "Mets Give Sierra Minor League Pact," *New York Times*, June 21, 1998.

53. Quoted in Ed Barmakian, "Not High on Sierra Signing," *Star-Ledger*, June 21, 1998.

54. Quoted in Sean Brennan, "For Mets, Al's Not Well," *Daily News*, June 27, 1998.

55. Quoted in Thomas Hill, "With Mel In, It's Leits Out," *Daily News*, June 27, 1998.

56. Quoted in "In Bizarre Finish, Mets Rule Yankees 2–1," *St. Petersburg Times*, June 29, 1998.

57. Quoted in Joel Sherman, "Piazza Feelin' Heat," *New York Post*, July 15, 1998.

58. Steve Campbell, "Piazza, Mets Fans Both Striking Out," *Albany Times Union*, August 9, 1998.

59. Quoted in Torre and Verducci, *The Yankee Years*, 51.

60. Quoted in Jack O'Connell, "There's More Power to 'Em," *Hartford Courant*, August 5, 1998.

61. Quoted in Joel Sherman, untitled article in *New York Post*, August 1, 1998.

62. Quoted in Rafael Hermoso, "Mets Wheel and Deal," *Daily News*, August 1, 1998.

63. Quoted in Ike Kuhns, "Mets: Bye-bye, Bernard," *Star-Ledger*, August 1, 1998.

64. Quoted in Thomas Hill, "Mets Survive Mac Attack," *Daily News*, August 12, 1998.

65. Quoted in Colin Stephenson, "Mets Order a Couple of Heroes," *Star-Ledger*, September 17, 1998.

66. Quoted in Shaun Powell, "Never-Say-Die Mets Feel Magic," *Newsday*, September 17, 1998.

67. Quoted in Marty Noble, "Catcher Clouts," *Newsday*, September 17, 1998.

68. Mike Vaccaro, "It's Franco for Mets, Because It Has to Be," *Star-Ledger*, September 19, 1998.

69. Quoted in Jason Diamos, "Expos Nudge Mets Back into a Tie with the Cubs," *New York Times*, September 23, 1998.

70. Quoted in Jason Diamos, "Another Loss Pushes Mets to the Brink of the Off Season," *New York Times*, September 27, 1998.

71. Quoted in Golenbock, *Amazin'*, 577.

72. Quoted in Marty Noble, "Mets Hopes End with Fifth Loss in Row," *Newsday*, September 28, 1998.

73. Quoted in T. J. Quinn, "Bitter End: Mets Go Quietly into Off-Season," *Bergen Record*, September 28, 1998.

74. Quoted in Jason Diamos, "Mets Lay Their Final Egg, and It Tastes Awful," *New York Times*, September 28, 1998.

75. Quoted in Pat Borzi, "Dejected Mets Bag the Season," *Star-Ledger*, September 29, 1998.

76. Quoted in "Toronto, New York Brawl before Yankees Fall," Associated Press, September 11, 1998.

77. Quoted in Buster Olney, "Yankees, Beaten Again, Leave Torre Fuming," *New York Times*, September 17, 1998.

78. Quoted in Jack Curry, "Yankees Make a Long Day Even Longer for Royals," *New York Times*, August 8, 1998.

79. Gregory Schutta, "Spencer Makes Postseason List," *Bergen Record*, September 28, 1998.

80. Quoted in Peter Botte, "Spencer's Not Left Out," *Daily News*, September 28, 1998.

81. Quoted in Ursula Reel, "Shane Offers Proof Perseverance Pays," *New York Post*, September 28, 1998.

82. Strawberry and Strausbaugh, *Straw*, 155.

83. Quoted in Jack O'Connell, "Yankees Outfielder Faces Cancer Surgery," *Hartford Courant*, October 2, 1998.

84. Quoted in Buster Olney, "Strawberry to Have Surgery for Colon Cancer," *New York Times*, October 2, 1998.

85. Quoted in Ken Davidoff, "Chucklehead," *Bergen Record*, October 8, 1998.

86. Quoted in George King, "Chuck Fiddles as Yanks Burn," *New York Post*, October 8, 1998.

87. Quoted in Mel Antonen, "Fans Let Knoblauch Hear What They Think of 12th-Inning Play," *USA Today*, October 8, 1998.

88. Quoted in Tim Brown, "Yankees Show Some Zip," *Star-Ledger*, October 11, 1998.

89. Quoted in "Hernandez Calmly Lifts Yankees Out of Hole," Mercury News Services, October 11, 1998.

90. Quoted in Lawrence Rocca, "Duque Gets Yanks Even," *Newsday*, October 11, 1998.

91. Quoted in Buster Olney, "For 35th Time, Yankees Reach the World Series," *New York Times*, October 14, 1998.

92. Quoted in Jack O'Connell, "First in a Series," *Hartford Courant*, October 14, 1998.

93. Quoted in Richard Justice, "Yanks Go on Power Trip in Game 1," *Washington Post*, October 18, 1998.

94. Author's interview with Jim Leyritz, March 10, 2020.

95. Quoted in Murray Chass, "3,000 Miles and 9 Innings Away," *New York Times*, October 21, 1998.

96. Quoted in Richard Justice, "Great Scott: Brosius Rocks Padres," *Washington Post*, October 21, 1998.

97. Quoted in Sam Borden, "The Yankees, Overshadowed? Why the 'Best Team Ever' Never Got Its Due," ESPN, June 15, 2020, https://www.espn.com/mlb/story/_/id/29302265/the-yankees-overshadowed-why-best-team-ever-never-got-due.

98. Quoted in Jack Curry, "3 Cheers and a Toast for the Straw Man, Too," *New York Times*, October 22, 1998.

5. "I PLAY BASEBALL"

1. All quotes in this chapter are from author's interview with Dave Mlicki, August 25, 2023. See also Buster Olney, "Puzzle of a Pitcher Leaves Yankees Scratching Heads," *New York Times*, June 17, 1997.

6. MR. MOJO RISIN'

1. Quoted in Buster Olney, "1998 World Champions: Jubilant Today, but Who's Gone Tomorrow," *New York Times*, October 24, 1998.
2. Murray Chass, "American League Suspends Belle for Five Games," *New York Times*, June 4, 1996.
3. Quoted in Madden, *Steinbrenner*, 381.
4. Quoted in Peter Botte and Dave Goldiner, "Bye, Boomer—And Hi, Rocket," *Daily News*, February 19, 1999.
5. Quoted in O'Connor, *The Captain*, 153.
6. Randolph, *The Yankee Way*, 168.
7. Quoted in Madden, *Steinbrenner*, 384.
8. Quoted in Botte and Goldiner, "Bye, Boomer—And Hi, Rocket."
9. Quoted in Jack O'Connell, "Cy Yank," *Hartford Courant*, February 19, 1999.
10. Quoted in George King, "Yankee Prank Catches Roger," *New York Post*, February 27, 1999.
11. Posada, *The Journey Home*, 233.
12. Quoted in Ken Davidoff, "Torre's Biggest Battle," *Bergen Record*, March 11, 1999.
13. Quoted in Lawrence Rocca, "I Feel Fine," *Newsday*, March 11, 1999.
14. Quoted in Buster Olney, "Irabu's Effort Seems Lacking, So Yankees Push Pitchers Hard," *New York Times*, March 29, 1999.
15. Quoted in George King, "Cashman Butts in on Irabu," *New York Post*, March 28, 1999.
16. Quoted in Tim Brown, "Irabu's Behavior Is Sorry," *Star-Ledger*, March 29, 1999.
17. All quotes in this paragraph are in George King, "George Rips 'Fat Toad' Irabu," *New York Post*, April 2, 1999.
18. Buster Olney, "For Zimmer and Yanks, It's Play Ball (Please)," *New York Times*, April 5, 1999.
19. Strawberry and Strausbaugh, *Straw*, 173.
20. Jason Stark, "And the Rich Get . . . ," *Philadelphia Inquirer*, February 19, 1999.
21. Quoted in Joel Sherman, "At His Finest, David Was No Match for Roger," *New York Post*, February 19, 1999.
22. Quoted in Adian Wojnarowski, "Mercenary Mike," *Bergen Record*, October 27, 1998.
23. Quoted in Marty Noble, "Mike Loves NY," *Newsday*, October 27, 1998.

24. Quoted in Hal Bodley, "Mets GM Phillips Goes on Leave after Threat of Suit," *USA Today*, November 9, 1998.

25. Quoted in "Mets Give Up Hundley, Get Benitez in Round-About Trade," Associated Press, December 2, 1998.

26. Quoted in T. J. Quinn, "Met-Amorphosis," *Bergen Record*, December 2, 1998.

27. Quoted in Don Burke, "Hundley Shipped to Dodgers," *Star-Ledger*, December 2, 1998.

28. Bryant, *Rickey*, 337.

29. Quoted in Lawrence Rocca, "He's Leading the Way," *Newsday*, December 14, 1998.

30. Quoted in Tom Keegan, "Rickey Wearing 24 Irks Mays," *New York Post*, December 15, 1998.

31. T. J. Quinn, "Rickey Is Final Piece in Remodeling of Mets," *Bergen Record*, December 14, 1998.

32. Quoted in T. J. Quinn, "Mets in Orel Stage," *Bergen Record*, March 26, 1999.

33. Quoted in Rafael Hermoso, "Mets OK Orel Contract," *Daily News*, March 26, 1999.

34. Quoted in Mark Herrmann, "Orel Agreement," *Newsday*, March 26, 1999.

35. Quoted in Mike Lupica, "Triumph for Yogi and Yankees," *Daily News*, April 10, 1999.

36. Quoted in Ken Davidoff, "Yankees Swinging in the Rain," *Bergen Record*, April 10, 1999.

37. Quoted in George King, "Chili's Wealth of Knowledge Comes from School of Hard Knocks," *New York Post*, May 23, 1999.

38. Quoted in George Vecsey, "Todd Pratt Can Stand the Heat," *New York Times*, October 12, 1999.

39. Quoted in Rafael Hermoso, "Franco Reels in 400th," *Daily News*, April 15, 1999.

40. Author's interview with Bobby Valentine, January 31, 2024.

41. Quoted in Buster Olney, "Yankees Show the Mets How to Win in New York," *New York Times*, June 5, 1999.

42. Tim Brown, "Rivalry Makes Yanks Healthy," *Star-Ledger*, June 5, 1999.

43. Joe Gergen, "Fun City? Not for Everyone," *Newsday*, June 6, 1999.

44. David Waldstein, "Adopdaca, Duo Canned but Bobby V Is Spared," *New York Post*, June 6, 1999.

45. Quoted in Josh Durbow, "Mets Fire Three Coaches," Associated Press, June 5, 1999.

46. Quoted in Mark Herrmann, "Fighting Back," *Newsday*, June 7, 1999.

47. Quoted in Mark Herrmann, "Change in Air," *Newsday*, June 14, 1999.

48. Quoted in T. J. Quinn, "Agbayani's Homer Lights Mets Fuse," *Bergen Record*, June 14, 1999.

49. Quoted in Golenbock, *Amazin'*, 581.

50. Author's interview with Bobby Valentine, January 31, 2024.

51. "Yips," Mayo Clinic, https://www.mayoclinic.org/diseases-conditions/yips/symptoms-causes/syc-20379021#:~:text=Overview,always%20associated%20with%20performance%20anxiety.

52. The Torre quote is from the live broadcast on FOX, July 10, 1999.

53. Quoted in David Waldstein, "Franco Heroics Cap Amazin' Day," *New York Post*, July 11, 1999.

54. Quoted in Buster Olney, "Pure Storybook," *New York Times*, July 11, 1999.

55. Quoted in Thomas Hill, "Mets Blast Off Rocket," *Daily News*, July 10, 1999.

56. Quoted in Lisa Olson, "In Pinch, Mets Roll Out Welcome Matt," *Daily News*, July 11, 1999.

57. Quoted in Waldstein, "Franco Heroics Cap Amazin' Day."

58. Dave Anderson, "The Greatest 24 Hours in the Mets' History," *New York Times*, July 11, 1999.

59. Quoted in Howard Bryant, "Did the A's Fold 'Em?" *San Jose Mercury News*, July 24, 1999.

60. Quoted in Ralph Vacchiano, "Jones' Return Set Back," *Daily News*, July 24, 1999.

61. Quoted in Murray Chass, "Yanks' Cone Baffles Expos," *New York Times*, July 19, 1999.

62. Quoted in Chass, "Yanks' Cone Baffles Expos."

63. Quoted in "Chad Feisty but Foolish," editorial in *New York Post*, August 9, 1999.

64. Quoted in Jack O'Connell, "So Much for Yanks' Strong Pitch," *Hartford Courant*, July 29, 1999.

65. Quoted in Torre, *The Yankee Years*, 76.

66. Quoted in Olney, *The Last Night of the Yankee Dynasty*, 124.

67. Quoted in Tom Keegan, "Boo-nilla Hits New Low," *New York Post*, June 10, 1999.

68. Quoted in David Waldstein, "Bo Denies He Asked to Join DL," *New York Post*, July 5, 1999.

69. Quoted in Bob Klapisch, "Turner for Worse," *Bergen Record*, September 24, 1999.

70. Mike Lupica, "Talk Sends Mets on Wild Goose Chase," *Daily News*, September 24, 1999.

71. Quoted in Tom Keegan, "Lady Luck's No Fan of the Mets," *New York Post*, September 27, 1999.

72. Quoted in Rafael Hermoso, "Mets Drop in the Red after Phlop in Philly, Cincinnati Surges Ahead," *Daily News*, September 27, 1999.

73. Quoted in Marty Noble, "Early & Awful," *Newsday*, September 29, 1999.

74. Quoted in "Braves Surprised by Mets Fold," *Asbury Park Press*, September 29, 1999.

75. Quoted in David Waldstein, "Hanging by Thread," *New York Post*, October 1, 1999.

76. Quoted in Ronald Blum, "Rocker All Smiles for Mets Fans," Associated Press, October 15, 1999.

77. Bon Klapisch, "Time to Let Go of a Dying Season," *Bergen Record*, October 1, 1999.

78. Quoted in Josh Dubow, "Mets 2, Pirates 1," Associated Press, October 4, 1999.

79. Quoted in David Waldstein, "'Wild' Finish Gives Amazins New Life," *New York Post*, October 4, 1999.

80. Author's interview with Bobby Valentine, January 31, 2024.

81. Quoted in Mark Kriegel, "For Mets, Let There Be Leit," *Daily News*, October 5, 1999.

82. Quoted in Paul Doyle, "Completely Wild," *Hartford Courant*, October 5, 1999.

83. Quoted in T. J. Quinn, "October Fest," *Bergen Record*, October 5, 1999.

84. Mark Kriegel, "Fear & Loathing in . . . Phoenix," *Daily News*, October 6, 1999.

85. Quoted in Judy Battista, "The Mets Eliminate Cincinnati, the Doubts and the Frustration," *New York Times*, October 5, 1999.

86. Quoted in Lawrence Rocca, "The Rocket Gets Roasted," *Newsday*, October 17, 1999.

87. Quoted in Ken Davidoff, "Easy As 1-2-3," *Bergen Record*, October 10, 1999.

88. Quoted in Jamie Aron, "Yankees 3, Rangers 0," Associated Press, October 10, 1999.

89. Quoted in Bill Finley, "After Allowing Game-Winning HR, Beck Tips His Cap," *Daily News*, October 14, 1999.

90. Quoted in Don Amore, "Curse of the Bam Berno," *Hartford Courant*, October 14, 1999.

91. Quoted in Jeff Goodman, "Sleeping Beauty," Associated Press, October 6, 1999.

92. Quoted in S. L. Price, "Valentine's Day," *Sports Illustrated*, October 11, 1999.

93. Quoted in T. J. Quinn, "More Turmoil for Valentine," *Bergen Record*, October 9, 1999.

94. Quoted in Jeff Goldberg and Jack O'Connell, "Rojas Takes Hands-On Approach," *Hartford Courant*, October 10, 1999.

95. Author's interview with Bobby Valentine, January 31, 2024.

96. Quoted in Jose de Jesus Ortiz, "Franco Savors the Day," *Star-Ledger*, October 10,1999.

97. Quoted in "Pratt's Enough," Associated Press, October 10, 1999.

98. Quoted in Kevin Kernan "Rocker Rips Shea Fans Once More," *New York Post*, October 16, 1999.

99. Quoted in David Waldstein, "Now Pratt's the Way We Like It," *New York Post*, October 10, 1999.

100. Quoted in Mark Kriegel, "Haven't Met Match Yet," *Daily News*, October 17, 1999.

101. Quoted in Kernan, "Rocker Rips Shea Fans Once More."
102. Quoted in Anthony McCarron, "Braves Tell Rocker to Save Breath," *Daily News*, October 20, 1999.
103. Quoted in Bob Klapisch, "Mets Get to Braves in the End," *Bergen Record*, October 17, 1999.
104. Quoted in Mark Kriegel, "Mets Bullpen Comes Up Aces," *Daily News*, October 18, 1999.
105. Quoted in "Atlanta Braves Pitcher John Rocker Renowned for His Insults to Mets Fans," CBS *Morning News*, October 19, 1999.
106. Author's interview with Bobby Valentine, January 31, 2024.
107. Quoted in Marty Noble, "A Grand Single," *Newsday*, October 18, 1999.
108. Quoted in "Leiter's Long Night," *Asbury Park Press*, October 20, 1999.
109. Author's interview with Bobby Valentine, January 31, 2024.
110. Quoted in Marty Noble, "Negating the Pen," *Newsday*, October 24, 1999.
111. O'Neill, *Swing and a Hit*, 128.
112. Quoted in Lawrence Rocca, "O'Neill's Hit Well-Times Single of Rocker in 8th Keys Win in Opener," *Newsday*, October 24, 1999.
113. Quoted in Ben Walker, "Yankees 6, Braves 5, 10 innings," Associated Press, October 27, 1999.
114. Quoted in Thomas Stinson, "Curtis Home Run Thunder Rips Braves Asunder," *Atlanta Journal and Constitution*, October 27, 1999.
115. Quoted in George Solomon and Dave Sheinin, "Gray's Apology Is Not Enough for Players," *Washington Post*, October 27, 1999.
116. Quoted in Dom Amore, "Yanks Chad All Over," *Hartford Courant*, October 27, 1999.
117. Author's interview with Jim Leyritz, March 10, 2020.
118. Quoted in Rod Beaton, "Yankees Sweep into History," *USA Today*, October 28, 1999.

8. UNTIL SOMEONE BEATS US

1. Bob Klapisch, "Valentine Left Hanging," *Bergen Record*, November 24, 1999.
2. Quoted in Scott MacGregor, "Mets Notes," *Cincinnati Enquirer*, October 5, 1999.
3. Quoted in Bob Klapisch, "A Pair of Jokers Draw Team's Wrath," *Bergen Record*, October 21, 1999.
4. Quoted in Bryant, *Rickey*, 341.
5. Quoted in Lisa Olsen, "Throw the Bums Out!" *Daily News*, October 24, 1999.
6. Quoted in Peter Botte, "Mets Fold on Bonilla," *Daily News*, January 4, 2000.
7. Valentine and Golenbock, *Valentine's Way*, 224.
8. Quoted in Bob Klapisch, "Mets Striking Out on Griffey," *Bergen Record*, December 14, 1999.

9. Quoted in Ronald Blum, "Griffey Rejects Deal to Mets," Associated Press, December 14, 1999.

10. Quoted in Jose de Jesus Ortiz, "Hampton Is the Jewel in Deal with Astros," *Star-Ledger*, December 24, 1999.

11. Quoted in Shawn Courchesne, "This Ace Is High for Mets," *Hartford Courant*, December 24, 1999.

12. T. J. Quinn, "Holiday Cheering," *Bergen Record*, December 24, 1999.

13. Quoted in Marty Noble, "Mets Tell Orosco: So Long, It's Been Good to Know You," *Newsday*, March 19, 2000.

14. Quoted in Andrew Marchand, "Sorry, Charlie: Hayes Released," *New York Post*, March 21, 2000.

15. Andrew Marchand, "Mets 2000—It's All or Nothing," *New York Post*, March 30, 2000; Wallace Matthews, "The Flushing Zoo," *New York Post*, March 30, 2000.

16. Quoted in Joel Sherman, "Yanks Rally 'Round Down & Out Darryl," *New York Post*, February 24, 2000.

17. Quoted in Ken Davidoff, "The Boss Not Ready to Give up on Darryl," *Bergen Record*, February 24, 2000.

18. Quoted in Richard Justice, "Strawberry Out on Third Strike," *Washington Post*, February 29, 2000.

19. Quoted in Buster Olney, "Emotions Intact, Raines Ends a 21-Year Career," *New York Times*, March 24, 2000.

20. Quoted in Ronald Blum, "Officials Likely to OK Mets, Cubs in Japan," Associated Press, August 18, 1999.

21. Quoted in John Harnes, "Alarm Clocks Call Fans to Opener," *Asbury Park Press*, March 30, 2000.

22. Quoted in Rafael Hermoso, "Openers Foreign Affairs for Hamilton," *Daily News*, March 30, 2000.

23. Quoted in Kit Stier, "Cubs' Baylor Fumes over Mets' Protest," *Journal News*, March 30, 2000.

24. Quoted in David Lennon, "Long Trip and Faces," *Newsday*, March 30, 2000.

25. Quoted in Marty Noble, "No Joy in Metsville," *Newsday*, April 13, 2000.

26. Marty Noble, "No Joy in Metsville," *Newsday*, April 13, 2000.

27. Valentine and Golenbock, *Valentine's Way*, 248–49.

28. Quoted in Andrew Marchand, "Who the f-k Is Brad34?" *New York Post*, June 30, 2020.

29. Quoted in Steve Jacobsen, "Mets' Tolerance of Rickey Hits Wall," *Newsday*, May 14, 2000.

30. Quoted in Gregory Schutta, "Mets Finally Let Rickey Go," *Bergen Record*, May 14, 2000.

31. Quoted in Andrew Marchand, "Run Out of Town," *New York Post*, May 14, 2000.

32. Quoted in Rafael Hermoso, "Rey's Loss Bigger Than Defeat," *Daily News*, May 30, 2000.

33. Rivera with Coffey, *The Closer*, 117.

34. Quoted in Torre and Verducci, *The Yankee Years*, 56.

35. Quoted in O'Connor, *The Captain*, 170.

36. Quoted in Shawn Courchesne, "Knoblauch Story Not a Highlight," *Hartford Courant*, June 19, 2000.

37. George King, "Bombers Deal Leyritz to Dodgers for the Viz," *New York Post*, June 21, 2000.

38. Quoted in Tom Withers, "Trade for Juan Gonzalez Falls Apart," *Wichita Eagle*, June 27, 2000.

39. Quoted in Josh Dubow, "Yanks Get Justice in Deal with Cleveland," Associated Press, June 30, 2000.

40. Here and in the following paragraph, Pearlman quotes are from author's interview with Jeff Pearlman, October 13, 2023.

41. Quoted in Jeff Pearlman, "A Reporter's Tale," *Bleacher Report*, April 4, 2014.

42. Quoted in "Mayor Says John Rocker's Hometown Should Stand by Him," Associated Press, January 5, 2000.

43. Quoted in Tracy Connor, "Shrinks Are on Deck to Face Punk Rocker," *New York Post*, January 7, 2000.

44. Quoted in Ronald Blum, "Psychological Tests for Rocker," Associated Press, January 6, 2000.

45. Quoted in Ronald Blum, "Mets 11, Braves 8," Associated Press, July 1, 2000.

46. Quoted in Jose de Jesus Ortiz, "Huge Eighth-Inning Rally Ends Braves' Dominance," *Star-Ledger*, July 1, 2000.

47. Quoted in Rafael Hermoso, "Piazza Caps Fireworks," *Daily News*, July 1, 2000.

48. Quoted in "D-Rays Show Gooden the Door," CBS News, May 25, 2000.

49. Quoted in Darren Everson, "Sweeping Beauty for Bombers," *Daily News*, July 9, 2000.

50. Quoted in Ronald Blum, "Two Games, Two Ballparks, One Long Day," Associated Press, July 9, 2000.

51. Posada with Brozek, *The Journey Home*, 225.

52. Quoted in Ben Walker, "Yankees 4, Mets 2, 1st Game," Associated Press, July 9, 2000.

53. Quoted in Walker, "Yankees 4, Mets 2, 1st Game."

54. Quoted in Bob Klapisch, "Teams Share History—and Some Venom," *Bergen Record*, July 9, 2000.

55. Quoted in Torre and Verducci, *The Yankee Years*, 129.

56. Quoted in Lawrence Rocca, "Mets Lose More Than 2 Games," *Newsday*, July 9, 2000.

57. Quoted in Tara Sullivan, "Bombers Acquire Hill from Cubs," *Bergen Record*, July 22, 2000.

58. Quoted in Lawrence Rocca, "Yanks Win Race to Arm," *Newsday*, July 13, 2000.

59. Quoted in "Yankees Get Help," Associated Press, July 13, 2000.

60. Author's interview with Mike Stanley, April 7, 2020.

61. Quoted in Josh Dubow, "Torre 'Stunned' by Canseco Acquisition," Associated Press, August 8, 2000.

62. Quoted in Torre and Verducci, *The Yankee Years*, 100.

63. Quoted in Thomas Hill, "Larkin Decides to Stay," *Daily News*, July 24, 2000.

64. David Waldstein, "The Prospects Are Good; Deal for Bordick Is Better," *Star-Ledger*, July 29, 2000.

65. Quoted in T. J. Quinn, "Mets Secure Playoffs," *Daily News*, September 28, 2000.

66. Quoted in Jack O'Connell, "You Bet, Mets," *Hartford Courant*, September 28, 2000.

67. Quoted in Peter Botte, "Teammates Get One Hill of a Show," *Daily News*, August 25, 2000.

68. Quoted in George King, "Cone Done for Season?" *New York Post*, September 6, 2000.

69. Quoted in Anthony McCarron, "Bombers Pan Fall Preview," *Daily News*, September 18, 2000.

70. Quoted in McCarron, "Bombers Pan Fall Preview."

71. Quoted in Anthony McCarron, "Jeter's Not at a Loss," *Daily News*, September 30, 2000.

72. Quoted in Dom Amore, "When It Reigns, It Pours," *Hartford Courant*, September 30, 2000.

73. Jack Curry, "Real Yankees Need to Stand and Deliver," *New York Times*, September 30, 2000.

74. Quoted in Jon Heyman, "Destiny May Have Switched Dugouts," *Newsday*, October 6, 2000.

75. Kevin Kernan, "Confident Kent Still Says Giants Are Better," *New York Post*, October 8, 2000.

76. Quoted in Jon Heyman, "Benny and the Mets a 'W' Away," *Newsday*, October 8, 2000.

77. Quoted in Valentine and Golenbock, *Valentine's Way*, 257.

78. Quoted in David Heuschkel, "Mets' One-Hit Wonder," *Hartford Courant*, October 9, 2000.

79. Quoted in Chuck Johnson, "Mets Bring Down Giants 4–0," *USA Today*, October 9, 2000.

80. Quoted in Josh Dubow, "Mets 4, Giants 0," Associated Press, October 9, 2000.

81. Quoted in Tyler Kepner, "Coast to Coast, Mets and Yankees Celebrate," *New York Times*, October 9, 2000.

82. Quoted in Rob Gloster, "Athletics 5, Yankees 3," Associated Press, October 4, 2000.

83. Quoted in Buster Olney, "Return to Glory? No, but Yankees Win," *New York Times*, October 5, 2000.

84. Quoted in Steve Jacobson, "Lineup Shakeup Produces Wakeup," *Newsday*, October 5, 2000.

85. Quoted in Bob Raissman, "TV Sked Has Boss Fit to Be Tied," *Daily News*, October 4, 2000.

86. Quoted in Ursula Reel, "Chavez Regrets Yank Insult," *New York Post*, October 9, 2000.

87. Quoted in Dan Graziano, "Reaching ALCS Again Is a Relief," *Star-Ledger*, October 9, 2000.

88. Quoted in Graziano, "Reaching ALCS Again Is a Relief."

89. Quotes from Stearns and Hampton are in Ben Walker, "Mets 6, Cardinals 2," Associated Press, October 12, 2000.

90. Quoted in "Mets GM, La Russa Have Spat," *Contra Costa Times*, October 13, 2000.

91. Quoted in David Waldstein, "La Russa-Phillips War of Words Is Something to Talk About," *Star-Ledger*, October 13, 2000.

92. Quoted in Tim Leonard, "Perez: Just Call Me 'Timo,'" *Bergen Record*, September 10, 2000.

93. Quoted in Jose de Jesus Ortiz, "Shea by Way of Japan," *Star-Ledger*, September 15, 2000.

94. Quoted in Marty Noble, "Mets Halfway to Series," *Newsday*, October 13, 2000.

95. Quoted in Marty Noble, "The 7 Train Is Ready," *Newsday*, October 17, 2000.

96. Quoted in Andrew Marchand, "Mets Reserve Subway Seat," *New York Post*, October 17, 2000.

97. Kepner, "Coast to Coast, Mets and Yankees Celebrate."

98. Mike Lupica, "Both Teams Taking Us on Amazin' Ride," *Daily News*, October 15, 2000.

99. Daniel Sforza, "Cyberspace Buzzing over Mets and Yanks," *Bergen Record*, October 10, 2000.

100. Quoted in John Hickey, "Bronx Bombed," *Seattle Post-Intelligencer*, October 12, 2000.

101. Quoted in Ronald Blum, "Yankees 7, Mariners 1," Associated Press, October 12, 2000.

102. Quoted in Tom Spousta, "The Scorecard: One Double, Some Anger and a Slew of Baffled Batters," *New York Times*, October 15, 2000.

103. Quoted in Anthony McCarren, "Clemens Is a 1-Hit Wonder," *Daily News*, October 15, 2000.

104. Quoted in Dom Amore, "Retro Rocket," *Hartford Courant*, October 15, 2000.

105. Quoted in Lawrence Rocca, "Roger Redeems Himself," *Newsday*, October 15, 2000.

106. Quoted in Mike Lupica, "Heartbreak Kid Takes Look Back at What Might've Been," *Daily News*, October 18, 2000.

107. Quoted in Larry McShane, "All Aboard—Maybe—for First Subway Series in 44 Years," Associated Press, October 17, 2000.

108. Quoted in Mel Antonen, "Yankees Jump on Subway 9–7," *USA Today*, October 18, 2000.

109. John Hickey, "It's Over," *Seattle Post-Intelligencer*, October 18, 2000.

110. Quoted in Mike Berardino, "How 'Bout Them Apples," *South Florida Sun-Sentinel*, October 18, 2000.

9. JOY IN METSVILLE

1. Quote from Chip Caray on FX, June 16, 1997.

2. Author's interview with Dave Mlicki, August 25, 2023.

3. Quoted in Buster Olney, "Puzzle of a Pitcher Leaves Yankees Scratching Heads," *New York Times*, June 17, 1997.

10. UP THE MIDDLE

1. Mark Bradley, "New York Teams Not One," *Atlanta Journal and Constitution*, October 22, 2000.

2. Skip Bayless, "Chicago Teams Need Their Own Steinbrenner," *Chicago Tribune*, October 22, 2000.

3. Patrick Reusse, "Yankees' Latest Run Should End after Series," *Star Tribune*, October 26, 2000.

4. O'Neill and Curry, *Swing and a Hit*, 192.

5. Randolph, *The Yankee Way*, 177.

6. Quoted in Robert Ingrassia, "Renewing Old, Even Ancient, Ties in Quest for Tix," *Daily News*, October 25, 2000.

7. Quoted in Leonard Greene, "Benny's Boast: Amazin's in Five," *New York Post*, October 20, 2000.

8. Quoted in Larry McShane, "Fans Draw Line as World Series Begins in New York," *Florida Times-Union*, October 22, 2000.

9. Quoted in Ohm Youngmisuk, "Derek Is Nothing Short of World Class," *Daily News*, October 22, 2000.

10. Quoted in Peter Botte, "Mets Blunder on Basepaths Run Selves Right Out of Series Opener," *Daily News*, October 22, 2000.

11. O'Neill and Curry, *Swing and a Hit*, 130.

12. Quoted in Buster Olney, "Finally, Mets and Yankees Are Good Enough to Be the Best," *New York Times*, October 22, 2000.

13. O'Neill and Curry, *Swing and a Hit*, 133.

14. Quoted in Golenbock, *Amazin'*, 621.

15. Quoted in Don Amore, "Wild Ride!" *Hartford Courant*, October 22, 2000.

16. Quoted in Marc Topkin, "World Series Game 1," *St. Petersburg Times*, October 22, 2000.

17. Quoted in Lawrence Rocca, "Mike's Unsplendid Splinter Incident," *Newsday*, October 23, 2000.

18. Randolph, *The Yankee Way*, 183.

19. Quoted in "Rocket Still Not a Favorite with Mets," *Times Herald-Record*, October 19, 2000.

20. Quoted in Ben Walker, "Yankees 6, Mets 5," Associated Press, October 23, 2000.

21. Quoted in T. J. Quinn, "Harris Would Like A Piece of Clemens," *Daily News*, October 23, 2000.

22. O'Neill and Curry, *Swing and a Hit*, 194.

23. Rivera with Coffey, *The Closer*, 126.

24. Quoted in Gary Shelton, "Clemens: Nasty Duality," *St. Petersburg Times*, October 23, 2000.

25. Quoted in Olney, *The Last Night of the Yankee Dynasty*, 68.

26. Quoted in Bob Hohier, "L-Duque Hernandez Is Finally Beaten in Postseason as Mets Derail Yankees," *Boston Globe*, October 25, 2000.

27. Quoted in Ronald Blum, "Ben-ny Leads Mets over Yankees," Associated Press, October 25, 2000.

28. Quoted in Thomas Hill, "Mets Sidetrack Bronx Express," *Daily News*, October 25, 2000.

29. Quoted in Jim Caple, "Mets Battle Back," *Seattle Post-Intelligencer*, October 25, 2000.

30. Quoted in Pete Caldera, "Mets Finally Show Yankees Are Human," *Bergen Record*, October 26, 2000.

31. Quoted in Madden, *Steinbrenner*, 392.

32. Quoted in Tara Sullivan, "George Takes a Seat," *Bergen Record*, October 26, 2000.

33. Author's interview with Rick Cerrone, April 11, 2021.

34. Quoted in Jim Abbott, "Mets Counting on the Power of Music," *Orlando Sentinel*, October 21, 2000.

35. Quoted in "Strawberry Arrested Again," *Orlando Sentinel*, October 26, 2000.

36. Quoted in Bill Jensen, "Name Recognition for Baha Men," *Newsday*, October 23, 2000.

37. Quoted in O'Connor, *The Captain*, 167.

38. Quoted in Marc Topkin, "Yankees Are on the Verge," *St. Petersburg Times*, October 26, 2000.

39. Quoted in Buster Olney, "Subway Series; Rivera & Co. in 3–2 Nailbiter at Shea," *New York Times*, October 26, 2000.

40. O'Neill with Curry, *Swing and a Hit*, 67.

41. Quoted in "Jeter Takes Over," *Asbury Park Press*, October 26, 2000.

42. Quoted in Buster Olney, "Rivera & Co. Shut Door in 3–2 Nail-Biter at Shea," *New York Times*, October 26, 2000.

43. Quoted in O'Connor, *The Captain*, 175.

44. Quoted in Peter Botte, "Shea Hey, Yankee Fans in House," *Daily News*, October 26, 2000.

45. Quoted in Jim Salisbury and Bob Brookover, "Pettitte Says Series Has Lost Its Luster," *Philadelphia Inquirer*, October 26, 2000.

46. Quoted in Mike DiGiovana, "Yankees' Edge Is a Lot of Bullpen," *Los Angeles Times*, October 26, 2000.

47. Quoted in Torre and Verducci, *The Yankee Years*, 137.

48. Quoted in Josh Dubow, "Perez and Alfonzo Missing in Action for Mets," Associated Press, October 26, 2000.

49. Quoted in Kepner, *K*, 262.

50. Quoted in Bob Hohler, "Yankees, Jeter Are in Driver's Seat, Mets May Get Off at Next Stop," *Boston Globe*, October 26, 2000.

51. Olney, *The Last Night of the Yankee Dynasty*, 31.

52. Quoted in Bob Klapisch, "When Bombers Sweat, Mets Smile," *Bergen Record*, October 27, 2000.

53. Quoted in Thomas Stinson, "There's No Explaining Williams' Series Slump," *Atlanta Journal and Constitution*, October 26, 2000.

54. Quoted in Wayne Coffey, "Jorge, Yankees Hand Al, Mets Walking Papers," *Daily News*, October 27, 2000.

55. Quoted in Jim Caple, "Yankees Beat Mets in Five, Earning Third Consecutive World Series Title," *Seattle Post-Intelligencer*, October 27, 2000.

56. Quoted in Andrew Marchand, "No Stopping Yank Express—Bombers Derail Mets for Historic Three-Peat," *New York Post*, October 27, 2000.

57. Quoted in Thomas Stinson, "Three-Peat Sojo Sweet for Yankees," *Atlanta Journal and Constitution*, October 27, 2000.

58. Quoted in Mike Lupica, "Stroke of Midnight, Shea Goodbye," *Daily News*, October 27, 2000.

59. Quoted in Mike Klis, "Yankees 4, Mets 2," *Denver Post*, October 27, 2000.

60. Quoted in Rivera with Coffey, *The Closer*, 129.

61. Posada with Brozek, *The Journey Home*, 256.

Bibliography

Materials and quotes gathered from interviews with the following people were used for this book: Jim Abbott, Mike Blowers, Wade Boggs, Homer Bush, Brian Butterfield, Frank Cashen, Rick Cerrone, Russ Davis, Rick Down, Tony Fernández, Jeff Idelson, Moss Klein, Jim Leyritz, Bill Madden, Dave Magadan, Don Mattingly, Jim Mecir, Alan Mills, Dave Mlicki, Rich Monteleone, Charlie O'Brien, Paul O'Neill, Jesse Orosco, Jeff Pearlman, Lou Piniella, Eric Plunk, Glen Sherlock, Buck Showalter, Ken Singleton, Luis Sojo, Mike Stanley, John Sterling, Mel Stottlemyre, David Sussman, Tony Tarasco, Bobby Valentine, Randy Velarde, Wally Whitehurst, Mookie Wilson.

Angell, Roger. *A Pitcher's Story: Innings with David Cone*. New York: Warner Books, 2001.

Bryant, Howard. *Rickey: The Life and Legend of an American Original*. New York: Mariner Books, 2022.

Curry, Jack. *The 1998 Yankees*. New York: Twelve, 2023.

Golenbock, Peter. *Amazin': The Miraculous History of New York's Most Beloved Baseball Team*. New York: St. Martin's Griffin, 2002.

——. *George: The Poor Little Rich Boy Who Built the Yankee Empire*. Hoboken: John Wiley & Sons, 2009.

Gooden, Dwight, and Bob Klapisch. *Heat: My Life On and Off the Diamond*. New York: William Morrow, 1999.

Kepner, Tyler. *K: A History of Baseball in Ten Pitches*. New York: Doubleday, 2019.

Klapisch, Bob. *High and Tight: The Rise and Fall of Dwight Gooden and Darryl Strawberry*. New York: Villard Books, 1996.

Klapisch, Bob, and Pail Solotaroff. *Inside the Empire: The True Power behind the New York Yankees*. New York: Houghton Mifflin Harcourt, 2019.

Madden, Bill. *Steinbrenner: The Last Lion of Baseball*. New York: HarperCollins, 2010.

O'Connor, Ian. *The Captain: The Journey of Derek Jeter*. New York: Houghton Mifflin Harcourt, 2011.

Olney, Buster. *The Last Night of the Yankee Dynasty: The Game, the Team, and the Cost of Greatness*. New York: Echo, 2004.

O'Neill, Paul, and Jack Curry. *Swing and a Hit*. New York: Grand Central, 2023.

Pepe, Phil. *Core Four: The Heart and Soul of the Yankees Dynasty*. Chicago: Triumph Books, 2013.

Pessah, Jon. *The Game: Inside the Secret World of Major League Baseball's Power Brokers*. New York: Back Bay Books, 2015.

Posada, Jorge, with Gary Brozek. *The Journey Home: My Life in Pinstripes*. New York: Dey Street Books, 2016.

Randolph, Willie. *The Yankee Way: Playing, Coaching, and My Life in Baseball*. New York: It Books, 2014.

Rivera, Mariano, with Wayne Coffey. *The Closer*. New York: Little, Brown, 2014.

Sherman, Joel. *Birth of a Dynasty*. Emmaus PA: Rodale, 2006.

Stottlemyre, Mel, with John Harper. *Pride and Pinstripes: The Yankees, Mets, and Surviving Life's Challenges*. New York: Harper Entertainment, 2007.

Strawberry, Darryl, and John Strausbaugh. *Straw: Finding My Way*. New York: HarperCollins, 2009.

Torre, Joe, and Tom Verducci. *The Yankee Years*. New York: Doubleday, 2009.

Valentine, Bobby, and Peter Golenbock. *Valentine's Way: My Adventurous Life and Times*. New York: Simon & Schuster, 2021.

Index